THE CLAY SANSKRIT LIBRARY
FOUNDED BY JOHN & JENNIFER CLAY

GENERAL EDITOR

SHELDON POLLOCK

EDITED BY

ISABELLE ONIANS

WWW.CLAYSANSKRITLIBRARY.ORG
WWW.NYUPRESS.ORG

Artwork by Robert Beer.
Typeset in Adobe Garamond at 10.25 : 12.3+pt.
XML-development by Stuart Brown.
Editorial input from Dániel Balogh, Ridi Faruque,
Chris Gibbons, Tomoyuki Kono & Eszter Somogyi.
Printed and Bound in Great Britain by
TJ International, Cornwall on acid free paper

MAHĀBHĀRATA

BOOK TEN

DEAD OF NIGHT

BOOK ELEVEN

THE WOMEN

TRANSLATED BY

Kate Crosby

NEW YORK UNIVERSITY PRESS

JJC FOUNDATION

2009

First Edition 2009

ISBN 978-0-8147-1727-1

The Clay Sanskrit Library is co-published by
New York University Press
and the JJC Foundation.

Further information about this volume
and the rest of the Clay Sanskrit Library
is available on the following websites:
www.claysanskritlibrary.org
www.nyupress.org

Library of Congress Cataloging-in-Publication Data
Mahābhārata. Sauptikaparvan. English & Sanskrit.
Mahābhārata. Book ten, Dead of night. Book eleven, The women /
translated by Kate Crosby. -- 1st ed.
p. cm. – (The Clay Sanskrit library)
Sanskrit texts with parallel English translations on facing pages.
Includes bibliographical references.
ISBN 978-0-8147-1727-1
1. Epic poetry, Sanskrit--Translations into English. I. Crosby, Kate.
II. Mahabharata. Striparvan. English & Sanskrit. III. Title.
IV. Title: Mahabharata, Book X-XI. V. Title: Mahabharata X-XI.
VI. Title: Dead of night.
BL1138.242.S28E5 2009
294.5'923045--dc22
2009023490

CONTENTS

CSL Conventions vii

Introduction xvii

MAHA·BHÁRATA X – DEAD OF NIGHT

1–5 The Owl in the Banyan 5

6–8 Merciless Slaughter 47

9 Balm for Duryódhana 97

10–11 Dráupadi's Demand 111

12–15 The Brink of Apocalypse 127

16–18 Strategies Revealed 151

MAHA·BHÁRATA XI – THE WOMEN

1–9 Counseling the Ineffectual King 175

10–15 Farewells and Reconciliation 229

16–25 Mothers and Widows in the Carnage 263

26–27 The Funerary Rites 325

Notes 345

Emendations to the Sanskrit Text 361

Glossary of Proper Names and Epithets 365

CSL CONVENTIONS

Sanskrit Alphabetical Order

Vowels:	*a ā i ī u ū ṛ ṝ ḷ ḹ e ai o au ṃ ḥ*
Gutturals:	*k kh g gh ṅ*
Palatals:	*c ch j jh ñ*
Retroflex:	*ṭ ṭh ḍ ḍh ṇ*
Dentals:	*t th d dh n*
Labials:	*p ph b bh m*
Semivowels:	*y r l v*
Spirants:	*ś ṣ s h*

Guide to Sanskrit Pronunciation

a	b*u*t
ā, â	f*a*ther
i	s*i*t
ī, î	f*ee*
u	p*u*t
ū, û	b*oo*
ṛ	vocalic *r*, American p*ur*dy or English p*re*tty
ṝ	lengthened *ṛ*
ḷ	vocalic *l*, ab*le*
e, ê, ē	m*a*de, esp. in Welsh pronunciation
ai	b*i*te
o, ô, ō	r*o*pe, esp. Welsh pronunciation; Italian s*o*lo
au	s*ou*nd
ṃ	*anusvāra* nasalizes the preceding vowel
ḥ	*visarga*, a voiceless aspiration (resembling the English *h*), or like Scottish lo*ch*, or an aspiration with a faint echoing of the last element of the preceding vowel so that *taiḥ* is pronounced *taih[i]*
k	lu*ck*
kh	blo*ckh*ead
g	*g*o
gh	bi*gh*ead
ṅ	a*n*ger
c	*ch*ill
ch	mat*chh*ead
j	*j*og
jh	aspirated *j*, he*dgeh*og
ñ	ca*ny*on
ṭ	retroflex *t*, *t*ry (with the tip of tongue turned up to touch the hard palate)
ṭh	same as the preceding but aspirated
ḍ	retroflex *d* (with the tip

	of tongue turned up to touch the hard palate)
ḍh	same as the preceding but aspirated
ṇ	retroflex *n* (with the tip of tongue turned up to touch the hard palate)
t	French *t*out
th	ten*t h*ook
d	*d*inner
dh	guil*dh*all
n	*n*ow
p	*p*ill
ph	u*ph*eaval
b	*b*efore
bh	a*bh*orrent
m	*m*ind
y	*y*es
r	trilled, resembling the Italian pronunciation of *r*
l	*l*inger
v	*w*ord
ś	*sh*ore
ṣ	retroflex *sh* (with the tip of the tongue turned up to touch the hard palate)
s	hi*ss*
h	*h*ood

CSL Punctuation of English

The acute accent on Sanskrit words when they occur outside of the Sanskrit text itself, marks stress, e.g., Ramáyana. It is not part of traditional Sanskrit orthography, transliteration, or transcription, but we supply it here to guide readers in the pronunciation of these unfamiliar words. Since no Sanskrit word is accented on the last syllable it is not necessary to accent disyllables, e.g., Rama.

The second CSL innovation designed to assist the reader in the pronunciation of lengthy unfamiliar words is to insert an unobtrusive middle dot between semantic word breaks in compound names (provided the word break does not fall on a vowel resulting from the fusion of two vowels), e.g., Maha·bhárata, but Ramáyana (not Rama·áyana). Our dot echoes the punctuating middle dot (·) found in the oldest surviving samples of written Indic, the Ashokan inscriptions of the third century BCE.

The deep layering of Sanskrit narrative has also dictated that we use quotation marks only to announce the beginning and end of every direct speech, and not at the beginning of every paragraph.

CSL Punctuation of Sanskrit

The Sanskrit text is also punctuated, in accordance with the punctuation of the English translation. In mid-verse, the punctuation will not alter the sandhi or the scansion. Proper names are capitalized. Most Sanskrit meters have four "feet" (*pāda*); where possible we print the common *śloka* meter on two lines. In the Sanskrit text, we use French *Guillemets* (e.g., *«kva saṃcicīrṣuḥ?»*) instead of English quotation marks (e.g., "Where are you off to?") to avoid confusion with the apostrophes used for vowel elision in sandhi.

SANDHI

Sanskrit presents the learner with a challenge: *sandhi* (euphonic combination). Sandhi means that when two words are joined in connected speech or writing (which in Sanskrit reflects speech), the last letter (or even letters) of the first word often changes; compare the way we pronounce "the" in "the beginning" and "the end."

In Sanskrit the first letter of the second word may also change; and if both the last letter of the first word and the first letter of the second are vowels, they may fuse. This has a parallel in English: a nasal consonant is inserted between two vowels that would otherwise coalesce: "a pear" and "an apple." Sanskrit vowel fusion may produce ambiguity.

The charts on the following pages give the full sandhi system.

Fortunately it is not necessary to know these changes in order to start reading Sanskrit. All that is important to know is the form of the second word without sandhi (pre-sandhi), so that it can be recognized or looked up in a dictionary. Therefore we are printing Sanskrit with a system of punctuation that will indicate, unambiguously, the original form of the second word, i.e., the form without sandhi. Such sandhi mostly concerns the fusion of two vowels.

In Sanskrit, vowels may be short or long and are written differently accordingly. We follow the general convention that a vowel with no mark above it is short. Other books mark a long vowel either with a bar called a macron (*ā*) or with a circumflex (*â*). Our system uses the

VOWEL SANDHI

Final vowels:

a	ā	i	ī	u	ū	ṛ	e	ai	o	au	*Initial vowels:*
' â	" â	y a	y a	v a	v a	r a	e '	ā a	o '	āv a	a
' ā	" ā	y ā	y ā	v ā	v ā	r ā	a ā	ā ā	a ā	āv ā	ā
' ê	" ê	' î	" î	v i	v i	r i	a i	ā i	a i	āv i	i
' ē	" ē	' ī	" ī	v ī	v ī	r ī	a ī	ā ī	a ī	āv ī	ī
' ô	" ô	y u	y u	' û	" û	r u	a u	ā u	a u	āv u	u
' ō	" ō	y ū	y ū	' ū	" ū	r ū	a ū	ā ū	a ū	āv ū	ū
a' r	a" r	y ṛ	y ṛ	v ṛ	v ṛ	' ṝ	a ṛ	ā ṛ	a ṛ	āv ṛ	ṛ
' âi	" âi	y e	y e	v e	v e	r e	a e	ā e	a e	āv e	e
' āi	" āi	y ai	y ai	v ai	v ai	r ai	a ai	ā ai	a ai	āv ai	ai
' âu	" âu	y o	y o	v o	v o	r o	a o	ā o	a o	āv o	o
' āu	" āu	y au	y au	v au	v au	r au	a au	ā au	a au	āv au	au

CONSONANT SANDHI

Permitted finals: k	ṭ	t	p	ṅ	n	m	(Except āḥ/aḥ) ḥ/r	āḥ	aḥ	Initial letters:
k	ṭ	t	p	ṅ	n	ṃ	ḥ	āḥ	aḥ	k/kh
g	ḍ	d	b	ṅ	n	ṃ	r	ā	o	g/gh
k	ṭ	c	p	ṅ	ṃś	ṃ	ś	āś	aś	c/ch
g	ḍ	j	b	ṅ	ñ	ṃ	r	ā	o	j/jh
k	ṭ	ṭ	p	ṅ	ṃṣ	ṃ	ṣ	āṣ	aṣ	ṭ/ṭh
g	ḍ	ḍ	b	ṅ	ṇ	ṃ	r	ā	o	ḍ/ḍh
k	ṭ	t	p	ṅ	ṃs	ṃ	s	ās	as	t/th
g	ḍ	d	b	ṅ	n	ṃ	r	ā	o	d/dh
k	ṭ	t	p	ṅ	n	ṃ	ḥ	āḥ	aḥ	p/ph
g	ḍ	d	b	ṅ	n	ṃ	r	ā	o	b/bh
ṅ	ṇ	n	m	ṅ	n	ṃ	r	ā	o	*nasals* (n/m)
g	ḍ	d	b	ṅ	n	ṃ	r	ā	o	y/v
g	ḍ	d	b	ṅ	n	ṃ	*zero*[1]	ā	o	r
g	ḍ	l	b	ṅ	l̃[2]	ṃ	r	ā	o	l
k	ṭ	c ch	p	ṅ	ñ ś/ch	ṃ	ḥ	āḥ	aḥ	ś
k	ṭ	t	p	ṅ	n	ṃ	ḥ	āḥ	aḥ	ṣ/s
gg h	ḍḍ h	dd h	bb h	ṅ	n	ṃ	r	ā	o	h
g	ḍ	d	b	ṅ/ṅṅ[3]	n/nn[3]	m	r	ā	a[4]	*vowels*
k	ṭ	t	p	ṅ	n	m	ḥ	āḥ	aḥ	*zero*

[1]ḥ or r disappears, and if a/i/u precedes, this lengthens to ā/ī/ū. [2]e.g. tān+lokān=tāl̃ lokān.
[3]The doubling occurs if the preceding vowel is short. [4]Except: aḥ+a=o '.

macron, except that for initial vowels in sandhi we use a circumflex to indicate that originally the vowel was short, or the shorter of two possibilities (*e* rather than *ai*, *o* rather than *au*).

When we print initial *â*, before sandhi that vowel was *a*

î or *ê*,	*i*
û or *ô*,	*u*
âi,	*e*
âu,	*o*
ā,	*ā*
ī,	*ī*
ū,	*ū*
ē,	*ī*
ō,	*ū*
ai,	*ai*
āu,	*au*

', before sandhi there was a vowel *a*

When a final short vowel (*a*, *i*, or *u*) has merged into a following vowel, we print ' at the end of the word, and when a final long vowel (*ā*, *ī*, or *ū*) has merged into a following vowel we print " at the end of the word. The vast majority of these cases will concern a final *a* or *ā*. See, for instance, the following examples:

What before sandhi was *atra asti* is represented as *atr' âsti*

atra āste	*atr' āste*
kanyā asti	*kany" âsti*
kanyā āste	*kany" āste*
atra iti	*atr' êti*
kanyā iti	*kany" êti*
kanyā īpsitā	*kany" ēpsitā*

Finally, three other points concerning the initial letter of the second word:

(1) A word that before sandhi begins with *ṛ* (vowel), after sandhi begins with *r* followed by a consonant: *yatha" rtu* represents pre-sandhi *yathā ṛtu*.

(2) When before sandhi the previous word ends in *t* and the following word begins with *ś*, after sandhi the last letter of the previous word is *c*

and the following word begins with *ch*: *syāc chāstravit* represents pre-sandhi *syāt śāstravit*.

(3) Where a word begins with *h* and the previous word ends with a double consonant, this is our simplified spelling to show the pre-sandhi form: *tad hasati* is commonly written as *tad dhasati*, but we write *tadd hasati* so that the original initial letter is obvious.

COMPOUNDS

We also punctuate the division of compounds (*samāsa*), simply by inserting a thin vertical line between words. There are words where the decision whether to regard them as compounds is arbitrary. Our principle has been to try to guide readers to the correct dictionary entries.

Exemplar of CSL Style

Where the Devanagari script reads:

कुम्भस्थली रक्षतु वो विकीर्णसिन्धूररेणुर्द्विरदाननस्य ।
प्रशान्तये विघ्नतमश्छटानां निष्ठ्यूतबालातपपल्लवेव ॥

Others would print:

kumbhasthalī rakṣatu vo vikīrṇasindūrareṇur dviradānanasya /
praśāntaye vighnatamaśchaṭānāṃ niṣṭhyūtabālātapapallaveva //

We print:

kumbha|sthalī rakṣatu vo vikīrṇa|sindūra|reṇur dvirad'|ānanasya
praśāntaye vighna|tamaś|chaṭānāṃ niṣṭhyūta|bāl'|ātapa|pallav" êva.

And in English:

May Ganésha's domed forehead protect you! Streaked with vermilion dust, it seems to be emitting the spreading rays of the rising sun to pacify the teeming darkness of obstructions.

("Nava·sáhasanka and the Serpent Princess" I.3)

Wordplay

Classical Sanskrit literature can abound in puns (*śleṣa*). Such paronomasia, or wordplay, is raised to a high art; rarely is it a *cliché*. Multiple meanings merge (*śliṣyanti*) into a single word or phrase. Most common are pairs of meanings, but as many as ten separate meanings are attested. To mark the parallel senses in the English, as well as the punning original in the Sanskrit, we use a *slanted* font (different from *italic*) and a triple colon (⁝) to separate the alternatives. E.g.

> yuktaṃ Kādambarīṃ śrutvā kavayo maunam āśritāḥ
> *Bāṇa|dhvanāv* an|adhyāyo bhavat' îti smṛtir yataḥ.
>
> It is right that poets should fall silent upon hearing the Kadámbari, for the sacred law rules that recitation must be suspended when *the sound of an arrow* ⁝ *the poetry of Bana* is heard.
>
> (Soméshvara·deva's "Moonlight of Glory" I.15)

To those who decline blindfolds

INTRODUCTION

Two books of the "Maha·bhárata" epic are presented here, 'Dead of Night' (*Sauptikaparvan*) and 'The Women' (*Strīparvan*). They mark the turning point from war to peace at the culmination of eighteen days of military engagement between the Káurava and Panchála clans in the mythic past of north India. These eighteen days are the climax to years of proxy wars, maneuvering, one-upmanship and deliberate provocation, in which personal loyalties and rivalries have been forged across tribal divides in a struggle over sovereignty and territory. A subgroup of the Káuravas, the five Pándava brothers and those loyal to them, have been shoring up alliances for the past thirteen years in order to stake a claim to the Káurava throne. Thus the Pándavas fight alongside the Panchálas against their own Káurava cousins and kin, and even—unbeknown to them—their own brother. The highly personalized portrayal of the war in the "Maha·bhárata" focuses on this feud between the Pándava and Káurava cousins, and pays close attention to the psychology of grief, indignation, bitterness and the quest for understanding that betrayal within the bonds of family and community entails.

Voices of the Victors, Voices of the Vanquished

Though the war has already been won, and the Panchálas and Pándavas are celebrating their victory, the indignation and bitterness of the surviving Káuravas explodes in further, unanticipated slaughter. The final hostilities take place in these two books and the reckoning of peace begins.[1] The overall voice of the "Maha·bhárata" is that of the Pándava side, of their ultimate military and moral superiority, their prior claim to the throne and their favor with the gods, each of which excuses their behavior—even where it is as treacherous as that of their enemies—and vindicates their seizure of the Káurava kingdom.

While 'Dead of Night' and 'The Women' are also set within this framework of Pándava propaganda, and indeed are located in the very context of the Pándava victory, here it is the voices of the defeated we hear most keenly. The main protagonist of 'Dead of Night,' Ashva·tthaman, rails against the injustice of the Pándavas' victory, losing all sight of the future welfare both of himself and of the world in his obsessive acts of revenge. King Dhrita·rashtra, father of the losing Káurava brothers, now all dead, struggles to comprehend the extent of his defeat and humiliation. His wife Gandhári has to relinquish the years of scheming she has invested to no gain. Survivors learn of their place in the new world order. They learn to swallow their bitterness and anger. The unfulfilled vengeance of women on both sides—Dráupadi's against Ashva·tthaman for the loss of her sons, Gandhári against the Pándavas for the loss of hers, and the anticipated curses of Karna's widows against the Pándavas—must now be reined in for there to be any hope of reconciliation or even of a future for the world. The women of both sides enter the battlefield to piece together the remnants of their men, stupefied by the horror and the extent of their loss.

The End of an Age

Within the broader framework of Indian eschatology, in which the universe is successively renewed, and each universe is marked by four ages or periods, *yuga*, 'Dead of Night' and 'The Women' mark the cosmic dissolution of the old world order between these ages. Ashva·tthaman's horrific slaughter of living and unborn Panchála warriors, related and anticipated in 'Dead of Night,' ends the previous world period, the Dvápara *yuga*. The cremation of the corpses and scattering of ashes into the river Ganges clears the way for the new era. This is our own era, the Kali *yuga*, which begins with the birth of the sole male heir to the Pándava-Káurava line: Paríkshit.[2] Paríkshit's son, Janam·éjaya, is the ultimate beneficiary of the Pándavas' victory and the final audience to whom the entire tale is told in the cumulative framework of narrative layers. He hears how much his ancestors sacrificed and lost in the internecine war that ensured his kingship.

Shameful Victory

'Dead of Night' opens with three exhausted warriors returning to their camp to find it over-run by their enemies who are rejoicing and looting. The three realize that all their fellow soldiers are dead. Their entire army has been slaughtered and they alone survive. Their enemies, the five sons of Pandu, the Pándavas, with their allies the Panchálas, have finally won the great war of the "Maha·bhárata." But their victory has come at a cost, not just the cost of human lives, but of human dignity. The age-old history of war remains unchanged: while each side appeals to mutually agreed conventions of warfare to restrict and demonize the activities of the other, each succumbs to a fight of no-holds-barred in their desperation to win the contest. The Pándava allies targeted the most powerful assets of the Káuravas, using trickery and treachery in every case to destroy their finest warriors, invincible through any fair means. Since this is a war between cousins, a single family embroiled in conflict, this treachery entails patricide, fratricide and the murder of teachers. The victorious side has lost its innocence and the stain of their own debasement will follow them into peace, delivering a Pyrrhic victory.

Agents of Death

It falls to Ashva·tthaman, to whom command has been transferred by Duryódhana, the dying leader of the Káurava side, to be the instrument of destruction, to foil the victors of this deceptive peace. That this should be Ashva·tthaman's fate is no coincidence. He is the son of Drona, the brahmin teacher of martial arts to the entire Káurava-Pándava clan. Drona has been murdered on the battlefield. Tricked into thinking his son Ashva·tthaman is dead and deceived by his former pupil Yudhi·shthira, the only combatant who till that moment could be relied on to speak the truth, Drona had nothing left to fight for. He gave up his weapons and sat in meditative trance, awaiting death. We, the privileged audience, know that his spirit has already departed to heaven, but his archenemy, Dhrishta·dyumna, general of the Panchála forces, snatches that moment of apparent vulnerability and decapitates him. Only five days later, Duryódhana, the oldest of the Káurava brothers, to whom Ashva·tthaman is fiercely loyal, is also dealt a mortal blow in an illegal move by Bhima, one of the Pándava brothers. Ashva·tthaman wishes to avenge his father's and his leader's death.

Untenable Dharma

But it is Ashva·tthaman's status as one whose dharma, whose social and religious identity and duty, is confused that makes him the fitting catalyst of the apocalyptic climax of the war. Ashva·tthaman is brahmin—ritual and educational expert—by birth, but kshatriya—warrior—by training and livelihood. He can fulfill perfectly neither role and therefore neither the affirmation nor the constraints of maintaining one's dharmic duty apply to him. Just as Yudhi·shthira, the king of the Pándava side, represents the inherent frustration of dharma, when it meets with the pragmatics of reality, and Árjuna—especially in the 'Bhagavad Gita' of Book Six of the "Maha·bhárata"—represents the inherent conflict of dharma when two dharmic duties conflict, namely that of warrior and of dutiful son and student, so Ashva·tthaman represents the impossibility of an ambiguous dharma: he has nothing to gain or maintain, and so nothing to lose. His final destiny, once he has wreaked his revenge, to wander the earth ever restless, unrecognized and homeless, is but an external manifestation of his internal dissonance.

The Night

'Dead of Night' is a dark book. Night reigns over all activity, inspires every act. The language throughout invokes apocalypse. The motivation of the protagonist throughout is to wreak perpetual night on those who thought they had won the day.

Stealth and Hubris

The three surviving combatants of the Káurava side, Ashva·tthaman, Krita·varman and Kripa, have taken shelter in a particularly wild and entangled forest. While the other two succumb to their exhaustion, Ashva·tthaman's blood boils at all the injustice and treachery used to bring about the death of his father and of Duryódhana, the leader of the Káurava side. In this state he gazes at a banyan tree where crows sleep peacefully on each branch. The banyan tree symbolizes the kingdom, the known world, over which the battle is fought.[3] When an owl attacks the sleeping crows, filling the entire orb of the tree with their corpses, Ashva·tthaman is not horrified by this destruction of the peace, but inspired by the potential symbolism of the owl's deadly stealth. Against the protestations of his companions about the illegality of his plans, he discards the convention of fighting only by day to play owl to the Panchála crows. He leads the two other surviving combatants, Kripa and Krita·varman, to attack the Panchála-Pándava camp that very night, where the Panchálas sleep off-guard, prematurely jubilant at their victory. The divine Krishna, aide to the Pándavas, who as it turns out is aware of the impending massacre, advises the Pándavas not to spend the night in their allies' camp, leaving the remaining victors to their fate. The Pándavas, Krishna and his charioteer Sátyaki, are the only combatants out of harm's way.

Divine Intervention

But Ashva·tthaman's access to the camp is not straightforward. The way is barred and the action is interrupted by the magnificent vision of a wrathful god, which displays attributes first of wrathful Shiva and the troops of monstrous beings associated with him, and then attributes of

Vishnu. Until this point, the two gods have co-operated to protect the Pándava-Panchála troops. Not recognizing the opponent, which swallows all the weapons Ashva·tthaman throws at it, Ashva·tthaman offers himself in sacrifice to Shiva, placing himself on a sacrificial fire that appears before him. Here the conflict and concurrence of human effort and divine intervention (*daiva*) are worked out. Ashva·tthaman cannot succeed without divine approval. At the same time he is already part of the plan: the fate of the Panchálas and other allies of the Pándavas was already sealed, as indeed was the entire devastation. We come to hear this at the end of 'Dead of Night,' when the sage Nárada reveals that the slaughter of all the warriors was a favor granted by the assembly of gods to the overburdened earth goddess, weary of her weight of warriors. Ashva·tthaman, transformed into an incarnation of the god Shiva who possesses him, is fulfilling Shiva's role in bringing an end to the current age. The entire massacre is a sacrifice, and the divine Krishna will, once Ashva·tthaman is defeated, relate the story of Shiva's destruction of the sacrifice celebrated by the entire world at the creation of the universe, in his wrath at being excluded from it. It is this sacrifice—the parallels between sacrifice and war for warriors are made throughout the "Maha·bhárata"—which the excluded Ashva·tthaman mirrors in his savage attack on the victorious Panchálas.[4]

Destructive Heat and the Spark of Hope

The camp, the entire Panchála army and all the remaining sons of the Pándava line are annihilated. But the destruction is not over. The entire world stands on the brink of complete obliteration as a missile crisis develops in a standoff between Ashva·tthaman, who has been tracked to the banks of the Ganges, and the middle Pándava brother, Árjuna. The missiles have the potential to devastate the entire country. Here the Pándavas' essential moral right to rule is once more emphasized as Árjuna's spiritual purity is revealed through his ability to recall his missile, following the intervention of the divine sages Nárada and Vyasa. Ashva·tthaman is too angry, too ill-disciplined and too vengeful to recall his own. The subjugation and exile of Ashva·tthaman is the final successful act of revenge in the epic, revenge in the name of the Pándavas' wife Dráupadi for the murder of her sons, but the world is now blighted. Ashva·tthaman directs his missile into the wombs of the Bhárata women. They all miscarry and—their husbands dead—have no hope to bear more children. It is divine intervention by Krishna, the incarnation of the creator god Vishnu, that gives hope of a renewed world order. He promises he will revive the stillborn grandson of Árjuna, Paríkshit, to restore life to the devastated clans.

From Darkness to Dust

Just as the dominant mood of 'Dead of Night' is darkness, *tamas* in every sense, the dominant mood of 'The Women' is passion and dust, *rajas*, the passions of grief and anger, the dust of the deserted battlefield, a mass of dead bodies.

The eponymous women of this book only make an appearance once the passion and anger among the men have been resolved. 'The Women' opens with king Dhrita·rashtra's ineffectiveness as a physically, spiritually and paternally blind man. He must accept that his fatherly partiality for his war-mongering son Duryódhana undermined his judgment as regent of the kingdom and gave room for the rivalry to escalate to all-out war. Again, a conflict of dharma creates the tension of this scene: Dhrita·rashtra is a man of wisdom who knew right from wrong and knew his duty as head of the entire Káurava clan, but he allowed his paternal partiality and personal ambition to intercede.[5] Two characters representative of untarnished wisdom, his half-brother Vídura and their shared natural father, the sage Vyasa, now point out his failings. They also offer him spiritual teachings about the nature and inevitability of loss, and the heaven won by those who die in action. Finally, Vyasa offers him the comfort that the massive slaughter was all part of a divine plan. Now Dhrita·rashtra must accept defeat, which he can only do by acknowledging his responsibility and understanding that loss is inherent in life. Finally, his acceptance of his new position, and that the Pándavas will welcome him as a father in spite of all that has happened, paves the way for a tense reconciliation between the Pándavas and Dhrita·rashtra's wife Gandhári, the mother of the Káuravas. This episode marks the shift from the hostilities to the clearing up of the battle, taming the women's appetite for revenge and curbing their potent curses in order to enable peace.

It is a conscious decision on the part of the redactors of the "Maha·bhárata" to mark a clear division between the continued violence of 'Dead of Night' and the process of laying both the enmity of the living and the bodies of the deceased to rest in 'The Women.' This is achieved through a non-consecutive narrative. Overlapping events are divided between the two books, according to violence or reconciliation. Thus part of the action that in fact precedes the missile launch related at the end of 'Dead of Night' is recorded afterwards in 'The Women,' at the beginning of book eleven. This allows the three remaining combatants of the Káurava side to take their leave of Dhrita·rashtra and Gandhári in the context of the clean-up and reconciliation after the end of all hostilities, and brings Ashva·tthaman's final act of revenge forward into 'Dead of Night.' This overlap is made clear by the narrator Vaishampáyana at the end of the eleventh canto of 'The Women,' where he links the flight of three remaining Káuravas to the lead-up to the missile contest between Ashva·tthaman and Árjuna.

Extreme Grief

The mood of grief, the grief of failure, of lost status and of lost loved ones, dominates 'The Women.' The grief is so terrible that in places people can only express it through imagining the grief of others and grieving on another's account. The greatest example of this is Gandhári's expression of grief to Krishna, in which she surveys the blighted battlefield, using the divine eye granted to her by the sage Vyasa. The description she paints of the innocent wives of the deceased warriors confronted by the mangled corpses of their men is a masterpiece of horror and pathos. It is taut with the tension of contrasts between what was and could have been with what now is. Recalling the former virility of the warriors accentuates their now pitiable state. This virility is recalled with reference to three key components of manhood: the commander of status, the champion fighter and the passionate lover. The tension over status is drawn out by comparing the former comforts each warrior enjoyed, and his now lowly state compelled to lie in the mud, gore and dust of the battlefield. The martial tension is created by comparing the warrior's former apparent invincibility—an opportunity for the brief recapitulation of favored episodes so beloved of the "Maha·bhárata"—with his actual fall. A sexual tension is brought out between the women's reminiscences of and attempts to recreate their love-making with their now lifeless husbands, with the actual carnal relationship between the fallen warriors and the predators now consuming them, especially the she-jackals.

Signs of Mourning

Two physical indicators of affection and grief described in order to heighten the pathos might without special mention be missed by the reader new to Indian tragedy. The first of these is sniffing as a sign of affection. Although it does not come up much in modern Western imagery—in spite of the experience of parents—sniffing a child as a sign of affection is also found in Western classical drama, for example in the heart-wrenching speech of Andromache in Euripides' "The Trojan Women," where she sniffs the sweet scent of her infant son who is about to be killed by the Greeks.[6] The second is loose hair as a sign of mourning, leading to the repeated mention both of the unbound hair of the war widows, and to warriors whose hair is down. The latter is an indicator that the warrior in question is non-combatant during a period of mourning. It recurs as a theme in Ashva·tthaman's anger at the murder of his own father who—thinking him dead—had laid down his weapons and loosened his hair, unassailable by the rules of war, but vulnerable to Dhrishta·dyumna who chose to break those rules.

Narrators

While the composition of the "Maha·bhárata" is attributed to the sage Vyasa, also known as Krishna Dvaipáyana, the biological father of Dhrita·rashtra, Pandu and Vídura, and so grandfather to the warring Káurava and Pándava cousins, we hear two narrators in these books. One is Vyasa's pupil Vaishampáyana, who tells the entire epic to King Janam·éjaya, the grandson of Árjuna, the middle Pándava, and second successor to the Káurava throne after the war is over and the Pándavas have departed to heaven. The other narrator is Sánjaya, who uses the divine eye bestowed on him by Vyasa to describe the entire battle to the blind king Dhrita·rashtra. This task completed, his divine vision departs and the narrative returns to Vaishampáyana.

The *suta*

Sánjaya's role as narrator is in accord with his status as Dhrita·rashtra's charioteer, or *suta*. The *suta* is a class of mixed caste, supposedly derived originally from brahmin and warrior (kshatriya) intermarriage. Their allocated profession as charioteer brings with it the roles of bard, witnessing, reporting and eulogizing the heroic deeds of battle, as well as the role of advisor, consoling, reinvigorating and spotting strategic advantage for the warrior they attend. Thus the fact that the divine Krishna takes up the position of Árjuna's charioteer in order to give him both practical and spiritual advice fits with the expectations of the *suta* role, even though there is no suggestion that Krishna is of that class.

Conflicting Codes of Conduct

The advice Krishna gives the Pándavas straddles the brahmin and warrior codes. On the one hand he dispenses wisdom based on the spiritual teachings that focus on the underlying nature of the universe. On the other hand, he gives strategic, military advice, the sole aim of which is military advantage. The former lies more within the traditional realm of the priestly brahmin class, the latter within the traditional realm of the warrior and regal kshatriya class. At times the priorities of the two are in conflict. Eventually the Pándavas succeed only by taking illicit advantage of weaknesses that conventions of war or filial duty protect.

This conflict between ideals of conduct, and between ideal and actual conduct, pervades the "Maha·bhárata." Seen as a conflict between the code of two castes, it can be attributed to the different layers of the authorship of the "Maha·bhárata." Just as the *suta* straddles the brahmin-kshatriya divide, so the text as a whole, in the form we have it, seems to shift between a kshatriya record of warring clans to a brahmanical record of cosmogonic, sacrificial and spiritual teachings. The action of battle is put to one side for long periods during the text, to allow various sages and advisors to proclaim lengthy teachings of the ultimate meaning or cosmogonic significance of events, to recast the sacrifice of battle in terms of brahmanical sacrifice.

The text's ongoing development—the main composition dating from as early as the beginning of the first millennium BCE and continuing to the middle of the first millennium CE—also led to the need to reconcile conduct acceptable, or even advocated in a bygone era, with the expectations of the current time (current to whichever period of composition the reconciliation takes place). We can see this very clearly with the explanations given for the apparently scandalous polyandrous marriage of Dráupadi to all five Pándavas. A mythical explanation is given. She is reborn to marry the "five Indras," the five manifestations of the god Indra a part of whom is incarnated in each of the Pándava brothers. The five are in fact really one. A practical explanation is given. When the brothers return home with her, the middle Pándava, Árjuna, having won her in an archery contest, they call to their mother to come and see what they have brought. She, thinking they have gone to find food, tells them, without looking, to share it between them. Since whatever she says must be true, and they, in their filial perfection, must be obedient to their mother, they share the new bride. Yet we know that polyandry used to be an acceptable form of marriage in north India, and is still found in some Himalayan regions. The code of a later era necessitates the reconciliation. We have to wonder if this applies to other stories of reconciliation in the epic.

The reconciliation of acts that go against dharma, the code of conduct which should govern each person, is often about reconciling the ideals of dharmic duty with military necessity. For the sin of killing a teacher, Dhrishta·dyumna is torn apart by Ashva·tthaman and thus denied the heaven that awaits warriors who die by the sword. Yudhi·shthira also must pay for this part in Drona's death and see hell (in the final book of the "Maha·bhárata"). When Bhima, the second and most savage of the Pándavas, illegally breaks Duryódhana's thigh, it is explained in terms of the latter's former despicable conduct in displaying himself to Dráupadi. Yet when Bhima sanitizes his drinking of Duhshásana's blood by telling Gandhári he only pretended to, claiming the blood "did not pass my lips," is he in fact sanitizing a practice of drinking the blood, or consuming the flesh, of the conquered victim still found even in modern societies, for an audience for whom this was now beyond the pale?

Agency and Privileged Knowledge

A final dilemma which the "Maha·bhárata" seeks to accommodate is the extent to which one acts consciously or is merely an agent of Fate. On one level Ashva·tthaman is made responsible for his actions and pays the price for them. His destructiveness stems from his own corruption. On another level, he is entirely the agent of a divine plan to rid the earth of all its warriors. At the same time, he is the instrument of a vengeful god weary of protecting the Panchálas, in his embodiment of Shiva, or his waywardness is deliberately permitted by the knowing but fickle Krishna, who saves only his favored few. The same Krishna kept counsel over a secret that could have, in human terms, quashed the very reason for the war—the disputed right to the throne. Only at the end of the 'The Women' does the Pándavas' mother Kunti reveal that Yudhi·shthira, now the undisputed king as oldest of her victorious sons, was not in fact the oldest. Karna, the closest ally of their enemy Duryódhana, oldest of the Káuravas, was in fact their first-born brother. They had killed the key to a successful, bloodless resolution to their agonizing conflict.

With so many layers of unseen and compromised causality, the characters struggle in their moment, seeking lights amid the darkness and passion, yet cornered by Fate, their outlook fatefully obscured. The full picture, the well worked out plan of the gods, is visible only to the divine and to the favored audience to whom they choose to bestow this revelation.

A Note on Non-classical Grammar

While epic Sanskrit is on the whole simpler than classical Sanskrit, we also find some deviations from classical norms: the use of *iti*, the marker of the end of speech, before the actual end of the speech, e.g. *Sauptika* ('Dead of Night') 16.29; the relationship between a noun outside the compound with a subordinate member of the compounds, e.g. *putra|hantā jitaḥ sa te* at *Sauptika* 16.27 where *te* relates to *putra*; the use of *katham* to mean "so that," e.g. *Strī* ('The Women') 8.20 and 8.40; the loss of the verbal augments *a-* in the aorist, imperfect and conditional tense e.g. *svapatām* (*Sauptika* 8.4); occasional non-grammatical agreement of participle and agent, e.g. with present participle (*anusmaran Sauptika* 4.23) and absolutive *baddhvā* (*Sauptika* 8.70; see relevant notes); and sandhi being performed twice to remove a hiatus that would be left to stand in classical Sanskrit, e.g. *hateti* for *hata iti*, which is *hataḥ iti* before sandhi (*Sauptika* 4.26).

Concordance of Canto Numbers with the Critical Edition

SAUPTIKAPARVAN

CSL and CE versions correspond fairly closely.

STRĪPARVAN

CSL	CE
1.1	1.1
9.2	–
10.1	9.2
15.1	14.1
15.24	15.1
16.1	16.1

A large part of canto 9 is in fact repetition from canto 5, but accepted by the commentary as intentional repetition and not an error.

Acknowledgements

I rejoice in the following virtues: the *dāna* of John & Jennifer Clay, the *śīla* of Richard Gombrich, the *kṣānti* and *vīrya* of Isabelle Onians and Chris Gibbons, the *samādhi* of Daniel Bálogh, Stuart Brown and Tomoyuki Kono, and the *prajñā* of Andrew Skilton. This would be nowhere without them.

Notes

1 Although the hostilities within the Káurava clan come to an end here, the war continues to have a knock-on effect among other groups involved, leading to the eventual implosion of Krishna's

clan, the Vrishnis, which fought divided between the two sides in the war ('Book of the Maces' in the volume 'Final Departures' of this series).

2 This interpretation of the "Maha·bhárata" in terms of cosmic dissolution reflecting myths of cosmic destruction and renewal that receive far more explicit expression in Puranic literature has received some attention in scholarship, most notably by MADELEINE BIARDEAU, *Études de mythologie hindou*, Paris 1–5. *Bulletin de l'École d'Extrême-Orient* 54 (1968) 19–45; 55 (1969) 59–105; 58 (1971) 17–89; 63 (1976) 111–263; 65 (1978) 87–238. HILTEBEITEL (1976, part 4: 310–11) discusses this theme in depth and notes BIARDEAU's identification of this section of the epic—Ashva·tthaman's embodiment of Shiva and complete destruction of possible renewal without divine intervention through his killing of the Pándavas' unborn children—with specific stages of cosmic dissolution.

3 See SCHEUER (1982: 295–96 with note 5) on the traditional symbolism of the banyan tree for the universe and the possible equation here of the owl with the sage Naráyana, agent of the destruction and renewal of the universe.

4 For an analysis of the extensive parallels between Ashva·tthaman's massacre of the Panchálas and the myth of Shiva's destruction of the sacrifice, see HILTEBEITEL (1976: 312–35).

5 Conflicts within dharma and between dharma and personal weakness are a recurring theme throughout the "Maha·bhárata" and have received much attention in scholarship, particularly in the cases of Yudhi·shthira and Árjuna. For a discussion of some of the issues, including the case of Dhrita·rashtra, see MATILAL (2002: chapter 5).

6 "Thou little thing / That curlest in my arms, what sweet scents cling / All round thy neck!." GILBERT MURRAY: "The Trojan Women of Euripides." London: George Allen, 1905, p. 49.

Bibliography

THE "MAHA·BHÁRATA" IN SANSKRIT

The text used for this edition is based mainly on:

The Mahabharatam with the Bharata Bhawadeepa Commentary of Nilakantha, RAMACHANDRASHASTRI KINJAWADEKAR (ed.) Poona: Chitrashala press 1929–36; repr. New Delhi: Oriental Books Reprint Corporation 1978, 2nd ed. 1979. Vols. 10 and 11 [= CSL = K]

Comparison is made with, and occasional emendation introduced on the basis of:

The Mahābhārata, for the first time critically edited, V.S. SUKTHANKAR, S.K. BELVALKAR, P.L. VAIDYA, et al. (eds.) 19 vols. plus 6 vols. of indices (Poona Bhandarkar Oriental Research Institute 1933–72). Vol. XII. [= CE]

A list of emendations to this text can be found on pp. 361ff.

THE "MAHA·BHÁRATA" IN TRANSLATION

GANGULI, KISARI MOHAN (trans.) [early editions ascribed to the publisher, P.C. Roy]. 1884–99. *The Mahabharata of Krishna-Dwaipayana Vyasa*, 12 vols. (2nd edn. Calcutta 1970; repr. New Delhi: Munshiram Manoharlal, 1970 (5th edn.1990)).

FITZGERALD, JAMES L. 2004. *The Mahābhārata 11. The Book of the Women 12. The Book of Peace, Part One*. Chicago: Chicago University Press. Extensive introduction and annotations, particularly useful in terms of Dharmashastra.

JOHNSON, W.J. 1998. *The Sauptikaparvan of the Mahābhārata: The Massacre at Night*. Oxford World's Classics. Oxford: Oxford University Press. Extensive introduction and annotations, particularly useful in terms of Dharmashastra.

OTHER WORKS

HILTEBEITEL, ALF. *The Ritual of Battle: Krishna in the Mahabharata*, Ithaca: Cornell University Press. Part Four analyses the *Sauptikaparvan* in terms of ritual and eschatological symbolism, summarising important earlier work on the subject, including that of DUMÉZIL and BIARDEAU.

KATZ, RUTH CECILY. 1989. *Arjuna in the Mahabharata*, Columbia: University of South Carolina Press; reprinted Delhi: Motilal Banarsidass Publishers 1990.

MATILAL, BIMAL KRISHNA and JONARDON GANERI (ed.) 2002. *Ethics and Epics. The Collected Essays of Bimal Krishna Matilal*. New Delhi: Oxford University Press.

PARGITER, FREDERICK. 1972. *Ancient Indian Historical Tradition*. London: Oxford University Press 1922; reprinted Delhi: Motilal Banarsidass 1962 and 1972.

OBERLIES, THOMAS. 2003. *A Grammar of Epic Sanskrit*. Berlin: Walter de Gruyter.

SØRENSEN, SØREN. 1904–25. *An Index to the Names in the Mahābhārata*. London: Williams and Norgate (issued in 13 parts); reprinted Delhi: Motilal Banarsidass 2006.

SCHEUER, JACQUES. 1982. *Śiva dans le Mahābhārata*. Paris: Presses Universitaires de France. Chapter Nine is devoted to an analysis of Shiva in the *Sauptikaparvan*.

MAHA·BHÁRATA

BOOK TEN

DEAD OF NIGHT

Nārāyaṇaṃ namas|kṛtya
Naraṃ c' âiva nar'|ôttamam,
devīṃ Sarasvatīṃ c' âiva,
tato jayam udīrayet.

Honor Naráyana, most exalted Nara,
and blessed Sarásvati, and spur on "Victory!"*

1–5
THE OWL IN THE BANYAN

SAÑJAYA uvāca:

1.1 TATAS TE SAHITĀ vīrāḥ prayātā dakṣiṇā|mukhāḥ
upāstamana|velāyāṃ śivir'|ābhyāśam āgatāḥ.
vimucya vāhāṃs tvaritā bhītā samabhavaṃs tadā;
gahanaṃ deśam āsādya pracchannā nyaviśanta te.
senā|niveśam abhito n' âtidūram avasthitāḥ
nikṛttā niśitaiḥ śastraiḥ samantāt kṣata|vikṣatāḥ.
dīrgham uṣṇaṃ ca niḥśvasya Pāṇḍavān eva cintayan,
śrutvā ca ninadaṃ ghoraṃ Pāṇḍavānāṃ jay'|âiṣiṇāṃ,
1.5 anusāra|bhayād bhītāḥ prāṅ|mukhāḥ prādravan punaḥ.
te muhūrtāt tato gatvā, śrānta|vāhāḥ, pipāsitāḥ
n' âmṛṣyanta mah"|êṣv|āsāḥ krodh'|âmarṣa|vaśaṃ* gatāḥ,
rājño vadhena saṃtaptā muhūrtaṃ samavasthitāḥ.

DHṚTARĀṢṬRA uvāca:

a|śraddheyam idaṃ karma kṛtaṃ Bhīmena, Sañjaya,
yat sa nāg'|âyuta|prāṇaḥ putro mama nipātitaḥ,
a|vadhyaḥ sarva|bhūtānāṃ, vajra|saṃhanano, yuvā
Pāṇḍavaiḥ samare putro nihato mama, Sañjaya.
na diṣṭam abhyatikrāntaṃ śakyaṃ, Gāvalgaṇe, naraiḥ,
yat sametya raṇe Pārthaiḥ putro mama nipātitaḥ.
1.10 adri|sāra|mayaṃ nūnaṃ hṛdayaṃ mama, Sañjaya,
hataṃ putra|śataṃ śrutvā yan na dīrṇaṃ sahasradhā.
kathaṃ hi vṛddha|mithunaṃ hata|putraṃ bhaviṣyati?
na hy ahaṃ Pāṇḍaveyasya viṣaye vastum utsahe.

SÁNJAYA continued:*

AS ONE THOSE warriors then set off, heading south. As 1.1
the sun began to set, they approached their encampment. But they sensed danger and, hurriedly releasing their
mounts, they took cover and kept down low, hidden from
view. All around the army camp on every side lay in their
places, at no great distance, the maimed and wounded,
hewn down by whetted weapons. As they let out long,
burning groans of grief, it was on the Pándavas that our
men's thoughts fixed, and hearing the terrible roar of the
Pándavas bent on victory, they pushed on again, driven by 1.5
the terror of pursuit, heading east. When they had ridden
but a short while, their mounts exhausted and their throats
parched, those great archers could bear it no longer. Sub-
mitting to their insufferable rage, seething at the slaughter
of their king,* they halted a moment.

DHRITA·RASHTRA interrupted:

It's impossible to believe that Bhima could achieve this feat, Sánjaya; that my son, who had the vitality of ten thousand elephants, could be brought down; that my son, invincible to all beings, Sánjaya, impenetrably armored and in his prime, could be slain by Pándavas in combat. But men can't overturn the ordinance of Fate, son of Gaválgana, which sealed that my son, on confronting Pritha's sons in battle, would be brought down.

My heart must be stone to the core, Sánjaya, since it does 1.10
not shatter in a thousand pieces on hearing my hundred
sons are slain. For what becomes of an old couple whose
sons are slain? For sure I cannot endure vassalage to Pandu's

kathaṃ rājñaḥ pitā bhūtvā, svayaṃ rājā ca, Sañjaya,
preṣya|bhūtaḥ pravarteyaṃ Pāṇḍaveyasya śāsanāt,
ājñāpya pṛthivīṃ sarvāṃ, sthitvā mūrdhani, Sañjaya,
yena putra|śataṃ pūrṇam ekena nihataṃ mama?
kṛtaṃ satyaṃ vacas tasya Vidurasya mah"|ātmanaḥ†
a|kurvatā vacas tena mama putreṇa, Sañjaya.
1.15 katham asya bhaviṣyāmi preṣya|bhūto dur|anta|kṛt?
kathaṃ Bhīmasya vākyāni śrotuṃ śakṣyāmi, Sañjaya?
a|dharmeṇa hate, tāta, putre Duryodhane mama,
Kṛtavarmā, Kṛpo, Drauṇiḥ kim akurvata, Sañjaya?

SAÑJAYA uvāca:

gatvā tu tāvakā, rājan, n' âtidūraṃ avasthitāḥ
apaśyanta vanaṃ ghoraṃ nānā|druma|lat"|āvṛtam.
te muhūrtaṃ tu viśramya labdha|toyair hay' ôttamaiḥ,
sūry'|āstamana|velāyāṃ samāsedur mahad vanaṃ
nāna|mṛga|gaṇair juṣṭaṃ, nānā|pakṣi|gaṇ'|āvṛtam,
nānā|druma|lat"|ācchannaṃ, nānā|vyāla|niṣevitam,
1.20 nānā|toyaiḥ samākīrṇaṃ, nānā|puṣp'|ôpaśobhitam,
padmanī|śata|saṃchannaṃ, nīl'|ôtpala|samāyutam.
praviśya tad vanaṃ ghoraṃ vīkṣamāṇāḥ samantataḥ,
śākhā|sahasra|saṃchannaṃ nyagrodhaṃ dadṛśus tataḥ.
upetya tu tadā, rājan, nyagrodhaṃ te mahā|rathāḥ
dadṛśur dvi|padāṃ śreṣṭhāḥ śreṣṭhaṃ taṃ vai vanas|patim.
te 'vatīrya rathebhyaś ca, vipramucya ca vājinaḥ,
upaspṛśya yathā|nyāyaṃ sandhyām anvāsataḥ, prabho.

son. Sánjaya, how can someone once the father of a king, nay a king himself, continue now a slave at the beck of Pandu's son? When I have directed the entire world, have stood at its head, Sánjaya, and he has single-handedly slain the full century of my sons? Sánjaya, by that son of mine not acting on the words of the noble Vídura, those words have been actualized.

How can I fulfill such an ignoble end, as his slave? How 1.15
will I endure the sound of Bhima's words, Sánjaya? Now, Sánjaya, when my son Duryódhana had been so treacherously slain, dear man, what did Krita·varman, Kripa and Drona's child do?

SÁNJAYA continued:

Your men, sire, had come to a halt after no great distance, whereupon they spied a fearsome forest, shrouded in vines trailing from the various trees. After resting a moment, while their sterling steeds took water, they advanced to that great forest, just as the sun slipped from the sky. It was home to many a herd, veiled by various flocks of birds, swathed by the vines trailing from an array of different trees, frequented by every kind of wild beast, swamped 1.20
by stretches of water, lush with a wealth of blossoms, pocketed by a hundred lotus pools brimming with blue lotuses. As they entered that terrible forest and looked about them, they caught sight of a banyan tree screened within a thousand rooted limbs. Now, sire, coming up close to the banyan, those mighty warriors, surveyed it—the most magnificent of men, that most magnificent forest giant. They alighted from their chariots and unharnessed their steeds.

tato 'staṃ parvata|śreṣṭham anuprāpte divā|kare
sarvasya jagato dhātrī śarvarī samapadyata.
1.25 graha|nakṣatra|tārābhiḥ saṃpūrṇābhir alaṃkṛtam
nabho 'ṃśukam iv' ābhāti prekṣaṇīyaṃ samantataḥ.
icchayā te pravalganti ye sattvā rātri|cāriṇaḥ;
divā|carāś ca ye sattvās te nidrā|vaśam āgatāḥ.
rātriṃ|carāṇāṃ sattvānāṃ nirghoṣo 'bhūt su|dāruṇaḥ;
kravyādāś ca pramuditā, ghorā prāptā ca śarvarī.
tasmin rātri|mukhe ghore duḥkha|śoka|samanvitāḥ
Kṛtavarmā, Kṛpo, Drauṇir upopaviviśuḥ samam.
tatr' ôpaviṣṭāḥ śocanto nyagrodhasya samīpataḥ
tam ev' ârtham atikrāntaṃ Kuru|Pāṇḍavayoḥ kṣayam.
1.30 nidrayā ca parīt'|āṅgā niṣedur dharaṇī|tale
śrameṇa su|dṛḍhaṃ yuktā, vikṣatā vividhaiḥ śaraiḥ.
tato nidrā|vaśaṃ prāptau Kṛpa|Bhojau mahā|rathau
sukh' ôcitāv, a|duḥkh'|ārhau, niṣaṇṇau dharaṇī|tale,
tau tu suptau, mahā|rāja, śrama|śoka|samanvitau
mah"|ārha|śayan'|ôpetau bhūmāv eva hy anāthavat.
krodh'|âmarṣa|vaśaṃ† prāpto Droṇa|putras tu, Bhārata,
na vai sma sa jagām' âtha nidrāṃ, sarpa iva śvasan.
na lebhe sa tu nidrāṃ vai dahyamāno hi manyunā.
vīkṣāṃ cakre mahā|bāhus tad vanaṃ ghora|darśanam.

Then, after ablution, they performed the proper prayers of twilight, Lord. At that moment, when the bringer of day had reached the exalted western mountain, the star-spangled night, nurse to all the world, appeared.

Dressed in the full complement of planets, constellations 1.25
and stars, the sky shimmered softly like muslin drape, the vision good on every side.* As the urge took them the creatures of the night stirred, while those beings busy by day succumbed to sleep. Pitiless were the sounds of the creatures that prowled the shadows, as the feeders on flesh were filled with glee and that gory, starry night progressed.

Side by side in the dreadful maw of that night, overwhelmed by misery and grief, sat Krita·varman, Kripa and Drona's son together. There they sat close to the banyan, grieving for what had come to pass, the destruction of both the Kuru and Pándava sides.

Their limbs overwhelmed by weariness they slumped to 1.30
the bare ground, sore-pressed by exhaustion, injured by countless arrows. Then the two great chariot-warriors Kripa and Bhoja, so accustomed to comfort, so undeserving of such wretchedness, yet slumped on the bare ground, succumbed to sleep. But, Your Majesty, while those two, overcome by exhaustion and grief, slept on the bare earth like the dispossessed, though owners of the most luxurious beds, Drona's son, by contrast, fell mercy to wrath and indignation, scion of Bhárata's line, and he no more fell asleep than a hissing serpent. No, he got no sleep at all, burning as he was with pride. The strapping warrior cast his eyes about that terrifying forest.

1.35 vīkṣamāṇo van'|ôddeśaṃ nānā|sattvair niṣevitam
apaśyata mahā|bāhur nyagrodhaṃ vāyasair yutam.
tatra kāka|sahasrāṇi tāṃ niśāṃ paryaṇāmayan.
sukhaṃ svapanti, Kauravya, pṛthak|pṛthag|upāśrayāḥ.
supteṣu teṣu kākeṣu viśrabdheṣu samantataḥ,
so 'paśyat sahasā yāntam ulūkaṃ ghora|darśanam,
mahā|svanaṃ, mahā|kāyaṃ, hary|akṣaṃ, babhru|piṅgalam,
su|dīrgha|ghoṇā|nakharaṃ, Suparṇam iva veginam.
so 'tha śabdaṃ mṛduṃ kṛtvā līyamāna iv' âṇḍajaḥ
nyagrodhasya tataḥ śākhāṃ prārthayām āsa, Bhārata.
1.40 saṃnipatya tu śākhāyāṃ nyagrodhasya vihaṃ|gamaḥ
suptāñ jaghāna su|bahūn vāyasān vāyas'|ântakaḥ.
keṣāñ cid acchinat pakṣāñ, śirāṃsi ca cakarta ha,
caraṇāṃś caiva keṣāñ cid babhañja caraṇ'|āyudhaḥ.
kṣaṇen' âhan sa† balavān ye 'sya dṛṣṭi|pathe sthitāḥ.
teṣāṃ śarīr'|âvayavaiḥ śarīraiś ca, viśāṃ|pate,
nyagrodha|maṇḍalaṃ sarvaṃ
saṃchannaṃ sarvato 'bhavat.
tāṃs tu hatvā tataḥ kākān
kauśiko mudito 'bhavat,
pratikṛtya yathā|kāmaṃ śatrūṇāṃ śatru|sūdanaḥ.
tad dṛṣṭvā s'|ôpadhaṃ karma kauśikena kṛtaṃ niśi,
1.45 tad|bhāve kṛta|saṃkalpo Drauṇir eko 'nvacintayat:†
«upadeśaḥ kṛto 'nena pakṣiṇā mama saṃyuge,
śatrūṇāṃ kṣapaṇe yuktaḥ, prāpta|kālaś ca me mataḥ.
n' âdya śakyā mayā hantuṃ Pāṇḍavā jita|kāśinaḥ,
balavantaḥ, kṛt'|ôtsāhāḥ, prāpta|lakṣāḥ, prahāriṇaḥ.
rājñaḥ sakāśāt teṣāṃ tu pratijñāto vadho mayā.

Looking at the spot in the forest frequented by many 1.35
different creatures, the strapping warrior observed that the banyan tree was full of crows. Thousands of crows were spending the night there. They slept peacefully, king of Kurus, each roosting in its place. As those crows slept unsuspecting all about, he saw all of a sudden an owl swoop, a ghostly sight, with its loud screech, vast body, yellow eyes, and tawny hew, its long hooked beak and talons, deft in flight as fine-winged Gáruda.* Now making a soft sound, as if melting away, that egg-born creature then sought out a branch of the banyan, scion of Bhárata's line.

Now that rider of the sky, falling upon the banyan bough, 1.40
killed many a crow in slumber, bringing the crows their end. He ripped the wings off some, the heads off others. Of some he broke the feet, whose own feet were his weapon, full of power, slaying in an instant all those within his line of sight. Their dismembered limbs and corpses, lord of all peoples, carpeted the entire circle of the banyan bole in every direction, while the taloned murderer of those black crows exulted in his work, at wreaking havoc on his prey at whim, his prey's executioner.

On seeing the taloned owl dispatch that deed so stealthily
in the night, in Drona's lone son the resolve formed to be- 1.45
come just like it, as he realized: "This winged bird has given me a lesson in the art of war tailored to the obliteration of my enemies and I deem the time has come. Today I was not able to kill the Pándavas. They seemed victorious, powerful, their mission fulfilled, their target struck, the champions. Yet I have sworn their slaughter in the presence of the king. Resorting to a course of self-destruction like a moth toward

patang'|âgni|samāṃ vṛttim āsthāy' ātma|vināśinīm
nyāyato yudhyamānasya prāṇa|tyāgo, na saṃśayaḥ.
chadmanā tu bhavet siddhiḥ śatrūṇāṃ ca kṣayo mahān.

    tataḥ saṃśayitād arthād yo 'rtho niḥsaṃśayo bhavet,
1.50 taṃ janā bahu manyante ye ca śāstra|viśāradāḥ.
yac c' âpy atra bhaved vācyaṃ,† garhitaṃ, loka|ninditaṃ,
kartavyaṃ tan manuṣyeṇa kṣatra|dharmeṇa vartatā.
ninditāni ca sarvāṇi kutsitāni pade pade
s'|ôpadhāni kṛtāny eva Pāṇḍavair a|kṛt'|ātmabhiḥ.
asminn arthe purā gītāḥ śrūyante dharma|cintakaiḥ
ślokā nyāyam avekṣadbhis tattv'|ârthās tattva|darśibhiḥ:

    ‹pariśrānte, vidīrṇe vā,
        bhuñjāne v" âpi śatrubhiḥ,
    prasthāne ca, praveśe ca
        prahartavyaṃ ripor balam;
    nidr"|ārtam ardha|rātre ca,
        tathā naṣṭa|praṇāyakam,
1.55 bhinna|yodhaṃ balaṃ yac ca,
        dvidhā yuktaṃ ca yad bhavet.› »

    ity evaṃ niścayaṃ cakre suptānāṃ niśi māraṇe
Pāṇḍūnāṃ saha Pāñcālair Droṇaputraḥ pratāpavān.
sa krūrāṃ matim āsthāya, viniścitya muhur muhuḥ,
suptau prābodhayat tau tu mātulaṃ Bhojam eva ca.
tau prabodhau mah"|ātmanau Kṛpa|Bhojau mahā|balau
n' ôttaraṃ pratipadyetāṃ tatra yuktaṃ hriyā vṛtau.

a flame, I would throw away my life if I fought them lawfully, that's not in doubt. But through stealth could come success, and massive loss to our enemy.

In preference to an uncertain outcome an objective that
is certain to succeed is deemed better by many people in- 1.50
cluding experts in tracts on polity. Furthermore, whatever
aspect of this might be culpable, reprehensible, or scorned
by the world, is also the very thing a man committed to the
role of a soldier must do. Anyway, at every step such blameworthy, contemptible acts have already been treacherously
committed by the Pándavas who have no self-restraint. On
this subject of old, heeded by those pondering righteous
duty as they considered the nature of reality and realized
the truth, were sung these verses, these epitomes of truth:

'Exhausted, wounded, at mess; about to march,
or when the march is but done;
Succumbed to sleep in the night's middle watch,
or when its commander is gone;
When the troops are dispersed or divided, 1.55
when they should be together as one,
That is when hostile forces can ensure
their foe's army's undone.'"*

As he thought along these lines Ashva·tthaman resolved to kill at night the sleeping sons of Pandu along with the Panchálas. That splendid son of Drona, committed to that cruel plan, growing more determined by the minute, woke his two sleeping companions, his uncle and the Bhoja king. Once awake those noble-souled, mighty warriors Kripa and the Bhoja king, could make no reply, justly hindered as they

sa muhūrtam iva dhyātvā bāṣpa|vihvalam abravīt:

«hato Duryodhano rājā eka|vīro mahā|balaḥ
yasy' ârthe vairam asmābhir āsaktaṃ Pāṇḍavaiḥ saha.
1.60 ekākī bahubhiḥ kṣudrair āhave śuddha|vikramaḥ
pātito Bhīmasenena ekādaśa|camū|patiḥ.
Vṛkodareṇa kṣudreṇa su|nṛśaṃsam idaṃ kṛtam
mūrdh'|âbhiṣiktasya śiraḥ pādena parimṛdnatā.

vinardanti ca Pāñcālāḥ, kṣvelanti ca hasanti ca,
dhamanti śaṅkhāñ śataśo, hṛṣṭā ghnanti ca dundubhīn.
vāditra|ghoṣas tumulo vimiśraḥ śaṅkha|nisvanaiḥ
anilen' ērito ghoro diśaḥ pūrayat' îva ha.
aśvānāṃ heṣamāṇānāṃ, gajānāṃ c' âiva bṛṃhatām,
siṃha|nādaś ca śūrāṇāṃ śrūyate su|mahān ayam.
1.65 diśaṃ prācīṃ samāśritya hṛṣṭānāṃ gacchatāṃ bhṛśam
ratha|nemi|svanāś c' âiva śrūyante loma|harṣaṇāḥ.

Pāṇḍavair Dhārtarāṣṭrāṇāṃ yad idaṃ kadanaṃ kṛtam,
vayam eva trayaḥ śiṣṭās tasmin mahati vaiśase.
ke cin nāga|śata|prāṇāḥ. ke cit sarv'|âstra|kovidāḥ.
nihatāḥ Pāṇḍaveyais te. manye kālasya paryayam.
evam etena bhāvyaṃ hi. nūnaṃ kāryeṇa tattvataḥ,
yathā hy asy' ēdṛśī niṣṭhā kṛta|kārye 'pi duṣkare.
bhavatos tu† yadi prajñā na mohād apanīyate,
vyāpanne 'smin mahaty arthe yan naḥ śreyas, tad ucyatām.»

were by shame at what he said. He seemed to reflect for a moment, then, choking back the tears, he said:

"King Duryódhana, our eminent hero and mighty warrior, in whose cause we engaged in this hostility with the
Pándavas, is slain. Though the commander of eleven bat- 1.60
talions,* his own valor never sullied, he was all-alone on
the battlefield when Bhima·sena and his many vile helpers
brought him down. The vile Wolf-belly committed a further most pernicious crime when he rubbed his foot upon
his head, his consecrated head.

The Panchálas, they whoop and leap for joy and cheer.
They blow their conches and beat their drums a hundred
times in jubilation. Carried by the wind, the horrific tumult
of their drums intermingled with the calls of their conches
seems to fill the horizon. Above the neighing horses and
trumpeting elephants, this great lion's roar from the champions of the battle can be heard. The spine-chilling grind 1.65
made by the rims of their chariot wheels as they drive off
briskly in jubilation is audible even here as it reaches the
eastern horizon.

The Pándavas carried out this slaughter of Dhrita·rashtra's men. From that monstrous massacre only the three of us survive. Some had the vitality of a hundred elephants. Others were skilled in every missile. They were slain by the Pándavas' men. I consider this the alteration of time.* For this is how it was meant to be. Surely it is really through that act that a fate just like it shall also befall the evil man who carried out that act. Now, if bewilderment has not removed your ability to think, tell me what course of action would be best for us in our great quest, given our current misfortune."

KṚPA uvāca:

2.1 ŚRUTAṂ TE vacanaṃ sarvaṃ yad yad uktaṃ tvayā, vibho.
mam' âpi tu vacaḥ kiñ cic chṛṇuṣv' âdya, mahā|bhuja:
ābaddhā mānuṣāḥ sarve nibaddhāḥ karmaṇor dvayoḥ:
daive puruṣa|kāre ca. paraṃ tābhyāṃ na vidyate.
na hi daivena sidhyanti kāryāṇy ekena, sattama,
na c' âpi karmaṇ" âikena. dvābhyāṃ siddhis tu yogataḥ.
tābhyām ubhābhyāṃ sarv|ârthā nibaddhā adham|ôttamāḥ
pravṛttāś caiva dṛśyante nivṛttāś caiva sarvaśaḥ.
2.5 Parjanyaḥ parvate varṣan kiṃ nu sādhayate phalam?
kṛṣṭe kṣetre tathā varṣan kiṃ na sādhayate phalam?
utthānaṃ c' âpi daivasya hy an|utthānaṃ ca daivatam
vyarthaṃ bhavati sarvatra pūrvas tatra viniścayaḥ.
su|vṛṣṭe ca yathā deve samyak kṣetre ca karṣite
bījaṃ mahā|guṇaṃ bhūyāt tathā siddhir hi mānuṣī.
tayor daivaṃ viniścitya svayaṃ c' âiva pravartate
prājñāḥ puruṣa|kāreṣu vartante dākṣyam āśritāḥ.
tābhyāṃ sarve hi kāry' ârthā manuṣyāṇāṃ, nara'|rṣabha.
viceṣṭantaḥ sma, dṛśyante nivṛttās tu tath" âiva ca.
2.10 kṛtaḥ puruṣa|kāraś ca, so 'pi daivena sidhyati,
tath" âsya karmaṇaḥ kartur abhinirvartate phalam.
utthānaṃ ca manuṣyāṇāṃ dakṣāṇāṃ daiva|varjitam
a|phalaṃ dṛśyate loke samyag apy upapāditam.
tatr' âlasā manuṣyāṇāṃ ye bhavanty a|manasvinaḥ,
utthānaṃ te vigarhanti. prājñānāṃ tan na rocate.

KRIPA replied:

I HAVE LISTENED to your every word, powerful lord. Now, mighty hero, listen in turn to what I have to say: 2.1

All humans are confined, restricted by two types of action: divine intervention and the effort wrought by man. There is nothing other than these two. Excellent man, goals are not accomplished through divine intervention alone, nor through human effort by itself. Rather success comes from the two combined. All goals, from the lowest to the highest, determined by both these factors are universally seen to succeed or fail. When the cloud-god releases rain on 2.5
a mountain does he produce a crop? Yet when he releases rain in exactly the same way on a tilled field, does he not produce a crop? For if human exertion is against divine will or divine will is unmet by exertion, anything one had determined to achieve would fail. Just as a correctly tilled field which god* has watered well would have a high yield, so it is with human achievement. Of the two, divine will, once decided, proceeds automatically, whereas insightful men succeed in human ventures on the basis of their diligence. Absolutely all aims of man are achieved on the basis of these two, bull of men. We see some progress while others fall by the way.

Now the profit of the effort made by man, though it de- 2.10
pends on the divine to succeed, still yields to the performer of that deed. On the other hand, the endeavor of diligent men, even when correctly applied, is known to be in vain in this world, if divine will shuns it. The idle among men who lack wisdom in this matter despise endeavor. That doesn't

prāyaśo hi kṛtaṃ karma n' â|phalaṃ dṛśyate bhuvi.
a|kṛtvā ca punar duḥkhaṃ karma paśyen mahā|phalam.
ceṣṭām akurval̃ labhate yadi kiṃ cid yadṛcchayā,
yo vā na labhate kṛtvā, dur|darśau tāv ubhāv api.
2.15 śaknoti jīvituṃ dakṣo. n' âlasaḥ sukham edhate.
dṛśyante jīva|loke 'smin dakṣāḥ prāyo hit'|âiṣiṇaḥ.
yadi dakṣaḥ samārambhāt
karmaṇo n' âśnute phalam,
n' âsya vācyaṃ bhavet kiñ cil,
labdhavyaṃ v" âdhigacchati.
a|kṛtvā karma yo loke phalaṃ vindati dhiṣṭhitaḥ,
sa tu vaktavyatāṃ yāti, dveṣyo bhavati bhūyaśaḥ.
evam etad an|ādṛtya vartate yas tv ato 'nyathā,
sa karoty ātmano 'n|arthān. eṣa buddhimatāṃ nayaḥ.
hīnaṃ puruṣa|kāreṇa yadi daivena vā punaḥ,
kāraṇābhyām ath' âitābhyām utthānam a|phalaṃ bhavet.
2.20 hīnaṃ puruṣa|kāreṇa karma tv iha na sidhyati.
daivatebhyo namas|kṛtya yas tv arthān samyag īhate
dakṣo, dākṣiṇya|saṃpanno, na sa moghair vihanyate.
samyag īhā punar iyaṃ: yo vṛddhān upasevate,
āpṛcchati ca yac chreyaḥ, karoti ca hitaṃ vacaḥ.
utthāy' ôtthāya hi sadā praṣṭavyā vṛddha|saṃmatāḥ.
te sma yoge paraṃ mūlaṃ. tan|mūlā siddhir ucyate.
vṛddhānāṃ vacanaṃ śrutvā yo 'bhyutthānaṃ prayojayet,
utthānasya phalaṃ samyak tadā sa labhate 'cirāt.

please those with insight. For it's generally agreed that an action done is not without result on earth. Moreover, by failing to act, one might see a disastrous outcome of great magnitude. One rarely sees either a man who achieves something by chance without making any effort, or a man who achieves nothing in spite of all he does. The industrious 2.15
man flourishes. The idle man does not prosper comfortably. The industrious in this world of the living are generally seen to be striving for some advantage.

Regardless of whether a diligent man fails to attain the anticipated result of his undertaking, or achieves the goal he sought, he would be beyond any reproach. The audacious person who reaps benefit in the world without doing anything for it, by contrast, is the subject of reproach and in most cases an object of hatred. Now anyone who disregards this fact and acts in defiance of it, brings misfortunes on himself. Such is the prudence of the wise.

Whether it's from lack of human effort or lack of divine will, an endeavor can fail due to either of these factors. On the one hand an act lacking human effort never suc- 2.20
ceeds in this world. On the other hand, when first he honors the gods before striving appropriately toward his goals, the diligent man, imbued with a sense of devotion, is not disappointed by failures. And this is appropriate diligence: when someone honors his seniors, asks them which course of action is better, and acts on their good advice. At each and every endeavor one should solicit the approval of one's seniors. It is they who are the best foundation in any plan. Success is said to be founded on them. Anyone who undertakes an endeavor listening to the counsel of his seniors,

rāgāt krodhād bhayāl lobhād yo 'rthān īhati mānavaḥ
2.25 an|īśaś c' âvamānī ca, sa śīghraṃ bhraśyate śriyaḥ.

so 'yaṃ Duryodhanen' ârtho lubdhen' â|dīrgha|darśinā
a|samarthaḥ samārabdho mūḍhatvād a|vicintitaḥ,
hita|buddhīn an|ādṛtya, saṃmantry' â|sādhubhiḥ saha.
vāryamāṇo 'karod vairaṃ Pāṇḍavair guṇavattaraiḥ.
pūrvam apy atiduḥśīlo na dhairyaṃ kartum arhati.
tapaty arthe vipanne hi mitrāṇām a|kṛtaṃ vacaḥ.
anuvartāmahe yat tu taṃ vayaṃ pāpa|pūruṣam
asmān apy a|nayas tasmāt prāpto 'yaṃ dāruṇo mahān.

anena tu mam' âdy' âpi vyasanen' ôpatāpitā
2.30 buddhiś cintayate kiñ cit, svaṃ śreyo n' âvabudhyate.
muhyatā tu manuṣyeṇa praṣṭavyāḥ suhṛdo janāḥ.
tatr' âsya buddhir vinayas, tatra śreyaś ca paśyati.
tato 'sya mūlaṃ kāryāṇāṃ buddhyā niścitya vai budhāḥ
te 'tra pṛṣṭā yathā brūyus, tat kartavyaṃ tathā bhavet.
te vayaṃ Dhṛtarāṣṭraṃ ca Gāndhārīṃ ca sametya ha,
upapṛcchāmahe gatvā Viduraṃ ca mahā|matim.
te pṛṣṭā ca vadeyur yac chreyo naḥ samanantaram.
tad asmābhiḥ punaḥ kāryam. iti me naiṣṭhikī matiḥ.
an|ārambhāt tu kāryāṇāṃ n' ârthaḥ saṃpadyate kva cit.
2.35 kṛte puruṣa|kāre tu yeṣāṃ kāryaṃ na sidhyati,
daiven' ôpahatās te tu, n' âtra kāryā vicāraṇā.

soon achieves the appropriate outcome of that endeavor.
But the man who aspires to his ambitions out of passion,
anger, fear or greed, refusing all counsel and contemptuous, 2.25
he quickly falls from glory.

This goal that Duryódhana has foolishly pursued, in his greed and shortsightedness, was unjustified and not thought through. Heedless of those who discerned what is best, he took counsel with bad men. Though people tried to stop him, he stirred up enmity with the Pándavas who excel in virtue. Even before that, he was completely unruly in his atrocious conduct. Now his plan is thwarted, he repents the advice of friends which he chose to ignore. Meanwhile, because we follow that evil man, this severe and harsh misfortune has overtaken us as well.

But even now, when oppressed by this disaster my mind, 2.30
however much it tries to work it out, can't comprehend
what might be in our own best interest. Now when a man
is bewildered, he should consult well-meaning people. In
this, discernment should be his guide for it identifies the
best option. Therefore whatever wise people, who have an-
alyzed with their discernment the heart of the tasks ahead
of him, advise him when they are consulted on this matter,
that is the course of action he should take. So let us meet
with Dhrita·rashtra and Gandhári, then let us go and consult also Vídura, steeped in wisdom. If we ask them, they
will immediately explain what would be in our best interest. Moreover, that is what we are bound to do. This is my
final opinion. No purpose is ever served by avoiding doing
those things one should. Since those whose intended task 2.35
is not achieved, in spite of all humanly possible effort, have

SAÑJAYA uvāca:

3.1 KṚPASYA VACANAṂ śrutvā
dharm'|ârtha|sahitaṃ śubham
Aśvatthāmā, mahā|rāja,
duḥkha|śoka|samanvitaḥ,
dahyamānas tu śokena pradīpten' âgninā yathā
krūraṃ manas tataḥ kṛtvā tāv ubhau pratyabhāṣata:
«puruṣe puruṣe buddhir yā yā bhavati śobhanā,
tuṣyanti ca pṛthak sarve prajñayā te svayā svayā.
sarvo hi manyate loka ātmānaṃ buddhimattaram.
sarvasy' ātmā bahu mataḥ. sarv' ātmānaṃ* praśaṃsati.
3.5 sarvasya hi svakā prajñā sādhu|vāde pratiṣṭhitā.
para|buddhiṃ ca nindanti, svāṃ praśaṃsanti c' â|sakṛt.
kāraṇ'|ântara|yogena yoge yeṣāṃ samā gatiḥ,
anyonyena ca tuṣyanti, bahu manyanti c' â|sakṛt.
tasy' âiva tu manuṣyasya sā sā buddhis tadā tadā,
kāla|yoga|viparyāsaṃ prāpy' ânyonyaṃ vipadyate.
vicitratvāt tu cittānāṃ manuṣyāṇāṃ viśeṣataḥ
citta|vaiklavyam āsādya sā sā buddhiḥ prajāyate.
yathā hi vaidyaḥ kuśalo jñātvā vyādhiṃ yathā|vidhi
bhaiṣajyaṃ kurute yogāt ‹praśam'|ârtham› iti, prabho,
3.10 evaṃ kāryasya yog'|ârthaṃ buddhiṃ kurvanti mānavāḥ
prajñayā hi svayā yuktās; tāṃ ca nindanti mānavāḥ.
anyayā yauvane martyo buddhyā bhavati mohitaḥ,
madhye 'nyayā, jarāyāṃ tu so 'nyāṃ rocayate matim.

been thwarted by divine will, there is no need to debate this matter further.

SÁNJAYA continued:

ON HEARING Kripa's good words, replete with morality and sense, Ashva·tthaman was filled with misery and grief, great king. Then, inflamed by his grief as if by a fire flaring up, he formed his cruel resolve and replied to the two of them: 3.1

"In each man shines forth his own personal perspective and they are all contented with that personal insight of theirs. For every person regards himself the most intelligent in the world. Everyone holds himself in high esteem. Each praises himself.

For everyone thinks their own insight is based on sound 3.5
theory. They find fault with the opinions of others, and praise their own repeatedly. Those who are engaged in a common purpose, though the purpose stems from different causes, are exceedingly smug about each other and repeatedly engage in mutual admiration. But each man holds different opinions at different times, which are mutually contradictory, according to alteration of time or purpose. And, because of the variation in views, according to the different specifics of people, each different opinion arises as the result of a confusion of views. Just as a skilled doctor on recognizing an illness in line with medical understanding, prepares medicine appropriate to its treatment, thinking 'This will sort it out,' Lord, in the same way men form their opinions 3.10

vyasanaṃ vā mahā|ghoraṃ, samṛddhiṃ v' âpi tādṛśīm
avāpya puruṣo, Bhoja, kurute buddhi|vaikṛtam.
ekasminn eva puruṣe sā sā buddhis tadā tadā
bhavaty; a|kṛta|dharmatvāt sā tasy' âiva na rocate.
niścitya tu yathā|prajñaṃ yāṃ matiṃ sādhu paśyati,
tayā prakurute bhāvaṃ. sā tasy' ôdyoga|kārikā.

3.15 sarvo hi puruṣo, Bhoja, ‹sādhv etad› iti niścitaḥ
kartum ārabhate prīto maraṇ'|âdiṣu karmasu.
sarve hi buddhiṃ ājñāya prajñāṃ v' âpi svakāṃ narāḥ
ceṣṭante vividhāṃ ceṣṭāṃ, hitam ity eva jānate.
upajātā vyasana|jā y" êyam adya matir mama,
yuvayos tāṃ pravakṣyāmi mama śoka|vināśinīm.
prajā|patiḥ prajāḥ sṛṣṭvā,
karma tāsu vidhāya ca,
varṇe varṇe samādhatte hy
ek'|âikaṃ guṇa|bhāg guṇam:
brāhmaṇe vedam agryaṃ tu; kṣatriye teja uttamam;
dākṣyaṃ vaiśye ca; śūdre ca sarva|varṇ'|ânukūlatām.

3.20 ‹a|dānto brāhmaṇo 'sādhur.
nis|tejāḥ kṣatriyo 'dhamaḥ.
a|dakṣo nindyate vaiśyaḥ,
śūdraś ca pratikūlavān.›

in relation to their intended outcome, but based on their personal view, with which, however, other men find fault. Mortal man is deluded by one set of opinions in his youth, another in middle age, and in old age he prefers another perspective still. A man changes his perspective according to whether he encounters horrendous misfortune or enjoys prosperity, Bhoja king. Even a single man forms this or that opinion which at another time, being subject to change by nature, he finds distasteful. Yet on formulating a decision which one regards as good, in accordance with one's views, one forms one's inclinations on the basis of it. It molds one's endeavor.

Everyone, Bhoja king, once he's decided that 'this is 3.15
right,' is happy to engage in the corresponding deeds, even if it means death. All men, on ascertaining their own perspective or view, exert themselves in their differing undertakings, convinced that it's for the best. This resolve that I've formed today has arisen out of misfortune. I shall explain to the two of you how it will end my grief. The Lord of Beings* on creating every creature, allotted to each his role and, as the distributor of qualities, he allocated to each different class a particular asset: to the priestly class the supreme Text of Wisdom; to the warrior class the ultimate prowess; to the mercantile and agricultural class their expertise; to the servant class, the disposition to serve all the other classes.*

'An ill-disciplined priest is no good. 3.20
Beneath contempt is a warrior without prowess.
An unskilled vaishya is criticized, so too
a refractory servant who fails to do his best.'

so 'smi jātaḥ kule śreṣṭhe brāhmaṇānāṃ su|pūjite
manda|bhāgyatay" âsmy etaṃ kṣatra|dharmam anuṣṭhitaḥ.
kṣatra|dharmaṃ viditv' âhaṃ yadi brāhmaṇyam āśritaḥ
prakuryāṃ sumahat karma, na me tat sādhu saṃmatam.
dhārayaṃś ca dhanur divyaṃ divyāny astrāṇi c' āhave,
pitaraṃ nihataṃ dṛṣṭvā kiṃ nu vakṣyāmi saṃsadi?
so 'ham adya yathā|kāmaṃ kṣatra|dharmam upāsya tam
gant" âsmi padavīṃ rājñaḥ pituś c' âpi mah"|ātmanaḥ.
3.25 adya svapsyanti Pāñcālā viśvastā, jita|kāśinaḥ:
vimukta|yugya|kavacā, harṣeṇa ca samanvitāḥ,
jayaṃ matv" ātmanaś c' âiva, śrāntā, vyāyāma|karśitāḥ.
teṣāṃ niśi prasuptānāṃ su|sthānāṃ śibire svake,
avaskandaṃ kariṣyāmi śibirasy' âdya duṣkaram.
tān avaskandya śibire preta|bhūta|vicetasaḥ
sūdayiṣyāmi vikramya, Maghavān iva Dānavān.
adya tān sahitān sarvān Dhṛṣṭadyumna|purogamān
sūdayiṣyāmi vikramya, kakṣaṃ dīpta iv' ânalaḥ.
nihatya c' âiva Pāñcālāñ śāntiṃ labdh" āsmi, sattama.
3.30 Pāñcāleṣu cariṣyāmi sūdayann adya saṃyuge
Pināka|pāṇiḥ saṃkruddhaḥ svayaṃ Rudraḥ paśuṣv iva.
ady' âhaṃ sarva|Pāñcālān nihatya ca nikṛṣya ca
ardayiṣyāmi saṃhṛṣṭo raṇe Pāṇḍu|sutāṃs tathā.
ady' âhaṃ sarva|Pāñcālaiḥ kṛtvā bhūmiṃ śarīriṇīm,

Now I was born into the highest, greatly honored family, that of the priests, yet it was my ill-fated lot to follow the vocation of the warrior.* Having known the warrior's vocation, if now I were, by reverting to the brahmin way, to accomplish something, however great, I wouldn't be respected for it. While I bear the divine bow and divine arrows in battle, and have seen my father slain, what account could I give of myself at court? Here I am, someone who has willingly walked the way of the warrior, and for that reason today I shall pursue the path taken by the king and by my noble father.

Now they will be sleeping, the Panchálas, unsuspecting, 3.25
showing all the traits of victors: they will have taken off their armor, unharnessed their chariots, and be replete with joy, believing the victory theirs, exhausted, worn out after their exertions. As they sleep through the night happily in their own camp I shall carry out a daunting assault on their encampment before this night is out. I shall overwhelm them in their camp, as they lie as senseless as the dead. Tonight I shall overpower them all, as the bounteous Indra did the Dánava demons,* and slay them all together, Dhrishta·dyumna first in line. I shall engulf them as I dispatch them, as a blazing fire dry wood. And once I have killed the Panchálas, your excellency, I shall find peace.

Careening among the Panchálas as I slaughter them in 3.30
battle before the night is out, I shall be like wrathful Rudra himself among the beasts, Pináka bow in hand.* This very night, once I have slain and laid waste every Panchála, I shall take great delight applying the same method and executing Pandu's sons in battle. This very night, when I have decked

prahṛty' âik'|âikaśas teṣu bhaviṣyāmy an|ṛṇaḥ pituḥ,
Duryodhanasya Karṇasya Bhīṣma|Saindhavayor api.
gamayiṣyāmi Pāñcālān padavīm adya durgamām.
adya Pāñcāla|rājasya Dhṛṣṭadyumnasya vai niśi
na cirāt pramathiṣyāmi paśor iva śiro balāt.
3.35 adya Pāñcāla|Pāṇḍūnāṃ śayitān ātmajān niśi
khaḍgena niśiten' ājau pramathiṣyāmi, Gautama.
adya Pāñcāla|senāṃ tāṃ nihatya niśi sauptike
kṛta|kṛtyaḥ sukhī caiva bhaviṣyāmi, mahā|mate.»

KṚPA uvāca:

4.1 DIṢṬYĀ TE PRATIKARTAVYE matir jāt" êyam, a|cyuta.
na tvāṃ vārayituṃ śakto Vajrapāṇir api svayam.
anuyāsyāvahe tvāṃ tu prabhāte sahitāv ubhau.
adya rātrau viśramasva vimukta|kavaca|dhvajaḥ.
ahaṃ tvām anuyāsyāmi, Kṛtavarmā ca Sātvataḥ,
parān abhimukhaṃ yāntaṃ, rathāv āsthāya daṃśitau.
āvābhyāṃ sahitaḥ śatrūñ śvo 'si hantā samāgame
vikramya, rathināṃ śreṣṭha, Pāñcālān sa|pad'|ânugān.
4.5 śaktas tvam asi vikramya. viśramasva niśām imām.
ciraṃ te jāgratas, tāta. svapa tāvan niśām imām.
viśrāntaś ca vinidraś ca svastha|cittaś ca, māna|da,
sametya samare śatrūn vadhiṣyasi. na saṃśayaḥ.
na hi tvāṃ rathināṃ śreṣṭhaṃ pragṛhīta|var'|āyudham

the earth with the corpses of every Panchála, when I have hewn down each in turn, I shall be released from my debt to my father, to Duryódhana, Karna, Bhishma and the king of Sindh. This very night I shall dispatch the Pándavas on the hardest path for them to travel. This very night, ere long, I shall violently rip off the head of Dhrishta·dyumna, the Panchála king, as I would a beast's.

This very night with sharpened sword I shall torment the 3.35
Panchálas' and Pandu's own flesh and blood on the battle ground, as they lie sleeping, scion of Gótama. This very night, when I have slain the Panchála army as they sleep, I shall have performed my duty, and only then, wise man, shall I be happy."

KRIPA replied:

IT IS BY PROVIDENCE that this determination for revenge 4.1
has gained life within you, unyielding man. Even the thunderbolt-wielding Indra himself hasn't the power to hold you back. But at dawn the two of us together will accompany you. For now, take off your armor and your ensign and rest for the night. I'll follow you, as will Krita·varman of the Satvats, dressed for battle, mounted on our chariots, as you go to face our foes. Tomorrow, flanked by us, you, the most excellent of chariot fighters, will attack and kill the Panchálas and their followers in battle.

You can succeed when you attack them, but rest this 4.5
night. It has been a long time since you slept, my son. Sleep through this night. Rested, refreshed, your senses restored, you who inspire honor, there is no doubt that, when you meet your enemies in the fray, you will destroy them.

jetum utsahate śaśvad api deveṣu Vāsavaḥ.
Kṛpeṇa sahitaṃ yāntaṃ, yuktaṃ ca Kṛtavarmaṇā,
ko Drauṇiṃ yudhi saṃrabdhaṃ yodhayed, api deva|rāṭ?
te vayaṃ pariviśrāntā, vinidrā, vigata|jvarāḥ,
prabhātāyāṃ rajanyāṃ vai nihaniṣyāma śātravān.
4.10 tava hy astrāṇi divyāni mama c' âiva, na saṃśayaḥ.
Sātvato 'pi mah"|êṣv|āso nityaṃ yuddheṣu kovidaḥ.
te vayaṃ sahitās, tāta, sarvāñ śatrūn samāgatān
prasahya samare hatvā prītiṃ prāpsyāma puṣkalām.
viśramasva tvam a|vyagraḥ, svapa c' êmāṃ niśāṃ sukham:
ahaṃ ca Kṛtavarmā ca tvāṃ prayāntaṃ nar' ôttamam
anuyāsyāva sahitau dhanvinau, para|tāpinau,
rathinaṃ tvarayā yāntaṃ ratham āsthāya daṃśitau.
sa gatvā śibiraṃ teṣāṃ, nāma viśrāvya c' āhave,
tataḥ kart" âsi śatrūṇāṃ yudhyatāṃ kadanaṃ mahat.
4.15 kṛtvā ca kadanaṃ teṣāṃ prabhāte vimale 'hani
viharasva yathā Śakraḥ sūdayitvā mah"|âsurān.
tvaṃ hi śakto raṇe jetuṃ Pāñcālānāṃ varūthinīm,
daitya|senām iva kruddhaḥ sarva|Dānava|sūdanaḥ.
mayā tvāṃ sahitaṃ saṃkhye, guptaṃ ca Kṛtavarmaṇā
na saheta vibhuḥ sākṣād Vajrapāṇir api svayam.
na c' âhaṃ samare, tāta, Kṛtavarmā na c' âiva hi
a|nirjitya raṇe Pāṇḍūn na ca yāsyāmi karhi cit.
hatvā ca samare kruddhān Pāñcālān Pāṇḍubhiḥ saha

For among the gods even Indra, chief of the Vasu gods, could never defeat you—you are the best chariot-fighter; you wield the most powerful weapons. And who but the king of gods would dare to fight Drona's enraged son advancing in battle, in company with Kripa, in unison with Krita·varman? Once night has become dawn, the three of us, rested and refreshed, our weariness dispelled, will kill our enemies.

For you have divine weapons as do I, without a doubt. 4.10
The lord of the Satvats also is a great archer, always skilled in battles. Together we will overpower all our assembled enemies in battle, my son, and slay them to our resounding delight. Rest, do not fret, but sleep this night contented: as you, the best of men, set out, Krita·varman and I shall follow you, together, fully armored, bows in hand, the torment of our enemy, with all speed aboard our chariots, as you go in yours. Arriving at their encampment, you will make the battle ground resound to your name, and then will you visit total havoc upon your enemies as they fight.

When you have wreaked havoc on them in the clear light 4.15
of day, enjoy yourself as powerful Indra did after slaughtering the mighty Titans. For you have the power to defeat in battle the fully armored Panchála troops, like the wrathful slayer of all the Dánavas did to defeat the demon army. I reckon that even the thunderbolt-wielding Lord Indra in person would be useless against you, with me as your attendant and Krita·varman as your guard. And I won't depart the battlefield, my son, nor indeed will Krita·varman, until we've crushed Pandu's sons in combat. We'll desist only when we've killed the fierce Panchálas as well as Pandu's

nivartiṣyāmahe sarve, hatā vā svarga|gā vayam.
4.20 sarv'|ôpāyaiḥ sahāyās te prabhāte vayam āhave.
satyam etan, mahā|bāho, prabravīmi tav', ân|agha.

evam uktas tato Drauṇir mātulena hitaṃ vacaḥ
abravīn mātulaṃ, rājan, krodha|saṃrakta|locanaḥ:

«āturasya kuto nidrā, narasy' âmarṣitasya ca,
arthāṃś cintayataś c' âpi, kāmayānasya vā punaḥ?
tad idaṃ samanuprāptaṃ paśya me 'dya catuṣṭayam.
paśya: bhāgaś caturtho me svapnam ahnāya nāśayet,
kiṃ nāma duḥkhaṃ loke 'smin pitur vadham anusmaran.*
hṛdayaṃ nirdahan me 'dya rātry|ahāni na śāmyati,
yathā ca nihataḥ pāpaiḥ pitā mama viśeṣataḥ,
4.25 pratyakṣam api te sarvaṃ tan me marmāṇi kṛntati.
kathaṃ hi mādṛśo loke muhūrtam api jīvati?
‹Droṇo hat'› êti,* yad vācaḥ Pāñcālānāṃ śṛṇomy aham.
Dṛṣṭadyumnam a|hatv" ājau n' âhaṃ jīvitum utsahe.

sa me pitṛ|vadhād vadhyaḥ, Pāñcālā ye ca saṅgatāḥ.
vilāpo bhagna|sakthasya yas tu rājño mayā śrutaḥ,
sa punar hṛdayaṃ kasya krūrasy' âpi na nirdahet?
kasya hy a|karuṇasy' âpi netrābhyām aśru n' āvrajet?
nṛ|pater bhagna|sakthasya śrutvā tādṛg vacaḥ punaḥ,
yaś c' âyaṃ mitra|pakṣo me mayi jīvati nirjitaḥ,
4.30 śokaṃ me vardhayaty eṣa, vāri|vega iv' ârṇavam.

sons, or when we ourselves are killed and have made our way to heaven. At dawn, we shall be your allies with every- 4.20
thing we can throw at them, powerful and sinless warrior. This is the truth I tell you.

Your Majesty, when Drona's son received these well-intended words from his uncle, he replied to him, his eyes bloodshot with rage:

"How can there be sleep for a man tormented or driven to anger, for the man obsessively reviewing his plans, or for one driven by love? Look at me, right now all four in one! Look: even one of the four would immediately put an end to sleep for me, let alone this, the worst suffering in this world as I remember my father's murder. My heart burns night and day, never abating. The particular way those evil
men slew my father, the entire event cuts me to the quick 4.25
as if still before my eyes. Given that, how can someone in my state continue alive in this world, even for a moment? 'Drona is dead,' I hear the Panchálas announce. I cannot bear to continue living unless I kill Dhrishta·dyumna in battle.*

For the murder of my father, I must murder him, and those Panchálas in his alliance. I heard too the king's scream as his thigh was shattered.* Who is so cruel their heart would not burn at that sound? Who so lacks passion that their eyes would not flood with tears? Hearing a cry like that from our sovereign as his thigh was shattered, the loyalty that lives on unvanquished within me swells my grief, 4.30
as swells the force of the waves the restless ocean.

ek'|âgra|manaso me 'dya kuto nidrā, kutaḥ sukham?
Vāsudev'|Ârjunābhyāṃ ca tān ahaṃ parirakṣitān
a|viṣahyatamān manye Mahendreṇ' âpi, sattama.
na c' âpi śaktaḥ saṃyantum kopaṃ etaṃ samutthitam.
taṃ na paśyāmi loke 'smin yo māṃ kopān nivartayet.
tath" âiva niścitā buddhir eṣā sādhu|matā mama.
vārttikaiḥ kathyamānas tu mitrāṇāṃ me parābhavaḥ
Pāṇḍavānāṃ ca vijayo hṛdayaṃ dahat' îva me.
ahaṃ tu kadanaṃ kṛtvā śatrūṇām adya sauptike
tato viśramitā c' âiva svaptā ca vigata|jvaraḥ.»

KṚPA uvāca:

5.1 ŚUŚRŪṢUR API dur|medhāḥ puruṣo '|niyat'|êndriyaḥ
n' âlaṃ vedayituṃ kṛtsnau dharm'|ârthāv. iti me matiḥ.
tath" âiva tāvan medhāvī vinayaṃ yo na śikṣate,
na ca kiṃ cana jānāti so 'pi dharm'|ârtha|niścayam.
ciraṃ hy api jaḍaḥ śūraḥ paṇḍitaṃ paryupāsya hi
na sa dharmān vijānāti, darvī sūpa|rasān iva.
muhūrtam api taṃ prājñaḥ paryupāsya hi
kṣipraṃ dharmān vijānāti jihvā sūpa|rasān iva
5.5 śuśrūṣus tv eva medhāvī puruṣo niyat'|êndriyaḥ
jānīyād āgamān sarvān, grāhyaṃ ca na virodhayet.
a|neyas tv avamānī yo durātmā pāpa|pūruṣaḥ,
diṣṭam utsṛjya kalyāṇaṃ karoti bahu|pāpakam.
nāthavantaṃ tu suhṛdaḥ pratiṣedhanti pātakāt.

When my emotions are brought to a single head how can I now find sleep or content? I recognize that those who are protected by Árjuna and Krishna, son of Vasu·deva, are pretty inaccessible, your excellency. But I can't curb the rage that has welled up in me and I see no one in this world who could hold me back from venting it. So my mind is made up, and I value my decision. As the defeat of my friends and the victory of the Pándavas is described by the heralds, I feel it set my heart on fire. But when I've brought carnage to the sleeping camp of my enemies, that's when I'll rest and sleep, my weariness dispelled."

KRIPA replied:

EVEN IF A MAN is keen to learn, if he is also slow-witted 5.1
or not master of his own senses, he will be capable of understanding neither duty nor sound strategy in their entirety. This is my opinion. On the same count, however sharp he is, if a man doesn't practice discipline, he can know nothing of the purpose of duty or sound strategy. Even if a dull-witted warrior studies for a long time with a wise teacher, he no more comes to understand his teachings than a ladle the flavors of soup. But if an intelligent man studies with that same teacher just for a short time, he quickly understands the teachings, as a tongue the flavors of soup.

Now should a quick-witted man, who has mastered his 5.5
senses, be keen to learn, he would be able to understand all the transmitted teachings and wouldn't contradict what should be accepted. A man who can't accept guidance, who's arrogant, malicious or evil, who rejects useful instructions, does much harm. Someone who has people to guide

nivartate tu lakṣmīvān; n' â|lakṣmīvān nivartate.
yathā hy ucc'|âvacair vākyaiḥ kṣipta|citto niyamyate,
tath" âiva suhṛdā śakyo, na|śakyas tv avasīdati.
tath" âiva suhṛdaṃ prājñaṃ kurvāṇaṃ karma pāpakam
prājñāḥ saṃpratiṣedhante yathā|śakti punaḥ punaḥ.
5.10 sa kalyāṇe matiṃ kṛtvā, niyamy' ātmānam ātmanā,
kuru me vacanaṃ, tāta, yena paścān na tapyase.
na vadhaḥ pūjyate loke suptānām iha dharmataḥ,
tath" âiv' âpāsta|śastrāṇāṃ, vimukta|ratha|vājinām,
ye ca brūyus, «tav' âsm' îti,» ye ca syuḥ śaraṇ'|āgatāḥ,
vimukta|mūrdhajā ye ca, ye c' âpi hata|vāhanāḥ.
adya svapsyanti Pāñcālā† vimukta|kavacā, vibho,
viśvastā rajanīṃ sarve, pretā iva vicetasaḥ.
yas teṣāṃ tad|avasthānāṃ druhyeta puruṣo 'n|ṛjuḥ
vyaktaṃ sa narake majjed a|gādhe vipule '|plave.
5.15 sarv'|âstra|viduṣāṃ loke śreṣṭhas tvam asi viśrutaḥ,
na ca te jātu loke 'smin su|sūkṣmam api kilbiṣam.
tvaṃ punaḥ sūrya|saṃkāśaḥ śvo|bhūta udite ravau,
prakāśe sarva|bhūtānāṃ vijetā yudhi śātravān.
a|saṃbhāvita|rūpaṃ hi tvayi karma vigarhitam
śukle raktam iva nyastaṃ bhaved. iti matir mama.

him is held back from anything to his discredit by those well disposed to him. The fortunate man desists, while one without such good fortune doesn't. Just as someone who is distracted is called to attention by raised or lowered voices, so can a man be influenced by a well-disposed friend, while the man who remains unaffected is ruined. So it is that men of insight prevent their insightful friend from engaging in any bad act, as far as they are able, every time.

Give me your word, my son, that you have set your heart 5.10
on good action and restrained yourself on your own account, so that you don't regret it later. According to sacred law on this matter, the world offers no respect for killing those who are asleep; or who have put down their weapons; or who have unharnessed their chariots and horses, as also those who try to say, "I'm yours," or those who have sought asylum, or those whose hair is loose* or whose mount has been killed. Powerful lord, right now all the Panchálas will be sleeping, off-guard for the night, as unconscious as the dead. An underhanded man who would do them harm while they are in such a condition, would without doubt sink without a raft in a vast, unfathomable hell.

You are renowned as the greatest expert in weaponry in 5.15
the world, and you have never committed even the slightest wrong. Once tomorrow has come and the sun has risen, you like the sun in broad daylight before all beings, can defeat your enemies in battle. But a blameworthy act from you would be as insufferable as blood splattered on the white surface of the moon. This is what I think.

AŚVATTHĀM" ôvāca:

evam etad yath" āttha tvam, mātul', êha na saṃśayaḥ.
tais tu pūrvam ayaṃ setuḥ śatadhā vidalī|kṛtaḥ.
pratyakṣaṃ bhūmi|pālānāṃ bhavatāṃ c' âpi saṃnidhau
nyasta|śastro mama pitā Dhṛṣṭadyumnena pātitaḥ.
5.20 Karṇaś ca patite cakre rathasya rathināṃ varaḥ
uttame vyasane sanno hato Gāṇḍīva|dhanvanā.
tathā Śāntanavo Bhīṣmo nyasta|śastro nir|āyudhaḥ
Śikhaṇḍinaṃ puras|kṛtya hato Gāṇḍīva|dhanvanā.
Bhūriśravā mah"|êṣv|āsas tathā prāya|gato raṇe
krośatāṃ bhūmi|pālānāṃ Yuyudhānena pātitaḥ.
Duryodhanaś ca Bhīmena sametya gadayā raṇe
paśyatāṃ bhūmi|pālānām a|dharmeṇa nipātitaḥ.
ekākī bahubhis tatra parivārya mahā|rathaiḥ
a|dharmeṇa nara|vyāghro Bhīmasenena pātitaḥ.
5.25 vilāpo bhagna|sakthasya yo me rājñaḥ pariśrutaḥ
vārttikānāṃ kathayatāṃ, sa me marmāṇi kṛntati.
evaṃ c' â|dhārmikāḥ pāpāḥ Pañcālā bhinna|setavaḥ.
tān evaṃ bhinna|maryādān kiṃ bhavān na vigarhati?
pitṛ|hantṝn ahaṃ hatvā Pāñcālān niśi sauptike,
kāmaṃ kīṭaḥ pataṃgo vā janma prāpya bhavāmi vai.

ASHVA·TTHAMAN replied:

Everything that you have said is true, uncle. There is no doubt about it. But the line has already been torn up a hundred times from their side. Even though the protectors of the world were all looking on, before their eyes Dhrishta·dyumna killed my father, who had already laid down his weapons.

In the same way Árjuna, bearer of the bow Gandíva, 5.20
killed Karna, the best of the chariot-fighters, after the wheel had fallen from his chariot, so that he'd sunk down in a position of extreme vulnerability. In the same way, the bearer of the bow Gandíva, by allowing Shikhándin to go ahead of him, killed Bhishma, son of Shántanu, even though he had laid down his arms and was without weapon.* In the same way, the great lord Bhuri·shravas, even though he was fasting to the death on the battlefield, was killed by Yuyu·dhána, son of Sátyaka, in spite of the protectors of the earth screaming at him to stop.* Then Duryódhana, when he had met with Bhima in the mace fight, was brought down with an illegal blow, while the protectors of the earth looked on. The tiger among men was completely isolated, though many great chariot-warriors stood around him, and Bhima·sena brought him down with his foul blow.

When I hear about the wail the king let out when his 5.25
thigh was shattered, as the heralds report it, it cuts me to the quick. That's how unfair those evil Panchálas are, they have broken every restriction. When they have crossed the line like this, why, sir, don't you criticize them? If I succeed in killing those patricidal Panchálas while they sleep this night I'll gladly accept rebirth as a worm or a moth. I must

tvare c' âham anen' âdya yad idaṃ me cikīrṣitam.
tasya me tvaramāṇasya kuto nidrā, kutaḥ sukhaṁ?
na sa jātaḥ pumā̃l loke kaś cin, na sa bhaviṣyati,
yo me vyāvartayed etāṃ vadhe teṣāṃ kṛtāṃ matiṃ.

SAÑJAYA uvāca:

5.30 evam uktvā, mahā|rāja, Droṇa|putraḥ pratāpavān
ekānte yojayitv" âśvān prāyād abhimukhaḥ parān.
tam abrūtāṃ mah"|ātmānau Bhoja|Śāradvatāv ubhau:
«kim|arthaṃ syandano yuktaḥ? kiṅ ca kāryaṃ cikīrṣitam?
eka|sārtha|prayātau svas tvayā saha, nara'|rṣabha,
sama|duḥkha|sukhau c' âpi. n' āvāṃ śaṅkitum arhasi.»

Aśvatthāmā tu saṃkruddhaḥ pitur vadham anusmaran
tābhyāṃ tathyaṃ tad" ācakhyau yad asy' ātma|cikīrṣitam:
«hatvā śata|sahasrāṇi yodhānāṃ niśitaiḥ śaraiḥ
nyasta|śastro mama pitā Dhṛṣṭadyumnena pātitaḥ.
5.35 taṃ tath" âiva haniṣyāmi nyasta|dharmāṇam adya vai
putraṃ Pāñcālarājasya pāpaṃ pāpena karmaṇā.
kathaṃ ca nihataḥ pāpaḥ Pāñcālyaḥ paśuvan mayā
śastreṇa vijitā̃l lokān prāpnuyād? iti me matiḥ.
kṣipraṃ saṃnaddha|kavacau, sa|khaḍgāv, ātta|kārmukau
mām āsthāya pratīkṣetāṃ, rathavaryau, paraṃ|tapau.»

hurry now, to do my chosen task. Since I must hurry, how can I sleep, how rest content? In this world, the man is not born nor will he ever be, who could hold me back from this decision that I have made to kill them.

SÁNJAYA continued:

When Drona's son had done speaking, Your Great Majes- 5.30
ty, he harnessed his horses and valiantly set out alone to face the enemy. The noble-souled Bhojan and the son of Sharádvat both cried out to him: "Why have you yoked your war-chariot? And what have you decided to do? Tomorrow we'll go with you, as one in common purpose, bull among men. We've come through good and bad together and you shouldn't give up on us."

But the furious Ashva·tthaman, mindful of his father's murder, then called back to them the nature of the task he had chosen for himself:

"My father who had slain a hundred thousand soldiers with his tipped arrows, had laid down his arms when
Dhrishta·dyumna killed him. Now that he has discarded 5.35
justice, I shall kill him in exactly the same way, that evil son of the Panchála king, with an evil act in return. When I have slaughtered that evil Panchálan like an animal, how will he be able to reach the realms that are won only by the sword? This is my thinking. Quickly, you tormenters of the enemy, gird on your armor, seize your swords, take up your bows, stick with me, my excellent chariot-fighters, and keep your eyes on me."

ity uktvā ratham āsthāya prāyād abhimukhaḥ parān.
tam anvagāt Kṛpo, rājan, Kṛtavarmā ca Sātvataḥ.
te prayātā vyarocanta parān abhimukhās trayaḥ,
hūyamānā yathā yajñe samiddhā havya|vāhanāḥ.
5.40 yayuś ca śibiraṃ teṣāṃ saṃprasupta|janaṃ, vibho.
dvāra|deśaṃ tu saṃprāpya Drauṇis tasthau mahā|rathaḥ.

Saying this, he mounted his chariot and set off to face the enemy. Kripa followed on behind him, sire, as did Krita·varman of the Satvats. The three men, now on their way to face the enemy, shone bright like the oblation-bearing sacrificial flames into which the offerings are poured at the sacrifice. Powerful lord, they went to the camp of the other 5.40
side, full of sleeping people. But on reaching the path in, the great chariot-fighter, Drona's son, stopped still.

6–8

MERCILESS SLAUGHTER

DHṚTARĀṢṬRA uvāca:

6.1 DVĀRA|DEŚE TATO Drauṇim avasthitam avekṣya tau
akurvatāṃ Bhoja|Kṛpau kiṃ, Saṃjaya? vadasva me.

SAÑJAYA uvāca:

Kṛtavarmāṇam āmantrya Kṛpaṃ ca sa mahā|ratham
Drauṇir manyu|parīt'|ātmā śibira|dvāram āgamat.
tatra bhūtaṃ mahā|kāyaṃ candr'|ârka|sadṛśa|dyutim
so 'paśyad dvāram āśritya tiṣṭhantaṃ loma|harṣaṇam,
vasānaṃ carma vaiyāghraṃ mahā|rudhira|visravam,
kṛṣṇ'|âjin'|ôttar'|āsaṅgaṃ, nāga|yajñ'|ôpavītinam;
6.5 bāhubhiḥ sv|āyataiḥ† pīnair nānā|praharaṇ'|ôdyataiḥ;
baddh'|âṅgada|mahā|sarpaṃ; jvālā|māl"|ākul'|ānanam,
daṃṣṭrā|karāla|vadanaṃ, vyādit'|āsyaṃ, bhayānakam,
nayanānāṃ sahasraiś ca vicitrair abhibhūṣitam.
n' âiva tasya vapuḥ śakyaṃ pravaktuṃ, veṣa eva ca.
sarvathā tu tad ālakṣya sphuṭeyur api parvatāḥ.
tasy' āsya|nāsikābhyāṃ ca, śravaṇābhyāṃ ca sarvaśaḥ,
tebhyaś c' âkṣi|sahasrebhyaḥ prādur āsan mah"|ârciṣaḥ.
tathā tejo|marīcibhyaḥ śaṅkha|cakra|gadā|dharāḥ
prādur āsan Hṛṣīkeśāḥ śataśo 'tha sahasraśaḥ.
6.10 tad aty|adbhutam ālokya bhūtaṃ loka|bhayaṃ|karam
Drauṇir a|vyathito divyair astra|varṣair avākirat.
Drauṇi|muktāñ śarāṃs tāṃs tu tad bhūtaṃ mahad agrasat,
udadher iva vāry|oghān pāvako vaḍavā|mukhaḥ.
agrasat tāṃs tathā bhūtaṃ Drauṇinā prahitāñ śarān.

DHRITA·RASHTRA interrupted:

SO WHEN THE Bhojan and Kripa saw the son of Drona 6.1
stood at the entrance way, what did they do, Sánjaya?
Tell me.

SÁNJAYA replied:

After he had called Krita·varman and the great chariot-fighter Kripa to join him, the son of Drona, his soul engulfed by fury, came to the entrance of the encampment. As he came to the entry he saw standing there a hair-raising sight—a giant of enormous dimensions, as bright as the sun and moon, wearing the skin of a tiger dripping with blood; a black antelope skin was his upper garment and a
cobra was his sacred thread;* With many very long, mus- 6.5
cular arms, each holding raised a different weapon; a great serpent twisted round his biceps as an ornament; a garland of flames played about his face. His terrifying, gaping face, a maw of gruesome fangs, was covered with a thousand eyes, glinting myriad colors. Indescribable in body and apparel, were even mountains to catch a glimpse of him in his entirety, they would split asunder. Great rays of light beamed on all sides, from his mouth and nostrils, from his two ears and from his thousand eyes. Again from the rays of light appeared Vishnu-gods, a hundred, nay a thousand of them, each bearing the conch, discus and mace.

Seeing that extraordinary creature that could instill fear 6.10
in the whole world, Drona's son stood firm and discharged volleys of his divine missiles upon it. But that enormous being simply swallowed the arrows Drona's son had shot, as the submarine fire at the gateway to the underworld swal-

Aśvatthāmā tu saṃpreksya śar'|âughāṃs tān nir|arthakān,
ratha|śaktiṃ mumoc' âsau dīptām agni|śikhām iva.
sā tam āhatya dīpt'|âgrā ratha|śaktir adīryata,
yug'|ânte† sūryam āhatya mah"|ôlk" êva divaś cyutā.
atha hema|tsaruṃ divyaṃ khaḍgam ākāśa|varcasam
6.15 kośāt samudbabarh' āśu, bilād dīptam iv' ôragam.
tataḥ khaḍga|varaṃ dhīmān bhūtāya prāhiṇot tadā.
sa tad āsādya bhūtaṃ vai bilaṃ nakulavad yayau.
tataḥ sa kupito Drauṇir Indra|ketu|nibhāṃ gadām
jvalantīṃ prāhiṇot tasmai. bhūtaṃ tām api c' âgrasat.
tataḥ sarv'|āyudh'|â|bhāve vīkṣamāṇas tatas tataḥ
apaśyat kṛtam ākāśam an|ākāśaṃ Janārdanaiḥ.
tad adbhutatamaṃ dṛṣṭvā Droṇa|putro nir|āyudhaḥ
abravīd abhisaṃtaptaḥ Kṛpa|vākyam anusmaran:
«bruvatām a|priyaṃ pathyaṃ suhṛdāṃ na śṛṇoti yaḥ,
6.20 sa śocaty āpadaṃ prāpya, yath" āham ativartya tau.
śāstra|dṛṣṭān a|vidvān yaḥ samatītya jighāṃsati,
sa pathaḥ pracyuto dharmyāt, ku|pathe pratihanyate.
‹go|brāhmaṇa|nṛpa|strīṣu, sakhyur, mātur, guros tathā,
hīna|prāṇa|jaḍ'|ândheṣu, supta|bhīt'|ôtthiteṣu ca,
matt'|ônmatta|pramatteṣu na śastrāṇy upadhārayet.›
ity evaṃ gurubhiḥ pūrvam upadiṣṭaṃ nṛṇāṃ sadā.
so 'ham utkramya panthānaṃ śāstra|dṛṣṭaṃ sanātanam,

lows the currents of water from the ocean. That apparition swallowed those arrows Drona's son delivered. Now, when Ashva·tthaman saw his volleys of arrows fail to make any impact, he launched the flagpole of his chariot set ablaze like a rocket. But when the chariot flagpole struck against him, it shattered, like a great meteor colliding into the sun at the end of the eon and falling from the sky, or a divine sword with a golden hilt against the luster of the sky.

Then the cunning warrior drew from its scabbard his 6.15
prized sword like a blazing serpent slipping from its lair, and hurled it at that creature. But when the sword struck him, it disappeared, as if down the burrow of a mongoose.* At that, Drona's son, incensed, hurled at it his blazing mace, resplendent as the banner of Indra. But the giant swallowed that too. At that, with all his weapons used up, Drona's son, casting his eyes about him, saw that the whole sky had been entirely filled by Vishnu in wrathful form. At that most extraordinary sight, Ashva·tthaman, now weaponless, recalled with regret the words of Kripa and said:

"Whoever fails to heed the salutary advice of friends,
however unwelcome, repents on finding himself in trouble, 6.20
as do I after ignoring those two. Whoever disregards the injunctions found in the law books and sets out to kill in violation of them has fallen from the path of good and is driven onto the path of evil. 'To cow, brahmin, king, friend, mother and teacher, to the impaired, idiots, the blind, the sleeping, the terrified or one getting up from sleep, to the drunk, deranged or unconscious, one should never raise a weapon.' These are the words of the eternal path found in the law books, always taught in this way to men by their

a|mārgeṇ' âivam ārabhya ghorām āpadam āgataḥ.
tāṃ c' āpadaṃ ghorataraṃ pravadanti manīṣiṇaḥ,
6.25 yad udyamya mahat kṛtyaṃ bhayād api nivartate.
a|śakyaś c' âiva tat kartuṃ karma śakti|balād iha,
na hi daivād garīyo vai mānuṣaṃ karma kathyate.
mānuṣaṃ kurvataḥ karma yadi daivān na sidhyati,
sa pathaḥ pracyuto dharmyād vipadaṃ pratipadyate.
pratijñānaṃ hy a|vijñānaṃ pravadanti manīṣiṇaḥ,
yad ārabhya kriyāṃ kāñ cid bhayād iha nivartate.
tad idaṃ duṣ|praṇītena bhayaṃ māṃ samupasthitam
—na hi Droṇa|sutaḥ saṃkhye nivarteta kathañ cana—
idaṃ ca su|mahad bhūtaṃ daiva|daṇḍam iv' ôdyatam.
6.30 na c' âitad abhijānāmi cintayann api sarvathā.
dhruvaṃ y" êyam a|dharmaṃ me pravṛttā kaluṣā matiḥ,
tasyāḥ phalam idaṃ ghoraṃ pratighātāya kalpate.
tad idaṃ daiva|vihitaṃ mama saṃkhye nivartanam.
n' ânyatra daivād udyantum iha śakyaṃ kathañ cana.
so 'ham adya Mahādevaṃ prapadye śaraṇaṃ vibhum.
daiva|daṇḍam imaṃ ghoraṃ sa hi me nāśayiṣyati.
kapardinaṃ, deva|devam, Umā|patim, an|āmayam,
kapāla|mālinaṃ, rudraṃ, Bhaga|netra|haraṃ Haram.
sa hi devo 'tyagād devāṃs tapasā vikrameṇa ca
tasmāc charaṇam abhyemi giri|śaṃ śūla|pāṇinam.»

teachers of old, and I have strayed from that. Now that I've lost my way by trying to do such a thing, I have brought terrible disaster upon myself. But the wise rate it as a disaster more terrible still when out of cowardice someone gives up 6.25
the great mission they have undertaken. Moreover, in this world nobody can achieve anything on the basis of ability, for it's said that human effort can't outmatch divine will. If the effort of a man who has tried fails due to divine will, he has met misfortune after falling from the path of righteousness. The wise declare that in this world when someone gives up the task they had undertaken out of fear then their vow to do it was based on ignorance. But this fear that has come upon me comes from my misconduct—for otherwise the son of Drona would never give up on the battlefield—and this fantastic creature has risen up as a kind of divine retribution.

Aye, no matter how hard I think, I don't recognize it at 6.30
all, surely this is the terrifying result of my corrupt mind engaging on an unjust path, serving to obstruct it. My failure on the battlefield like this is ordained by divine will. In this world it is impossible to strive against divine will. For this reason I now seek sanctuary in the powerful Great Deity. He will destroy this terrifying embodiment of divine retribution for me. The god of gods, Uma's matted-haired lord, who removes disease, the wrathful lord whose garland is a string of skulls, the Destroyer, who destroyed the eyes of Bhaga. He is the god that surpasses all gods in power and prowess. Therefore I seek sanctuary in him, the mountain-dweller, the holder of the trident."*

SAÑJAYA uvāca:

7.1 SA EVAṂ CINTAYITVĀ tu Droṇa|putro, viśāṃ pate,
avatīrya rath'|ôpasthād dev'|ēśaṃ praṇataḥ sthitaḥ.

DRAUṆIR uvāca:

ugraṃ, sthāṇuṃ, śivaṃ, rudraṃ,
śarvam, īśānam, īśvaram,
giri|śaṃ, vara|daṃ, devaṃ,
bhava|bhāvanam, īśvaram,
śiti|kaṇṭham, ajaṃ, śukraṃ, Dakṣa|kratu|haraṃ Haram,
viśva|rūpaṃ, virūp'|âkṣaṃ, bahu|rūpam Umā|patim,
śmaśāna|vāsinaṃ, dṛptaṃ mahā|gaṇa|patiṃ, vibhum,
khaṭvāṅga|dhāriṇaṃ rudraṃ, jaṭilaṃ brahmacāriṇam,
7.5 manasā su|viśuddhena duṣ|kareṇ' âlpa|cetasā
so 'ham ātm"|ôpahāreṇa yakṣye tripura|ghātinam.
stutaṃ, stutyaṃ, stūyamānam, a|moghaṃ, kṛtti|vāsasam,
vilohitaṃ, nīla|kaṇṭham, a|sahyaṃ, dur|nivāraṇam,
śukraṃ Brahma|sṛjaṃ, brahma, brahmacāriṇam eva ca,
vratavantaṃ, tapo|niṣṭham, an|antaṃ tapatāṃ gatim,
bahu|rūpaṃ gaṇ'|âdhyakṣaṃ, try|akṣaṃ, pāriṣada|priyam,
dhan'|âdhyakṣaṃ, kṣiti|mukhaṃ, Gaurī|hṛdaya|vallabham,
Kumāra|pitaraṃ, piṅgaṃ, go|vṛṣ'|ôttama|vāhanam,
tanu|vāsasam, atyugram, Umā|bhūṣaṇa|tatparam,
7.10 paraṃ parebhyaḥ, paramaṃ, paraṃ yasmān na vidyate,
iṣv|astr'|ôttama|bhartāraṃ, dig|antaṃ, deśa|rakṣiṇam,

SÁNJAYA continued:

SUCH WERE THE thoughts of Drona's son, lord of the re- 7.1
gions, whereupon he stepped down from the platform of his chariot and stood bowed before the lord of gods.

DRONA'S SON continued:

To the formidable, firm, auspicious, fierce, deadly-arrowed sovereign lord, mountain-dweller, bestower of favors, the creator of the universe, to the blue-throated, unborn, radiant, destroyer of Daksha's sacrifice, the Destroyer, to the omnipresent, to the uneven-eyed,* many-formed Lord of Uma, who lives in cremation grounds, the wild overlord of demigods, the powerful, the wrathful holder of the skull-topped staff, the celibate ascetic with matted
locks, to the god that razed the three citadels in one,* with 7.5
a truly pure mind I shall make a sacrifice, with difficulty, with my own self as the offering, even though I can barely cling to consciousness.

To the one who has been praised, will be praised, and is praised even now, the infallible, the wearer of the antelope hide, the red, the blue-throated, invincible, irresistible, to the resplendent creator of the Creator, the supreme being, and celibate devotee of the supreme being, the keeper of the vow, devoted to austerities, the eternal objective of ascetics, to the multiform leader of the demigods, the three-eyed, beloved of his retinue, the overseer of treasures, whose mouth spells destruction, the darling of Gauri's* heart, to the father of Karttikéya, the tawny one, whose mount is the

hiraṇya|kavacaṃ devaṃ, candra|mauli|vibhūṣitam
prapadye śaraṇaṃ devaṃ parameṇa samādhinā.
imāṃ ced āpadaṃ ghorāṃ tarāmy adya su|duṣkarām,
sarva/bhūt'|ôpahāreṇa yakṣye 'haṃ śucinā śucim.»

iti tasya vyavasitaṃ jñātvā yogāt su|karmaṇaḥ
purastāt kāñcanī vediḥ prādur āsīn mah"|ātmanaḥ.
tasyāṃ vedyāṃ tadā, rājaṃś, citra|bhānur ajāyata
sa diśo vidiśaḥ khaṃ ca jvālābhir iva pūrayan.

7.15 dīpt'|āsya|nayanāś c' âtra, n'|âika|pāda|śiro|bhujāḥ,
ratna|citr'|âṅgada|dharāḥ, samudyata|karās tathā,
dvīpa|śaila|pratīkāśāḥ prādur āsan mahā|gaṇāḥ
śva|varāh'|ôṣṭra|rūpāś ca, haya|gomāyu|gomukhāḥ,
ṛkṣa|mārjāra|vadanā, vyāghra|dvīpi|mukhās tathā,
kāka|vaktrāḥ, plava|mukhāḥ, śuka|vaktrās tath" âiva ca,
mah"|âjagara|vaktrāś ca, haṃsa|vaktrāḥ, śita|prabhāḥ,
dārv|āghāṭa|mukhāś c' âpi, cāṣa|vaktrāś ca, Bhārata,
kūrma|nakra|mukhāś c' âiva, śiśumāra|mukhās tathā,
mahā|makara|vaktrāś ca, timi|vaktrās tath" âiva ca,
7.20 hari|vaktrāḥ, krauñca|mukhāḥ, kapot'|êbha|mukhās tathā,
pārāvata|mukhāś c' âiva, madgu|vaktrās tath" âiva ca,

most excellent bull,* to the one who wears a corpse as clothing, the extremely fierce, the one preoccupied with deck-
ing Uma in jewelry, to the one beyond all others, beyond 7.10
whom there is no one, the bearer of the best bow, the extent of all horizons, the protector of all regions, to the god
in golden armor, the moon diadem adorning his hair—to
him I go for sanctuary, focused in sublime meditation. If I
survive this terrifying disaster, this insurmountable ordeal,
today I shall make a sacrifice to the pure one with the pure
offering of *all beings : my every element.*"

In recognition of the vow sworn in these words, in response to the religious act thus well-performed, a golden sacrificial fire altar appeared before that great-souled man. Then on that sacrificial altar, Your Majesty, a brilliant fire flared up, seeming to fill every corner of the compass and the firmament with flames.

Also in this place, with blazing mouths and eyes, with 7.15
many feet, heads and arms, their raised hands displaying
resplendent jeweled armlets, there appeared in great clusters
like towering craggy islands the demigods, in the forms of
dogs, boars, or donkeys, with the heads of horses, jackals or
cows, with the faces of bears or cats, or the maws of tigers or
leopards, the heads of crows, frog-faced, or with the heads
of parrots, with faces of boa constrictors or of geese, radiant
white, with faces of woodpeckers and jays, child of Bhárata's
line. With the heads of turtles and alligators, or the faces
of crocodiles, with the heads of great *mákaras*,* or the faces
of whales; monkey-faced, osprey-headed, with the faces of 7.20
pigeons or elephants, with the faces of turtle-doves, or the
heads of cormorants, with ears shaped like hands, and a

pāṇi|karṇāḥ, sahasr'|âkṣās, tath" âiva ca śat'|ôdarāḥ,
nir|māṃsāḥ, kāka|vaktrāś ca, śyena|vaktrāś ca, Bhārata,
tath" âiv' â|śiraso, rājan, ṛkṣa|vaktrāś ca, Bhārata,
pradīpta|netra|jihvāś ca, jvālā|varṇās tath" âiva ca,
jvālā|keśāś ca, rāj'|êndra, jvalad|roma|catur|bhujāḥ,
meṣa|vaktrās tath" âiv' ânye, tathā chāga|mukhā, nṛpa,
śaṅkh'|ābhāḥ, śaṅkha|vaktrāś ca,
śaṅkha|karṇās tath" âiva ca,
śaṅkha|mālā|parikarāḥ,
śaṅkha|dhvani|sama|svanāḥ,
7.25 jaṭā|dharāḥ, pañca|śikhās, tathā muṇḍāḥ, kṛś'|ôdarāḥ,
catur|daṃṣṭrāś, catur|jihvāḥ, śaṅku|karṇāḥ, kirīṭinaḥ,
mauñjī|dharāś ca, rāj'|êndra, tathā kuñcita|mūrdhajāḥ,
uṣṇīṣiṇo, mukuṭinaś, cāru|vaktrāḥ, sv|alaṃkṛtāḥ,
padm'|ôtpal'|āpīḍa|dharās, tathā mukuṭa|dhāriṇaḥ,
māhātmyena ca saṃyuktāḥ śataśo 'tha sahasraśaḥ,
śata|ghnī|vajra|hastāś ca, tathā musala|pāṇayaḥ,
bhuśuṇḍī|pāśa|hastāś ca, daṇḍa|hastāś ca, Bhārata,
pṛṣṭheṣu baddh'|êṣudhayaś, citra|bāṇ'|ôtkaṭās tathā,
sa|dhvajāḥ, sa|patākāś ca, sa|ghaṇṭāḥ, sa|paraśvadhāḥ,
7.30 mahā|pāś'|ôdyata|karās, tathā laguḍa|pāṇayaḥ,
sthūṇā|hastāḥ, khaḍga|hastāḥ, sarp'|ôcchrita|kirīṭinaḥ,
mahā|sarp'|âṅgada|dharāś, citr'|ābharaṇa|dhāriṇaḥ,
rajo|dhvastāḥ, paṅka|digdhāḥ, sarve śukl'|âmbara|srajaḥ,
nīl'|âṅgāḥ, piṅgal'|âṅgāś ca, muṇḍa|vaktrās tath"|âiva ca.

thousand eyes, with one hundred bellies, fleshless, with the faces of crows and of hawks, scion of Bhárata's line.

Some were even headless, or bear-mawed, king of Bhárata's line, their eyes and tongues gleaming and flame-colored. The hair of their heads was flame, chief of kings, and the hairs on their four arms ablaze. Some had the heads of sheep, others the faces of goats, protector of men. Some gleamed like conches, had conches for heads, or conch ears, or festooned in conch-garlands, they emitted sound the
same as conches. Some wore matted locks or had five crests 7.25
while others were bald, with lean bellies, four fangs, four tongues, with darts through their ears, wearing diadems. Some wore sacred threads of sacred grass, with frizzy hair, chief of kings, with royal turbans or crowns, with elegant faces, well-adorned. Some wore chaplets of red or pale blue lotuses or bore crowns. They possessed greatness a hundredfold, nay a thousandfold. Some brandished the hundred-slaying spikes and thunderbolt weapons in their hands. Some clasped clubs. Some brandished missiles and nooses or clasped rods, scion of Bhárata's line. The quivers strapped to their backs thronged with different colored arrows and they held aloft pennons and standards, bells and battle-
axes. Their outstretched arms were slung with nooses while 7.30
cudgels rested in their hands, or they brandished anvils or clasped swords, their diadems raised up like snakes. Bearing great serpents as armlets, sporting ornaments of every color, their resplendent garments and garlands were all covered with dust and daubed with mud. Some had bodies blue or tawny, some had shaven heads.

bherī|śaṅkha|mṛdaṅgāṃś ca, jharjhar'|ānaka|gomukhān
avādayan pāriṣadāḥ prahṛṣṭā kanaka|prabhāḥ.
gāyamānās tath" âiv' ânye, nṛtyamānās tath" âpare,
laṅghayantaḥ, plavantaś ca, valgantaś ca mahā|rathāḥ,
dhāvanto, javanā, muṇḍāḥ, pavan'|ôddhūta|mūrdhajāḥ,
7.35 mattā iva mahā|nāgā vinadanto muhur muhuḥ,
su|bhīmā, ghora|rūpāś ca, śūla|paṭṭiśa|pāṇayaḥ,
nānā|virāga|vasanāś, citra|māly'|ânulepanāḥ,
ratna|citr'|âṅgada|dharāḥ, samudyata|karās tathā,
hantāro dviṣatāṃ, śūrāḥ, prasahy' â|sahya|vikramāḥ,
pātāro 'sṛg|vas"|āughānāṃ, māṃs'|ântra|kṛta|bhojanāḥ,
cūḍālāḥ karṇikārāś ca, prahṛṣṭāḥ, piṭhar'|ôdarāḥ,
atihrasv", âtidīrghāś ca, prabalāś c', âtibhairavāḥ,
vikaṭāḥ, kāla|lamb'|ôṣṭhā, bṛhac|cheph'|âṇḍa|piṇḍikāḥ,
mah"|ārha|nānā|vikaṭā, muṇḍāś ca, jaṭilāḥ pare.
7.40 s'|ârk'|êndu|graha|nakṣatrāṃ dyāṃ kuryur ye mahī|tale,
utsaherаṃś ca ye hantuṃ bhūta|grāmaṃ catur|vidham,
ye ca vīta|bhayā nityaṃ Harasya bhrukuṭī|sahāḥ,
kāma|kāra|karā nityaṃ, trailokyasy' ēśvar'|ēśvarāḥ,
nity'|ānanda|pramuditā, vāg|īśā, vīta|matsarāḥ,
prāpy' âṣṭa|guṇam aiśvaryaṃ ye na yānti ca vismayam,
yeṣāṃ vismayate nityaṃ bhagavān karmabhir Haraḥ,
mano|vāk|karmabhir yuktair nityam ārādhitaś ca yaiḥ,
mano|vāk|karmabhir bhaktān pāti putrān iv' āurasān.

These thrilled throngs, radiant as gold, sounded their instruments: kettle drums, conches, tambours, drums, dhols and cow-faced horns, while others sang and still others danced, great warriors prancing, leaping and jumping, running and racing, their heads shaven or their hair blown about by the wind. Like incensed cobras they hissed con- 7.35
stantly. Terrifying, horrific to see, they brandished pikes and spears, clothed in a variety of changing hues, wearing dazzling garlands and paints, their outstretched arms sported armlets encrusted with gems of every color.

The valiant foe-slayers, violent, unbeatable and bold, drinkers of streams of blood and bodily juices, who have feasted on flesh and entrails, sporting topknots and earrings, potbellied, were thrilled. Whether dwarfish or gargantuan, their power was immense and they were terrifying in the extreme. Hideous, with black, drooping lips, with enormously swollen penises and scrota, some had diadems of inestimable value, some were bald and others had matted locks.

Those who might bring the very firmament to earth, 7.40
bringing with it the sun and moon, the planets and the constellations, and those who could slay the entire community of the four kinds of living beings, and the fearless ones who forever endure the frown of the Destroyer, perpetually indulging their desires, lords of the lords of the tripartite universe,* those lords of speech, ever in raptures of joy, who, beyond selfishness and having attained the eight kinds of supremacy,* are never dismayed, at whose deeds the bounteous lord, the Destroyer, is always amazed, by whom he is ever worshipped with thought, word and deed:

pibanto 'sṛg|vasās tv anye kruddhā brahma|dviṣāṃ sadā,
7.45 catur|vidh'|ātmakaṃ somaṃ ye pibanti ca sarvadā;
śrutena, brahma|caryeṇa, tapasā ca, damena ca
ye samārādhya śūl'|âṅkaṃ Bhava|sāyujyam āgatāḥ,
yair ātma|bhūtair bhagavān, Pārvatyā ca mah"|ēśvaraḥ,
mahā|bhūta|gaṇān bhuṅkte bhūta|bhavya|bhavat|prabhuḥ.

nānā|vāditra|hasita|kṣveḍit'|ôtkruṣṭa|garjitaiḥ
santrāsayantas te viśvam Aśvatthāmānam abhyayuḥ,
saṃstuvanto Mahādevaṃ, bhāḥ kurvāṇāḥ su|varcasaḥ.
vivardhayiṣavo Drauṇer mahimānaṃ mahātmanaḥ,
jijñāsamānās tat|tejaḥ, sauptikaṃ ca didṛkṣavaḥ,
7.50 bhīm'|ôgra|parigh'|âlāta|śūla|paṭṭiśa|pāṇayaḥ,
ghora|rūpāḥ samājagmur bhūta|saṅghāḥ samantataḥ.
janayeyur bhayaṃ ye sma trailokyasy' âpi darśanāt,
tān prekṣamāṇo 'pi vyathāṃ na cakāra mahā|balaḥ.
atha Drauṇir dhanuṣ|pāṇir, baddha|godh'|âṅgulitravān,
svayam ev'|âtman" ātmānam upahāram upāharat.

dhanūṃṣi samidhas tatra, pavitrāṇi śitāḥ śarāḥ,
havir ātmavataś c' ātmā tasmin, bhārata, karmaṇi.
tataḥ saumyena mantreṇa Droṇa|putraḥ pratāpavān
upahāraṃ mahā|manyur ath' ātmānam upāharat.

them he protects as his own sons, who adore him with body, speech and mind. Now some, ever cruel, drink the blood
and marrow of the enemies of sacrificial power, those who 7.45
always drink the four types of Soma juice; those who, on propitiating the one whose insignia is the trident, with their learning, celibacy, austerity or restraint enter union with the Being;* with these who are one with him, the bounteous Great Lord with Párvati, the master of all that has been, is and will be, enjoys all the great groups of beings.

Making the universe quake with their various forms of instrumental music, laughter, battle-cries, their clamoring and roaring, they closed in on Ashva·tthaman, praising the Great God, emitting a brilliant radiance. Seeking to increase the power of Drona's noble son, wanting to understand his glory, and longing to witness his deed in the dead
of that night, the groups of beings, terrible in appearance, 7.50
gathered around on all sides, clasping their fearsome and harsh iron cudgels, their pikes and spears in their hands. As he looked upon those creatures, who could instill fear throughout the entire tripartite universe by their appearance alone, the mighty man betrayed no anguish. Then Drona's son, bow in hand, a leathern archer's fence strapped across his fingers, made an offering of himself, by himself, alone.

In the offering the bows were the kindling, the purifying sacrificial tools were the sharpened arrows, and in that rite, son in Bhárata's line, the self of the self-possessed man was the oblation. Then uttering a soft ambrosial mantra, Drona's spirited son, replete with religious power, made an offering of himself.

7.55 taṃ Rudraṃ raudra|karmāṇaṃ
raudraiḥ karmabhir a|cyutam
abhiṣṭutya Mahātmānam,
ity uvāca kṛt'|âñjaliḥ:

DRAUṆIR uvāca:

imam ātmānam ady' âhaṃ jātam Āṅgirase kule
sv|agnau juhomi, bhagavan. pratigṛhṇīṣva māṃ balim.
bhavad|bhaktyā, Mahādeva, parameṇa samādhinā
asyām āpadi, Viśvātmann, upākurmi tav' âgrataḥ.
tvayi sarvāṇi bhūtāni, sarva|bhūteṣu c' âsi vai.
guṇānāṃ hi pradhānānām ekatvaṃ tvayi tiṣṭhati.
sarva|bhūt'|āśraya, vibho, havir|bhūtam avasthitam
pratigṛhāṇa† māṃ deva yady a|śakyāḥ pare mayā.
7.60 ity uktvā Drauṇir āsthāya tāṃ vedīṃ dīpta|pāvakām,
santyajy' ātmānam, āruhya kṛṣṇa|vartmany upāviśat.
tam ūrdhva|bāhuṃ, niśceṣṭaṃ dṛṣṭvā havir upasthitam,
abravīd bhagavān sākṣān Mahādevo hasann iva:
«satya|śauc'|ārjava|tyāgais, tapasā, niyamena ca,
kṣāntyā, bhaktyā ca, dhṛtyā ca, buddhyā ca, vacasā tathā
yathāvad aham ārāddhaḥ Kṛṣṇen' â|kliṣṭa|karmaṇā.
tasmād iṣṭatamaḥ Kṛṣṇād anyo mama na vidyate.
kurvatā tasya† saṃmānaṃ, tvāṃ ca jijñāsatā mayā
Pāñcālāḥ sahasā guptā, māyāś ca bahuśaḥ kṛtāḥ.
7.65 kṛtas tasy' âiva saṃmānaḥ Pāñcālān rakṣatā mayā.
abhibhūtās tu Kālena. n' âiṣām ady' âsti jīvitam.»

When he had worshipped with fearsome rites that im- 7.55
movable Fierce Lord of fearsome rites, he spoke as follows to the Great Soul, his hands pressed together in prayer.

DRONA'S SON said:

Today I offer this, my own self, born in the family of the Ángiras seers,* into the excellent fire as an oblation, bounteous lord. Please accept me as an offering. Out of devotion to you, Great God, in supreme meditation I perform this rite before you, Self of All, in my current misfortune. All beings reside in you, and you in turn reside in all beings. For the unitary nature of all the principal strands of existence abide in you. Refuge of all beings, powerful lord, accept this oblation that I have become, placed before you, since my enemies cannot be affected by me.

After saying this, Drona's son approached the altar that 7.60
blazed with purifying fire, and, abandoning himself he climbed upon it and sat on the blackening furnace. On seeing him positioned there with uplifted arms, a motionless oblation, the bounteous lord, the Great God appeared before him, seeming to smile, and spoke:

"With truth, purity, honesty, with renunciation, austerity and restraint, with forbearance, devotion, resolve, and understanding and speech, has Krishna, whose actions are unsullied, propitiated me. Therefore none is more favored by me than Krishna. To honor that dear man and to assess you I have intervened to protect the Panchálas and displayed multiple illusions. By protecting the Panchálas it is 7.65
him that I have respected. But they are overpowered by Time. Today their life runs out."

evam uktvā mah"|ātmānaṃ bhagavān ātmanas tanum
āviveśa, dadau c' âsmai vimalaṃ khaḍgam uttamam.
ath' āviṣṭo bhagavatā bhūyo jajvāla tejasā,
vegavāṃś c' âbhavad yuddhe deva|sṛṣṭena tejasā.
tam a|dṛśyāni bhūtāni rakṣāṃsi ca samādravan,
abhitaḥ śatru|śibiraṃ yāntaṃ, sākṣād iv' Īśvaram.

DHṚTARĀṢṬRA uvāca:

8.1 TATHĀ PRAYĀTE śibiraṃ Droṇa|putre mahā|rathe
kaccit Kṛpaś ca Bhojaś ca bhay'|ārtau na nyavartatām?
kaccin na vāritau, kṣudrai rakṣibhir n' ôpalakṣitau?
«a|sahyam» iti manvānau na nivṛttau mahā|rathau?
kaccid unmathya śibiraṃ hatvā somaka|Pāṇḍavān
Duryodhanasya padavīṃ gatau paramikāṃ raṇe?
Pāñcālair nihatau vīrau kaccit tu svapatāṃ kṣitau?*
kaccit tābhyāṃ kṛtaṃ karma? tan mam' ācakṣva, Saṃjaya.

SAṂJAYA uvāca:

8.5 tasmin prayāte śibiraṃ Droṇa|putre mah"|ātmani,
Kṛpaś ca Kṛtavarmā ca śibira|dvāry atiṣṭhatām.
Aśvatthāmā tu tau dṛṣṭvā yatnavantau mahā|rathau
prahṛṣṭaḥ śanakai, rājann, idaṃ vacanam abravīt:
«yat tau bhavantau paryāptau sarva|kṣatrasya nāśane,
kiṃ punar yodha|śeṣasya prasuptasya viśeṣataḥ!
ahaṃ pravekṣye śibiraṃ, cariṣyāmi ca Kālavat,

When he had said this to the noble warrior, the bounteous lord entered his body and bestowed on him an immaculate, supreme sword. Then, the bounteous lord within him, Ashva·tthaman shone with even greater splendor, and he became swift in battle on account of the splendor created by God. Invisible beings and protecting demons converged on him from all sides, as he entered the camp of the enemy, like the Lord incarnate.

DHRITA·RASHTRA interrupted:

WHEN THE GREAT chariot fighter, the son of Drona, had 8.1
set off into the encampment like that, did Kripa and the Bhojan not turn back, terrified? Were they not held in check, were they not observed by those useless sentinels? Did those two great chariot fighters not turn back thinking "We cannot win?" Or did they wreak dreadful havoc on the encampment, killing the Sómakas and Pándavas, before they took the highest path in battle,* the road taken by Duryódhana? Or did those two heroes, slain by the Panchálas, lie to rest upon the ground? What did the two of them do? Speak to me of that, Sánjaya.

SÁNJAYA replied:

When the noble-souled son of Drona set off into the en- 8.5
campment, both Kripa and Krita·varman remained standing at the camp gate. But then Ashva·tthaman saw those two valiant chariot-fighters, Your Majesty, and, thrilled, whispered to them these words: "Since the two of you are capable of destroying the entire warrior caste, how much more so the mere sleeping remnant of soldiers! I shall enter the camp, and wend my way like Time. The two of you

yathā† na kaś cid api vāṃ jīvan mucyeta mānavaḥ,
tathā bhavadbhyāṃ† kāryaṃ syād, iti me niścitā matiḥ.»
ity uktvā prāviśad Drauṇiḥ pārthānāṃ śibiraṃ mahat.
8.10 a|dvāreṇ'|âbhyavaskandya, vihāya bhayam ātmanaḥ,
sa praviśya mahā|bāhur, uddeśa|jñaś ca tasya ha
Dhṛṣṭadyumnasya nilayaṃ śanakair abhyupāgamat.
te tu kṛtvā mahat karma, śrāntāś ca balavad raṇe,
prasuptāś c' âiva vidhvastāḥ sametya paridhāvitāḥ.
atha praviśya tad veśma Dhṛṣṭadyumnasya, Bhārata,
Pāñcālyaṃ śayane Drauṇir apaśyat suptam antikāt
kṣaum'|âvadāte, mahati, spardhy'|āstaraṇa|saṃvṛte,
mālya|pravara|saṃyukte, dhūpaiś cūrṇaiś ca vāsite.
taṃ śayānaṃ mah"|ātmānaṃ visrabdham a|kuto|bhayam
8.15 prābodhayata pādena śayana|sthaṃ, mahī|pate.
saṃbudhya caraṇa|sparśād utthāya raṇa|durmadaḥ
abhyajānad a|mey'|ātmā Droṇa|putraṃ mahā|ratham.
tam utpatantaṃ śayanād Aśvatthāmā mahā|balaḥ
keśeṣv ālambya pāṇibhyāṃ niṣpipeṣa mahī|tale.
sa|balaṃ tena niṣpiṣṭaḥ, sādhvasena ca, Bhārata,
nidrayā c' âiva Pāñcālyo n' âśakac ceṣṭituṃ tadā.
tam ākramya padā, rājan, kaṇṭhe c' ôrasi c' ôbhayoḥ
nadantaṃ visphurantaṃ ca paśu|māram amārayat.
tudan nakhais tu sa Drauṇiṃ n' âtivyaktam udāharat:

must do whatever it takes to ensure that not a single man escapes your clutches alive. My heart is set on this." So saying, Drona's son entered the great camp of the sons of Pritha.

Gaining access without using the entranceway, casting 8.10
off his own fear, that strapping hero went in and, recognizing the place, he quietly approached Dhrishta·dyumna's quarters. Meanwhile those men who had gathered together to surround it were in a state of thorough exhaustion after all the action of the battle and now lay sprawled about, fast asleep.

Then, scion of Bhárata's line, Drona's son, on entering Dhrishta·dyumna's tent, espied the Panchálan king close by asleep on his cot, which was covered with a magnificent, large, immaculate silken cloth and dressed with fragrance and perfume paste, along with the finest garlands. As that noble warrior lay there relaxed, without a care in the world,
as he slumbered, Lord of the great earth, the other woke 8.15
him with his foot.

Waking from the touch of the other's foot and rising, the man who was so ferocious in battle, of immeasurable soul, recognized Drona's son, the great chariot-warrior. As he started up from his bed, Ashva·tthaman, great in strength, grabbed his hair in both hands and threw him against the ground. Thrown so violently, scion of Bhárata's line, and in sheer terror and in his sleepy state, the Panchálan king had no chance to react. Pinning him down with his foot, Your Majesty, planting one foot on his the neck, the other on his chest, Ashva·tthaman forced him to die the death of a slaughtered animal, squealing and quivering. But he in

8.20 «ācārya|putra, śastreṇa jahi māṃ! mā ciraṃ kṛthāḥ!
tvat|kṛte su|kṛtāl̄ lokān gaccheyaṃ, dvi|padāṃ vara.»
evam uktvā tu vacanaṃ virarāma paraṃ|tapaḥ
sutaḥ Pañcāla|rājasya ākrānto balinā bhṛśam.*
tasy' â|vyaktāṃ tu tāṃ vācaṃ saṃśrutya Drauṇir abravīt:
«ācārya|ghātināṃ lokā na santi, kula|pāṃsana.
tasmāc chastreṇa nidhanaṃ na tvam arhasi, dur|mate.»
evaṃ bruvāṇas taṃ vīraṃ, siṃho mattam iva dvipam,
marmasv abhyavadhīt kruddhaḥ pād'|âṣṭhīlaiḥ su|dāruṇaiḥ.
tasya vīrasya śabdena māryamāṇasya veśmani
8.25 abudhyanta, mahā|rāja, striyo ye c' âsya rakṣiṇaḥ.
te dṛṣṭvā dharṣayantaṃ tam atimānuṣa|vikramam,
bhūtam ev' âdhyavasyanto na sma pravyāharan bhayāt.
taṃ tu ten' âbhyupāyena gamayitvā Yama|kṣayam
adhyatiṣṭhata tejasvī rathaṃ prāpya su|darśanam.
sa tasya bhavanād, rājan, niṣkramy', ānādayan diśaḥ,
rathena śibiraṃ prāyāj jighāṃsur dviṣato balī.
apakrānte tatas tasmin Droṇa|putre mahā|rathe
saha tai rakṣibhiḥ sarvaiḥ praṇedur yoṣitas tadā.
rājānaṃ nihataṃ dṛṣṭvā bhṛśaṃ śoka|parāyaṇāḥ,
8.30 vyākrośan kṣatriyāḥ sarve Dhṛṣṭadyumnasya, Bhārata.

turn, tearing at Drona's son with his nails, gasped out none too clearly:

"Son of my teacher, dispatch me with the sword! Make it 8.20
quick! When you have done, most excellent of men, I can go to the heavens reserved for the righteous." Now when he had said this much, the son of the Panchálan king, router of his enemies, stopped, overwhelmed so completely was he by that powerful man. But when Drona's son caught his indistinct words, he replied: "You disgrace to your family, there are no heavens reserved for the murderers of teachers. That's why you don't deserve death by the sword, you stupid man." As he said these words to the hero, he kicked at his vitals with pitiless blows of his heels, like a lion striking an elephant in rut.

At the sound of the hero being murdered in his tent
the women and those who should have been guarding him 8.25
woke up, great king. Seeing Ashva·tthaman savaging their master with superhuman strength, and taking him for some kind of ghoul, they couldn't speak for fear. Meanwhile, once he had despatched him to the wastes of Death, he returned to his beautiful chariot and stood in it, glorious. On leaving the other man's quarters, Your Majesty, his roars booming against the horizons, that mighty man set out round the rest of the encampment, planning the slaughter of his enemies. At the departure of the son of Drona, that great chariot-fighter, the women and the guards echoed him in turn with their wails. Succumbing completely to their
grief at seeing their prince slain, all Dhrishta·dyumna's no- 8.30
bles began screaming, king of Bhárata's line.

tāsām tu tena śabdena samīpe kṣatriya'|rṣabhāḥ
kṣipraṃ ca samanahyanta, «kim etad?» iti c' âbruvan.
striyas tu, rājan, vitrastā Bhāradvājaṃ nirīkṣya tam,
abruvan dīna|kaṇṭhena, «kṣipram ādravat'» êti vai.
«rākṣaso vā manuṣyo vā, n' âinaṃ jānīmahe vayam,
hatvā Pāñcālarājaṃ yo ratham āruhya tiṣṭhati.»
tatas te yodha|mukhyās taṃ sahasā paryavārayan.
sa tān āpatataḥ sarvān Rudr'|âstreṇa vyapothayat.
Dhṛṣṭadyumnaṃ ca hatvā sa, tāṃś c' âiv' âsya pad'|ânugān,
8.35 apaśyac chayane suptam Uttamaujasam antike.
tam apy ākramya pādena kaṇṭhe c' ôrasi c' âujasā,
tath" âiva mārayām āsa vinardantam ariṃ|damam.
Yudhāmanyuś ca saṃprāpto matvā taṃ rakṣasā hatam,
gadām udyamya vegena hṛdi Drauṇim atāḍayat.
tam abhidrutya jagrāha, kṣitau c' âinam apātayat,
visphurantaṃ ca paśuvat tath" âiv' âinam amārayat.
tathā sa vīro hatvā taṃ tato 'nyān samupādravat
saṃsuptān eva, rāj'|êndra, tatra tatra mahā|rathān,
sphurato vepamānāṃś ca, śamit" êva paśūn makhe.
8.40 tato nistriṃśam ādāya jaghān' ânyān pṛthag|janān,
bhāgaśo vicaran mārgān asi|yuddha|viśāradaḥ.
tath" âiva gulme saṃprekṣya śayānān madhyagaulmikān
śrāntān nyast'|āyudhān, sarvān kṣaṇen' âiva vyapothayat.

At the sound coming from the women, all the bull-like nobles in the vicinity asked "What's that?" as they quickly girded on their armor. The women meanwhile, Your Majesty, staring at that descendent of Bharad·vaja in horror, cried through constricted throats, "Hurry here quickly. Be it a devil or a man, we can't tell, but the creature standing mounted on his chariot has killed the king of the Panchálas." Suddenly the leading soldiers had him surrounded.

But as they fell upon him, he overpowered them all with fierce Shiva's sword. Dhrishta·dyumna's killer now killed his infantry too. Then he came upon Uttamáujas, of utmost vi- 8.35
tality, asleep in his cot close by. He used his own vitality to pin him down too with one foot on his neck, the other on his chest, and in that way brought that queller of his foes, bellowing, to his death. At that point Yudha·manyu arrived, and, thinking that Dhrishta·dyumna must have been slain by a demon, hastily took up his mace and struck Drona's son in the solar plexus. But the other turned on him, seized hold of him and forced him to the ground and dispatched him like a quivering beast. When the hero had slain him like that, he then set upon the other great chariot warriors, still aslumber in their different stations, chief of kings, quivering and shuddering like animals at the sacrifice, and he the butcher.

Then taking up his cruel rapier, with deft swordsman- 8.40
ship, he slaughtered the other wretches, working his way along the pathways, section by section. In similar vein, on spotting the middle-ranking officers lying exhausted in the military base, their weapons discarded, he made short shrift

yodhān, aśvān, dvipāṃś c' âiva prācchinat sa var'|âsinā,
rudhir'|ôkṣita|sarv'|âṅgaḥ† Kāla|sṛṣṭa iv' Ântakaḥ.
visphuradbhiś ca tair Drauṇir, nistriṃśasy' ôdyamena ca,
ākṣepaṇena c' âiv' âses tridhā rakt'|ôkṣito 'bhavat.
tasya lohita|raktasya† dīpta|khaḍgasya yudhyataḥ
a|mānuṣa iv' ākāro babhau parama|bhīṣaṇaḥ.
8.45 ye tv ajāgrata,† Kauravya, te 'pi śabdena mohitāḥ
nirīkṣyamāṇā anyonyaṃ dṛṣṭvā dṛṣṭvā pravivyathuḥ.
tad rūpaṃ tasya te dṛṣṭvā kṣatriyāḥ śatru|karṣiṇaḥ.
rākṣasaṃ manyamānās taṃ nayanāni nyamīlayan.
sa ghora|rūpo vyacarat Kālavac chibire tataḥ.
apaśyad Draupadī|putrān avaśiṣṭāṃś ca Somakān.
tena śabdena vitrastā dhanur|hastā mahā|rathāḥ
Dhṛṣṭadyumnaṃ hataṃ śrutvā Draupadeyā, viśāṃ pate,
avākiran śara|vrātair Bhāradvājam a|bhītavat.
tatas tena ninādena saṃprabuddhāḥ Prabhadrakāḥ
8.50 śilīmukhaiḥ Śikhaṇḍī ca Droṇa|putraṃ samārdayan.
Bhāradvājas tu† tān dṛṣṭvā śara|varṣāṇi varṣataḥ
nanāda balavan nādaṃ jighāṃsus tān mahā|rathān.
tataḥ parama|saṃkruddhaḥ, pitur vadham anusmaran,
avaruhya rath'|ôpasthāt tvaramāṇo 'bhidudruve,
sahasra|candra|vimalaṃ gṛhītvā carma saṃyuge,
khaḍgaṃ ca vipulaṃ, divyaṃ, jāta|rūpa|pariṣkṛtam.
Draupadeyān abhidrutya khaḍgena vyadhamad balī.

of them all. Warriors, horses and elephants, he hacked apart with his prize sword, his every limb drenched in blood, like the god of Death issued forth by Time. From the spurting of his victims, from the impact of his sword, and again from the blade as he withdrew it, he was three times drenched in gore. Red with blood, his sword glinting as he waged battle, he glistened like some inhuman form, instilling the utmost terror.

Even those who did wake, Kuru king, were confused by 8.45
the noise. Looking to each other, they were terrified at what they saw each time. Seeing his appearance those warriors, more used to being the ones to instill fear in their enemies, took him for a demon and shut their eyes tightly. Then that gruesome form made his way through the camp like Time himself. He spotted the sons of Dráupadi and the surviving Sómakas. Alarmed by the commotion, Lord of the peoples, Dráupadi's sons, bows in hand, great chariot-warriors all, hearing that Dhrishta·dyumna had been slain, fearlessly showered curtains of arrows on Bharad·vaja's scion.

Woken by the whoosh as these fell, the Prabhádrakas
and Shikhándin assailed Drona's son with their dart-tipped 8.50
shafts. But seeing them send these showers of arrows raining down, Bharad·vaja's scion bellowed a tremendous roar in his impatience to kill these great chariot-warriors. Inflamed with fury at the memory of his father's murder, he then leaped down in a flash from the platform of his chariot and ran at them, seizing his shield, untainted as a thousand moons in battle, and his broad sword, a weapon fit for a god, fashioned from gold. Running headlong at the sons of Dráupadi, full of might, he scattered them with that sword.

tataḥ sa nara|śārdūlaḥ Prativindhyaṃ mah"|āhave
kukṣi|deśe 'vadhīd, rājan. sa hato nyapatad bhuvi.
8.55 prāsena viddhvā Drauṇiṃ tu Sutasomaḥ pratāpavān
punaś c' âsiṃ samudyamya Droṇa|putram upādravat.
Sutasomasya s'|âsiṃ tu bāhuṃ chittvā nara'|rṣabhaḥ
punar abhyahanat pārśve. sa bhinna|hṛdayo 'patat.
Nākulis tu Śatānīko ratha|cakreṇa vīryavān
dorbhyām utkṣipya vegena vakṣasy enam atāḍayat.
atāḍayac Chatānīkaṃ mukta|cakraṃ† dvijas tu saḥ.
sa vihvalo yayau bhūmiṃ. tato 'sy' âpāharac chiraḥ.
Śrutakarmā tu parighaṃ gṛhītvā samatāḍayat
abhidrutya tato Drauṇiṃ savye sa phalake bhṛśam.
8.60 sa tu taṃ Śrutakarmāṇam āsye jaghne var' âsinā.
sa hato nyapatad bhūmau vimūḍho vikṛt'|ānanaḥ.

tena śabdena vīras tu Śrutakīrtir mahā|rathaḥ
Aśvatthāmānam āsādya śara|varṣair avākirat.
tasy' âpi śara|varṣāṇi carmaṇā prativārya saḥ
sa|kuṇḍalaṃ śiraḥ kāyād† bhrājamānam upāharat.
tato Bhīṣma|nihantā taṃ† saha sarvaiḥ Prabhadrakaiḥ
ahanat sarvato vīraṃ nānā|praharaṇair balī.
śilīmukhena c' ânyena bhruvor madhye samārpayat.
sa tu krodha|samāviṣṭo Droṇa|putro mahā|balaḥ
8.65 Śikhaṇḍinaṃ samāsādya dvidhā ciccheda so 'sinā.

Next in the great battle, Your Majesty, that tiger of men plunged it into Prativíndhya's belly. Prativíndhya fell dead upon the ground.

Then Suta·soma the splendid, striking Drona's child with 8.55
a barbed missile, in turn raised his sword to attack Drona's son. But that bull of a man cut off Suta·soma's arm as it still clutched the sword, then struck him again through the now unprotected side of his body. Suta·soma, heart cleaved in two, fell. Shataníka, Nákula's valiant son, using two ropes swiftly hurled a chariot wheel at him, striking him in the chest. But the twice-born brahmin* struck back at Shataníka after he had released the wheel. Shataníka lurched to the ground. At that Ashva·tthaman hacked off his head. Shruta·karman in turn snatched up an iron bar and, rushing at Drona's son, struck him hard across the left temple. But he in turn hit Shruta·karman full in the 8.60
face with his prize sword. Shruta·karman fell dead upon the ground, staring, his features askew.

At the sound that made, heroic Shruta·kirti the great chariot-warrior, in his turn targeted Ashva·tthaman, firing a rain of arrows at him. The other deflected his raining arrows too, and severed his glittering head, earrings and all, from his body. Next the powerful slayer of Bhishma along with all the Prabhádrakas attacked our hero from all sides with different kinds of weapons. With another dart-tipped arrow, Shikhándin pierced him between his eyebrows. But Drona's son, full of strength, seething with fury, attacked 8.65
Shikhándin and, with his sword, cut him clean in two.

Śikhaṇḍinaṃ tato hatvā krodh'|āviṣṭaḥ paraṃ|tapaḥ
Prabhadraka|gaṇān sarvān abhidudrāva vegavān,
yac ca śiṣṭaṃ Virāṭasya balaṃ tu bhṛśam ādravat.
Drupadasya ca putrāṇāṃ, pautrāṇāṃ, suhṛdām api
cakāra kadanaṃ ghoraṃ. dṛṣṭvā dṛṣṭvā mahā|balaḥ,
anyān anyāṃś ca puruṣān abhisṛty' âbhisṛtya ca,
nyakṛntad asinā Drauṇir asi|mārga|viśāradaḥ

Kālīṃ rakt'|āsya|nayanāṃ, rakta|māly'|ânulepanām,
rakt'|âmbara|dharām, ekāṃ, pāśa|hastāṃ kuṭumbinīm
8.70 dadṛśuḥ kāla|rātriṃ te gāyamānām avasthitām,
nar' âśva|kuñjarān pāśair baddhvā* ghoraiḥ pratasthuṣīm,
vahantīṃ vividhān pretān pāśa|baddhān, vi|mūrdhajān,
tath" âiva ca sadā, rājan, nyasta|śastrān mahā|rathān.
svapne suptān nayantīṃ tāṃ rātriṣv anyāsu, māriṣa,
dadṛśur yodha|mukhyās te, ghnantaṃ Drauṇiṃ ca nityadā.
yataḥ prabhṛti saṃgrāmaḥ Kuru|Pāṇḍava|senayoḥ,
tataḥ prabhṛti tāṃ kanyām apaśyan, Drauṇim eva ca.

tāṃs tu daiva|hatān pūrvaṃ paścād Drauṇir nyapātayat,
trāsayan sarva|bhūtāni, vinadan bhairavān ravān.
8.75 tad anusmṛtya te vīrā darśanaṃ paurvakālikam,†
«idaṃ tad» ity amanyanta daiven'|ôpanipīḍitāḥ.
tatas tena ninādena pratyabudhyanta dhanvinaḥ
śibire Pāṇḍaveyānāṃ śataśo 'tha sahasraśaḥ.
so 'cchinat kasya cit pādau, jaghanaṃ c' âiva kasya cit.

After slaying Shikhándin, the seething dispatcher of his foes then rushed after all the cohorts of Prabhádrakas, and ferociously attacked what remained of Viráta's army. He wrought bloody carnage on the sons, grandsons and allies of Drúpada too. Every formation of men Drona's son saw, one after the other, he fell on them, full of strength, and diced them with his sword, sure of his sword's path.

They saw standing there the black goddess Kali with scarlet mouth and eyes, adorned in scarlet garlands, a matriarch
clothed in scarlet apparel, noose in hand, all alone, singing, 8.70
the embodiment of the night of doom, looking to make her way among them, trapping men, horses and elephants in her dreadful nooses, carrying off, trapped in her nooses, different kinds of departed spirits, hairless, as well as the great chariot warriors who had now laid down their arms forever, Your Majesty. On other nights, dear sir, the commanding combatants had repeatedly seen that lady in their dreams taking them away as they slept, and the son of Drona killing them. From the time that the battle between the Kuru and Pándava sides had commenced, they had seen that youthful woman and Drona's son.

Now those who first were marked for slaughter by divine Fate were then dispatched by Drona's son, who instilled fear in every living being as he roared blood-curdling
howls. Those valiant men recalling the vision they had had 8.75
at an earlier time, understood it for what it was, as they were struck by divine Fate. Then at the din the archers in the camp of the Pándavas awoke, in their hundreds and then thousands. He severed the feet of one and the hip of another. Others he smashed in the flanks, like the Bringer of

kāṃś cid bibheda pārśveṣu, Kāla|sṛṣṭa iv' Ântakaḥ.
atyugra|pratipiṣṭaiś ca nadadbhiś ca bhṛś'|ôtkaṭaiḥ
gaj'|âśva|mathitaiś c' ânyair mahī kīrṇ" âbhavat, prabho.
krośatāṃ, «kim idaṃ?» «ko 'yaṃ?»
«kiṃ śabdaḥ?» «kiṃ nu?» «kiṃ kṛtam?»
—evaṃ teṣāṃ tadā Drauṇir
Antakaḥ samapadyata

8.80 apeta|śastra|sannāhān sannaddhān Pāṇḍu|Sṛñjaān
prāhiṇon Mṛtyu|lokāya Drauṇiḥ praharatāṃ varaḥ.
tatas tac|chastra|vitrastā utpatanto, bhay'|āturāḥ,
nidr"|ândhā, naṣṭa|saṃjñāś ca tatra tatra nililyire.
ūru|stambha|gṛhītāś ca, kaśmal'|âbhihat'|âujasaḥ,
vinadanto bhṛśaṃ, trastāḥ samāsīdan parasparam.

tato rathaṃ punar Drauṇir āsthito bhīma|nisvanam,
dhanuṣ|pāṇiḥ śarair anyān preṣayad vai Yama|kṣayam.
punar utpatataś c' âpi dūrād api nar'|ôttamān
śūrān saṃpatataś c' ânyān Kāla|rātryai nyavedayat.

8.85 tath" âiva syandan'|âgreṇa pramathan sa vidhāvati,
śara|varṣaiś ca vividhair avarṣac chātravāṃs tataḥ.
punaś ca su|vicitreṇa śata|candreṇa carmaṇā
tena c' ākāśa|varṇena tad" ācarata so 'sinā.
tathā sa śibiraṃ teṣāṃ Drauṇir āhava|durmadaḥ
vyakṣobhayata, rāj'|êndra, mahā|hradam iva dvipaḥ

doom sent by Time. The earth was strewn with elephants and horses, whinnying wildly, and other animals caught up in the confusion, cruelly crushed against each other, Lord. Then, even as men were calling out, "What's this?," "Who's this?," "Why the noise?," "What's up?," "What's happened?," Drona's son, the End-maker, fell upon them.

Whether the Pandu and Srínjaya soldiers were still 8.80
dressed for battle or had earlier discarded both weapons and armor, their most fabulous of assailants, Drona's son, propelled them into the realm of Death. At that they started, terrified of his weapon and besieged by fear, but blinded by sleep and not fully conscious, they perished where they were. Paralysis gripped their thighs, their courage was smitten by confusion, and, howling wildly, in their panic, they set upon each other.

Then Drona's son remounted his chariot, its felloes grinding gruesomely, and, bow in hand, he banished others to Death's mansion with his arrows. As the noblest of men started up and other valiant men fell upon him, again, even from a distance, he delivered them to the Night of Time.*

So it was that he drove through them at top speed, crush- 8.85
ing his enemies beneath his felloes, and shot showers of the entire gamut of arrows into their midst. Again wielding his dazzling shield of a hundred moons and his sky-hued sword, he wrought his way. So it was, lord of kings, that Drona's son, frenzied by battle, churned up their camp, like a water-tossing elephant* a large lake.

utpetus tena śabdena yodhā, rājan, vicetasaḥ;
nidr"|ārtāś ca bhay'|ārtāś ca vyadhāvanta tatas tataḥ.
visvaraṃ cukruśuś c' ânye, bahv|a|baddhaṃ tath" âvadan,†
na ca sma pratipadyante śastrāṇi vasanāni ca.
8.90 vimukta|keśāś c' âpy anye n' âbhyajānan parasparam
utpatanto 'patan śrāntāḥ ke cit tatr' âbhramaṃs tadā.
purīṣam asṛjan ke cit, ke cin mūtraṃ prasusruvuḥ.
bandhanāni ca, rāj'|êndra, saṃchidya tura|gā, dvipāḥ
samaṃ paryapataṃś c' ânye kurvanto mahad ākulam.
tatra ke cin narā bhītā vyalīyanta mahī|tale;
tath" âiva tān nipatitān apiṃṣan gaja|vājinaḥ.

tasmiṃs tathā vartamāne rakṣāṃsi, puruṣa'|ṛṣabha,
hṛṣṭāni vyanadann uccair mudā, Bharata|sattama.
sa śabdaḥ pūrito, rājan, bhūtasaṃghair mudā yutaiḥ.
8.95 apūrayad diśaḥ sarvā, divaṃ c' âpi mahān svanaḥ.
teṣām ārta|ravaṃ śrutvā vitrastā gaja|vājinaḥ
muktāḥ paryapatan, rājan, mṛdnantaḥ śibire janam.
tais tatra paridhāvadbhiś caraṇ'|ôdīritaṃ rajaḥ
akaroc chibire teṣāṃ rajanyāṃ dvi|guṇaṃ tamaḥ.
tasmiṃs tamasi saṃjāte pramūḍhāḥ sarvato janāḥ.
n' âjānan pitaraḥ putrān, bhrātṝn bhrātara eva ca.

gajā gajān atikramya nir|manuṣyā, hayā hayān
atāḍayaṃs tath" âbhañjaṃs tath" âmṛdnaṃś ca, Bhārata.
te bhagnāḥ prapatantaś ca nighnantaś ca parasparam,
8.100 nyapātayaṃs tathā c' ânyān, pātayitvā tath" âpiṣan.

At the noise, Your Majesty, soldiers started up, half-conscious; still trapped in sleep and gripped by fear, they ran this way and that. Some shouted noiselessly, or babbled total nonsense, and they neither reached their weapons nor their clothes. With their hair loose over their faces, many 8.90
did not recognize one another. Some started up only to fall back again exhausted or stagger about where they were. Some shat themselves. Some wet themselves. Meanwhile stallions and elephants had broken their fetters, lord of kings, and were careening about, creating pandemonium. In the midst of that, some men slid to the ground in fear, so that the elephants and speeding horses crushed them where they had fallen.

While this was all going on, bull of a man, ogres let out high shrieks, bristling with delight, most excellent of the Bhárata line. That noise, Your Majesty, was echoed by gatherings of creatures brimming with relish. The tremendous 8.95
clamor resounded round the compass and the sky. Hearing their torturous howls, the terrified elephants and stampeding horses, untethered, careened about, Your Majesty, crushing the people in the camp. The dust churned up by their galloping hooves made their camp doubly dark that night. In the ensuing gloom people were totally disoriented. Fathers did not know their sons, nor brothers their brothers.

Riderless, elephants trampled on elephants, horses on horses and thus, son of Bhárata's line, they gored, broke and crushed each other. Wounded they careened about, swapping death blows. So doing they brought down others, and 8.100
after felling them crushed them too.

vicetasaḥ sa|nidrāś ca, tamasā c' āvṛtā narāḥ
jaghnuḥ svān eva tatr' âtha Kālen' âbhipracoditāḥ.
tyaktvā dvārāṇi ca dvāḥ|sthās, tathā gulmāni gaulmikāḥ,
prādravanta yathā|śakti kāṃdiśīkā vicetasaḥ.
vipranaṣṭāś ca te 'nyonyaṃ n' âjānanta tadā, vibho.
krośantas «tāta!» «putr'!» êti daiv'|ôpahata|cetasaḥ
palāyatāṃ diśas teṣāṃ svān apy utsṛjya bāndhavān;
gotra|nāmabhir anyonyam ākrandanta tato janāḥ,
hāhā|kāraṃ ca kurvāṇāḥ pṛthivyāṃ śerate pare.
8.105 tān buddhvā raṇa|madhye 'sau Droṇa|putro nyavārayat.
tatr' âpare vadhyamānā muhur muhur a|cetasaḥ
śibirān niṣpatanti sma kṣatriyā bhaya|pīḍitāḥ.
tāṃs tu niṣpatatas trastāñ śibirāj jīvit'|âiṣiṇaḥ
Kṛtavarmā Kṛpaś c' âiva dvāra|deśe nijaghnatuḥ.
visrasta|yantra|kavacān, mukta|keśān, kṛt'|âñjalīn,
vepamānān kṣitau, bhītān n' âiva kāṃś cid amuñcatām.
n' âmucyata tayoḥ kaś cin niṣkrāntaḥ śibirād bahiḥ.

Kṛpaś c' âiva, mahā|rāja, Hārdikyaś c' âiva dur|matiḥ
bhūyaś c' âiva cikīrṣantau Droṇa|putrasya tau priyam,
8.110 triṣu deśeṣu dadatuḥ śibirasya hut'|āśanam.
tataḥ prakāśe śibire khaḍgena pitṛ|nandanaḥ
Aśvatthāmā, mahā|rāja, vyacarat kṛta|hastavat.
kāṃś cid āpatato vīrān aparāṃś c' âiva dhāvataḥ
vyayojayata khaḍgena prāṇair dvija|var|ôttamaḥ.

Then the men there, steeped in darkness and barely conscious, still half asleep, killed their own men, impelled by Time. The guardsmen deserted their posts, as did troops their divisions, and rushed forward as far as they were able, but in the wrong direction, such was their confusion. Then, doomed, they did not recognize each other, powerful lord. Even as, their minds weakened by divine Fate, they called out "Dad!" "Son!" to those fleeing in every direction, they had in fact just dispatched their own relatives; some people cried out to each other by their clan names, while some lay upon the ground wailing in anguish.

Finding them out in the midst of the battle ground 8.105
the son of Drona blocked their escape. Some others there, slipping in and out of consciousness as they were being picked off, did manage to flee the camp, born warriors overwhelmed by fear. But as they fled the camp in terror and in hope of life, Krita·varman and Kripa slaughtered them at the threshold. Though they had dropped all means of protection, though their hair was loose and their hands pressed together in supplication, though they quaked on the ground in terror, the pair spared none. Not one who escaped the camp escaped those two.

Great king, both Kripa and Krita·varman the Good-in-heart, evil in intent, in their desperation to please Drona's
son further in what they did, started an oblation-eating fire 8.110
in three places in the camp. Then Ashva·tthaman, the joy of his fore-fathers,* put on a display with his sword on the parade ground, with his deft hand, great king. Whether the heroic men took aim or took flight, that most exalted of twice-born priests cut them off from their life breath

kāmś cid yodhān sa khaḍgena madhye saṃchidya vīryavān
apātayad Droṇa|sutaḥ saṃrabdhas tila|kāṇḍavat.
ninadadbhir bhṛś'|āyastair nar'|âśva|dvirad'|ôttamaiḥ
patitair abhavat kīrṇā medinī, Bharata'|rṣabha.
mānuṣāṇāṃ sahasreṣu hateṣu patiteṣu ca
8.115 udatiṣṭhan kabandhāni bahūny, utthāya c' âpatan.
s'|āyudhān s'|âṅgadān bāhūn vicakarta, śirāṃsi ca,
hasti|hast'|ôpamān ūrūn,
hastān, pādāṃś ca, Bhārata,
pṛṣṭha|cchinnān pārśva|cchinnāñ
śiraś|chinnāṃs tath" âparān
sa mah"|ātm" âkarod Drauṇiḥ
kāṃś cic c' âpi parāṅ|mukhān.
madhya|kāyān† narān anyāṃś
cicched', ânyāṃś ca karṇataḥ.
aṃsa|deśe nihaty' ânyān kāye prāveśayac chiraḥ.
evaṃ vicaratas tasya nighnataḥ su|bahūn narān
tamasā rajanī ghorā babhau dāruṇa|darśanā.
kiñ|cit|prāṇaiś ca puruṣair, hataiś c'|ânyaiḥ sahasraśaḥ,
8.120 bahunā ca gaj'|âśvena bhūr abhūd bhīma|darśanā.
yakṣa|rakṣaḥ|samākīrṇe, rath'|âśva|dvipa|dāruṇe
kruddhena Droṇa|putreṇa saṃchinnāḥ prāpatan bhuvi.
bhrātṝn anye, pitṝn anye, putrān anye vicukruśuḥ.
ke cid ūcur, «na tat kruddhair Dhārtarāṣṭraiḥ kṛtaṃ raṇe,
yat kṛtaṃ naḥ prasuptānāṃ rakṣobhiḥ krūra|karmabhiḥ.
a|sānnidhyādd hi Pārthānām idaṃ vaḥ kadanaṃ kṛtam.
na c' âsurair, na gandharvair, na yakṣair, na ca rākṣasaiḥ
śakyo vijetuṃ Kaunteyo, goptā yasya Jan'|ārdanaḥ,

with his sword. Some soldiers the incensed son of Drona felled by slashing them vigorously across their midriff, like so many sesamum stalks.

The fat earth overflowed with the fallen, glorious men, horses and tuskers, bellowing as they thrashed about, bull of Bhárata's line.

Amid the thousands of slain and toppled men, many 8.115
of their decapitated torsos still stood back up, then on standing, fell down again. That great-spirited son of Drona severed arms still bearing weapons and armlets, as well as heads; likewise thighs, hands and feet, all like flailing trunks of elephants, son of Bhárata's line. From some, as they turned their backs, he excised their backs, or flanks or heads. Other men, he sliced through the midriff, and others at the ears. After hacking others between the shoulders, he forced their heads inside their bodies. As he cavorted about in this manner, slaughtering untold numbers of men, the dark black night gleamed with gore, a gruesome spectacle.

With men in their thousands slain or scarcely breathing,
and with the mass of horses and elephants, the ground was a 8.120
horrific sight. Upon a floor crowded with goblins and ogres, pitiful with chariots, horses and tuskers, those hewn down by the cruel son of Drona lay writhing. They screamed for their brothers, others for their fathers, others their sons. Some said, "Even the cruel men of Dhrita·rashtra did not do to us in battle what the torturing ogres have done to us in our sleep, this massacre, wreaked on you in the absence of Pritha's sons. For Kunti's son, whose protector is Krishna, the rouser of men, the pious speaker of the truth, mild and

brahmaṇyaḥ, satya|vāg, dāntaḥ, sarva|bhūt'|ânukampakaḥ.
8.125 na ca suptaṃ, pramattaṃ vā,
nyasta|śastraṃ, kṛt'|âñjalim,
dhāvantaṃ, mukta|keśaṃ vā
hanti Pārtho Dhanaṃjayaḥ.
tad idaṃ naḥ kṛtaṃ ghoraṃ rakṣobhiḥ krūra|karmabhiḥ.»
iti lālapyamānāḥ sma śerate bahavo janāḥ,
stanatāṃ ca manuṣyāṇām, apareṣāṃ ca kūjatām.
tato muhūrtāt prāśāmyat sa śabdas tumulo mahān.
śoṇita|vyatiṣiktāyāṃ vasudhāyāṃ ca, bhūmi|pa,
tad rajas tumulaṃ ghoraṃ kṣaṇen' ântar|adhīyata
sa ceṣṭamānān, udvignān, nir|utsāhān sahasraśaḥ
nyapātayan narān kruddhaḥ, paśūn Paśupatir yathā
8.130 anyonyaṃ saṃpariṣvajya śayānān, dravato 'parān,
saṃlīnān, yudhyamānāṃś ca sarvān Drauṇir apothayat.
dahyamānā hut'|āśena, vadhyamānāś ca tena te
parasparaṃ tadā yodhā anayan† Yama|sādanam.
tasyā rajanyās tv ardhena Pāṇḍavānāṃ mahad balam
gamayām āsa, rāj'|êndra, Drauṇir Yama|niveśanam.
niśā|carāṇāṃ sattvānāṃ sā rātrir harṣa|vardhinī
āsīn nara|gaj'|âśvānāṃ raudrī kṣaya|karī bhṛśam.
tatr' âdṛśyanta rakṣāṃsi piśācāś ca pṛthag|vidhāḥ
khādanto nara|māṃsāni, pibantaḥ śoṇitāni ca.

compassionate to all beings, cannot be beaten by demons, heavenly minions, goblins or ogres.

And yet the spoil-winning son of Pritha, Árjuna, never 8.125
resorted to killing anyone who was asleep or deranged, who had laid down their weapon, who was pleading for mercy, or fleeing, or had hair untied. Such horrific treatment has been inflicted on us by ogres, acting in sheer cruelty."

Many men lay there, babbling such things, while other men mumbled inarticulately and still others groaned incoherently. Then all at once that great tumult abated. Once the wealth-bestowing world was completely splattered in blood, protector of the earth, then the horrific, tumultuous darkness was suddenly dispelled. As men in their thousands writhed about, some agitated, some beyond exertion, he slaughtered them cruelly like animals, as the Lord of Animals.*

Some lay hugging each other, others were trying to es- 8.130
cape. Some lay hiding, while others fought. Drona's son annihilated all. Then as they were engulfed by the oblation-consuming fire or slain by him, the warriors led each other towards Yama's resting place. Now in the course of just half that dark night, lord of kings, Drona's son sent the mighty army of the Pándavas to the residence of the Lord of Death. That night furnished delight for the creatures that fare at night, so dreadful and destructive was it for men, elephants and horses alike. There appeared in that place ogres and goblins, of every possible kind, gobbling the flesh of men, slurping at their blood.

8.135 karālāḥ, piṅgalāś c' âiva, śaila|dantā, rajasvalāḥ,
jaṭilā, dīrgha|śaṅkhāś ca, pañca|pādā, mah"|ôdarāḥ,
paścād|aṅgulayo,† rūkṣā, virūpā, bhairava|svanāḥ,
ghaṇṭā|jāl'|âvasaktāś ca, nīla|kaṇṭhā, vibhīṣaṇāḥ,
sa|putra|dārāḥ, su|krūrā, su|durdarśāḥ, su|nirghṛṇāḥ—
vividhāni ca rūpāṇi tatr' âdṛśyanta rakṣasām.
pītvā ca śoṇitaṃ hṛṣṭā prānṛtyan gaṇaśo 'pare,
«idaṃ param,† idaṃ medhyam, idaṃ svādv» iti c' âbruvan.
medo|majj'|âsthi|raktānāṃ vasānāṃ ca bhṛś'|âśitāḥ
paraṃ māṃsāni khādantaḥ kravy'|ādā māṃsa|jīvinaḥ.
8.140 vasāś c' âiv' âpare pītvā paryadhāvan vikukṣikāḥ
nānā|vaktrās tathā raudrāḥ kravy'|ādāḥ piśit'|āśinaḥ.
ayutāni ca tatr' āsan, prayutāny, arbudāni ca
rakṣasāṃ ghora|rūpāṇāṃ mahatāṃ krūra|karmaṇām
muditānāṃ vitṛptānāṃ, tasmin mahati vaiśase
sametāni bahūny āsan bhūtāni ca, jan'|âdhipa.

pratyūṣa|kāle śibirāt pratigantum iyeṣa saḥ.
nṛ|śoṇit'|âvasiktasya Drauṇer āsīd asi|tsaruḥ
pāṇinā saha saṃśliṣṭa ekī|bhūta iva, prabho.
dur|gamāṃ padavīṃ gatvā virarāja jana|kṣaye,
8.145 yug'|ânte sarva|bhūtāni bhasma kṛtv" êva pāvakaḥ.

yathā|pratijñaṃ tat karma kṛtvā Drauṇāyaniḥ, prabho,
dur|gamāṃ padavīṃ gacchan pitur, āsīd gata|jvaraḥ.
yath" âiva saṃsupta|jane śibire prāviśan niśi
tath" âiva hatvā niḥ|śabde niścakrāma nara'|rṣabhaḥ.

Deformed, discolored, craggy-toothed, streaked with 8.135
dirt, fur matted, brows protruding, five-footed, swollen-
bellied, with backwards pointing fingers, ragged, hideous,
emitting frightful sounds, with nets of gongs hanging down,
blue-throated, terrifying, accompanied by their mates and
offspring, vicious, dreadful to see, merciless, these were the
various features of the ogres' appearance that could be seen
there too. Gleefully quaffing blood, some danced forth in
droves and commented, "This is excellent. This is fresh. This
is tasty stuff." The voracious feasters on entrails, the fat, the
marrow, the bones and blood, the carrion-consumers that
thrive on flesh, then tucked further into that flesh. Some of 8.140
the many-mouthed, fierce carrion-consuming flesh-eaters,
having gorged their fill of entrails, capered around with
bloated bellies. There were tens of thousands, millions, nay
tens of millions of gargantuan, torturing *rákshasa*s, delighted and sated, and many were the ghouls gathered together
at that great butchery, sovereign of the people.

As dawn approached, Drona's son decided to quit the
camp. It was as if, with him drenched in the blood of men,
the hilt of his sword had become one with his hand, so fast
they stuck together, Lord. Having carved its unforgiving
path it shone resplendent over the destruction of the people
like the purifying flames that reduce all beings to ashes at 8.145
the end of the world.

Drona's heir had fulfilled his sworn task, lord. While he followed this unforgiving path for the sake of his father his fever passed. Just as that prize bull of a man had entered the silent camp of slumbering men that night, so he departed, the killing done, the once more silent camp.

niṣkramya śibirāt tasmāt, tābhyāṃ saṃgamya vīryavān,
ācakhyau karma tat sarvaṃ hṛṣṭaḥ, saṃharṣayan, vibho.
tāv ath' ācakhyatus tasmai priyaṃ priya|karau tadā,
Pāñcālān Sṛñjayāṃś c' âiva vinikṛttān sahasraśaḥ.
prītyā c' ôccair udakrośaṃs, tath" âiv' āsphoṭayaṃs talān.
8.150 evaṃ|vidhā hi sā rātriḥ Somakānāṃ jana|kṣaye
prasuptānāṃ pramattānām āsīt su|bhṛśa|dāruṇā.
a|saṃśayaṃ hi kālasya paryāyo dur|atikramaḥ,
tādṛśā nihatā yatra kṛtv" âsmākaṃ jana|kṣayam.

DHṚTARĀṢṬRA uvāca:

prāg eva su|mahat karma Drauṇir etan mahā|rathaḥ
n' âkarod īdṛśaṃ kasmān mat|putra|vijaye dhṛtaḥ?
atha kasmādd hate kṣatre† karm' êdaṃ kṛtavān asau
Droṇa|putro mah"|ātmā sa? tan me śaṃsitum arhasi.

SAṂJAYA uvāca:

teṣāṃ nūnaṃ bhayān n' âsau kṛtavān, Kuru|nandana.
a|sāṃnidhyādd hi Pārthānāṃ, Keśavasya ca dhīmataḥ,
8.155 Sātyakeś c' âpi karm' êdaṃ Droṇa|putreṇa sādhitam.
ko hi teṣāṃ samakṣaṃ tān hanyād, api Marut|patiḥ?
etad īdṛśakaṃ vṛttaṃ, rājan, supta|jane, vibho.

Leaving the camp, the heroic man met up with the other two, powerful lord, whereupon he told them of all that he had done, delighted and delighting them. Those two in turn then told him that they had done as he had hoped. In exultation, they yelled at the tops of their voices that the Panchálas and Sríñjayas had been dismembered into a thousand pieces, and their voices reverberated across the surface of earth and sky.

Such indeed was that brutal night, that sealed the anni- 8.150
hilation of the Sómakas, while they were asleep and unprepared. There can be no doubt that the unraveling of Destiny is inescapable, when men of such ilk are slain even after their own destruction of our people.

DHRITA·RASHTRA interrupted:

Why did the great chariot-fighter, Drona's son, not perform a great feat like this before, to serve victory for my son? Come to that, why has the noble-souled son of Drona performed this feat only now, after our warriors have already been wiped out? You must explain that to me.

SÁNJAYA replied:

For sure it was because he was afraid of them that he did not do it earlier, delight of the Kurus. For it was only in
the absence of Pritha's sons and cunning Krishna, as well as 8.155
Sátyaki, that Drona's son could achieve this feat. After all who, including the lord of the wind gods,* could kill these people while they were around? Moreover, Your Majesty, this event overtook these people while they were asleep, powerful lord.

tato jana|kṣayaṃ kṛtvā Pāṇḍavānāṃ mah"|âtyayam
diṣṭyā diṣṭy" âiva c' ânyonyaṃ samety' ōcur mahā|rathāḥ.
paryaṣvajat tato Drauṇis tābhyāṃ saṃpratinanditaḥ.
idaṃ harṣāt tu su|mahad ādade vākyam uttamam:
«Pāñcālā nihatāḥ sarve, Draupadeyāś ca sarvaśaḥ.
Somakā Matsya|śeṣāś ca sarve vinihatā mayā.
idānīṃ kṛta|kṛtyāḥ sma. yāma tatr' âiva mā ciram.
yadi jīvati no rājā, tasmai śaṃsāmahe vayam.»

Now then, after the three great chariot warriors had wrought the massacre of those people, a great injury to the Pándavas, they reunited and congratulated one another. Then Drona's son joyously embraced his two companions. In his delight, he offered these great and noble words:

"The Panchálas are all slain, as are the sons of Dráupadi, every one. The Sómakas and the surviving Matsyas, I have killed them all. Now our duty is done. Let us return without delay to our king, and if he lives still, let us tell him."

9
BALM FOR DURYÓDHANA

SAÑJAYA uvāca:

9.1 TE HATVĀ SARVA|Pāñcālān Draupadeyāṃś ca sarvaśaḥ,
āgacchan sahitās tatra, yatra Duryodhano hataḥ.
gatvā c' âinam apaśyanta kiñ|cit|prāṇaṃ jan'|âdhipam.
tato rathebhyaḥ praskandya parivavrus tav' ātmajam.
taṃ bhagna|sakthaṃ, rāj'|êndra,
kṛcchra|prāṇam, a|cetasam,
vamantaṃ rudhiraṃ vaktrād
apaśyan vasudhā|tale,
vṛtaṃ samantād bahubhiḥ śvāpadair ghora|darśanaiḥ,
śālā|vṛka|gaṇaiś c' âiva bhakṣayiṣyadbhir antikāt.
9.5 nivārayantaṃ kṛcchrāt tāñ śvāpadāṃś ca cikhādiṣūn,
viceṣṭamānaṃ mahyāṃ ca, su|bhṛśaṃ gāḍha|vedanam.
taṃ śayānaṃ tathā dṛṣṭvā bhūmau sva|rudhir'|ôkṣitam,
hata|śiṣṭās trayo vīrāḥ śok'|ārtāḥ paryavārayan
Aśvatthāmā, Kṛpaś c' âiva, Kṛtavarmā ca Sātvataḥ.
tais tribhiḥ śoṇit'|ādigdhair niḥśvasadbhir mahā|rathaiḥ
śuśubhe saṃvṛto rājā, vedī tribhir iv' âgnibhiḥ.
te taṃ śayānaṃ saṃprekṣya rājānam a|tath"|ôcitam,
a|viṣahyena duḥkhena tatas te rurudus trayaḥ.
tatas tu rudhiraṃ hastair mukhān nirmṛjya tasya hi,
raṇe rājñaḥ śayānasya kṛpaṇaṃ paryadevayan.

SÁNJAYA spoke:

WHEN THEY HAD killed all the Panchálas and every 9.1
one of Dráupadi's sons, together they came back to the place where Duryódhana lay dying. As they reached the sovereign of the people, they could see that he was still breathing faintly, so they leaped down from their chariots and rushed to your son's side. Lord of kings, they gazed on the man whose thigh had been shattered. He was scarcely breathing, barely conscious. Blood oozed from his mouth down onto the rich earth. He was circled on all sides by a great gathering of gruesome wild beasts, with packs of jackals and wolves closing in, in anticipation of their approaching meal.

So far, he had, with great difficulty, managed to ward 9.5
off the drooling beasts, as he struggled, writhing in agony, on the ground. Seeing him lying there in that state on the ground, soaked in his own blood, the three valiant men, the sole survivors of our army, stood round him, overcome by grief, Ashva·tthaman and Kripa and Krita·varman of the Satvat tribe. These three great chariot-fighters, streaked with blood, sighing in grief, surrounded the king and he shone like an altar reflecting the sacrificial fires. Seeing their king lying there barely recognizable, the three of them found it unbearably painful and broke down in tears. But they wiped the blood from his mouth with their hands, heartbroken at the king's pitiful state as he lay on the battle field.

KṚPA uvāca:

9.10 na daivasy' âtibhāro 'sti yad ayaṃ rudhir'|ôkṣitaḥ
ekādaśa|camū|bhartā śete Duryodhano hataḥ.
paśya cāmīkar'|ābhasya cāmīkara|vibhūṣitām
gadāṃ gadā|priyasy' êmāṃ samīpe patitāṃ bhuvi.
iyam enaṃ gadā śūraṃ na jahāti raṇe raṇe,
svargāy' âpi vrajantaṃ hi na jahāti yaśasvinam.
paśy' êmāṃ saha vīreṇa jāmbūnada|vibhūṣitām
śayānāṃ, śayane harmye bhāryāṃ prītimatīm iva.
yo 'yaṃ mūrdh'|âvasiktānām agre jātaḥ paraṃ|tapaḥ,
sa hato grasate pāṃsūn. paśya Kālasya paryayam.
9.15 yen' ājau nihatā bhūmāv aśerata hata|dviṣaḥ,
sa bhūmau nihataḥ śete Kuru|rājaḥ parair ayam.
bhayān namanti rājāno yasya sma śata|saṃghaśaḥ,
sa vīra|śayane śete kravy'|âdbhiḥ parivāritaḥ.
upāsata dvijāḥ pūrvam artha|hetor yam īśvaram,
upāsate ca taṃ hy adya kravy'|ādā māṃsa|hetavaḥ.

SAMJAYA uvāca:

taṃ śayānaṃ Kuru|śreṣṭhaṃ tato, Bharata|sattama,
Aśvatthāmā samālokya karuṇaṃ paryadevayat.
«āhus tvāṃ, rāja|śārdūla, mukhyaṃ sarva|dhanuṣmatām,
dhan'|âdhyakṣ'|ôpamaṃ yuddhe, śiṣyaṃ Saṃkarṣaṇasya ca.

KRIPA spoke:

No fate is harder to bear than this—that fierce-fighting 9.10
Duryódhana, who sustained eleven battalions, lies here, struck down, soaked in blood. See how his mace, gleaming like gold, adorned in gold, lies close to her tender master, fallen on the ground. Battle after battle, this mace has not once forsaken her champion and even as he makes the final journey to heaven, she remains loyal to that glorious man. See how she lies here with her hero, adorned in gold, like a satisfied bride on a sumptuous bed. Here the first-born among the consecrated kings,* a veritable blight upon the foe, now lies slain, eating dust. Observe the fickle nature of Time!

He who slew his enemies on the battlefield, leaving their 9.15
bodies prostrate on the ground, now lies here on the ground himself, this king of the Kurus, slain by his enemies. To him kings in their hundreds once bowed low in fear; now he lies supine on the bed of valor, only scavenging beasts adore him. The lord whom brahmins formerly attended in the hope of wealth, is today attended by scavengers in the hope of flesh.

SÁNJAYA spoke:

Most excellent of Bhárata's line, it was then the turn of Ashva·tthaman, gazing on the most glorious of the Kurus lying there, to express his sadness at his pitiful fate: "You are a tiger of a king. They say you were the best of all bowmen, like the God of Treasure* embodied in battle, a fit apprentice of the Powerful Plowman.*

9.20 kathaṃ vivaram adrākṣīd Bhīmasenas tav', ân|agha,
balinaṃ kṛtinaṃ nityaṃ, sa ca pāp'|ātmavān, nṛpa?
kālo nūnaṃ, mahā|rāja, loke 'smin balavattaraḥ,
paśyāmo nihataṃ tvāṃ ca Bhīmasenena saṃyuge.
kathaṃ tvāṃ sarva|dharma|jñaṃ kṣudraḥ pāpo Vṛkodaraḥ
nikṛtyā hatavān mando? nūnaṃ kālo dur|atyayaḥ.
dharma|yuddhe hy a|dharmeṇa samāhūy' âujasā mṛdhe
gadayā Bhīmasenena nirbhagne sakthinī tava.
a|dharmeṇa hatasy' ājau mṛdyamānaṃ padā śiraḥ
ya upekṣitavān, kṣudraṃ dhik Kṛṣṇaṃ, dhig Yudhiṣṭhiram!
9.25 yuddheṣv apavadiṣyanti yodhā nūnaṃ Vṛkodaram,
yāvat sthāsyanti bhūtāni. nikṛtyā hy asi pātitaḥ.
nanu Rāmo 'bravīd, rājaṃs, tvāṃ sadā Yadu|nandanaḥ,
‹Duryodhana|samo n' âsti gadayā› iti vīryavān.
ślāghate tvāṃ hi Vārṣṇeyo rāja|saṃsatsu, Bhārata,
‹su|śiṣyo† mama Kauravyo gadā|yuddha› iti, prabho.
yāṃ gatiṃ kṣatriyasy' āhuḥ† praśastāṃ parama'|rṣayaḥ
hatasy' âbhimukhasy' ājau, prāptas tvam asi tāṃ gatim.
Duryodhana, na śocāmi tvām ahaṃ, puruṣa'|rṣabha,
hata|putrau tu śocāmi Gāndhārīṃ pitaraṃ ca te.
9.30 bhikṣukau vicariṣyete śocantau pṛthivīm imām.

Faultless one, how did Bhima·sena find out a weakness 9.20
in you, when you have always been strong and competent, protector of men, and he wicked to the core? Surely it's Fate that is the stronger combatant here, that we have seen you slain by Bhima·sena in the fight. How else could the mean and evil Wolf-belly,* who's so stupid, succeed in using a trick to slay you, when you're so conscious of all the rules of combat. Surely it's Fate that can't be beat. Though challenging you to a lawful contest it was with an illegal move in the fight that Bhima·sena broke your thighs with his mace. Then with you struck down on the battlefield, he ground your head with his sacrilegious foot in a cruel display of contempt. Damn Krishna and damn Yudhi·shthira!

Surely, as long as there's life on earth, soldiers in battle 9.25
will revile Wolf-belly for the treachery with which he managed to kill you. Hadn't the heroic Rama, ever the joy of the Yadu line, declared of you, 'There is none equal to Duryódhana at fighting with the mace?' Indeed, son of Bhárata's line, Vrishni's descendant praised you in the royal assemblies, declaring, 'the Káuravan is my best student in the art of mace fighting,' powerful lord. The most exalted sages have declared as the prized destiny of the warrior, the destiny which you, slain in action on the battlefield, have now won. So it's not for you that I grieve, Duryódhana, you who are a prize bull among men, but rather it's for Gandhári
and your father, who've lost their son, that I grieve. As they 9.30
mourn, they will wander this earth as beggars.

dhig astu Kṛṣṇaṃ Vārṣṇeyam Arjunaṃ c' âpi dur|matim,
dharma|jña|māninau yau tvāṃ vadhyamānam upekṣatām!*
Pāṇḍavāś c' âpi te sarve kiṃ vakṣyanti, nar'|âdhipa?
kathaṃ ‹Duryodhano 'smābhir hata› ity an|apatrapāḥ?
dhanyas tvam asi, Gāndhāre, yas tvam āyodhane hataḥ,
prāyaśo 'bhimukhaḥ śatrūn dharmeṇa, puruṣa'|rṣabha.
hata|putrā hi Gāndhārī nihata|jñāti|bāndhavā.
Prajñācakṣuś ca dur|dharṣaḥ kāṃ gatiṃ pratipatsyate?
dhig astu Kṛtavarmāṇaṃ, māṃ, Kṛpaṃ ca mahā|ratham,
9.35 ye vayaṃ na gatāḥ svargaṃ tvāṃ puras|kṛtya pārthivam.
dātāraṃ sarva|kāmānāṃ, rakṣitāraṃ prajā|hitam
yad vayaṃ n' ânugacchāmas†
tvāṃ, dhig asmān nar'|âdhamān.
Kṛpasya, tava vīryeṇa,
mama c' âiva, pituś ca me
sa|bhṛtyānāṃ, nara|vyāghra, ratnavanti gṛhāṇi ca.
tava prasādād asmābhiḥ sa|mitraiḥ saha|bāndhavaiḥ
avāptāḥ kratavo mukhyā bahavo, bhūri|dakṣiṇāḥ.
kutaś c' âp' īdṛśaṃ pāpāḥ pravartiṣyāmahe vayam,
yādṛśena puras|kṛtya tvaṃ gataḥ sarva|pārthivān.
vayam eva trayo, rājan, gacchantaṃ paramāṃ gatim
9.40 yad vai tvāṃ n' ânugacchāmas, tena dhakṣyāmahe vayam,
tat|svarga|hīnā hīn'|ârthāḥ smarantaḥ su|kṛtasya te.
kiṃ nāma tad bhavet karma yena tvāṃ na vrajāma vai?
duḥkhaṃ nūnaṃ, Kuru|śreṣṭha, cariṣyāmo mahīm imām.
hīnānāṃ nas tvayā, rājan, kutaḥ śāntiḥ, kutaḥ sukham?

Damn Krishna of the line of Vrishni and the evil minded
Árjuna! Those two, so proud in their knowledge of the laws
of war, made no attempt to intervene as you were killed.
And all the Pándavas, what will they say, Lord of men? How
can they declare, 'We have killed Duryódhana,' without
feeling mortified by shame? You are blessed, son of Gandhári, in being slain in action, departing life facing your enemies with dignity, prize bull among men. But Gandhári has
lost her son. Those familiar and family to her are all killed.
And the proud Dhrita·rashtra with his eyes of understanding, what will become of him? Accursed are Krita·varman,
Kripa the great chariot-fighter and I, that we aren't follow- 9.35
ing you, the lord of the earth, to heaven. When you've been
the one to fulfill all our desires, the guardian of your subjects, that we can't follow you shows how we are as cursed
as the most wretched of men. Through our heroism, yours,
Kripa's, mine and my father's, we filled the homes of everyone with gems, tiger among men. Thanks to you we, and
our friends and relatives, were able to sponsor plenty of sacrifices, bestowing largesse liberally on the priests. So why
has such a dreadful fate now befallen us misfortunates, that 9.40
you abandon us here, ushering all the other rulers of the
earth ahead of you? Your Majesty, as you go to the highest
destiny, what will torment us is that we three alone won't
be following you. We are deprived of that heaven and deprived of our purpose, bereft of you who did so much good.
What misdeed could it have been that now prevents us from
treading after you? Best of the Kuru clan, surely we shall
wander this earth in misery. How can we, robbed of you,
find peace, Your Majesty, how happiness?

gatv" âiva tu, mahā|rāja, sametya tvaṃ mahā|rathān,
yathā|jyeṣṭhaṃ yathā|śreṣṭhaṃ pūjayer vacanān mama.
ācāryaṃ pūjayitvā ca ketuṃ sarva|dhanuṣmatām,
hataṃ may" âdya śaṃsethā Dhṛṣṭadyumnaṃ, nar'|âdhipa.
pariṣvajethā rājānaṃ Bāhlikaṃ su|mahā|ratham,
9.45 Saindhavaṃ, Somadattaṃ ca, Bhūriśravasam eva ca.
tathā pūrva|gatān anyān svarge pārthiva|sattamān
asmad|vākyāt pariṣvajya saṃpṛcches tvam an|āmayam.»

SAÑJAYA uvāca:

ity evam uktvā rājānaṃ bhagna|saktham a|cetasam
Aśvatthāmā samudvīkṣya punar vacanam abravīt.
«Duryodhana, jīvasi ced, vācaṃ śrotra|sukhāṃ śṛṇu:
sapta Pāṇḍavataḥ śeṣā, Dhārtarāṣṭrās trayo vayam.
te c' âiva bhrātaraḥ pañca, Vāsudevo, 'tha Sātyakiḥ;
ahaṃ ca, Kṛtavarmā ca, Kṛpaḥ Śāradvatas tathā.
9.50 Draupadeyā hatāḥ sarve, Dhṛṣṭadyumnasya c' ātmajāḥ.
Pāñcālā nihatāḥ sarve, Matsya|śeṣaṃ ca, Bhārata.
kṛte pratikṛtaṃ paśya. hata|putrā hi Pāṇḍavāḥ.
sauptike śibiraṃ teṣāṃ hataṃ sa|nara|vāhanam.
mayā ca pāpa|karm" âsau Dhṛṣṭadyumno, mahī|pate,
praviśya śibiraṃ rātrau paśu|māreṇa māritaḥ.»
Duryodhanas tu tāṃ vācaṃ niśamya manasaḥ priyām,
pratilabhya punaś ceta, idaṃ vacanam abravīt:
«na me 'karot tad Gāṅgeyo, na Karṇo, na ca te pitā,
yat tvayā Kṛpa|Bhojābhyāṃ sahiten' âdya me kṛtam.

Now when you do depart, great king, and meet up with the great chariot-warriors, please honor them in my name, according to age and rank. Please give due honor to our teacher,* the emblem of all archers, and report to him, sovereign, that I killed Dhrishta·dyumna today. Embrace the king of the Báhlika people, the supreme chariot-fighter,
as well as the king of Sindh, Soma·datta and Bhuri·shravas, 9.45
and all the other rulers of this earth who have preceded you to heaven. Embrace them in my name and wish them well."

SÁNJAYA continued:

When Ashva·tthaman had said these words to the unconscious king whose thighs had been smashed, he looked closely at him and spoke again: "Duryódhana, if you're alive, hear my news—you'll like what you hear: seven of the Pándava side survive, and we three on the side of Dhrita·rashtra. On that side it is the five brothers, as well as Krishna, son of Vasu·deva, and Sátyaki. On this it is Krita·varman, Kripa of the Sharádvatas and myself.

All Dráupadi's sons are killed, as are Dhrishta·dyumna's 9.50
offspring. All the Panchálas are slain, as is the remaining group of Matsyas, son of Bhárata's line. Know that you have been avenged. Now the Pándavas have lost all their sons, and their camp containing all their men and mounts has been slaughtered while they slept in the dead of night. Lord of this earth, know that Dhrishta·dyumna, a man of evil deeds, has been forced to die the death of an animal at my hands, after I went to their camp in the night." Now Duryódhana did hear what he had said, so pleasing to his heart, and, regaining consciousness, spoke these words: "Not even

9.55 sa cet senā|patiḥ kṣudro hataḥ sārdhaṃ Śikhaṇḍinā,
tena manye Maghavatā samam ātmānam adya vai.
svasti prāpnuta, bhadraṃ vaḥ.
svarge naḥ saṃgamaḥ punaḥ.»
ity evam uktvā tūṣṇīṃ sa
Kuru|rājo mahā|manāḥ
prāṇān upāsṛjad vīraḥ suhṛdāṃ duḥkham utsṛjan.
apākrāmad divaṃ puṇyāṃ; śarīraṃ kṣitim āviśat.
evaṃ te nidhanaṃ yātaḥ putro Duryodhano, nṛpa.
agre yātvā raṇe śūraḥ paścād vinihataḥ paraiḥ.
tath" âiva te pariṣvaktāḥ, pariṣvajya ca te nṛpam,
punaḥ punaḥ prekṣamāṇāḥ svakān āruruhū rathān.
9.60 ity evaṃ tava† putrasya niśamya karuṇāṃ giram
pratyūṣa|kāle śok'|ārtaḥ prādhāvaṃ† nagaraṃ prati.
evam eṣa kṣayo vṛttaḥ Kuru|Pāṇḍava|senayoḥ,
ghoro viśasano raudro, rājan, dur|mantrite tava.
tava putre gate svargaṃ śok'|ārtasya mam', ân|agha,
ṛṣi|dattaṃ pranaṣṭaṃ tad divya|darśitvam adya vai.

VAIŚAMPĀYANA uvāca:

iti śrutvā sa nṛ|patiḥ putrasya nidhanaṃ tadā,
niḥśvasya dīrgham uṣṇaṃ ca tataś cintā|paro 'bhavat.

Bhishma, Karna or your father did for me what you have done for me today, with Kripa's and Krita·varman of the Bhojas' help.

If that vile general has been slain, along with Shikhándin, 9.55
I consider myself today as blessed as the king of the gods. You should all be rewarded. May good fortune be yours. We shall meet again in heaven." After uttering these words, that noble king of the Kurus fell silent. The hero had breathed his last, to the great distress of his friends. He departed to the paradise of the pure while his body turned to dust. This is how your son Duryódhana met his end, Your Majesty. At the outset he was a champion in battle. In the end his enemies killed him. As he died these men held him in their embrace, and when they had released the king from their embrace, they mounted their chariots again, constantly looking back to him.

So it was that, with the heart-wrenching voice of your 9.60
son resounding in their ears, they drove on towards the city as day broke, stricken by grief.

And so it was that the devastation of the Káuravan and the Pándavan armies was wrought, a bloody and savage slaughter, all down to your bad counsel, Your Majesty. With your son gone, I am wracked by grief, unharmed sire. And, now my account has been related, the divine vision that the seer bestowed on me has gone.

VAISHAMPÁYANA continued:

This is the account that the lord of men received about the passing of his son, at which he became lost in his thoughts, his breathing reduced to long, hot gasps.

10–11
DRÁUPADI'S DEMAND

VAIŚAMPĀYANA uvāca:

10.1 TASYĀṂ RĀTRYĀṂ vyatītāyāṃ
Dhṛṣṭadyumnasya sārathiḥ
śaśaṃsa dharma|rājāya
sauptike kadanaṃ kṛtam.

SŪTA uvāca:

Draupadeyā hatā, rājan, Drupadasy' ātmajaiḥ saha
pramattā niśi viśvastāḥ, svapantaḥ śibire svake.
Kṛtavarmaṇā nṛśaṃsena, Gautamena Kṛpeṇa ca,
Aśvatthāmnā ca pāpena hataṃ vaḥ śibiraṃ niśi.
etair nara|gaj'|âśvānāṃ prāsa|śakti|paraśvadhaiḥ
sahasrāṇi nikṛntadbhir niḥ|śeṣaṃ te balaṃ kṛtam.
10.5 chidyamānasya mahato vanasy'|êva paraśvadhaiḥ
śuśruve su|mahāñ śabdo balasya tava, Bhārata.
aham eko 'vaśiṣṭas tu
tasmāt sainyān, mahā|mate,
muktaḥ kathaṃ cid, dharm'|ātman,
vyagrāc ca Kṛtavarmaṇaḥ.
tac chrutvā vākyam a|śivaṃ Kuntī|putro Yudhiṣṭhiraḥ
papāta mahyāṃ dur|dharṣaḥ putra|śoka|samanvitaḥ.
patantam taṃ atikramya parijagrāha Sātyakiḥ,
Bhīmaseno, 'rjunaś c' âiva, Mādrī|putrau ca Pāṇḍavau.
labdha|cetās tu Kaunteyaḥ śoka|vihvalayā girā
jitvā śatrūñ jitaḥ paścāt paryadevayad ārtavat:

VAISHAMPÁYANA continued:

WHEN THAT NIGHT had passed, Dhrishta·dyumna's charioteer reported to the righteous king the slaughter carried out on the camp while it slept in the dead of night. 10.1

THE CHARIOTEER said:

Slain were the sons of Dráupadi, Your Majesty, as well as those born to Drúpada, as they lay unconscious and unsuspecting, asleep in their own camp at night. Your camp was wiped out in the night, by Krita·varman the cruel, by Kripa of the clan of Gótama and by the evil Ashva·tthaman. They hacked your entire force of men, elephants and horses, into a thousand pieces using missiles, pikes and hatchets, leaving no survivors.

Tremendous was the noise heard from your forces, king 10.5
of Bhárata's line, like that of axes felling an enormous forest. Now only I survive, alone of all that army, king of great understanding—somehow, righteous lord, I managed to slip past Krita·varman while he was momentarily distracted.

On hearing this terrible news, Kunti's son, Yudhi·shthira the invincible, swooned to the ground, succumbing to grief for his sons. As he fell Sátyaki stepped in the way and caught hold of him, aided then by Bhima·sena, Árjuna and Pandu's two sons born of Madri. When he came to, Kunti's son who, having first defeated his enemies, was now defeated in turn, mourned in his misery, in a voice unsteady with grief:

10.10 «dur|vidā gatir arthānām, api ye divya|cakṣuṣaḥ.
jīyamānā jayanty anye, jayamānā vayaṃ jitāḥ.
hatvā bhrātṝn vayasyāṃś ca, pitṝn, putrān, suhṛd|gaṇān,
bandhūn, amātyān, pautrāṃś ca, jitvā sarvāñ, jitā vayam.
an|artho hy artha|saṃkāśas, tath" ân|artho 'rtha|darśanaḥ.
jayo 'yam a|jay'|ākāro. jayas tasmāt parājayaḥ.
yaj jitvā tapyate paścād āpanna iva dur|matiḥ,
kathaṃ manyeta vijayaṃ tato jitataraḥ paraiḥ?
yeṣām arthāya pāpaṃ syād vijayasya suhṛd|vadhaiḥ,
nirjitair a|pramattair hi vijitā jita|kāśinaḥ.
10.15 karṇi|nālīka|daṃṣṭrasya, khaḍga|jihvasya saṃyuge,
cāpa|vyāttasya, raudrasya, jyā|tala|svana|nādinaḥ,
kruddhasya nara|siṃhasya, saṃgrāmeṣv a|palāyinaḥ
ye vyamucyanta Karṇasya, pramādāt ta ime hatāḥ.
ratha|hradaṃ śara|varṣ'|ōrmimantaṃ,
  ratn'|ācitaṃ, vāhana|vāji|yuktam,
śakty|ṛṣṭi|mīna|dhvaja|nāga|nakraṃ,
  śar'|âsan'|āvarta|mah"|êṣu|phenam,
saṃgrāma|candr'|ôdaya|vega|velaṃ
  Droṇ'|ârṇavaṃ jyā|tala|nemi|ghoṣam
ye terur ucc'|âvaca|śastra|naubhis,
  te rāja|putrā nihatāḥ pramādāt.
na hi pramādāt paramo 'sti† kaś cid

"The course of affairs is hard to discern, even for those 10.10
with divine sight. Our opponents though beaten are really the winners, while we, the victorious, have lost. Slaying all our brothers, our peers, our fathers and scores of friends, our relatives, advisers and grandsons, we are the ones worse off. Fortune looks no different from misfortune and misfortune dons fortune's guise. Our victory defeats us. Victory, thereby, is defeat. When a man rues his victory afterwards, sick at heart, like someone who has succumbed to disaster, how can he regard it as victory, when he is more the loser than his enemies? For we, whose advantage this sin of a victory should have served, seem to be the losers, defeated by those we had beaten but who never lost their guard and killed our friends.

Those who survived the battle with fierce Karna, a cruel 10.15
lion of a man, whose open mouth was a bow resounding with the twang of the bowstring, his teeth barbed pikes, his tongue a sword, were never caught off guard in their skirmishes. Yet now being off guard has killed them. Those royal princes, who by means of boats that were various weapons crossed over the churning ocean of Drona, the pools of which are chariots, rippling with the torrents of arrows, replete with gems, harnessed to the swift steeds, with fish that are spears and javelins and banners that are serpents and crocodiles, resounding with the thrum of bowstrings and the rumble of the rims of their chariot wheels, rushing back and forth with tides of the moonrise over the battles, whose foam is the archers volleying forth their arrows, with swords and pikes darting like fish: but today they have been slain, simply being caught off guard. In this world of the

vadho narāṇām iha jīva|loke.
pramattam arthā hi naraṃ samantāt
tyajanty, an|arthāś ca samāviśanti.
10.20 dhvaj'|ôttam'|âgr'|ôcchrita|dhūma|ketuṃ,
śar'|ârciṣaṃ, kopa|mahā|samīram,
mahā|*dhanur*|jyā|tala|nemi|ghoṣaṃ,
tanutra|nānā|vidha|śastra|homam,
mahā|camū|kakṣa|dav'|âbhipannaṃ
mah'|āhave Bhīṣmamay'|âgni|dāham
ye sehur ātt'|āyudha|tīkṣṇa|vegaṃ,
te rāja|putrā nihatāḥ pramādāt.
na hi pramattena nareṇa śakyaṃ
vidyā, tapaḥ, śrīr, vipulaṃ yaśo vā.
paśy' â|pramādena nihatya śatrūn
sarvān mah"|Êndraṃ sukham edhamānam.
Indr' ôpamān, pārthiva, putra|pautrān
paśy' â|viśeṣeṇa hatān pramādāt.
tīrtvā samudraṃ vaṇijaḥ samṛddhā
magnāḥ ku|nadyām iva helamānāḥ.
a|marṣitair ye nihatāḥ śayānā,
niḥ|saṃśayaṃ te tri|divaṃ prapannāḥ.
Kṛṣṇāṃ tu śocāmi. kathaṃ nu sādhvī
śok'|ârṇavaṃ s" âdya viśalya|bhītā,
10.25 bhrātṝṃś ca putrāṃś ca hatān niśamya,
Pāñcāla|rājaṃ pitaraṃ ca vṛddham—
dhruvaṃ visaṃjñā patitā pṛthivyāṃ

living nothing kills men more than inattentiveness. Fortune abandons the inattentive and misfortunes rush down upon him.

Those royal princes who bore the harsh rush of weapons raised against them, the burning of the fire fueled by Bhishma, which caught hold of the forest of dry wood that was the mighty army in the great battle, whose pennants are the drifts of smoke high aloft the tallest banners, with arrows as sparks and a hurricane of wrath blowing up, the great noise of felloes and strings against the *bow: thunderbolts* across the sky, an oblation of armor and every kind of weapon, are now slain simply being caught off guard. Skill, austerity, glory and extensive prowess are all worthless to an inattentive man. 10.20

See how great Indra was able to kill all his enemies and enjoy happiness, once he was attentive, and how, king of the earth, our sons and grandsons, who so resembled Indra, have been slain without survivor, because of their inattention. They are like the merchants who have managed to cross the ocean and are now wealthy, but then sink in a mere trickle of a river through their lack of attention.

Those who have been slaughtered in their sleep by these unforgivable men, doubtless they have reached the third heaven, but it is for dark Dráupadi that I mourn their loss. But how will that good woman who is now free of pain and fear receive the news, the ocean of grief, that her brothers and her sons are all slain, as well as her father the venerable king of the Panchálas—surely she will fall to the ground unconscious, and her slender body will shrivel with grief? How will she ever reach an end to the suffering that such grief will 10.25

sā śoṣyate śoka|kṛś'|âṅga|yaṣṭiḥ.
tac choka|jaṃ duḥkham a|pārayantī
kathaṃ bhaviṣyaty ucitā sukhānām
putra|kṣaya|bhrātṛ|vadha|praṇunnā,
pradahyamān" êva hut'|āśanena?»
ity evam ārtaḥ paridevayan sa
rājā Kurūṇāṃ Nakulaṃ babhāṣe,
«gacch', ānay' âinām iha manda|bhāgyāṃ
sa|mātṛ|pakṣām iti rāja|putrīm.»
Mādrī|sutas tat parigṛhya vākyaṃ
dharmeṇa dharma|pratimasya rājñaḥ
yayau rathen' ālayam āśu devyāḥ,
Pāñcālarājasya ca yatra dārāḥ.
prasthāpya Mādrī|sutam Ājamīḍhaḥ
śok'|ârditas taiḥ sahitaḥ suhṛdbhiḥ
rorūyamāṇaḥ prayayau sutānām
āyodhanaṃ bhūta|gaṇ'|ânukīrṇam.

10.30 sa tat praviśy' â|śivam ugra|rūpaṃ
dadarśa putrān suhṛdaḥ sakhīṃś ca
bhūmau śayānān rudhir'|ārdra|gātrān
vibhinna|dehān prahṛt'|ôttam'|âṅgān
sa tāṃs tu dṛṣṭvā bhṛśam ārta|rūpo
Yudhiṣṭhiro dharma|bhṛtāṃ variṣṭhaḥ
uccaiḥ pracukrośa ca Kaurav'|āgryaḥ,
papāta c' ôrvyāṃ sa|gaṇo visaṃjñaḥ.

VAIŚAMPĀYANA uvāca:

11.1 SA DṚṢṬVĀ nihatān saṃkhye
putrān, bhrātṝn, sakhīṃs tathā,
mahā|duḥkha|parīt'|ātmā
babhūva, Janamejaya.

bring her and how take pleasure in any happiness again? She is devastated by the loss of her sons and the murder of her brothers, as if burned alive by the oblation-eating fire." So it was that the distraught king spoke to kind Nákula in his grief, saying, "Go, bring the princess, the poor woman, with her mother and attendants." Madri's son dutifully accepted that order from the king who is the image of duty, and made his way swiftly by chariot to the place where the royal ladies and the wives of the king of the Panchálas were staying. After he had sent Madri's son on this mission, Yudhi·shthira, the descendent of Ajamídha the Goat-Sacrificer, churned up by grief, set out for the ghoul-infested site of his sons' slaughter, accompanied by his friends, and weeping all the way.

On entering that inauspicious place he saw a dreadful 10.30
sight—his sons, friends, and beloved companions lying on the ground, their limbs damp with blood, their bodies broken, decapitated. On seeing them, his body was violently affected, and Yudhi·shthira, the best of those who uphold righteousness and now the head of the Káurava clan, wailed aloud. Then he and those with him fell upon the broad earth, their senses overwhelmed.

VAISHAMPÁYANA continued:

WHEN HE SAW his sons, brothers and friends who had 11.1
been slain in conflict, his very being was wholly overpowered by unimaginable suffering, Janam·éjaya. Then a profound grief overwhelmed the noble king, as he recalled his sons, grandsons and brothers, and his people. As his eyes

tatas tasya mahāñ śokaḥ prādur āsīn mah"|ātmanaḥ
smarataḥ putra|pautrāṇāṃ, bhrātṝṇāṃ, sva|janasya ha.
tam aśru|paripūrṇ'|âkṣaṃ, vepamānam, a|cetasam
suhṛdo bhṛśa|saṃvignāḥ sāṃtvayāṃ cakrire tadā.
tatas tasmin kṣaṇe kalpo rathen' āditya|varcasā
Nakulaḥ Kṛṣṇayā sārdham upāyāt param'|ārtayā.
11.5 Upaplavyaṃ gatā sā tu śrutvā su|mahad a|priyam.
tadā vināśaṃ sarveṣāṃ putrāṇāṃ vyathit" âbhavat.
kampamān" êva kadalī vāten' âbhisamīritā,
Kṛṣṇā rājānam āsādya śok'|ārtā nyapatad bhuvi.
babhūva vadanaṃ tasyāḥ sahasā śoka|karśitam
phulla|padma|palāś'|âkṣyās, tamo|grasta iv' âṃśumān.
tatas tāṃ patitāṃ dṛṣṭvā saṃrambhī, satya|vikramaḥ
bāhubhyāṃ parijagrāha samupetya Vṛkodaraḥ.
sā samāśvāsitā tena Bhīmasenena bhāminī
rudatī Pāṇḍavaṃ Kṛṣṇā sā hi bhrātaram abravīt.
11.10 «diṣṭyā, rājann, avāpy' êmām a|khilāṃ bhokṣyase mahīm,
ātmajān kṣatra|dharmeṇa saṃpradāya Yamāya vai.
diṣṭyā tvaṃ kuśalī, Pārtha, matta|mātaṅga|gāminam
avāpya pṛthivīṃ kṛtsnāṃ Saubhadraṃ na smariṣyasi.
ātmajān kṣatra|dharmeṇa śrutvā śūrān nipātitān,
Upaplavye mayā sārdhaṃ diṣṭyā tvaṃ na smariṣyasi.
prasuptānāṃ vadhaṃ śrutvā Drauṇinā pāpa|karmaṇā,
śokas tapati māṃ, Pārtha, hut'|âśana iv' āśayam.†
tasya pāpa|kṛto Drauṇer na ced adya tvayā raṇe
hriyate s'|ânubandhasya yudhi vikramya jīvitam,
11.15 ih' âiva prāyam āsiṣye. tan nibodhata, Pāṇḍavāḥ—

filled with tears, quaking and distraught, his friends, deeply shocked, tried to comfort him. It was at that moment, that the capable Nákula, in his chariot resplendent as the sun, drew up with dark Dráupadi at his side, her distress extreme.

Now she was already in Upaplávya when she heard the 11.5
really terrible news that all her sons had perished, which reduced her to agony. Trembling like a vine at the mercy of the wind, reaching the king, dark Dráupadi fell grief-stricken to the ground. The eyes of that lady had been like fully opened lotuses on their pads, but now her face was of a sudden furrowed with grief, like the radiant sun swallowed by darkness. Seeing her fall, the irascible Wolf-Bellied Bhima, bold in pursuit of his oaths, stepped up and gathered her in his arms. Bhima·sena revived that passionate woman. And she, dark Dráupadi, turned in tears to his brother Pándava and said:

"Congratulations, Your Majesty, on winning this great 11.10
earth in its entirety. May you enjoy it, having made your own sons an offering to Yama, god of Death, as is the duty of a warrior. Congratulations, son of Pritha, that on skillfully winning this entire earth, you will not recall Subhádra's son Abhimányu, who walked proud as an elephant in rut. Congratulations that on hearing that our valiant sons had met their deaths, in accordance with their duty as warriors, you will not recall them with me at Upaplávya. Son of Pritha, since I heard of their massacre, while they slept, at the hands of Drona's evil son, grief has consumed me, just as the oblation-eating fire consumes its own foundation. If you do not this day extract the very life of that evil son of

na cet phalam avāpnoti Drauṇiḥ pāpasya karmaṇaḥ!»

evam uktvā tataḥ Kṛṣṇā Pāṇḍavaṃ pratyupāviśat
Yudhiṣṭhiraṃ Yājñasenī dharma|rājaṃ yaśasvinī.
dṛṣṭv" ôpaviṣṭāṃ rāja'|rṣiḥ Pāṇḍavo mahiṣīṃ priyām,
pratyuvāca sa dharm'|ātmā Draupadīṃ cāru|darśanām.

«dharmyaṃ dharmeṇa, dharma|jñe,
prāptās te nidhanaṃ, śubhe,
putrās te bhrātaraś c' âiva.
tān na śocitum arhasi.
sa, kalyāṇi, vanaṃ dur|gaṃ dūraṃ Drauṇir ito gataḥ.
tasya tvaṃ pātanaṃ saṃkhye kathaṃ jñāsyasi, śobhane?»

DRAUPADY uvāca:

11.20 Droṇa|putrasya sahajo maṇiḥ śirasi me śrutaḥ.
nihatya saṃkhye taṃ pāpaṃ paśyeyaṃ maṇim āhṛtam.
rājañ, śirasi taṃ kṛtvā jīveyam iti me matiḥ.

ity uktvā Pāṇḍavaṃ Kṛṣṇā rājānaṃ cāru|darśanā
Bhīmasenam ath' āgatya paramaṃ vākyam abravīt:

trātum arhasi māṃ, Bhīma, kṣatra|dharmam anusmaran.
jahi taṃ pāpa|karmāṇaṃ, Śaṃbaraṃ Maghavān iva.
na hi te vikrame tulyaḥ pumān ast' îha kaś cana.
śrutaṃ tat sarva|lokeṣu, parama|vyasane yathā

Drona along with that of his children, after engaging him in battle, I shall take leave of my own life on this very spot. 11.15
Mark what I say, Pandu's sons—unless Drona's son reaps the consequences of his evil action!"

So saying, dark Dráupadi, the glorious lady, daughter of Yajña·sena, then placed herself before the Pándavan king facing the righteous king Yudhi·shthira, steadfast in battle. On seeing his beloved chief queen seated there before him, the royal seer, the king of the Pándavas, dutiful to the core, replied to Dráupadi, the apple of his eye:

"You are a pure lady, who recognizes duty. Your sons and brothers did win a dutiful end, dutifully. You should not grieve for them. Virtuous woman, the son of Drona has left this area and entered a distant, well nigh impenetrable forest. How will you know when he has fallen in battle, pure lady?"

DRÁUPADI replied:

I have heard that Drona's son was born with a gem on 11.20
his head. When that evil man is slain in battle, I would see the gem brought here before me. Your Majesty, my mind is made up—I shall only carry on with life if I have placed that gem upon my own head.

Once dark Dráupadi, the apple of his eye, had said this to the Pándavan king, she then turned back to Bhima and spoke these final words:

You should protect me, Bhima, mindful of your duty as a warrior. Kill the man who committed this atrocity, just as powerful Indra killed Shámbara. No man in this world is your match in valor. Indeed, it is famed through every

dvīpo 'bhūs tvaṃ hi Pārthānāṃ nagare Vāraṇāvate;
11.25 Hiḍimba|darśane c' âiva tathā tvam abhavo gatiḥ;
tathā Virāṭa|nagare Kīcakena bhṛś'|ârditām
mām apy uddhṛtavān kṛcchrāt, Paulomīṃ Maghavān iva.
yath" âitāny akṛthāḥ, Pārtha, mahā|karmāṇi vai purā,
tathā Drauṇim a|mitra|ghnaṃ vinihatya sukhī bhava.
tasyā bahu|vidhaṃ duḥkhaṃ niśamya paridevitam
na c' âmarṣata Kaunteyo Bhīmaseno mahā|balaḥ.
sa kāñcana|vicitr'|âṅgam āruroha mahā|ratham,
ādāya ruciraṃ citraṃ sa|mārgaṇa|guṇaṃ dhanuḥ,
Nakulaṃ sārathiṃ kṛtvā Droṇaputra|vadhe dhṛtaḥ,
11.30 visphārya sa|śaraṃ cāpaṃ tūrṇam aśvān acodayat.
te hayāḥ, puruṣa|vyāghra, coditā vāta|raṃhasaḥ,
vegena tvaritā jagmur harayaḥ, śīghra|gāminaḥ.
śibirāt svād gṛhītvā sa rathasya padam a|cyutaḥ.

region how you were the one who rescued your brothers when the terrible disaster struck in the city of Varanávata;* and how you were the means of escape in your encounter 11.25
with the ogre Hidímba; how, when Kíchaka pursued me in Viráta's capital, you managed to rescue me, just as bounteous Indra rescued his lover, the daughter of the demon Pulóman. These are the great feats you have performed before, son of Pritha.* Follow them up with the satisfaction of killing the son of Drona, who has murdered his adversaries.

Witnessing the many painful emotions that came over her, Kunti's son, the powerful Bhima·sena, could endure it no longer. He mounted his great chariot, with its flashing golden car, and, grabbing his beautiful, brightly colored bow, ready strung, with arrows at the ready, taking Nákula as his charioteer, resolved to kill the son of Drona. With 11.30
the shot of an arrow from his bow, he set his horses rushing forward. Those steeds, pressed forward, flew like the wind, tiger of a man. At a gallop they sped away, his swift paced steeds. Guiding them away from the camp, he stood fast at the helm of his chariot.

12–15
THE BRINK OF APOCALYPSE

VAIŚAMPĀYANA uvāca:

12.1 TASMIN PRAYĀTE dur|dharṣe Yadūnām ṛṣabhas tataḥ
abravīt Puṇḍarīkākṣaḥ Kuntī|putraṃ Yudhiṣṭhiram:

«eṣa, Pāṇḍava, te bhrātā putra|śoka|parāyaṇaḥ
jighāṃsur Drauṇim ākrande eka ev' âbhidhāvati.
Bhīmaḥ priyas te sarvebhyo bhrātṛbhyo, Bharata'|rṣabha.
taṃ kṛcchra|gatam adya tvaṃ kasmān n' âbhyavapadyase?
yat tad ācaṣṭa putrāya Droṇaḥ para|puraṃ|jayaḥ
astraṃ Brahma|śiro nāma, daheta pṛthivīm api.

12.5 tan mah"|ātmā mahā|bhāgaḥ, ketuḥ sarva|dhanuṣmatām
pratyapādayad ācāryaḥ prīyamāṇo Dhanaṃjayam.
taṃ putro 'py eka ev' âinam anvayācad a|marṣaṇaḥ.
tataḥ provāca putrāya n' âtihṛṣṭa|manā iva.

viditaṃ cāpalaṃ hy āsīd ātmajasya dur|ātmanaḥ.
sarva|dharma|vid ācāryo so 'nvaśāt sva|sutaṃ tataḥ:
‹param'|āpad|gaten' âpi na sma, tāta, tvayā raṇe
idam astraṃ prayoktavyaṃ, mānuṣeṣu viśeṣataḥ›
ity uktavān guruḥ putraṃ Droṇaḥ paścād ath' ôktavān:
‹na tvaṃ jātu satāṃ mārge sthāt"› êti, puruṣa'|rṣabha.

12.10 sa tad ājñāya duṣṭ'|ātmā pitur vacanam a|priyam,
nir|āśaḥ sarva|kalyāṇaiḥ śocan paryacaran mahīm.
tatas tadā, Kuru|śreṣṭha, vana|sthe tvayi, Bhārata,
avasad Dvārakām etya Vṛṣṇibhiḥ param'|ârcitaḥ.
sa kadā cit samudr'|ânte vasan Dvāravatīm anu,

VAISHAMPÁYANA continued:

WHEN THAT uncrushable warrior had departed, the bull of the Yadu tribe, lotus-eyed Krishna, spoke to Kunti's son Yudhi·shthira: 12.1

"Son of Pandu, your brother, is consumed by grief for his sons, and is bent on killing Drona's son in combat. He has set off to attack him all alone. Of all your brothers, Bhima is your favorite, bull of the Bhárata line. Now he's in danger. Why aren't you by his side, especially given that Drona, who captured the city of his enemies, told his son how to use the missile called Brahma's head, which can consume the entire earth in flames?

Your teacher, the noble illustrious emblem of all archers, 12.5
when he was well-disposed had bestowed this gift on spoil-winning Árjuna.* He was then implored impatiently by his only son for this same gift, to whom he did then impart it, though none too pleased.

For the capriciousness of his ignoble son was clear to see. So the teacher, who could recognize everyone's character, went on to advise his son: 'Even if you are in the direst straits in battle my son, you must not, whatever you do, employ this missile against any humans.' Saying this, teacher Drona cautioned his son further, bull of men, with these words: 'You will never stand in the way of good people.'

When he understood what his father was saying, it upset 12.10
him and, with his very soul disturbed, despairing of any happiness, he wandered the earth, bereft. It was after that, when you, the best of the Kurus in the line of Bhárata, were staying in the forest, that he arrived at the many-gated city of Dváraka, where he lived with my own clan, the Vrishnis,

eka ekaṃ samāgamya mām uvāca hasann iva:
‹yat tad ugraṃ tapaḥ, Kṛṣṇa, caran satya|parākramaḥ
Agastyād Bhārat'|ācāryaḥ pratyapadyata me pitā
astraṃ Brahma|śiro nāma deva|gandharva|pūjitam,
tad adya mayi, Dāśārha, yathā pitari me tathā.
12.15 asmattas tad upādāya
divyam astraṃ, Yad'|ûttama,
mam' âpy astraṃ prayaccha tvaṃ
cakraṃ ripu|haraṃ† raṇe.›
sa, rājan, prīyamāṇena may" âpy uktaḥ kṛt'|âñjaliḥ
yācamānaḥ prayatnena matto 'straṃ, Bharata'|rṣabha:
‹deva|dānava|gandharva|manuṣya|patag'|ôragāḥ
na samā mama vīryasya śat'|âṃśen' âpi piṇḍitāḥ.
idaṃ dhanur, iyaṃ śaktir, idaṃ cakram, iyaṃ gadā,
yad yad icchasi ced astraṃ mattas, tat tad dadāmi te.
yac chaknoṣi samudyantuṃ prayoktum api vā raṇe,
tad gṛhāṇa vin" âstreṇa yan me dātum abhīpsasi.›
12.20 sa su|nābhaṃ sahasr'|âraṃ vajra|nābham ayas|mayam
vavre cakraṃ mahā|bhāgo mattaḥ spardhan mayā saha.
‹gṛhāṇa cakram,› ity ukto mayā tu tad|anantaram
jagrāh' ôpetya sahasā cakraṃ savyena pāṇinā.
na c' âinam aśakat sthānāt sañcālayitum apy uta.
ath' âinaṃ dakṣiṇen' âpi grahītum upacakrame.

who showed him the utmost regard. While he was living off the many gated city, at the ocean's edge, at some point he visited me in person by himself when I was alone and, with a slight smile, said:

'Dark lord Krishna, my father, the truly powerful teacher of the descendants of Bhárata, while he was practicing the harshest austerity, received from the sage Agástya the Brahma-head missile, worshipped by gods and heavenly musicians alike. Now, descendant of Dashárha, just as my father possessed that weapon so now do I. Please accept that 12.15
divine missile from us, most exalted of the Yadu tribe, in exchange for your discus missile that annihilates the enemy in battle.'

Your Majesty, I was won over by him as he besought me with hands raised in supplication, trying to get that weapon from me, and, bull of Bhárata's line, I replied to him, 'The combined force of gods, demons, celestial spirits, humans, bird and serpent deities cannot match even a hundredth of my strength. This bow, this pike, this discus, this conch, if you want any one of them from me, I shall give it to you. Take whichever one you can lift up and put it to use in battle; never mind the weapon you offer to give to me.'

That distinguished man, thinking he could vie with me, 12.20
chose my discus, wrought of iron, with its beautiful center of diamond and its one thousand spokes. 'Take the discus,' I told him, whereon he rushed forward and laid hold of it with his left hand. But he couldn't even move it from its place. Then he changed position to take hold of it also with his right hand. But though he applied all his effort grasping hold of it, and applied all his strength, it wasn't possible for

sarva|yatna|balen' âpi gṛhṇann evam idaṃ tataḥ,
tataḥ sarva|balen' âpi yad" âinaṃ na śaśāka saḥ
udyantuṃ vā cālayituṃ Drauṇiḥ parama|dur|manāḥ,
kṛtvā yatnaṃ pariśrāntaḥ sa nyavartata, Bhārata.
12.25 nivṛtta|manasaṃ tasmād abhiprāyād, vicetasam
aham āmantrya saṃvignam Aśvatthāmānam abruvam:
‹yaḥ sad" âiva manuṣyeṣu pramāṇaṃ paramaṃ gataḥ,
Gāṇḍīva|dhanvā, śvet'|âśvaḥ, kapi|pravara|ketanaḥ,
yaḥ sākṣād deva|dev'|ēśaṃ śiti|kaṇṭham Umā|patim
dvaṃdva|yuddhe parājiṣṇus toṣayām āsa Śaṃkaram,
yasmāt priyataro n' âsti mam' ânyaḥ puruṣo bhuvi,
n' â|deyaṃ yasya me kiñ cid, api dārāḥ sutās tathā,
ten' âpi suhṛdā, brahman, Pārthen' â|kliṣṭa|karmaṇā
n' ôkta|pūrvam idaṃ vākyaṃ yas tvaṃ mām abhibhāṣase.
12.30 brahma|caryaṃ mahad ghoraṃ tīrtvā dvādaśa|vārṣikam,
Himavat|pārśvam āsthāya yo mayā tapas" ârjitaḥ,
samāna|vrata|cāriṇyāṃ Rukmiṇyāṃ yo 'nvajāyata
Sanatkumāras tejasvī Pradyumno nāma me sutaḥ,
ten' âpy etan mahad divyaṃ cakram a|pratimaṃ raṇe
na prārthitam abhūn, mūḍha, yad idaṃ prārthitaṃ tvayā.
Rāmeṇ' âtibalen' âitan n' ôkta|pūrvaṃ kadā cana,
na Gadena, na Sāmbena, yad idaṃ prārthitaṃ tvayā.
Dvārakā|vāsibhiś c' ânyair Vṛṣṇy|Andhaka|mahārathaiḥ
n' ôkta|pūrvam idaṃ jātu, yad idaṃ prārthitaṃ tvayā.
12.35 Bhārat'|ācārya|putras tvaṃ mānitaḥ sarva|Yādavaiḥ.
cakreṇa, rathināṃ śreṣṭha, kaṃ nu, tāta, yuyutsase?›

that exceedingly malevolent son of Drona to lift it up or move it. Finally, exhausted by the effort he had made, he relented, scion of Bhárata.

At this change of heart about his purpose, Ashva·tthaman 12.25
was confounded and I addressed him in his agitated state, saying: 'There is no man on earth more dear to me than the man who always reaches the greatest heights of human achievement, who wields the Gandíva bow, who is drawn by white horses, and whose lofty insignia is the monkey; the one who, in seeking to outdo in a dual the blue-throated lord of Uma, the lord of highest gods, the beneficent Shiva, succeeded in gaining his favor. There is nothing I would not give him, even my wives and sons, but even that dear friend, Pritha's son of unblemished conduct, has never asked of me what you have in addressing me today, brahmin.

My son the brilliant Eternal Youth, Pradyúmna by name, 12.30
who was procured by my asceticism when I had completed a great feat of awesome spiritual austerity for twelve years while living on the slopes of the Himalaya, and was born to Rúkmini* who had been practicing the same vow as me, even he did not request this divine discus, that is unmatched in battle, and which you, stupid man, have asked for. Never before at any time has such a request as you have made been expressed even by stupendously strong Rama or by Gada or by Samba.* Neither the inhabitants of the Gated Citadel nor the great chariot fighters among the Vrishnis and Ándhakas,* have ever before expressed the request
which you have dared to make. Son of the teacher to Bhá- 12.35
rata's line, you are highly regarded by all Yadu's descendants.

evam ukto mayā Drauṇir mām idaṃ pratyuvāca ha:
‹prayujya bhavate pūjāṃ yotsye, Kṛṣṇa, tvayā saha.
prārthitaṃ te mayā akraṃ deva|dānava|pūjitam,
a|jeyaḥ syām iti, vibho. satyam etad bravīmi te.
tvatto 'haṃ dur|labhaṃ kāmam an|avāpy' âiva, Keśava,
pratiyāsyāmi. Govinda, śiven' âbhivadasva mām.
etat su|bhīmaṃ, bhīmānām ṛṣabheṇa, tvayā dhṛtam
cakram a|praticakreṇa bhuvi n' ânyo 'bhipadyate.›

12.40 etāvad uktvā Drauṇir māṃ yugyān aśvān dhanāni ca
ādāy' ôpayayau kāle, ratnāni vividhāni ca.
sa saṃrambhī, dur|ātmā ca, capalaḥ, krūra eva ca,
veda c' âstraṃ Brahma|śiras. tasmād rakṣyo Vṛkodaraḥ.»

VAIŚAMPĀYANA uvāca:

13.1 EVAM UKTVĀ yudhāṃ śreṣṭhaḥ sarva|Yādava|nandanaḥ
sarv'|āyudha|var'|ôpetam āruroha, rath'|ôttamam
yuktaṃ parama|Kāmbojais turagair hema|mālibhiḥ.
ādity'|ôdaya|varṇasya dhuraṃ ratha|varasya tu
dakṣiṇām avahac Chaibyaḥ, Sugrīvaḥ savyato 'bhavat,
pārṣṇi|vāhau tu tasy' āstāṃ Meghapuṣpa|Balāhakau.
Viśvakarma|kṛtā divyā ratna|dhātu|vibhūṣitā
ucchrit" êva rathe māyā dhvaja|yaṣṭir adṛśyata.

Most excellent of chariot-fighters, against whom, my son, did you plan to fight with the discus?'

When I addressed Drona's son with these words, he gave me this reply: 'After worshipping your honor, it is against you, Krishna, that I had hoped to fight. I asked for your discus, that is revered by gods and demons, in the hope that I might become invincible, master. I am telling you the truth. Long-haired lord, given that I have not realized my unrealizable wish, I shall retreat. Lord of the cowherds, please bid me farewell with your blessing. No one else on this earth can procure this awesome discus of power wielded by you, to whom no power is hostile, bull of awesome gods.'

Having said this much, Drona's son, presenting in timely 12.40
fashion suitable horses and offerings of wealth and gems of many kinds, surrendered himself to me. He is impetuous, malevolent, capricious and cruel. What is more, he knows how to invoke the Brahma's Head missile. For these reasons, Wolf-Belly needs protecting."

VAISHAMPÁYANA continued:

WHEN THE MOST excellent of warriors, the delight of all 13.1
Yadu's descendants, had finished saying this, he mounted his excellent chariot equipped with all the best weapons. Now the fore-axle of that excellent chariot, the hue of the rising sun, was harnessed to the finest Kambójan horses* dressed in golden trappings. While the Stallion of Shibi led on its right, Fine-neck led the left, then Cloud Blossom and Thunder drew on the outside flanks.* Visible aloft the chariot was the magical flag pole encrusted with precious stones fashioned by the Crafter of All.*

13.5 Vainateyaḥ sthitas tasyāṃ prabhā|maṇḍala|raśmivān
tasya satyavataḥ ketur bhujag'|ârir adṛśyata.
anvārohadd Hṛṣīkeśaṃ† ketuḥ sarva|dhanuṣmatām
Arjunaḥ, satya|karmā ca Kuru|rājo Yudhiṣṭhiraḥ.
aśobhetāṃ mah"|ātmānau Dāśārham abhitaḥ sthitau
ratha|sthaṃ śārṅga|dhanvānam, Aśvināv iva Vāsavam.
tāv upāropya Dāśārhaḥ syandanaṃ loka|pūjitam,
pratodena jav'|ôpetān param'|âśvān acodayat.
te hayāḥ sahas" ôtpetur gṛhītvā syandan'|ôttamam
āsthitaṃ Pāṇḍaveyābhyāṃ Yadūnām ṛṣabheṇa ca.
13.10 vahatāṃ śārṅga|dhanvānam aśvānāṃ śīghra|gāminām
prādur āsīn mahāñ śabdaḥ, pakṣiṇāṃ patatām iva.
te samārchan nara|vyāghrāḥ kṣaṇena, Bharata'|ṛṣabha,
Bhīmasenaṃ mah"|êṣv|āsaṃ samanudrutya vegitāḥ.
krodha|dīptaṃ tu Kaunteyaṃ dviṣad|arthe samudyatam
n' âśaknuvan vārayituṃ samety' âpi mahā|rathāḥ.
sa teṣāṃ prekṣatām eva śrīmatāṃ dṛḍha|dhanvinām
yayau Bhāgīrathī|tīraṃ haribhir bhṛśa|vegitaiḥ,
yatra sma śrūyate Drauṇiḥ putra|hantā mah"|ātmanām.

At its tip could be seen the emblem of the preserver of truth, the standing figure of the son of Vínata,* the enemy of serpents, emitting a shining circle of rays. Then the emblem of all archers, Árjuna, mounted after the lord of the senses, as did the trustworthy king of Kurus, Yudhi·shthira. These two noble-souled men stood either side of Krishna Dashárha as he stood in the chariot, holding his bow of horn. They shone like the twin Ashvins, either side of the god Indra. The descendent of Dashárha, aiding them aboard his swift and universally revered war-chariot, started with the crack of his whip the fine horses, blessed with speed. At once those steeds flew off, drawing behind them the fine war-chariot, on which stood the two Pándavas and the bull of the Yadus. 13.5

From the fleet stallions drawing the archer with his horn 13.10
bow there emanated a mighty sound as of a flock of birds flying overhead. Bull of Bhárata's line, chasing after the great archer Bhima·sena at top speed, in an instant these tigers of mankind had caught up with him. But the great chariot-fighters, though they had caught up with him, could not hold back the son of Kunti, so inflamed with anger was he, so bent on the goal of his animosity. As they looked on, full of glory, sure of bow, he approached the bank of Bhagi·rathi, the western tributary of the Ganges, his horses pulling hard, for that was where they had heard that Drona's son, the murderer of the sons of the great, was to be found.

sa dadarśa mah"|ātmānam udak'|ânte yaśasvinam
13.15 Kṛṣṇadvaipāyanaṃ Vyāsam āsīnam ṛṣibhiḥ saha.
taṃ c' âiva krūra|karmāṇaṃ ghṛt'|âktaṃ, kuśa|cīriṇam,
rajasā dhvastam āsīnaṃ dadarśa Drauṇim antike.
tam abhyadhāvat Kaunteyaḥ pragṛhya sa|śaraṃ dhanuḥ
Bhīmaseno mahā|bāhus «tiṣṭha tiṣṭh'» êti c' âbravīt.
sa dṛṣṭvā bhīma|dhanvānaṃ pragṛhīta|śar'|âsanam,
bhrātarau pṛṣṭhataś c' âsya
Janārdana|rathe sthitau,
vyathit'|ātm" âbhavad Drauṇiḥ,
prāptaṃ c' êdam amanyata.
sa tad divyam a|dīn'|ātmā param'|âstram acintayat,
jagrāha ca sa c' Âiṣīkāṃ Drauṇiḥ savyena pāṇinā.
13.20 sa tām āpadam āsādya divyam astram udīrayat,
a|mṛṣyamāṇas tāñ śūrān divy'|āyudha|dharān sthitān.
«a|Pāṇḍavāy'!» êti ruṣā vyasṛjad dāruṇaṃ vacaḥ.
ity uktvā, rāja|śārdūla, Droṇa|putraḥ pratāpavān
sarva|loka|pramoh'|ârthaṃ tad astraṃ pramumoca ha.
tatas tasyām iṣīkāyāṃ pāvakaḥ samajāyata,
pradhakṣyann iva lokāṃs trīn kāl'|ântaka|Yam'|ôpamaḥ.

VAIŚAMPĀYANA uvāca:

14.1 IṄGITEN' ÂIVA Dāśārhas tam abhiprāyam āditaḥ
Drauṇer buddhvā mahā|bāhur Arjunaṃ pratyabhāṣata:
«Arjun', Ârjuna, yad divyam astraṃ te hṛdi vartate
Droṇ'|ôpadiṣṭaṃ, tasy' âyaṃ kālaḥ saṃprati, Pāṇḍava.

At the waters edge he saw, exuding glory, the noble-souled Vyasa, the dark lord of the island, seated with his sages. Close by he could see as well the one who had committed the cruel atrocity, the son of Drona, anointed with ghee, wearing a garment of sacred grass, sitting sprinkled with dust. Clasping his bow and arrows, Kunti's son rushed up to him. "Stay right where you are!" cried the strong-armed Bhima·sena. 13.15

Catching sight of the fearsome bowman clasping his arrow-shooting bow and the two brothers stood behind him in Janárdana's car, Ashva·tthaman was stricken to the core in agitation and realized, "the moment has come." His spirit undiminished, the mind of Drona's son turned to the supreme missile of the gods and he grasped the Seeker-missile in his left hand.

Caught in this dire situation, he raised the divine missile aloft, heedless of the heroes stood there bearing their divine weapons. Full of fury, he cried out the cruel command, "Destroy the race of Pandu!" With this cry, tiger of a king, the son of Drona, burning with passion, released the rocket intended to render all worlds unconscious. 13.20

At that, the missile set a tornado in motion, engulfing the three realms of the world in flames, like Yama, god of death, ushering in the end of time.

VAISHAMPÁYANA continued:

KRISHNA, THE powerful-armed descendant of Dashárha, realizing from the outset the intention of Drona's son from his demeanor, turned back to Árjuna, crying: "Árjuna, Árjuna, now is the time to use the weapon that lies within 14.1

bhrātṝṇām ātmanaś c' âiva paritrāṇāya, Bhārata,
visṛj' âitat tvam apy ājāv astram astra|nivāraṇam.»
Keśaven' âivam ukto 'tha Pāṇḍavaḥ para|vīra|hā
avātarad rathāt tūrṇam, pragṛhya sa|śaraṃ dhanuḥ.
14.5 pūrvam ācārya|putrāya, tato 'nantaram ātmane,
bhrātṛbhyaś c' âiva sarvebhyaḥ svast' îty uktvā paraṃ|tapaḥ,
devatābhyo namas|kṛtya, gurubhyaś c' âiva sarvaśaḥ,
utsasarja śivaṃ, dhyāyann, «astram astreṇa śāmyatām.»
tatas tad astraṃ sahasā sṛṣṭaṃ Gāṇḍīva|dhanvanā
prajajvāla mah"|ârciṣmad, yug'|ânt'|ânala|saṃnibham.
tath" âiva Droṇa|putrasya tad astraṃ tigma|tejasaḥ
prajajvāla mahā|jvālaṃ, tejo|maṇḍala|saṃvṛtam.
nirghātā bahavaś c' āsan, petur ulkāḥ sahasraśaḥ,
mahad bhayaṃ ca bhūtānāṃ sarveṣāṃ samajāyata.
14.10 sa|śabdam abhavad vyoma, jvālā|māl"|ākulaṃ bhṛśam
cacāla ca mahī kṛtsnā sa|parvata|vana|drumā.
te tv astre tejasī lokāṃs tāpayantī vyavasthite,
maharṣī sahitau tatra darśayām āsatus tadā—
Nāradaḥ sarva|bhūt'|ātmā, Bharatānāṃ pitāmahaḥ—
ubhau śamayituṃ vīrau Bhāradvāja|Dhanaṃjayau.
tau munī sarva|dharma|jñau, sarva|bhūta|hit'|âiṣiṇau
dīptayor astrayor madhye sthitau parama|tejasau.
tad|antaram ath' â|dhṛṣyāv upagamya yaśasvinau
āstām ṛṣi|varau tatra jvalitāv iva pāvakau,

your heart, son of Pandu, the one that Drona taught you.
To save your own brothers, son of Bhárata's line, you must
now fire that counter-missile that deflects other missiles in
war." When the long-haired lord told the son of Pandu to
do this, he, the slayer of enemy champions, quickly stepped
down from the chariot, snatching up his bow and arrows.

Uttering a blessing firstly on his teacher's son, then, with- 14.5
out interruption, on himself and all his brothers, the scourge
of foes, paying reverence to gods and teachers everywhere,
released his auspicious weapon, meditating, "May missile
be quelled by missile!" Thereupon this missile, released with
a rush by the wielder of the Gandíva bow, flared up with a
dazzling brightness like the inferno at the end of an eon. At
the same time the missile of Drona's fiery son, itself flared
up in a massive blaze surrounded by a halo of brilliant heat.
Countless tornados were whipped up and burning meteors
fell everywhere. Every living been was filled with immense
dread.

The sky was filled with fire as violent noise filled the air, 14.10
and the whole earth quaked down to every mountain, forest and tree. But even as the two blazing missiles look set to
set the worlds afire the two great seers suddenly appeared
there seated together—Nárada, the essence of all beings,
and the great grandsire of the Bhárata line—determined to
calm those two champions, Ashva·tthaman in the line of
Bharad·vaja and Árjuna, winner of spoils. These two sages,
who understand all things and pursue the benefit of all beings, stood resplendent in the highest spiritual power between those two blazing missiles. Then the excellent seers,
invincible and full of splendor, drew near and remained

14.15 prāṇa|bhṛdbhir an|ādhṛṣyau, deva|dānava|saṃmatau,
astra|tejaḥ śamayituṃ lokānāṃ hita|kāmyayā.

ṚṢĪ ūcatuḥ:

nānā|śastra|vidaḥ pūrve ye 'py atītā mahā|rathāḥ,
n' âitad astraṃ manuṣyeṣu taiḥ prayuktaṃ kathaṃ cana.
kim idaṃ sāhasaṃ vīrau kṛtavantau mah"|âtyayam?

VAIŚAṂPĀYANA uvāca:

15.1 DṚṢṬV" ÂIVA, nara|śārdūla, tāv Agni|sama|tejasau
saṃjahāra śaraṃ divyaṃ tvaramāṇo Dhanaṃjayaḥ.
uvāca, Bharata|śreṣṭha, tāv ṛṣī prāñjalis tadā:
«‹pramuktam astram astreṇa śāmyatām,› iti vai mayā
saṃhṛte param'|âstre 'smin sarvān asmān a|śeṣataḥ
pāpa|karmā dhruvaṃ Drauṇiḥ pradhakṣyaty astra|tejasā.
yad atra hitam asmākaṃ lokānāṃ c' âiva sarvathā,
bhavantau deva|saṃkāśau tathā saṃmantum arhataḥ!»
15.5 ity uktvā saṃjahār' âstraṃ punar eva Dhanaṃjayaḥ.
saṃhāro duṣkaras tasya devair api hi saṃyuge.
visṛṣṭasya raṇe tasya param'|âstrasya saṃgrahe,
a|śaktaḥ Pāṇḍavād anyaḥ sākṣād api Śatakratuḥ.
Brahma|tej'|ôdbhavaṃ tadd hi visṛṣṭam a|kṛt'|ātmanā
na śakyam āvartayituṃ Brahma|cāri|vratād ṛte.

there blazing fierily, both invincible to all who bear breath, 14.15
both revered by gods and demons, there in order to allay the impact of the missiles, in their desire to protect the peoples of the world.

THE SEERS said:

Previous great chariot-fighters of the past, even though they understood all the various weapons available, never at any point employed this missile against mankind. Why have these two champions so rashly committed such a terrible transgression?

VAISHAMPÁYANA continued:

TIGER OF A MAN, the moment Árjuna, winner of spoils, 15.1
saw those two, as splendid as Fire, he hastily recalled his divine rocket. He then addressed them, best of Bhárata's line, with his hands pressed together in prayer, saying, "I had wished 'The missile he released, may it be defused with mine.' With this supreme missile now withdrawn, the cruel son of Drona will surely use the power of his missile to reduce us all to ash. Please could the two of you, who have the appearance of gods, opine on what action can now be taken in the best interests not only of us but of all people everywhere!"

So saying the tormentor of the foes again recalled his 15.5
weapon. Its retrieval is a nigh impossible task even for gods waging war. When the ultimate missile is fired in battle, to call it back is beyond the capacity of anyone other than Pandu's son, even for Indra who had the power of a hundred sacrificial rites behind him, because that which arose from the brilliance of Brahma cannot be averted by anyone

a|cīrṇa|Brahma|caryo yaḥ sṛṣṭvā vartayate punaḥ,
tad astraṃ s'|ânubandhasya mūrdhānaṃ tasya kṛntati.
Brahma|cārī vratī c' âpi dur|avāpam avāpya tat
parama|vyasan'|ārto 'pi n' Ârjuno 'straṃ vyamuñcata.
15.10 satya|vrata|dharaḥ, śūro, Brahma|cārī ca Pāṇḍavaḥ,
guru|vartī ca. ten' âstraṃ sañjahār' Ârjunaḥ punaḥ.
Drauṇir apy atha saṃprekṣya tāv ṛṣī purataḥ sthitau
na śaśāka punar ghoram astraṃ saṃhartum ojasā.
a|śaktaḥ pratisaṃhāre param'|âstrasya saṃyuge,
Drauṇir dīna|manā, rājan, Dvaipāyanam abhāṣata:
«uttama|vyasan'|ārtena prāṇa|trāṇam abhīpsunā
may" âitad astram utsṛṣṭaṃ Bhīmasena|bhayān, mune.
a|dharmaś ca kṛto 'nena Dhārtarāṣṭraṃ jighāṃsatā
mithy"|ācāreṇa, bhagavan, Bhīmasenena saṃyuge.
15.15 ataḥ sṛṣṭam idaṃ, brahman, may" âstram a|kṛt'|ātmanā.
tasya bhūyo 'dya saṃhāraṃ kartuṃ n' âham ih' ôtsahe.
visṛṣṭaṃ hi mayā divyam etad astraṃ dur|āsadam
‹a|Pāṇḍavāy'› êti, mune, vahni|tejo 'numantrya vai.
tad idaṃ Pāṇḍaveyānām antakāy' âbhisaṃhitam
adya Pāṇḍu|sutān sarvāñ jīvitād bhraṃśayiṣyati.

with a single flaw in their character, without the vow of a spiritual life dedicated to Brahma. If someone who has not practiced Brahma's path releases that missile and then attempts to recall it again, it splits his head asunder, and that of every child who comes after him. But Árjuna had followed Brahma's path,* and had kept the vow and achieved that which is so hard to attain. So much so that even under extreme duress, he was able to prevent that missile from reaching its target.

So it was that the Pándava champion who kept the vow 15.10
of truth and had followed Brahma's path, acting out of respect for his elders, recalled the weapon again. But Drona's son, who also saw those two seers stood before him, did not have the strength to withdraw his terrible weapon. Lacking the ability to withdraw that ultimate missile in battle and sick at heart, Your Majesty, Drona's son spoke to Krishna of the Island: "It was under the utmost duress, desperate to defend my life, that I launched this missile, sage, in fear of Bhima·sena. In the battle Bhima·sena had committed an inadmissible maneuver, in his ambition to kill Dhrita·rashtra's son and acting in bad faith, Lord.

That is why I launched this missile, brahmin, though my 15.15
character is flawed. And now I don't have the power to recall it again. While employing the magical formula 'Destroy the race of Pandu,' I released this divine missile which is so hard to master, and which has the heat of sacrificial fire, sage. Now, charged with the destruction of the Pandu's heirs, it will deprive all his sons of life. Brahmin, my mind

kṛtaṃ pāpam idaṃ, brahman, roṣ'|āviṣṭena cetasā,
vadham āśāsya Pārthānāṃ may" âstraṃ sṛjatā raṇe.»

VYĀSA uvāca:

astraṃ Brahma|śiras, tāta, vidvān Pārtho Dhanaṃjayaḥ
utsṛṣṭavān na roṣeṇa, na nāśāya tav' āhave.
15.20 astram astreṇa tu raṇe tava saṃśamayiṣyatā
visṛṣṭam Arjunen' êdaṃ, punaś ca pratisaṃhṛtam.
Brahm'|âstram apy avāpy' âitad upadeśāt pitus tava
kṣatra|dharmān mahā|bāhur n' âkampata Dhanañ|jayaḥ.
evaṃ dhṛtimataḥ, sādhoḥ, sarv'|âstra|viduṣaḥ, sataḥ,
sa|bhrātṛ|bandhoḥ kasmāt tvaṃ vadham asya cikīrṣasi?
astraṃ Brahma|śiro yatra param'|âstreṇa vadhyate,
samā dvādaśa Parjanyas tad rāṣṭraṃ n' âbhivarṣati.
etad|arthaṃ mahā|bāhuḥ śaktimān api Pāṇḍavaḥ
na vihanyāt tad astraṃ tu prajā|hita|cikīrṣayā.
15.25 Pāṇḍavās tvaṃ ca rāṣṭraṃ ca sadā saṃrakṣyam eva hi.
tasmāt saṃhara divyaṃ tvam astram etan, mahā|bhuja.
a|roṣas tava c' âiv' âstu. Pārthāḥ santu nir|āmayāḥ.
na hy a|dharmeṇa rāja'|rṣiḥ Pāṇḍavo jetum icchati.
maṇiṃ c' âiva prayacch' âdya yas te śirasi tiṣṭhati.
etad ādāya te prāṇān pratidāsyanti Pāṇḍavāḥ.

in the grip of rage, I committed an act of evil, by launching this missile with hostility, ordering the slaughter of Pritha's sons."

VYASA replied:

Son, Pritha's son Árjuna, winner of spoils, had mastered the Brahma-head weapon, but didn't launch it in anger, nor to destroy you in combat. Rather Árjuna was aiming 15.20
to repel your missile with his on the battlefield when he released it, and he has now recalled it again. Since he had been granted the Brahma missile under your father's instruction, the powerfully built Árjuna, winner of spoils, did not transgress the warrior code. When he is so steadfast and so good, so well-versed in weaponry of every kind, how can you try to bring about his death and that of his brothers and kin? The god of rain refuses to release water for twelve years on a kingdom where the Brahma's head missile has been shot out of the sky by another ultimate missile. For this reason the powerfully built Pándava, though fully able to strike it out of the sky, would only proceed to do so with the higher aim of ensuring the safety of living beings.

The Pándavas, you and the kingdom can still be saved, so 15.25
call back the divine missile, great warrior. May you be free from anger, and may Pritha's sons be free from harm. For the royal seer of the Pándavas does not wish to be victorious through foul means. When you have done that, offer them the gem that sits upon your head. In return for taking it, the Pándavas will spare your life.

DRAUṆIR uvāca:

Pāṇḍavair yāni ratnāni, yac c' ânyat Kauravair dhanam
avāptam iha, tebhyo 'yaṃ maṇir mama viśiṣyate,
yam ābadhya bhayaṃ n' âsti śastra|vyādhi|kṣudh"|āśrayam
devebhyo dānavebhyo vā, nāgebhyo vā kathañ cana,
15.30 na ca rakṣo|gaṇa|bhayaṃ, na taskara|bhayaṃ tathā.
evaṃ|vīryo maṇir ayaṃ, na me tyājyaḥ kathaṃ cana.
yat tu me bhagavān āha, tan me kāryam an|antaram.
ayaṃ maṇir ayaṃ c' âham. Iṣīkā tu patiṣyati
garbheṣu Pāṇḍaveyānām, a|moghaṃ c' âitad uttamam.
na ca śakto 'smi, bhagavan, saṃhartuṃ punar udyatam.
etad astram ataś c' âiva garbheṣu visṛjāmy aham.
na ca vākyaṃ bhagavato na kariṣye, mahā|mune.

VYĀSA uvāca:

evaṃ kuru. na c' ânyā te buddhiḥ kāryā kadā cana.
garbheṣu Pāṇḍaveyānāṃ visṛjy' âitad, upārama!

VAIŚAMPĀYANA uvāca:

15.35 tataḥ paramam astraṃ tu Drauṇir udyatam āhave
Dvaipāyana|vacaḥ śrutvā garbheṣu pramumoca ha.

DRONA'S SON replied:

This gem here of mine is of greater worth than all the gems the Pándavas have acquired and any other spoils acquired by the Káuravas. For this gem gives total protection to its wearer against any risk from weapons, illness and
hunger, from gods, demons, and cobra-deities, from hosts 15.30
of goblins and from robbers. Such is the potency of this gem, that I should on no account relinquish it. Even so, I must carry out your behest immediately, lord. I surrender my gem here and I surrender myself. But this Seeker missile is set to strike the wombs of the Pándavas' women and this ultimate weapon unerringly hits its target. Lord, I can't call it back again, once launched. So I have directed this missile into their wombs and, great sage, I cannot refuse what your lordship has asked.

VYASA spoke:

Do it. It is the case that your mind can never be changed. But now that you have launched it into the wombs of the Pándava women, stand down!

VAISHAMPÁYANA continued:

Thereupon the son of Drona, heeding what Krishna of 15.35
the Island had said, directed that ultimate missile, launched in combat, into the women's wombs.

16–18
STRATEGIES REVEALED

VAIŚAMPĀYANA uvāca:

16.1 TAD ĀJÑĀYA Hṛṣīkeśo visṛṣṭaṃ pāpa|karmaṇā,
hṛṣyamāṇa idaṃ vākyaṃ Drauṇiṃ pratyabravīt tadā.
«Virāṭasya sutāṃ pūrvaṃ, snuṣāṃ Gāṇḍīva|dhanvanaḥ,
Upaplavya|gatāṃ dṛṣṭvā vratavān brāhmaṇo 'bravīt:
‹parikṣīṇeṣu Kuruṣu putras tava janiṣyati.
etad asya parikṣittvaṃ garbha|sthasya bhaviṣyati.›
tasya tad vacanaṃ sādhoḥ satyam etad bhaviṣyati.
Parikṣid bhavitā hy eṣāṃ punar vaṃśa|karaḥ sutaḥ.
16.5 evaṃ bruvāṇaṃ Govindaṃ Sātvatāṃ pravaraṃ tadā
Drauṇiḥ parama|saṃrabdhaḥ pratyuvāc' êdam uttaram:
«n' âitad evaṃ, yath" âttha tvaṃ pakṣa|pātena, Keśava,
vacanaṃ, puṇḍarīk'|âkṣa. na ca mad|vākyam anyathā.
patiṣyati tad astraṃ hi garbhe tasyā may" ôdyatam
Virāṭa|duhituḥ, Kṛṣṇa, yāṃ tvaṃ rakṣitum icchasi.»

ŚRĪ BHAGAVĀN uvāca:

a|moghaḥ param'|âstrasya pātas tasya bhaviṣyati.
sa tu garbho mṛto jāto dīrgham āyur avāpsyati.
tvāṃ tu kā|puruṣaṃ pāpaṃ viduḥ sarve manīṣiṇaḥ,
a|sakṛt pāpa|karmāṇaṃ, bāla|jīvita|ghātakam.
16.10 tasmāt tvam asya pāpasya karmaṇaḥ phalam āpnuhi.
trīṇi varṣa|sahasrāṇi cariṣyasi mahīm imām.
a|prāpnuvan kva cit kāñ cit saṃvidaṃ jātu kena cit,
nir|janān a|sahāyas tvaṃ deśān pravicariṣyasi.
bhavitrī na hi te, kṣudra, jana|madhyeṣu saṃsthitiḥ.

VAISHAMPÁYANA continued:

THEN KRISHNA, Lord of the Senses, watching the missile released by the evil-acting son of Drona, spoke exultantly to him in turn, with these words: 16.1

"When King Viráta's daughter,* the daughter-in-law of the bearer of the Gandíva bow, was in Upaplávya, a vow-keeping brahmin saw her and said: 'When the Kuru men are extensively wiped out, your son will be born. The one who lies in your womb will hold extensive sway.' The holy man's prediction will be fulfilled. For Paríkshit, the Extensive,* will survive, their scion holding sway once more.

While Krishna of the cowherds, the most eminent of the 16.5
Satvat tribe, was still saying this, Drona's son, flying into a passion, retorted with this reply: "Long-haired lord, it cannot be as you describe it, in your partiality, with your lotus eyes. My words will come true. Because, Krishna, that missile I launched will land in the womb of Viráta's daughter, whom you are trying to protect."

THE HOLY LORD spoke:

The flight of that ultimate missile will not miss its mark. Nonetheless, that still-born fetus will go on to live a lengthy life. You, on the other hand, will be known by all wise people as the evil man of evil deed who committed multiple infanticide.

Therefore you will harvest the fruit of this evil action. 16.10
For three thousand years you will wander this earth. You will wander from deserted place to place, never finding any comfort anywhere at any time by any means, never finding any companion. Reeking of pus and blood, consigned to

pūya|śoṇita|gandhī ca, durga|kāntāra|saṃśrayaḥ
vicariṣyasi pāp'|ātmā sarva|vyādhi|samanvitaḥ.
vayaḥ prāpya Parikṣit tu veda|vratam avāpya ca
Kṛpāc Chāradvatād śūraḥ sarv'|âstrāṇy upalapsyate.
viditvā param'|âstrāṇi kṣatra|dharma|vrate sthitaḥ,
16.15 ṣaṣṭiṃ varṣāṇi dharm'|ātmā vasu|dhāṃ pālayiṣyati.
itaś c' ōrdhvaṃ mahā|bāhuḥ Kuru|rājo bhaviṣyati
Parikṣin nāma nṛ|patir miṣatas te, su|dur|mate.
ahaṃ taṃ jīvayiṣyāmi dagdhaṃ śāstr'|âgni|tejasā.
paśya me tapaso vīryaṃ, satyasya ca, nar'|âdhama.

VYĀSA uvāca:

yasmād an|ādṛtya kṛtaṃ tvay' âsmān karma dāruṇam,
brāhmaṇasya sataś c' âiva yasmāt te vṛttam īdṛśam,
tasmād yad Devakī|putra uktavān uttamaṃ vacaḥ,
a|saṃśayaṃ te tad bhāvi. kṣatra|dharmas tvay" āśritaḥ.

AŚVATTHĀM" ôvāca:

sah" âiva bhavatā, brahman, sthāsyāmi puruṣeṣv iha.
satya|vāg astu bhagavān, ayaṃ ca puruṣ'|ôttamaḥ.

impenetrable wilderness, vile man, you will never be able to stay among people. Malevolent to the core, you will roam, plagued by every illness. Paríkshit, by contrast, will come of age and complete the undertaking of Vedic knowledge. He will be a champion, receiving all weaponry from Kripa, son of the sage Sharádvat.

He will acquire an understanding of the most sophisticated weaponry, and stand confident in his role as a warrior,
and righteous to the core, he will protect the bounteous 16.15
earth for sixty years. Thereafter, he will become the strong-armed king of the Kurus, the lord of men called Paríkshit, while you will look on helplessly, malicious man. Though he be burned, I shall restore him to life with the heat of the fire of scripture. See the vigor of my religious prowess and of the truth, vilest of men.

VYASA spoke:

Because of the atrocity you committed, your failure to respect us, and because you engaged in such behavior in spite of being a brahmin, what Krishna son of Dévaki has described will befall you, without doubt. You chose the career of a warrior.

ASHVA·TTHAMAN spoke:

I shall remain here among men with your excellency, brahmin. May these words of yours, Lord, and of this, the most exalted of men, come true.

VAIŚAMPĀYANA uvāca:

16.20 pradāy' âtha maṇim Drauṇiḥ
Pāṇḍavānāṃ mah"|ātmanām
jagāma vimanās, teṣāṃ
sarveṣāṃ paśyatāṃ, vanam.
Pāṇḍavāś c' âpi Govindaṃ puras|kṛtya hata|dviṣaḥ,
Kṛṣṇa|dvaipāyanaṃ c' âiva, Nāradaṃ ca mahā|munim,
Droṇa|putrasya saha|jaṃ maṇim ādāya, sa|tvarāḥ
Draupadīm abhyadhāvanta prāy'|ôpetāṃ manasvinīm.
tatas te puruṣa|vyāghrāḥ sad|aśvair anil'|ôpamaiḥ
abhyayuḥ saha|Dāśārhāḥ śibiraṃ punar eva ha.
avatīrya rathebhyas tu tvaramāṇā mahā|rathāḥ
dadṛśur Draupadīṃ Kṛṣṇām ārtām ārtatarāḥ svayam.
16.25 tām upetya nir|ānandāṃ, duḥkha|śoka|samanvitām,
parivārya vyatiṣṭhanta Pāṇḍavāḥ saha|Keśavāḥ.
tato rājñ" âbhyanujñāto Bhīmaseno mahā|balaḥ
pradadau tu maṇiṃ divyaṃ, vacanaṃ c' êdam abravīt:
«ayaṃ, bhadre, tava maṇiḥ. putra|hantā jitaḥ sa te.
uttiṣṭha śokam utsṛjya. kṣatra|dharmam anusmara.
prayāṇe Vāsudevasya śam'|ârtham, asit'|ēkṣaṇe,
yāny uktāni tvayā, bhīru, vākyāni Madhu|ghātinaḥ,
‹n' âiva me patayaḥ santi, na putrā, bhrātaro na ca,
na vai tvam iti, Govinda,› śamam icchati rājani
16.30 uktavaty asi tīvrāṇi vākyāni puruṣ'|ôttamam.
kṣatra|dharm'|ânurūpāṇi tāni saṃsmartum arhasi.
hato Duryodhanaḥ pāpo rājyasya paripanthikaḥ.

VAISHAMPÁYANA continued:

Drona's son bestowed his gem on the noble Pándavas, 16.20
then entered the wood, his spirit crushed, as they all looked on. Then the Pándavas, whose enemies were now all vanquished, paid honor to Krishna of the cowherds, Krishna of the island, and the great sage Nárada. They took the gem that Drona's son had been born with, then hastily rushed back to proud Dráupadi, who was fasting to the death. Then those tigers of men, on excellent horses swift as the wind, accompanied by Krishna of the Yadus, arrived again at the camp. The great chariot-warriors, dismounting from the chariots and rushing forward, saw the dark lady Dráupadi in torment, and were themselves tormented all the more.

Approaching the joyless woman who was overwhelmed 16.25
by anguish and grief, the Pándavas and Long-haired Krishna came to a stop in a circle around her. Then the broad-armed Bhima·sena, at the king's behest, presented the divine gem to her, and said these words: "Good lady, here is your gem. Your son's murderer is vanquished. Stand up, shrug off your grief. Be mindful of your duty as a warrior's wife. When Krishna, son of Vasu·deva, had set out 16.30
in pursuit of peace, dark-eyed lady, the words you, usually a timid woman, spoke to the slayer of Madhu when the king wanted to make peace, saying, 'I have no husbands, no sons, and no brothers any more, and not even you, Govínda,' were harsh words, and you addressed them to the highest of men. You should remember those words, fitting to the traditions of the warrior caste. Now the evil Duryódhana, dead set against our ruling, is dead himself. I drank

Duḥśāsanasya rudhiraṃ pītaṃ visphurato mayā.
vairasya gatam ānṛṇyaṃ. na sma vācyā vivakṣatām.
jitvā mukto Droṇa|putro brāhmaṇyād gauraveṇa ca.
yaśo 'sya patitaṃ, devi, śarīraṃ tv avaśeṣitam.
viyojitaś ca maṇinā, bhraṃśitaś c' āyudhaṃ bhuvi.»

DRAUPADY uvāca:

keval'|ānṛṇyam āpt" âsmi. guru|putro gurur mama.
śirasy etaṃ maṇiṃ rājā pratibadhnātu, Bhārata.
16.35 taṃ gṛhītvā tato rājā śirasy ev' âkarot tadā,
«guror ucchiṣṭam» ity eva, Draupadyā vacanād api.
tato divyaṃ maṇi|varaṃ śirasā dhārayan prabhuḥ
śuśubhe sa tadā rājā, sa|candra iva parvataḥ.
uttasthau putra|śok'|ārtā tataḥ Kṛṣṇā manasvinī.
Kṛṣṇaṃ c' âpi mahā|bāhuḥ paripapraccha dharma|rāṭ.

VAIŚAMPĀYANA uvāca:

17.1 HATEṢU SARVA|SAINYEṢU sauptike tai rathais tribhiḥ,
śocan Yudhiṣṭhiro rājā Dāśārham idam abravīt:
«kathaṃ nu, Kṛṣṇa, pāpena kṣudreṇ' â|kṛta|karmaṇā
Drauṇinā nihatāḥ sarve mama putrā mahā|rathāḥ,
tathā kṛt'|âstrā vikrāntāḥ sahasra|śata|yodhinaḥ
Drupadasy' ātmajāś c' âiva Droṇa|putreṇa pātitāḥ?
yasya Droṇo mah"|êṣv|āso

the blood of ill-counseled Duhshásana as he convulsed in the throes of death. The debt of enmity has been paid. We cannot be reproached by any seeking to fault us. When we overpowered Drona's son, we set him free because of his brahmin caste and out of respect for our teacher. But the glory has fallen from him, queen, and he has only his body now. He has been deprived of his gem and he has surrendered his weapon on the ground."

DRÁUPADI spoke:

I am avenged in full. The son of the teacher is as a teacher to me. May the king bind this gem upon his own head now, scion of Bhárata's line.

Then, at Dráupadi's request, the king Yudhi·shthira took 16.35
the gem and fastened it to his head, intoning "The sacred remains* of the teacher." At that, wearing the fabulous divine gem on his head, that powerful king shone like a mountain with the moon upon it. Whereupon the dark lady, afflicted by grief for her sons, but high-minded stood up, and the righteous, powerfully built king turned to question Krishna.

VAISHAMPÁYANA continued:

WITH ALL THE soldiers slain as they slept in the dead 17.1
of night by the three chariot-fighters, King Yudhi·shthira, in his grief, said this to Krishna, descendant of Dashárha: "Krishna, how is it that this vile and evil man, the son of Drona, who had never before achieved anything special, could kill all my sons, who were such established chariot-warriors? Not only them, but Drona's son also brought down a hundred thousand warriors, as well as the sons of

na prādād āhave mukham,
nijaghne rathinām śreṣṭhaṃ
Dhṛṣṭadyumnaṃ kathaṃ nu saḥ?
17.5 kiṃ nu tena kṛtaṃ karma tathā|yuktaṃ, nara'|rṣabha,
yad ekaḥ samare sarvān avadhīn no guroḥ sutaḥ?

VĀSUDEVA uvāca:

«nūnaṃ sa deva|devānām īśvar'|ēśvaram a|vyayam
jagāma śaraṇaṃ Drauṇir. ekas ten' âvadhīd bahūn.
prasanno hi Mahādevo dadyād amaratām api,
vīryaṃ ca Giriśo dadyād, yen' Êndram api śātayet.
ved' âhaṃ hi Mahādevaṃ tattvena, Bharata'|rṣabha,
yāni c' âsya purāṇāni karmāṇi vividhāny uta.
ādir eṣa hi bhūtānāṃ, madhyam, antaś ca, Bhārata.
viceṣṭate jagac c' êdaṃ sarvam asy' âiva karmaṇā.
17.10 evaṃ sisṛkṣur bhūtāni dadarśa prathamaṃ vibhuḥ
Pitāmaho, 'bravīc c' âinaṃ, «bhūtāni sṛja mā|ciram.»
hari|keśas «tath"» êty uktvā bhūtānāṃ doṣa|darśivān
dīrgha|kālaṃ tapas tepe, magno 'mbhasi mahā|tapāḥ.
su|mahāntaṃ tataḥ kālaṃ pratīkṣy' âinaṃ Pitāmahaḥ
sraṣṭāraṃ sarva|bhūtānāṃ sasarja manasā param.
so 'bravīt pitaraṃ, dṛṣṭvā Giriśaṃ magnam ambhasi,
«yadi me n' âgra|jo 'sty anyas, tataḥ srakṣyāmy ahaṃ prajāḥ.»
tam abravīt pitā, «n' âsti tvad anyaḥ puruṣo 'gra|jaḥ.
Sthāṇur eṣa jale magno. visrabdhaḥ kuru vai kṛtim!»

Drúpada, all skilled in missiles and brave. How could the one whom Drona would not allow to lead the van in battle, slay Dhrishta·dyumna, who was the best of chariot-warriors? What prior action had the son performed so to 17.5
the purpose, bull among men, that he could slay them all in single-handed combat?

KRISHNA SON OF VASU·DEVA replied:

"Surely Drona's son took refuge in the unchanging Lord of lords, the God of gods. That is how he could kill so many on his own. When he's propitiated the Great God can grant immortality itself. The Mountain-dweller could grant enough strength even to overthrow Indra. I recognize the Great God as he truly is, bull of Bhárata, and his former feats which are manifold. He is the beginning of all beings, their middle and culmination, son of Bhárata's line. In fact this entire realm of creatures functions through the work of him alone.

So it was that the powerful Grandfather Brahma, de- 17.10
siring to create creatures, saw that first being* and said to him, "Create living creatures ere long," and the yellow-haired lord at first consented, but then saw the failings of living creatures and practiced asceticism for a very long time, plunged in water, steeped deep in ascetic prowess. Then, giving up looking to him after almost an eternity, the Grandfather used his mind to create another, the supreme Creator of all creatures. Seeing the Mountain-dweller plunged in water, this latter said to his father, "If there is no other born ahead of me, then I shall create living beings born after me."* His father replied to him, "There is

17.15 bhūtāny anvasṛjat sapta Dakṣ'|ādīṃs tu prajā|patīn,
yair imaṃ vyakarot sarvaṃ bhūta|grāmaṃ catur|vidham.
tāḥ sṛṣṭa|mātrāḥ kṣudhitāḥ prajāḥ sarvāḥ Prajāpatim
bibhakṣayiṣavo, rājan, sahasā prādravaṃs tadā.
sa bhakṣyamāṇas trāṇ'|ârthī Pitāmaham upādravat.
«ābhyo māṃ Bhagavāṃs trātu. vṛttir āsāṃ vidhīyatām.»
tatas tābhyo dadāv annam, oṣadhīḥ sthāvarāṇi ca,
jaṅgamāni ca bhūtāni dur|balāni balīyasām.
vihit'|ânnāḥ prajās tās tu jagmuḥ sṛṣṭā yath"|āgatam.
tato vavṛdhire, rājan, prītimatyaḥ sva|yoniṣu.
17.20 bhūta|grāme vivṛddhe tu, tuṣṭe loka|gurāv api,
udatiṣṭhaj jalāj jyeṣṭhaḥ, prajāś c' êmā dadarśa saḥ,
bahu|rūpāḥ prajāḥ sṛṣṭā vivṛddhāś ca sva|tejasā.
cukrodha bhagavān Rudro, liṅgaṃ svaṃ c' âpy avidhyata.
tat praviddhaṃ tathā bhūmau tath" âiva pratyatiṣṭhata.
tam uvāc' â|vyayo Brahmā vacobhiḥ śamayann iva,
«kiṃ kṛtaṃ salile, Śarva, cira|kālaṃ sthitena te?
kim|arthaṃ c' âitad utpāṭya† liṅgaṃ bhūmau praveśitam?»
so 'bravīj jāta|saṃrambhas tathā loka|gurur gurum:
«prajāḥ sṛṣṭā pareṇ' êmāḥ. kiṃ kariṣyāmy anena vai?

no other man born ahead of you. This Immovable* person here is plunged in water. Go ahead and perform your creation with confidence!"

Now he produced seven living beings, that is, the Lords 17.15
of Creation beginning with Daksha the Adroit. With them he made this entire community of beings, of four types. No sooner than those beings were made they felt hunger and, the Lord of Creation arousing and tempting their appetites, they all at once attacked him, Your Majesty. As he was being eaten, he rushed to the Grandfather, in the hope of being saved. "May my Bountiful father protect me from these creatures. Please provide a means of subsistence for them." At that the latter provided them with food, the living plants that do not move, and the living creatures that do, the weaker for the stronger. Provided meanwhile with food the creatures he had created returned whence they had come. After which, Your Majesty, they delighted in procreating further in their own wombs.

Now when the assemblage of beings had increased in 17.20
number, and the forefather of the world was satisfied, the eldest stood up from the water and saw them, the many kinds of creatures that had been created and prospered through their own productivity. The wrathful lord became angry and tore off his own organ of generation, the *linga*.* He hurled it down in front of them and it became stuck in the ground like that. The everlasting Brahma, intending to soothe him with his words, said to him, "What have you, stood still so long in the flowing waters, to show for it? To what end have you torn out your *linga* and implanted it in the ground?" Full of rage the progenitor of the world spoke

17.25 tapas" âdhigatam̧ c' ânnam̧ praj"|ārtham̧ me, pitā|maha,
oṣadhyaḥ parivarteran yath" âiva satatam̧ prajāḥ,»
evam uktvā tu sam̧kruddho jagāma vimanā Bhavaḥ
girer muñjavataḥ pādam̧ tapas taptum̧ mahā|tapāḥ.

ŚRĪ BHAGAVĀN uvāca:

18.1 TATO DEVA|YUGE 'tīte devā vai samakalpayan
yajñam̧ veda|pramāṇena vidhivad yaṣṭum īpsavaḥ.
kalpayām āsur atha te sādhanāni havīm̧ṣi ca,
bhāg'|ârhā devatāś c' âiva, yajñiyam̧ dravyam eva ca.
tā vai Rudram a|jānantyo yāthātathyena devatāḥ,
n' âkalpayanta devasya Sthāṇor bhāgam̧, nar'|âdhipa.
so '|kalpyamāne bhāge tu kṛtti|vāsā makhe '|maraiḥ
tataḥ sādhanam anvicchan dhanur ādau sasarja ha.
18.5 loka|yajñaḥ, kriyā|yajño, gṛha|yajñaḥ sanātanaḥ,
pañca|bhūta|nṛ|yajñaś ca. yajñe sarvam idam̧ jagat.
loka|yajñair nṛ|yajñaiś ca Kapardī vidadhe dhanuḥ.
dhanuḥ sṛṣṭam abhūt tasya pañca|kiṣku|pramāṇataḥ.
vaṣaṭ|kāro 'bhavaj jyā tu dhanuṣas tasya, Bhārata,
yajñ'|âṅgāni ca catvāri tasya sam̧nahane 'bhavan.
tataḥ kruddho Mahādevas tad upādāya kārmukam
ājagām' âtha tatr' âiva, yatra devāḥ samījire.

these words to his progenitor: "These beings have been created by someone else, so what use is it to me now?

Moreover, grandfather, these creatures can replace for- 17.25
ever with plants the food I acquired for them through my religious austerity." With these words the incensed lord of life withdrew, offended, to his base on the mountain where the sacred *munja* reed thrives, to continue practicing asceticism, steeped deep in ascetic prowess.

THE HOLY LORD KRISHNA continued:

AT A LATER POINT, when the age of the gods had past, 18.1
the gods were deliberating together. They wanted to perform a sacrifice correctly according to the authority of the Vedas. Now they were deciding on the preparatory implements and the oblations, as well as on which divinities deserved a share and what the sacrificial object should be. But, sovereign, those deities, having no accurate knowledge of the wrathful Rudra, failed to allocate a share to the Immovable Lord. So then, when the allocation of the sacrifice was being apportioned by the immortals, the hide-clad lord, in his desire for a preparatory implement, first created a bow.

There is the universal sacrifice, the performance of occa- 18.5
sional rites, the constant performance of the daily household rites, and the offering that man makes on the basis of the five elements.* This entire universe relies on such sacrifice. The Lord with matted locks fashioned his bow using the acts of devotion to the world and the offerings man makes. The bow he created measured five spans.* The string of that bow became the mantra "*Vashat!*" that announces

tam āttaǀkārmukaṃ dṛṣṭvā brahmaǀcāriṇam aǀvyayam,
vivyathe pṛthivī devī, parvatāś ca cakampire
18.10 na vavau pavanaś c' âiva, n' âgnir jajvāla c' âidhitaḥ.
vyabhramac c' âpi saṃvignaṃ divi nakṣatraǀmaṇḍalam.
na babhau bhāskaraś c' âpi, somaḥ śrīǀmuktaǀmaṇḍalaḥ.
timireṇ' ākulaṃ sarvam ākāśaṃ c' âbhavad vṛtam.
abhibhūtās tato devā viṣayān na prajajñire.
na pratyabhāc ca yajñaḥ sa; devatās tresire tathā.
tataḥ sa yajñaṃ vivyādha raudreṇa hṛdi patriṇā.
apakrāntas tato yajño mṛgo bhūtvā saǀpāvakaḥ.†
sa tu ten' âiva rūpeṇa divaṃ prāpya vyarājata,
anvīyamāno Rudreṇa, Yudhiṣṭhira, nabhastale.
18.15 apakrānte tato yajñe saṃjñā na pratyabhāt surān.
naṣṭaǀsaṃjñeṣu deveṣu na prajñāyata kiṃ cana.
tryǀambakaḥ Savitur bāhū, Bhagasya nayane tathā,
Pūṣṇaś ca daśanān kruddho dhanuṣǀkoṭyā vyaśātayat.
prādravanta tato devā yajñ'ǀâṅgāni ca sarvaśaḥ.
ke cit tatr' âiva ghūrṇanto gat'ǀâsava iv' âbhavan.
sa tu vidrāvya tat sarvaṃ śitiǀkaṇṭho, 'vahasya ca,
avaṣṭabhya dhanuṣǀkoṭiṃ rurodha vibudhāṃs tataḥ.
tato vāg amarair uktā jyāṃ tasya dhanuṣo 'cchinat.
atha tat sahasā, rājaṃś, chinnaǀjyaṃ visphurad dhanuḥ

the oblation, king of Bhárata's line, while the four components of sacrifice were its fastenings at either end. Then the Great God, in his rage, took up the wooden bow and came to the site where the gods were performing the sacrifice. Seeing him, the unwavering celibate, with bow drawn, the goddess earth shuddered and the mountains quaked.

The purifying wind ceased to blow and the kindled fire 18.10
went out. The entire array of stars in the firmament reeled, shaken out of place. The radiant sun went black and the luster of the moon's orb vanished. The skies were completely concealed in darkness. At that the gods were overcome, their senses confused. In the gods' terror, the sacrifice was forgotten. Then he shot the sacrifice with a savage arrow through the heart. The sacrifice, now become a deer, then fled taking the fire with him. In that form he reached up to heaven, and shone brilliantly, Yudhi·shthira, as fierce Shiva pursued him along the surface of the sky.

At that point, with the sacrifice fled, the gods had lost 18.15
all perception. With their senses blinded, they could make out nothing. The three-eyed god, incensed, using the end of his bow, smashed the arms of Savítri the sun-god, the eyes of Bhaga, attendant god of dawn and the teeth of Pushan, conveyor of light.* At that the gods and the constituents of the sacrifice fled in all directions, while some stood trembling where they were, as if their vital breath had already forsaken them. Now once he had driven the entire world into a corner, the dark-throated god mocked them all, and, leaning on the tip of his bow, he blockaded the gods. The things the immortals said at this broke the string of his bow and then, its string snapping, the bow shuddered violently.

18.20 tato vidhanuṣaṃ devā deva|śreṣṭham upāgaman
śaraṇaṃ saha yajñena, prasādaṃ c' âkarot prabhuḥ.
tataḥ prasanno Bhagavān sthāpya kopaṃ jal'|āśaye.
sa jalaṃ pāvako bhūtvā śoṣayaty a|niśaṃ, prabho.
Bhagasya nayane c' âiva, bāhū ca Savitus tathā,
prādāt Pūṣṇaś ca daśanān, punar yajñāṃś ca, Pāṇḍava.
tataḥ su|stham idaṃ sarvaṃ babhūva† punar eva hi,
sarvāṇi ca havīṃṣy asya devā bhāgam akalpayan.
tasmin kruddhe 'bhavat sarvam
a|susthaṃ bhuvanaṃ, vibho,
prasanne ca punaḥ susthaṃ.
sa prasanno 'sya vīryavān.
18.25 tatas te nihatāḥ sarve tava putrā mahā|rathāḥ,
anye ca bahavaḥ śūrāḥ, Pāñcālāś ca sah'|ānugāḥ.
na tan manasi kartavyaṃ, na hi tad Drauṇinā kṛtam.
Mahādeva|prasādena kuru kāryam anantaram.

So the gods, together with the sacrifice, sought refuge 18.20
in the bowless best of gods, and the powerful lord was appeased. Then, in his appeased state, the Bountiful Lord stowed his anger in the water-cradling ocean, where, transformed into fire, it continues to drink away the water incessantly, lord.*

Now to Bhaga he restored his eyes, to Savítri his arms, and to Pushan his teeth and sacrifices, son of Pandu. That done, harmony reined throughout all the world once more, and the gods always remember to allocate the oblations and a share of the sacrifice to him. If he is ever angered, then the entire world is in trouble, lord, but once he is propitiated all is well again. Ashva·tthaman propitiated that potent god and won his favor.

That is how he managed to kill all your sons, even though 18.25
they were great chariot-warriors, as well as the many other champions, the Panchálas and their followers. You must not dwell on it, for it was not Drona's son that did it. With the Great God's good will, you must move on to the next task before you.

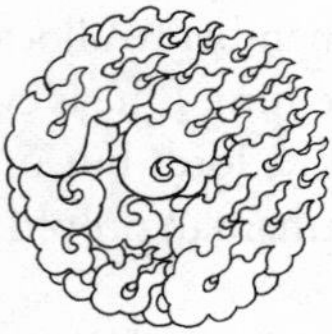

MAHA·BHÁRATA

BOOK ELEVEN

THE WOMEN

Nārāyaṇaṃ namas|kṛtya
Naraṃ c' âiva nar'|ôttamam,
devīṃ Sarasvatīṃ c' âiva,
tato jayam udīrayet.

Honor Naráyana, most exalted Nara,
and blessed Sarásvati, and spur on "Victory!"

1–9

COUNSELING THE INEFFECTUAL KING

JANAMEJAYA uvāca:

1.1 HATE DURYODHANE c' âiva, hate sainye ca sarvaśaḥ,
Dhṛtarāṣṭro mahā|rājaḥ śrutvā kim akaron, mune?
tath" âiva Kauravo rājā Dharma|putro mahā|manāḥ,
Kṛpa|prabhṛtayaś c' âiva—kim akurvata te trayaḥ?
Aśvatthāmnaḥ śrutaṃ karma. śāpād anyonya|kāritāt
vṛttāntam uttaraṃ brūhi, yad abhāṣata Sañjayaḥ.

VAIŚAṂPĀYANA uvāca:

hate putra|śate dīnaṃ, chinna|śākham iva drumam,
putra|śok'|âbhisaṃtaptaṃ Dhṛtarāṣṭraṃ mahī|patim
1.5 dhyāna|mūkatvam āpannaṃ, cintayā samabhiplutam
abhigamya, mahā|rāja, Saṃjayo vākyam abravīt.
«kiṃ śocasi, mahā|rāja? n' âsti śoke sahāyatā.
akṣauhiṇyo hatāś c' âṣṭau daśa c' âiva, viśāṃ pate.
nirjan" êyaṃ vasumatī, śūnyā saṃprati, kevalā.
nānā|digbhyaḥ samāgamya nānā|deśyā nar'|âdhipāḥ
sah" âiva tava putreṇa sarve vai nidhanaṃ gatāḥ.
pitṝṇāṃ, putra|pautrāṇāṃ, jñātīnāṃ, suhṛdāṃ tathā,
gurūṇāṃ c' ânupūrvyeṇa preta|kāryāṇi kāraya.»

JANAM·ÉJAYA spoke:

WHEN THE GREAT regent Dhrita·rashtra heard first 1.1
that Duryódhana and then that all the soldiers in his army had been murdered, what did he do, sage? What about Yudhi·shthira, the high-minded son of Dharma, now king of the Káuravas, and the group of three led by Kripa, what did they do? We have heard the account of what Ashva·tthaman did. Continue with what happened next, after Ashva·tthaman and the Pándavas had placed those curses on each other, just as Sánjaya told it.

VAISHAMPÁYANA continued:

Dhrita·rashtra, lord of the world, with his hundred sons slain was like a tree shorn of all branches. He was engulfed
by grief for his sons. As he remained stupefied in trance, 1.5
drowning in his own thoughts, Sánjaya approached him, Your Majesty, and addressed him with these words:

"Why succumb to grief, great king? Grieving won't help the situation. The eighteen divisions of your army have all been killed, lord of all peoples. This wealth-begetting earth has been robbed of her people, and now lies completely barren. The rulers of men from every direction, from every region, after joining forces with your son, have all been annihilated, to a man. You must arrange for their funeral rites to be performed, each in turn, be they fathers, sons or grandsons, relatives, friends or teachers."

VAIŚAMPĀYANA uvāca:

tac chrutvā karuṇaṃ vākyaṃ, putra|pautra|vadh'|ârditaḥ
papāta bhuvi, dur|dharṣo vāt'|āhata iva drumaḥ.

DHṚTARĀṢTRA uvāca:

1.10 hata|putro, hat'|āmātyo, hata|sarva|suhṛj|janaḥ.
duḥkhaṃ nūnaṃ bhaviṣyāmi vicaran pṛthivīm imām.
kiṃ nu bandhu|vihīnasya jīvitena mam' âdya vai,
lūna|pakṣasya iva me jarā|jīrṇasya pakṣiṇaḥ?
hṛta|rājyo, hata|bandhur, hata|cakṣuś ca vai tathā,
na bhrājiṣye, mahā|prājña, kṣīṇa|raśmir iv' âṃśumān.
na kṛtaṃ suhṛdāṃ vākyaṃ, Jāmadagnyasya jalpataḥ,
Nāradasya ca deva'|rṣeḥ, Kṛṣṇa|dvaipāyanasya ca.
sabhā|madhye tu Kṛṣṇena yac chreyo 'bhihitaṃ mama,
«alaṃ vaireṇa te, rājan. putraḥ saṃgṛhyatām» iti,
1.15 tac ca vākyam a|kṛtv" âhaṃ bhṛśaṃ tapyāmi dur|matiḥ,
na hi śrot" âsmi Bhīṣmasya dharma|yuktaṃ prabhāṣitam.
Duryodhanasya ca tathā. vṛṣabhasy' êva nardataḥ.
Duḥśāsana|vadhaṃ śrutvā, Karṇasya ca viparyayam.
Droṇa|sūry'|ôparāgaṃ ca, hṛdayaṃ me vidīryate.
na smarāmy ātmanaḥ kiṃ cit purā, Sañjaya, duṣ|kṛtam,
yasy' êdaṃ phalam ady' êha mayā mūḍhena bhujyate.
nūnaṃ vyapakṛtaṃ kiṃ cin mayā pūrveṣu janmasu
yena māṃ duḥkha|bhāgeṣu dhātā karmasu yuktavān.

VAISHAMPÁYANA continued:

When he heard those woeful words, already devastated by the slaughter of his sons and their sons in turn, Dhrita·rashtra toppled to the ground, like a tree of unassailable strength brought down in a hurricane.

DHRITA·RASHTRA spoke:

Killed are my sons, my ministers, and all those dear to 1.10
my heart. Surely I shall forever wander this earth in misery.
What purpose has my life, now stripped of all my relatives?
It is as worthless as that of a bird, shabby with age, shorn of
its wings. Robbed of my kingdom, my relatives wiped out,
my eyes rubbed out, I have as little hope of shining again,
my adviser steeped in wisdom, as the sun shorn of its rays.
I ignored the advice of my friends, of Jamad·agni's son, of
the divine seer Nárada and of Krishna of the island, when
they warned me. Even when Krishna counseled me to the
best course of action when, in the midst of the assembly,
he said, "Stop this antagonism, Your Majesty. Restrain your
son." I failed to act on that counsel, and now I am eaten 1.15
away by crippling remorse, my heart broken, because I was
not prepared to hear Bhishma's warning, so full of truth.
But now I have heard of the killing of my son Duhshásana,
of the catastrophe that befell Karna, and of the eclipse of
Drona, our radiant sun, for all Duryódhana's bellowing like
a bull, and my heart is rent apart.

Sánjaya, I do not recall any earlier misdeed of mine so great, that it could warrant me suffering such a disastrous outcome now, which leaves me so bewildered. Surely I did some dreadful things in former lives, to justify Fate allotting

pariṇāmaś ca vayasaḥ, sarva|bandhu|kṣayaś ca me,
1.20 suhṛn|mitra|vināśaś ca daiva|yogād upāgataḥ.
ko 'nyo 'sti duḥkhitataro matto 'nyo hi pumān bhuvi?
tan mām ady' âiva paśyantu Pāṇḍavāḥ saṃśita|vratam,
vivṛtaṃ Brahma|lokasya dīrgham adhvānam āsthitam.

VAIŚAMPĀYANA uvāca:

tasya lālapyamānasya, bahu|śokaṃ vitanvataḥ,
śok'|âpahaṃ nar'|êndrasya Sañjayo vākyam abravīt.
«śokaṃ, rājan, vyapanuda. śrutās te veda|niścayāḥ
śāstr'|āgamāś ca vividhā vṛddhebhyo, nṛpa|sattama,
Sṛñjaye putra|śok'|ārte yad ūcur munayaḥ purā.
yathā yauvana|jaṃ darpam āsthite te sute, nṛpa,
1.25 na tvayā suhṛdāṃ vākyaṃ bruvatām avadhāritam,
sv'|ârthaś ca na kṛtaḥ kaś cil lubdhena, phala|gṛddhinā.
asin" âiv' âika|dhāreṇa sva|buddhyā tu viceṣṭitam.
prāyaśo '|vṛtta|saṃpannāḥ satataṃ paryupāsitāḥ.
yasya Duḥśāsano mantrī Rādheyaś ca durātmavān,
Śakuniś c' âiva duṣṭ'|ātmā, Citrasenaś ca dur|matiḥ,
Śalyaś ca yena vai sarvaṃ śalya|bhūtaṃ kṛtaṃ jagat.
Kuru|vṛddhasya Bhīṣmasya, Gāndhāryā, Vidurasya ca,
Droṇasya ca, mahā|rāja, Kṛpasya ca Śaradvataḥ,
Kṛṣṇasya ca, mahā|bāho, Nāradasya ca dhīmataḥ,
1.30 ṛṣīṇāṃ ca tath" ânyeṣāṃ, Vyāsasy' â|mita|tejasaḥ

me to such hapless endeavors. My decline into old age, the
loss of all my relatives, the annihilation of my friends and 1.20
allies, are all the working of divine Fate. Is there any other man on earth more wretched than I? So let the Pándavas watch me right now, my resolve made, publicly taking the long road to the realm of God.*

VAISHAMPÁYANA continued:

As he continued to ramble, overwrought with the grief of so much loss, Sánjaya spoke to him, seeking to rouse the leader of men from his grief. "Put away your grief, Your Majesty. You have heard the determinations of the Veda and the different traditions of lore from the elders, most excellent of kings, and you have heard what the sages said to Srínjaya before, when he was overcome with grief for his son. Protector of men, when your son relied on an arrogance born of youth, you paid no attention to what your 1.25
friends were trying to tell you, and you declined to do anything actually to your own advantage, so greedy were you, so preoccupied by profit.

Instead you pursued your own whim, as inflexible as a knife made for a single job. Generally those surrounding your son have always been people of bad conduct. With Duhshásana the Ill-counseled as his advisor, along with the ignoble son of Radha, the corrupt Shákuni, malevolent Chitra·sena and Shalya the Spear, he turned the entire world into a spear leveled against him. To the advice of Bhishma, most senior of the Kurus, of Gandhári and of Vídura the Wise, of Drona, Your High Majesty, and to that

na kṛtaṃ vacanaṃ tena tava putreṇa, Bhārata.
na dharmaḥ sat|kṛtaḥ kaś cin nityaṃ yuddham abhīpsatā.
alpa|buddhir, ahaṃkārī, nityaṃ yuddhaṃ iti bruvan,
krūro, dur|marṣaṇo, nityam a|saṃtuṣṭaś ca, vīryavān.
śrutavān asi, medhāvī, satyavāṃś c' âiva nityadā.
na muhyant' īdṛśāḥ santo buddhimanto bhavādṛśāḥ.
na dharmaḥ sat|kṛtaḥ kaś cit tava putreṇa, māriṣa.
kṣapitāḥ kṣatriyāḥ sarve, śatrūṇāṃ vardhitaṃ yaśaḥ.
madhya|stho hi tvam apy āsīr, na kṣamaṃ kiṃ cid uktavān.
dur|dhareṇa tvayā bhāras tulayā na samaṃ dhṛtaḥ.

1.35 ādāv eva manuṣyeṇa vartitavyaṃ yathā kṣamam,
yathā n' ātītam arthaṃ vai paścāt|tāpena yujyate.
putra|gṛddhyā tvayā, rājan, priyaṃ tasya cikīrṣatā
paścāt|tāpam idaṃ prāptaṃ. na tvaṃ śocitum arhasi.
madhu yaḥ kevalaṃ dṛṣṭvā prapātaṃ n' ânupaśyati,
sa bhraṣṭo madhu|lobhena śocaty eva yathā bhavān.
arthān na śocan prāpnoti. na śocan vindate phalam.
na śocañ śriyam āpnoti. na śocan vindate param.

svayam utpādayitv" âgniṃ, vastreṇa pariveṣṭayan,
dahyamāno manas|tāpaṃ bhajate—na sa paṇḍitaḥ.
1.40 tvay" âiva sa|suten' âyaṃ vākya|vāyu|samīritaḥ
lobh'|ājyena ca saṃsikto jvalitaḥ Pārtha|pāvakaḥ.

of Kripa of the Sharádvata clan, that of the powerful Krishna and of Nárada the prudent, to that of Vyasa of im- 1.30
measurable splendor and of all the other sages, your son paid no heed, king of Bhárata's line. Not once did he honor his lawful duty, so set was he on war. Short-sighted and egotistical, he constantly clamored for it. Valiant as he was, he was also cruel, delinquent and always discontented. You are learned, intelligent and honest at all times. People like that, possessed of understanding as you are, always know the score. Not once did your son honor his lawful duty, noble friend. He has wrought destruction on all the warriors and enhanced the glory of your enemies. And through it all you stayed neutral, never speaking out as you should have. You never weighed their responsibility fairly, being reluctant to shoulder your own.

All men should from the outset behave correctly, so that 1.35
no past business ever warrants remorse. In favoring your son, Your Majesty, in your eagerness to please him, you brought this remorse upon yourself. You have no right to grieve. You are like the man who saw only the honey without paying attention to the drop. When finally he falls, he starts complaining, though it was his own greed for honey that pushed him. Not in grief does man achieve his goals. Not in grief does he find reward. Not in grief does he win glory. Not in grief does he find the higher realm.

A man kindles a fire and wraps it inside his clothes, then when he gets burned he indulges in remorse. He's no sage. Your sons have fallen like moths into the blaze you kindled. 1.40
When they are consumed by the fire of falling arrows, you

tasmin samiddhe patitāḥ śalabhā iva te sutāḥ.
tān vai śar' âgni|nirdagdhān na tvaṃ śocitum arhasi.
yac c' âśru|pātāt kalilaṃ vadanaṃ vahase, nṛpa,
a|śāstra|dṛṣṭam etadd hi na praśaṃsanti paṇḍitāḥ.
visphuliṅgā iva hy etān dahanti kila mānavān.
jahīhi manyuṃ buddhyā vai; dhāray' ātmānam ātmanā.»

VAIŚAMPĀYANA uvāca:

evam āśvāsitas tena Sañjayena mah"|ātmanā,
Viduro bhūya ev' āha buddhi|pūrvaṃ, paraṃ|tapa.

VAIŚAṂPĀYANA uvāca:

2.1 TATO 'MṚTA|SAMAIR vākyair hlādayan puruṣa'|rṣabham
Vaicitravīryaṃ Viduro yad uvāca, nibodha tat.

VIDURA uvāca:

uttiṣṭha, rājan. kiṃ śeṣe? dhāray' ātmānam ātmanā.
eṣā vai sarva|sattvānāṃ, lok'|ēśvara, parā gatiḥ:
sarve kṣay'|ântā nicayāḥ. patan'|ântāḥ samucchrayāḥ.
saṃyogā viprayog'|ântā. maraṇ'|ântaṃ ca jīvitam.

yadā śūraṃ ca bhīruṃ ca Yamaḥ karṣati, Bhārata,
tat kiṃ na yotsyanti hi te kṣatriyāḥ, kṣatriya'|rṣabha?

have no right to grieve. It is you and your son who are responsible for setting ablaze the raging sons of Pritha, fed by the wind of your words, doused in the incendiary of your greed. The face you wear wet from the falling of your tears, protector of men, is not recognized in the law books. Wise men give it no credit. For those tears are known to burn men as badly as sparks from a fire. Use this insight to cast aside your indignation and pull yourself together."

VAISHAMPÁYANA continued:

So it was that noble-souled Sánjaya brought the king to his senses. Then Vídura once again spoke words prompted by wisdom, torment of your enemies.

VAISHAMPÁYANA continued:

NOW PAY HEED to what Vídura said to Dhrita·rashtra, 2.1
son to Vichítra·virya, heartening that bull of a man with his nectar-like words.

VÍDURA said:

Stand up, Your Majesty. Why are you lying there? Pull yourself together. After all, the same final destiny awaits all living beings, lord of the world:

All that is assembled ends in disintegration. All that is raised on high ends up falling.
All that is joined ends in separation. And all that lives ends up dying.

The god of death drags each away, whether hero or coward, king of Bhárata's line, so why would men of the warrior class not fight, bull of that same class?

2.5 a|yudhyamāno mriyate, yudhyamānaś ca jīvati.
kālaṃ prāpya, mahā|rāja, na kaś cid ativartate.
a|bhāv'|ādīni bhūtāni, bhāva|madhyāni, Bhārata,
a|bhāva|nidhanāny eva. tatra kā paridevanā?
na śocan mṛtam anveti.† na śocan mriyate naraḥ.
evaṃ sāṃsiddhike loke kim|artham anuśocasi?
kālaḥ karṣati bhūtāni sarvāṇi vividhāny uta.
na kālasya priyaḥ kaś cin, na dveṣyaḥ, Kuru|sattama.
yathā vāyus tṛṇ'|âgrāṇi saṃvartayati sarvaśaḥ,
tathā kāla|vaśaṃ yānti bhūtāni, Bharata'|rṣabha.
2.10 eka|sārtha|prayātānāṃ sarveṣāṃ tatra gāminām
yasya kālaḥ prayāty agre, tatra kā paridevanā?
na c' âpy etān hatān yuddhe, rājañ, śocitum arhasi:
pramāṇaṃ yadi śāstrāṇi, gatās te paramāṃ gatim.
sarve svādhyāyavanto hi, sarve ca carita|vratāḥ,
sarve c' âbhimukhāḥ kṣīṇās. tatra kā paridevanā?
a|darśanād āpatitāḥ, punaś c' â|darśanaṃ gatāḥ.
n' âite tava, na teṣāṃ tvaṃ. tatra kā paridevanā?
hato 'pi labhate svargaṃ, hatvā ca labhate yaśaḥ.
ubhayaṃ no bahu|guṇaṃ. n' âsti niṣphalatā raṇe
2.15 teṣāṃ kāma|dughāl̄ lokān Indraḥ saṃkalpayiṣyati.
Indrasy' âtithayo hy ete bhavanti, puruṣa'|rṣabha.
na yajñair dakṣiṇāvadbhir, na tapobhir, na vidyayā
svargaṃ yānti tathā martyā, yathā śūrā raṇe hatāḥ.
śarīr'|âgniṣu śūrāṇāṃ juhuvus te śar'|āhutī,

Someone who doesn't fight still might die, while one who 2.5
fights might live. But once their time is up no one survives, Your Majesty. Beings begin in non-being. For the duration they have being. They culminate in non-being again. What is sad in that? Not by grieving does a man escort the dead. Not by grieving does he die. When the world is made this way, what purpose does sadness serve? Time drags away all beings of whatever kind. Time neither favors nor picks on anyone, most virtuous of Kurus. Just as the wind buffets the blades of grass twisting them this way and that, so living beings fall under the sway of Time, bull of Bhárata's line.

When all beings progress as a single caravan, traveling 2.10
along, why lament the one among them whom death meets first? Moreover you should not grieve for those who have been slain in this battle, Your Majesty, when, if the scriptures have authority, those men have reached the highest goal. For they had all completed their training. They had all fulfilled their vows, and they all died in action. What is sad in that? From beyond the visible realm they arrived and back to beyond the visible they have returned again. They do not belong to you, nor you to them. What is sad in that? The one who is killed attains heaven, while the one who kills attains glory. Both of these we value highly. So battle is never in vain.

Indra intends for them the worlds of the wish-fulfilling 2.15
cow. For now, bull of men, they are Indra's guests. The surest way for mortals to enter heaven is not through gift-laden sacrifice, nor through austerities, nor through learning, but as heroes slain in combat. They have performed their sacrifices by pouring arrows as oblations into the heroes

hūyamānāñ śarāṃś c' âiva sehus tejasvino mithaḥ.
evaṃ, rājaṃs, tav' ācakṣe svargyaṃ panthānam uttamam.
na yuddhād adhikaṃ kiñ cit kṣatriyasy' êha vidyate.
kṣatriyās te mah"|ātmānaḥ,† śūrāḥ, samiti|śobhanāḥ,
āśiṣaḥ paramāḥ prāptā; na śocyāḥ sarva eva hi.
2.20 ātmānam ātman" āśvāsya mā śucuḥ, puruṣa'|rṣabha.
n' âdya śok'|âbhibhūtas tvaṃ kāyam utsraṣṭum arhasi.
mātā|pitṛ|sahasrāṇi putra|dāra|śatāni ca
saṃsāreṣv anubhūtāni. kasya te? kasya vā vayam?
śoka|sthāna|sahasrāṇi bhaya|sthāna|śatāni ca
divase divase mūḍham āviśanti, na paṇḍitam.

na kālasya priyaḥ kaś cin, na dveṣyaḥ, Kuru|sattama.
na madhya|sthaḥ kva cit kālaḥ. sarvaṃ kālaḥ prakarṣati.
kālaḥ pacati bhūtāni. kālaḥ saṃharate prajāḥ.
kālaḥ supteṣu jāgarti. kālo hi dur|atikramaḥ.
2.25 a|nityaṃ yauvanaṃ, rūpaṃ, jīvitaṃ, dravya|saṃcayaḥ,
ārogyaṃ, priya|saṃvāso. gṛdhyed eṣu na paṇḍitaḥ.
na jānapadikaṃ duḥkham ekaḥ śocitum arhasi.

apy a|bhāvena yujyeta, tac c' âsya na nivartate;
a|śocan pratikurvīta yadi paśyet parākramam.
bhaiṣajyam etad duḥkhasya, yad etan n' ânucintayet.
cintyamānaṃ hi na vyeti, bhūyaś c' âpi pravardhate.

whose bodies were the fire. In return they, housing the fire within, bore the arrows oblated into them. This, I tell you, Your Majesty, is the surest path to heaven. For a warrior in this world nothing surpasses a war. Those warriors are noble-souled heroes, medallions of their society who have attained the highest blessing; not one of them warrants your grief.

Recover yourself and do not grieve, bull of mankind. 2.20
Not today should you succumb to grief and relinquish this life. Thousands of mothers and fathers, hundreds of children and wives are met within different stations of rebirth. Whose are they? Indeed whose are we? Thousands of opportunities for grief and hundreds of opportunities for fear day after day besiege the bewildered fool, but not the wise man.

Time favors none and picks on none, most virtuous of Kurus. But neither is Time ever indifferent. Time drags all away. Time removes all living beings. Time carries off all creatures. Time stays watchful amid the sleeping. No one escapes Time.

Youth, beauty, life, the accumulation of material things, 2.25
health, the company of loved ones—none of it lasts. No one in their right mind would covet them. You should not take on your shoulders alone the mourning for suffering that affects the entire populace.

Moreover, once something is destined for non-existence, your suffering does not bring it back and yet, if not preoccupied by grief, one can counteract an attack. What's more, the remedy for this suffering is not to dwell on it. For thinking about it does not diminish it; rather it encourages it to

an|iṣṭa|saṃprayogāc ca viprayogāt priyasya ca
mānuṣā mānasair duḥkhair dahyante c' âlpa|buddhayaḥ.
n' ârtho, na dharmo, na sukhaṃ, yad etad anuśocasi.
2.30 na ca n' âpaiti kāry'|ârthāt, tri|vargāc c' âiva hīyate.
anyām anyāṃ dhan'|âvasthāṃ prāpya vaiśeṣikīṃ narāḥ
a|saṃtuṣṭāḥ pramuhyanti; saṃtoṣaṃ yānti paṇḍitāḥ.
prajñayā mānasaṃ duḥkhaṃ hanyāc, chārīram auṣadhaiḥ.
etad vijñāna|sāmarthyaṃ. na bālaiḥ samatām iyāt.
śayānaṃ c' ânuśete hi, tiṣṭhantaṃ c' ânutiṣṭhati,
anudhāvati dhāvantaṃ karma pūrva|kṛtaṃ naram.
yasyāṃ yasyām avasthāyāṃ yat karoti śubh'|â|śubham,
tasyāṃ tasyām avasthāyāṃ tat tat phalam upāśnute.
yena yena śarīreṇa yad yat karma karoti yaḥ,
tena tena śarīreṇa tat phalaṃ samupāśnute.
2.35 ātm" âiva hy ātmano bandhur, ātm" âiva ripur ātmanaḥ,
ātm" âiva hy ātmanaḥ sākṣī kṛtasy' âpakṛtasya ca.
śubhena karmaṇā saukhyaṃ, duḥkhaṃ pāpena karmaṇā.
kṛtaṃ bhavati sarvatra. n' â|kṛtaṃ vidyate kva cit.
na hi jñāna|viruddheṣu bahv|apāyeṣu karmasu
mūla|ghātiṣu sajjante buddhimanto bhavad|vidhāḥ.

grow stronger. On contact with something unpleasant and separation from what is dear, people of weak understanding are consumed by torments of their own mind's making. No material benefit, no religious duty and no happiness is served by your succumbing to this grief.

One becomes further removed from the goal one must 2.30
achieve and is deprived of the three advantages in life.* Men, even when they have attained first one then another outstanding level of richness, stupidly remain discontented. Wise men attain content. One can remove the torments of the heart with understanding, as one can those of the body with medicines. Such is the power of knowledge. One should not sink to the level of fools. A man's previous actions share his bed when he lies down, stand by him when he stands and follow him when he runs. At whatever stage of life he does whatever good or bad thing, in the parallel stage of life he will reap the corresponding result. In whatever embodiment, whatever action anyone does, in a parallel embodiment he experiences the corresponding result.

One is both one's closest friend and one's own worst en- 2.35
emy, for it is one's self that witnesses one's good and bad deeds. A good act brings happiness; from an evil deed suffering ensues. One's actions always remain; never what one avoided doing. For people of insight, such as you sir, do not engage in acts that are at root damaging, in contravention of wisdom or greatly injurious.

DHṚTARĀṢṬRA uvāca:

3.1 SU|BHĀṢITAIR, mahā|prājña, śoko 'yaṃ vigato mama.
bhūya eva tu vākyāni śrotum icchāmi tattvataḥ.
an|iṣṭānāṃ ca saṃsargād iṣṭānāṃ ca vivarjanāt
kathaṃ hi mānasair duḥkhaiḥ pramucyante tu paṇḍitāḥ?

VIDURA uvāca:

yato yato mano duḥkhāt sukhād vā vipramucyate,
tatas tato niyamy' âitac chāntiṃ vindeta vai budhaḥ.
a|śāśvatam idaṃ sarvaṃ cintyamānaṃ, nara'|rṣabha,
kadalī|saṃnibho lokaḥ. sāro hy asya na vidyate.
3.5 yadā prājñāś ca mūḍhāś ca, dhanavanto 'tha nir|dhanāḥ
sarve pitṛ|vanaṃ prāpya svapanti vigata|jvarāḥ,
nir|māṃsair asthi|bhūyiṣṭhair gātraiḥ snāyu|nibandhibhiḥ,
kiṃ viśeṣaṃ prapaśyanti tatra teṣāṃ pare janāḥ,
yena pratyavagaccheyuḥ kula|rūpa|viśeṣaṇam?
kasmād anyonyam icchanti vipralabdha|dhiyo narāḥ?
gṛhāṇy eva hi martyānām āhur dehāni paṇḍitāḥ.
kālena viniyujyante; sattvam ekaṃ tu śāśvatam.
yathā jīrṇam a|jīrṇaṃ vā vastraṃ tyaktvā tu pūruṣaḥ,
anyad rocayate vastram—evaṃ dehāḥ śarīriṇām.

DHRITA·RASHTRA replied:

THANKS TO YOUR well-spoken words, friend of profound insight, I can put aside my grief. But I long to hear even more of what you have to say concerning reality. For instance, how is it that sensible men free themselves from the anguish of the mind that results from contact with what is disliked and from not having a hold on the things one does want? 3.1

VÍDURA answered:

As the mind is gradually released from both anguish and joy, so one with understanding, by restraining his mind, increasingly finds peace. All this that occupies our minds is transient, bull of men, for the world is like a plantain tree. It has no essence at its core.

When all men, be they wise or foolish, rich or poor, come to rest in the grove of their ancestors, all anguish cast aside, once their limbs are reduced to bone, the flesh gone, bound together only by sinews, what distinguishing feature of theirs can other people see in what remains, by which they might identify their particular family or appearance? 3.5

Why do men hanker after one another, robbed of their senses, when wise men have declared the bodies of mortals to be no different from houses. In the course of time they fall apart, while only one's essence is eternal. Just as a man discards his clothes, whether they are worn out or not, taking pleasure in a new item of clothing, so it is with bodies for those inhabiting them.

3.10 Vaicitravīrya, sādhyaṃ hi duḥkhaṃ vā yadi vā sukham,
prāpnuvant' îha bhūtāni sva|kṛten' âiva karmaṇā.
karmaṇā prāpyate svargaṃ, sukhaṃ, duḥkhaṃ ca, Bhārata.
tato vahati taṃ bhāram a|vaśaḥ sva|vaśo 'pi vā.

yathā ca mṛnmayaṃ bhāṇḍaṃ cakr'|ārūḍhaṃ vipadyate,
kiṃ cit prakriyamāṇaṃ vā, kṛta|mātram ath' âpi vā,
chinnaṃ v" âpy avaropyantam, avatīrṇam ath' âpi vā,
ārdraṃ v" âpy, atha vā śuṣkaṃ, pacyamānam ath' âpi vā,
uttāryamāṇam āpākād, uddhṛtaṃ v" âpi, Bhārata,
atha vā paribhṛjjantam—evaṃ dehāḥ śarīriṇām:
3.15 garbha|stho vā, prasūto v" âpy, atha vā divas'|ântaraḥ,
ardha|māsa|gato v" âpi, māsa|mātra|gato 'pi vā,
saṃvatsara|gato v" âpi, dvi|saṃvatsara eva vā,
yauvana|stho, 'tha madhya|stho, vṛddho v" âpi vipadyate.
prāk|karmabhis tu bhūtāni bhavanti na bhavanti ca.
evaṃ sāṃsiddhike loke kim|artham anutapyase?
yathā tu salile, rājan, krīḍ"|ârtham anusaṃcaran
unmajjec ca nimajjec ca kiṃ cit sattvaṃ, nar'|âdhipa,
evaṃ saṃsāra|gahane unmajjana|nimajjane
karma|bhogena badhyantaḥ kliśyante c' âlpa|buddhayaḥ.
3.20 ye tu prājñāḥ sthitāḥ sattve saṃsāre 'smin hit'|âiṣiṇaḥ,
samāgama|jñā bhūtānāṃ te yānti paramāṃ gatim.

Son to Vichítra·virya, whether it is suffering or pleasure 3.10
that is to be experienced, living beings harvest each on account of action that they themselves performed. Through
action is heaven reached, so too happiness and suffering,
king of Bhárata's line. Therefore, whether he likes it or not,
the burden a person carries is the one he put together.

Just as a clay pot might fall apart when just mounted on
the wheel, or while it is being shaped, or when it has just
been made, or perhaps it might be broken while being removed from the wheel, or once set down, while still dry-
ing, or once dry, or while it is being fired, when it is being
lowered or once removed from the kiln, king of Bhárata's
line, or even when it is already being used for cooking, so
it is with the bodies of those inhabiting them:

Some die while still in the womb, some are still-born, 3.15
some die after a day, some survive a fortnight, some just
a month, some die after a year, some after two, others in
their youth, their middle age or when old. People survive
or don't, in accordance with their deeds in former lifetimes.
When the world is made this way, what purpose is served
regretting it? Your Majesty, something swimming in the
waves for pleasure might bob to the surface or disappear
below, lord of men. When they are similarly coming to
the surface or submerging in the cycle of existence those
of little understanding are oppressed and weighed down
by the fruition of their actions. But those who do under- 3.20
stand, secure in the truth, seeking out good amid cyclic existence and recognizing how living beings come together,
they reach the highest destiny.

DHṚTARĀṢṬRA uvāca:

4.1 KATHAṂ SAṂSĀRA|gahanaṃ vijñeyaṃ, vadatāṃ vara?
etad icchāmy ahaṃ śrotuṃ. tattvam ākhyāhi pṛcchataḥ.

VIDURA uvāca:

janma|prabhṛti bhūtānāṃ kriyā sarv" ôpalakṣyate.
pūrvam ev' êha kalile vasate kiṃ cid antaram.
tataḥ sa pañcame 'tīte māse vā samakalpayat.
tataḥ sarv'|âṅga|saṃpūrṇo garbho vai sa tu jāyate.
a|medhya|madhye vasati māṃsa|śoṇita|lepane.
tatas tu vāyu|vegena ūrdhva|pādo hy adhaḥ|śirāḥ
4.5 yoni|dvāram upāgamya bahūn kleśān samṛcchati.
yoni|saṃpīḍanāc c' âiva pūrva|karmabhir anvitaḥ,
tasmān muktaḥ sa saṃsārād anyān paśyaty upadravān.
grahās tam anugacchanti sārameyā iv' āmiṣam.

tataḥ prāpt'|ôttare kāle vyādhayaś c' âpi taṃ tathā
upasarpanti jīvantaṃ, badhyamānaṃ sva|karmabhiḥ.
taṃ baddham indriyaiḥ pāśaiḥ saṅga|svādubhir āvṛtam
vyasanāny api vartante vividhāni, nar'|âdhipa.
badhyamānaś ca tair bhūyo n' âiva tṛptim upaiti saḥ.
tadā n' âvaiti c' âiv' âyaṃ prakurvan sādhv|a|sādhu vā,
4.10 tath" âiva parirakṣanti ye dhyāna|pariniṣṭhitāḥ.

DHRITA·RASHTRA asked:

MOST ELOQUENT of speakers, how is the abyss of cyclic 4.1
existence to be understood? This I want to hear. Please explain the reality of it to me now that I ask you.

VÍDURA replied:

I shall describe every process that living beings go through from the moment life begins. Right at the beginning it dwells for some time within the maternal fluid. Then when the fifth month has passed, it develops flesh. Then it becomes a proper fetus, with each limb completely formed. He lives in muck, smeared in flesh and blood. Next, through the effect of the wind element, the feet move upwards,
while the head points down. As he reaches the neck of the 4.5
womb, he undergoes many forms of distress. Upon the contractions of the womb he is delivered from there, now reassociated with his former actions, at which point as a result of the cycle of existence he witnesses other sources of distress. Disease-inducing spirits pursue him like dogs pursuing raw meat.

When some time has passed illnesses also pursue him, as long as he lives caught in the bonds of his own deeds. While he is bound by the fetters of the senses, entangled by attachment and pleasure, many kinds of misfortunes also beset him, lord of men. As he becomes ever more ensnared by them, he never feels satisfied. Then, though he performs
actions, he fails to understands right from wrong, which 4.10
is how those who are accomplished in profound reflection protect themselves.

ayaṃ na budhyate tāvad Yama|lokam ath' āgatam,
Yama|dūtair vikṛṣyaṃś ca mṛtyuṃ kālena gacchati.
vāgg|hīnasya ca yan|mātram iṣṭ'|ân|iṣṭaṃ kṛtaṃ mukhe,
bhūya ev' ātman" ātmānaṃ badhyamānam upekṣate.*
aho vinikṛto loko, lobhena ca vaśī|kṛtaḥ,
lobha|krodha|bhay' ônmatto n' ātmānam avabudhyate.
kulīnatve ca ramate, duṣ|kulīnān vikutsayan,
dhana|darpeṇa dṛptaś ca daridrān parikutsayan.
mūrkhān iti parān āha, n' ātmānaṃ samavekṣate.
doṣān kṣipati c' ânyeṣāṃ, n' ātmānaṃ śāstum icchati.

4.15 yadā prājñāś ca mūrkhāś ca, dhanavantaś ca nir|dhanāḥ,
kulīnāś c' â|kulīnāś ca, mānino 'th' âpy a|māninaḥ,
sarve pitṛ|vanaṃ prāptāḥ svapanti vigata|tvacaḥ.
nir|māṃsair asthi|bhūyiṣṭhair gātraiḥ snāyu|nibandhanaiḥ
viśeṣaṃ na prapaśyanti tatra teṣām pare janāḥ,
yena pratyavagaccheyuḥ kula|rūpa|viśeṣaṇam.
yadā sarve samaṃ nyastāḥ svapanti dharaṇī|tale,
kasmād anyonyam icchanti pralabdhum iha dur|budhāḥ?
pratyakṣaṃ ca parokṣaṃ ca yo niśamya śrutiṃ tv imāṃ,
a|dhruve jīva|loke 'smin yo dharmam anupālayan
janma|prabhṛti varteta, prāpnuyāt paramāṃ gatim.

He does not even understand that he has reached the realm of Yama, god of Death and, dragged this way and that by Yama's minions, in time he comes face to face with his mortality. He continues to disregard the way he is himself enmeshing himself, to the same extent that one pays no attention to the mumblings a mute forms in his mouth, regardless of whether it might be something one would want to hear or not. Alas the world is corrupt and under the control of greed. A person maddened by greed, hatred and fear has no understanding of himself. He delights in being a member of a good family, while he despises those of low status. He is complacent with the arrogance of wealth, while he reviles the poor. He labels others stupid, but fails to observe himself. He criticizes the faults of others, but has no desire to correct himself.

Whether wise or stupid, rich or penniless, from high 4.15
family or low, proud or humble, upon reaching the grove of the ancestors, all sleep, their skin gone. With their limbs reduced to bone, the flesh gone, bound together only by sinews, other people cannot see in what remains any of their distinguishing features, by which they might identify their particular family or appearance. Given that all people, when laid to rest, sleep on the bare earth equally, why do people, robbed of senses, hanker to cling to one another? But anyone who has paid attention to this sacred teaching, whether in public or secretly, and who, from the moment he is born, conducts himself in such a way that he maintains his righteous duty in this uncertain world of the living, will reach the supreme destiny.

4.20 evaṃ sarvaṃ viditvā vai yas tattvam anuvartate,
sa pramokṣāya labhate panthānaṃ, manu|j'|âdhipa.

DHṚTARĀṢṬRA uvāca:

5.1 YAD IDAṂ DHARMA|gahanaṃ buddhyā samanugamyate,
etad vistaraśaḥ sarvaṃ buddhi|mārgaṃ praśaṃsa me.

VIDURA uvāca:

atra te vartayiṣyāmi namas|kṛtvā Svayaṃbhuve,
yathā saṃsāra|gahanaṃ vadanti parama'|rṣayaḥ.
kaś cin mahati kāntāre vartamāno dvi|jaḥ kila
mahad dur|gam anuprāpto vanaṃ kravy'|āda|saṃkulam.
siṃha|vyāghra|gaja'|rkṣ'|âughair atighoraṃ mahā|svanaiḥ,
piśit'|âdair atibhayair mah"|ôgr'|ākṛtibhis tathā
5.5 samantāt saṃparikṣiptaṃ, yat sma dṛṣṭvā trased Yamaḥ.
tad asya dṛṣṭvā hṛdayam udvegam agamat param,
abhyucchrayaṃ ca romṇāṃ vai vikriyāś ca, paraṃ|tapa.
sa tad vanaṃ vyanusaran, saṃpradhāvan itas tataḥ,
vīkṣamāṇo diśaḥ sarvāḥ, «śaraṇaṃ kva bhaved?» iti;
sa teṣāṃ chidram anvicchan pradruto bhaya|pīḍitaḥ,
na ca niryāti vai dūraṃ, na vā tair vipramocyate.

The person who has really understood all this and be- 4.20
haves in accordance with the truth, finds the path that leads
to liberation, lord of primordial man's descendants.

DHRITA·RASHTRA said:

EXPLAIN TO ME more fully the entire path of that in- 5.1
sight which allows one to understand the profundity that is
Dharma.

VÍDURA replied:

After first paying homage to Brahma, the Self-Created, I
shall—by way of answer to your request—describe how the
supreme seers speak of the profundity of cyclic existence.
They relate how a certain twice-born was traveling in the
wilderness when he came upon a vast, impenetrable forest,
teeming with predators. Horrifying as it was with packs of 5.5
lions, tigers, elephants and wolves howling wildly and surrounded on all sides by the most fearsome goblins of ghastly
appearance, even the god of Death himself would have been
terrified at the sight of it.

At seeing those sights, his heart began pounding wildly, and his hair stood on end and bristled, torment of your enemy. He continued to make his way through the forest, running from one place to the next and looking all about him in the hope of finding shelter somewhere. Desperately searching for a way through them, he ran on, hard pressed by fear, but he could neither get out nor get free of them by much distance.

ath' âpaśyad vanaṃ ghoraṃ samantād vāgur"|āvṛtam,
bāhubhyāṃ saṃparikṣiptaṃ striyā parama|ghorayā,
pañca|śīrṣa|dharair nāgaiḥ śailair iva samunnataiḥ,
5.10 nabhaḥ|spṛśair mahā|vṛkṣaiḥ parikṣiptaṃ mahā|vanam.
vana|madhye ca tatr' âbhūd uda|pānaḥ samāvṛtaḥ,
vallībhis tṛṇa|channābhir dṛḍhābhir abhisaṃvṛtaḥ.
papāta sa dvi|jas tatra nigūḍhe salil'|āśaye,
vilagnaś c' âbhavat tasmin latā|saṃtāna|saṃkaṭe.
panasasya yathā jātaṃ vṛnta|baddhaṃ mahā|phalam.
sa tathā lambate tatra, ūrdhva|pādo hy adhaḥ|śirāḥ.
atha tatr' âpi c' ânyo 'sya bhūyo jāta upadravaḥ:
kūpa|madhye mahā|nāgam apaśyata mahā|balam,
kūpa|vīnāha|velāyām apaśyata mahā|gajam,
5.15 ṣaḍ|vaktraṃ, kṛṣṇa|śuklaṃ ca, dvi|ṣaṭka|pada|cāriṇam,
krameṇa parisarpantaṃ vallī|vṛkṣa|samāvṛtam.
tasya c' âpi praśākhāsu vṛkṣa|śākh'|âvalambinaḥ
nānā|rūpā madhu|karā ghora|rūpā bhay'|āvahāḥ
āsate madhu saṃvṛtya pūrvam eva. niketa|jāḥ
bhūyo bhūyaḥ samīhante madhūni, Bharata'|ṛṣabha,
svādanīyāni bhūtānāṃ, yair bālo viprakṛṣyate.
teṣāṃ madhūnāṃ bahu|dhā dhārā prasravate tadā.
ālambamānaḥ sa pumān dhārāṃ pibati sarvadā,
na c' âsya tṛṣṇā viratā pibamānasya saṅkaṭe.
5.20 abhīpsati tadā nityam a|tṛptaḥ sa punaḥ punaḥ.
na c' âsya jīvite, rājan, nirvedaḥ samajāyata.
tatr' âiva ca manuṣyasya jīvit'|āśā pratiṣṭhitā.

Then he realized that the horrific forest was surrounded on all sides by snares, that it was enclosed in the arms of a gruesome woman. Five-headed cobras, rearing up like
mountains and giant trees that touched the clouds also 5.10
hemmed in the great forest.

Now, in the midst of the forest, there was a well which was enclosed on all sides. It was covered by massive lianas, they in turn hidden by grass. Into that concealed tank of water fell our twice-born and there he remained, caught in that dense mesh of lianas, like a giant jackfruit hanging from its tree, attached by its stalk. That's how he hung there, feet up, head down. Whereupon a fresh misery assailed him in that place: in the middle of the well he could see a massive snake of colossal strength and at the rim at the top of the
well he could see an immense elephant, six-headed, piebald 5.15
and walking on six pairs of feet, steadily pacing around the opening concealed by the lianas and trees.

As he dangles down from the branch of the tree, bees of different shapes, grotesque and terrifying, move in and out of their hives amid the twigs, having earlier collected nectar. Those coming from the combs constantly seek out more nectar, bull of the Bhárata line, the taste of which, sweet to all beings, entices the fool astray. Now a rich stream of honey oozes from the combs. The man hanging there drinks constantly from that flow, but however much he drinks, in that perilous situation his thirst is never sated.

However much he tries to get he is never satisfied. Never- 5.20
theless, Your Majesty, he never became disenchanted with life. Though the man is in that situation, his desire to live remains unshaken.

kṛṣṇāḥ śvetāś ca taṃ vṛkṣaṃ kuṭṭayanti sma mūṣakāḥ.
vyālaiś ca vana|durg'|ânte, striyā ca param'|ôgrayā,
kūp'|âdhastāc ca nāgena, vīnāhe kuñjareṇa ca,
vṛkṣa|prapātāc ca bhayaṃ mūṣakebhyaś ca pañcamam,
madhu|lobhān madhukaraiḥ ṣaṣṭham āhur mahad bhayam.
evaṃ sa vasate tatra kṣiptaḥ saṃsāra|sāgare,
na c' âiva jīvit'|āśāyāṃ nirvedam upagacchati.

DHṚTARĀṢṬRA uvāca:

6.1 AHO KHALU MAHAD duḥkhaṃ kṛcchra|vāsaś ca tasya ha.
kathaṃ tasya ratis tatra, tuṣṭir vā, vadatāṃ vara?
sa deśaḥ kva nu, yatr' âsau vasate dharma|saṃkaṭe?
kathaṃ vā sa vimucyeta naras tasmān mahā|bhayāt?
etan me sarvam ācakṣva sādhu, ceṣṭāmahe tathā.
kṛpā me mahatī jātā tasy' âbhyuddharaṇena hi.

VIDURA uvāca:

upamānam idaṃ, rājan, mokṣa|vidbhir udāhṛtam,
su|kṛtaṃ vindate yena para|lokeṣu mānavaḥ.
6.5 ucyate yat tu kāntāraṃ, mahā|saṃsāra eva saḥ.
vanaṃ durgaṃ hi yac c' âitat, saṃsāra|gahanaṃ hi tat.
ye ca te kathitā vyālā, vyādhayas te prakīrtitāḥ.
yā sā nārī bṛhat|kāyā adhitiṣṭhati† tatra vai:
tām āhus tu jarāṃ prājñā rūpa|varṇa|vināśinīm.
yas tatra kūpo, nṛ|pate, sa tu dehaḥ śarīriṇām.

Meanwhile black and white rats were gnawing at that tree. From the wild animals in the impenetrable forest and from the gruesome woman, from the snake at the bottom of the well and from the elephant at its mouth, and fifthly from the prospect of the tree falling because of the rats, he was in peril. They say a sixth great peril came from the bees, because of his greed for the honey. And so he lives, stuck in that tumultuous ocean of cyclic existence, yet he never becomes disillusioned of his hope to go on living.

DHRITA·RASHTRA said:

WELL SURELY HIS discomfort must be extreme, remaining 6.1
in such a dire situation. How can he find any delight or satisfaction in it, most eloquent of speakers? But where is that place where he is trapped, that so restricts rightful life? Moreover, how can that man escape from that extremely precarious state? Explain all this to me clearly so that we might take action. For I feel great concern to haul him up out of there.

VÍDURA replied:

Your Majesty, this is but a metaphor, told by those who understand the path to liberation, so that a man might find the realm of virtue in the worlds to come.

Now what has been called the wilderness is in fact the 6.5
great whirl of cyclic existence. The impenetrable forest in the tale, that represents the quagmire of cyclic existence. The things I told you were beasts of prey, I reveal to you are diseases. That woman with the enormous body who was waiting there: wise men identify her as old age, who robs men of their physique and looks. Now the well in that

yas tatra vasate 'dhastān mah"|âhiḥ, kāla eva saḥ,
antakaḥ sarva|bhūtānāṃ dehināṃ sarva|hāry asau.
kūpa|madhye ca yā jātā vallī, yatra sa mānavaḥ
pratāne lambate lagno, jīvit'|āśā śarīriṇām.

6.10 sa yas tu kūpa|vīnāhe taṃ vṛkṣaṃ parisarpati
ṣaḍ|vaktraḥ kuñjaro, rājan, sa tu saṃvatsaraḥ smṛtaḥ.
mukhāni ṛtavo. māsāḥ pādā dvādaśa kīrtitāḥ.
ye tu vṛkṣaṃ nikṛntanti mūṣakāḥ panna|gās tathā,
rātry|ahāni tu tāny āhur bhūtānāṃ paricintakāḥ.
ye te madhu|karās tatra, kāmās te parikīrtitāḥ.
yās tu tā bahuśo dhārāḥ sravanti madhu|nisravam,
tāṃs tu kāma|rasān vidyād, yatra majjanti mānavāḥ.
evaṃ saṃsāra|cakrasya parivṛttiṃ vidur budhāḥ,
yena saṃsāra|cakrasya pāśāṃś chindanti vai budhāḥ.

DHṚTARĀṢṬRA uvāca:

7.1 AHO 'BHIHITAM ākhyānaṃ bhavatā tattva|darśinā.
bhūya eva tu me harṣaḥ śrotuṃ vāg|amṛtaṃ tava.

VIDURA uvāca:

śṛṇu, bhūyaḥ pravakṣyāmi mārgasy' âitasya vistaram,
yac chrutvā vipramucyante saṃsārebhyo vicakṣaṇāḥ.
yathā tu puruṣo, rājan, dīrgham adhvānam āsthitaḥ
kva cit kva cic chramāc chrāntaḥ kurute vāsam eva vā,
evaṃ saṃsāra|paryāye garbha|vāseṣu, Bhārata,

forest, lord of men, that's the body of those who become embodied. The deadly python living at its bottom, that is Time, which brings an end to all embodied beings, swallowing everything. The liana vine that grew down inside the well, onto the dangling tendril of which that man was caught suspended, that is the hope to continue living that embodied beings cling to.

Now treading about that tree close to the mouth of the 6.10
well was the six-headed elephant; that, Your Majesty, is now recognized as the year. His faces are the seasons. His twelve feet are revealed as the months. Now those who analyze the facts declare that the rats creeping down and chewing at the base of the tree are the days and nights. The bees in the story are explained as desires. The many different streams trickling down from the honey, one should know for the different indulgent pleasures in which men immerse themselves. This is how men of sense have seen the revolving of the wheel of cyclic existence, such that they can cut through the fetters of that wheel.

DHRITA·RASHTRA spoke:

OH, NOW THAT you have told me this story, seer of reality, 7.1
how I long to hear more of your ambrosial words.

VÍDURA replied:

Listen and I shall tell you more, in detail, of this path which, heeded by far-sighted men, liberates them from the realms of cyclic existence. In the same way, Your Majesty, that a man on a long journey becomes exhausted from the effort and so halts at many points along the way, so beings

kurvanti dur|budhā vāsaṃ. mucyante tatra paṇḍitāḥ.
7.5 tasmād adhvānam ev' âitam āhuḥ śāstra|vido janāḥ,
yat tu saṃsāra|gahanaṃ, vanam āhur manīṣiṇaḥ.
so 'yaṃ loka|samāvarto martyānāṃ, Bharata'|rṣabha,
carāṇāṃ sthāvarāṇāṃ ca. gṛdhyet tatra na paṇḍitaḥ.
śārīrā mānasāś c' âiva martyānāṃ ye tu vyādhayaḥ,
pratyakṣāś ca parokṣāś ca, te vyālāḥ kathitā budhaiḥ.
kliśyamānāś ca tair nityaṃ, hanyamānāś ca, Bhārata,
sva|karmabhir mahā|vyālair n' ôdvijanty alpa|buddhayaḥ.
ath' âpi tair vimucyeta vyādhibhiḥ puruṣo, nṛpa,
āvṛṇoty eva taṃ paścāj jarā rūpa|vināśinī.
7.10 śabda|rūpa|rasa|sparśair gandhaiś ca vividhair api
majjamānaṃ mahā|paṅke† nir|ālambe samantataḥ,
saṃvatsarāś ca māsāś ca pakṣ'|âho|rātra|sandhayaḥ
krameṇ' âsy' ôpayuñjanti rūpam āyus tath" âiva ca.
ete kālasya nidhayo. n' âitāñ jānanti dur|budhāḥ.
dhātr" âbhilikhitāny āhuḥ sarva|bhūtāni karmaṇā.
rathaṃ śarīraṃ bhūtānāṃ, sattvam āhus tu sārathim.
indriyāṇi hayān āhuḥ, karma buddhiś ca raśmayaḥ.
teṣāṃ hayānāṃ yo vegaṃ dhāvatām anudhāvati,
sa tu saṃsāra|cakre 'smiṃś cakravat parivartate.

of little understanding staying in the course of cyclic existence halt in different wombs, king of Bhárata's line. Men of understanding are freed from that.

That is why people who are versed in the scriptures call 7.5
this a journey, while men of wisdom liken the quagmire of cyclic existence to a forest. This assemblage that is the world, with its quick and its still, all destined for death, bull of Bhárata, no man in their right mind would covet any part of it. Now, the physical and mental illnesses that afflict mortals, both the obvious and the hidden, they are described as beasts of prey by the wise. People of little understanding show no alarm at those giant predators which come on account of their own actions, even though they are forever being maimed and killed by them, king of Bhárata's line. Suppose, protector of men, that a man does escape those illnesses, later old age still hems him in and destroys his physique.

And in the meantime, on account of sounds, sights, 7.10
tastes, sensual contacts and smells of many kinds, he remains submerged in a great mire with nothing to support him on any side. All the while the years and months, divided into fortnights, days and nights, eat up his physique and his lifespan bit by bit. These are the records of Time. Those weak in wisdom do not understand them.

It is said that the records of each and every being are set down by the Creator, according to their actions. The body is said to be a chariot, and the living essence the charioteer. The senses are said to be his horses. Action and understanding are the reins. Whoever pursues the speed of those

7.15 yas tān saṃyamate buddhyā, saṃyato na nivartate.
ye tu saṃsāra|cakre 'smiṃś cakravat parivartite
bhramamāṇā na muhyanti, saṃsāre na bhramanti te.
saṃsāre bhramatāṃ, rājan, duḥkham etadd hi jāyate.
tasmād asya nivṛtty|arthaṃ yatnam ev' ācared budhaḥ.
upekṣā n' âtra kartavyā. śata|śākhaḥ pravardhate.
yat'|êndriyo naro, rājan, krodha|lobha|nir|ākṛtaḥ,
saṃtuṣṭaḥ, satya|vādī yaḥ, sa śāntim adhigacchati.
Yāmyam āhū rathaṃ hy enaṃ, muhyante yena dur|budhāḥ.
sa c' âitat prāpnuyād, rājan, yat tvaṃ prāpto, nar'|âdhipa.
7.20 anutarṣulaṃ ev' âitad duḥkhaṃ bhavati, māriṣa,
rājya|nāśaṃ, suhṛn|nāśaṃ, suta|nāśaṃ ca, Bhārata.
sādhuḥ parama|duḥkhānāṃ duḥkha|bhaiṣajyam ācaret.
jñān'|āuṣadham avāpy' êha dūra|pāraṃ mah"|āuṣadhaṃ
chindyād duḥkha|mahā|vyādhim naraḥ saṃyata|mānasaḥ.
na vikramo, na c' âpy artho, na mitraṃ, na suhṛj|janaḥ
tath" ônmocayate duḥkhād, yath" ātmā sthira|saṃyamaḥ.
tasmān maitraṃ samāsthāya, śīlam āpadya, Bhārata,
damas, tyāgo '|pramādaś ca: te trayo Brahmaṇo hayāḥ.
śīla|raśmi|samāyukte sthito yo mānase rathe
tyaktvā mṛtyu|bhayaṃ, rājan, brahma|lokaṃ sa gacchati.

running horses, spins like a wheel in this circus of cyclic existence.

Whoever restrains them, restrained by his understanding, does not continue spinning. Even if they continue to roam in this circus of cyclic existence, as it continues to spin like a wheel, they are no longer misguided so do not become lost in cyclic existence. 7.15

But suffering afflicts those who wander in cyclic existence, Your Majesty. For that reason, a man with insight would make every effort not to return to it. It is crucial not to ignore it. It grows hundreds of branches. A man who restrains his senses, Your Majesty, and is never impelled by anger or greed, who is contented and speaks only truth, he finds peace. For they say this chariot belongs to Death. Those of little sense are deceived by it. This chariot brings you to the point at which you have now arrived, sovereign.

It is this greed for such things that turns to suffering, sire, 7.20
to the loss of kingdom, the loss of friends, the loss of sons, king of Bhárata's line. A good man would apply the remedy against suffering to these extreme sufferings. Having procured the remedy of understanding, that great remedy so difficult to reach in this world, the man who can keep his mind restrained, would excise this great illness of suffering. No courage, money, friend or loved one can release one from unhappiness as much as one's own self can, when full of firm restraint. That is why the three horses of God, which are harnessed to goodwill and yoked to good conduct, king of Bhárata's line, are restraint, relinquishment and vigilance. Stood in the chariot of mind, drawn by the

7.25 a|bhayaṃ sarva|bhūtebhyo yo dadāti, mahī|pate,
sa gacchati paraṃ sthānaṃ Viṣṇoḥ padam an|āmayam.
na tat kratu|sahasreṇa, n' ôpavāsaiś ca nityaśaḥ,
a|bhayasya ca dānena yat phalaṃ prāpnuyān naraḥ.
na hy ātmanaḥ priyataraṃ kiñ cid bhūteṣu niścitaṃ.
an|iṣṭaṃ sarva|bhūtānāṃ maraṇaṃ nāma, Bhārata.
tasmāt sarveṣu bhūteṣu dayā kāryā vipaścitā.
nānā|moha|samāyuktā, buddhi|jālena saṃvṛtāḥ,
a|sūkṣma|dṛṣṭayo mandā bhrāmyante tatra tatra ha.
susūkṣma|dṛṣṭayo, rājan, vrajanti Brahma śāśvatam.

VAIŚAMPĀYANA uvāca:

8.1 VIDURASYA TU tad vākyaṃ niśamya Kuru|sattamaḥ
putra|śok'|âbhisaṃtaptaḥ papāta bhuvi mūrchitaḥ.
taṃ tathā patitaṃ bhūmau,
nih|saṃjñaṃ prekṣya bāndhavāḥ,
Kṛṣṇadvaipāyanaś c' âiva,
kṣattā ca Viduras tathā,
Saṃjayaḥ, suhṛdaś c' ânye, dvāḥ|sthā ye c' âsya saṃmatāḥ.
jalena sukha|śītena, tāla|vṛntaiś ca, Bhārata,
paspṛśuś ca karair gātraṃ vījamānāś ca yatnataḥ,
anvāsya tu ciraṃ kālaṃ Dhṛtarāṣṭraṃ tathā|gatam.
8.5 atha dīrghasya kālasya labdha|saṃjño mahī|patiḥ
vilalāpa ciraṃ kālaṃ putr'|ādhibhir abhiplutaḥ:

reins of good conduct, a man who casts aside his fear of death, Your Majesty, arrives at the realm of God.

Lord of this earth, whoever provides freedom from fear 7.25
to all beings, enters the ultimate abode, the realm of Vishnu, free of all maladies. Neither a thousand sacrifices nor constant fasts bring a man as much benefit as that which he achieves through providing safety to others. For nothing is deemed dearer among living beings than their self. No one looks forward to death, king of Bhárata's line. For that reason a wise man should show pity to all living beings. They are caught up in various delusions, bound up in a net of different views. Those who lack subtle vision wander about aimlessly all over the place. But those of subtle vision, Your Majesty, follow the direct route to eternal Brahma.

VAISHAMPÁYANA continued:

NOW THOUGH THE most virtuous of the Kurus had lis- 8.1
tened to what Vídura said, consumed by grief for his sons, he fell to the ground in a faint. His relatives saw him fall senseless on the ground, as did Krishna the Dark Lord of the Island along with the latter's son with the slave girl, namely Vídura himself, so too did Sánjaya and other friends and his trusted doormen. Taking refreshing, cool water in their hands they dabbed it on Dhrita·rashtra's limbs and they fanned him vigorously with palm fans, king of Bhárata's line, attending him for some time while he remained
in a faint. Then, when after a considerable while the lord 8.5
of the earth had regained consciousness, he rambled for a long time, overwhelmed by anguish for his sons:

«dhig astu khalu mānuṣyaṃ, mānuṣye ca parigraham,
yato|mūlāni duḥkhāni saṃbhavanti muhur muhuḥ.
putra|nāśe, 'rtha|nāśe ca, jñāti|saṃbandhinām atha
prāpyate su|mahad duḥkhaṃ viṣ'|âgni|pratimaṃ, vibho,
yena dahyanti gātrāṇi, yena prajñā vinaśyati,
yen' âbhibhūtaḥ puruṣo maraṇaṃ bahu manyate.
tad idaṃ vyasanaṃ prāptaṃ mayā bhāgya|viparyayāt.
tasy' ântaṃ n' âdhigacchāmi ṛte prāṇa|vimokṣaṇāt.
8.10 tath" âiv' âhaṃ kariṣyāmi ady' âiva, dvi|ja|sattama.»

ity uktvā tu mah"|ātmānaṃ pitaraṃ brahmavittamam,
Dhṛtarāṣṭro 'bhavan mūḍhaḥ, śokaṃ ca paramaṃ gataḥ,
abhūc ca tūṣṇīṃ rāj" âsau dhyāyamāno, mahī|pate.

tasya tad vacanaṃ śrutvā Kṛṣṇa|dvaipāyanaḥ prabhuḥ
putra|śok'|âbhisaṃtaptaṃ putraṃ vacanam abravīt.

VYĀSA uvāca:

Dhṛtarāṣṭra mahā|bāho, yat tvāṃ vakṣyāmi, tac chṛṇu.
śrutavān asi, medhāvī, dharm'|ârtha|kuśalas tathā.
na te 'sty a|viditaṃ kiñ cid veditavyaṃ, paraṃ|tapa.
a|nityatāṃ hi martyānāṃ vijānāsi, na saṃśayaḥ.
8.15 a|dhruve jīva|loke ca, sthāne v" â|śāśvate sati,
jīvite maraṇ'|ânte ca kasmāc chocasi, Bhārata?
pratyakṣaṃ tava, rāj'|êndra, vairasy' âsya samudbhavaḥ
putraṃ te kāraṇaṃ kṛtvā kāla|yogena kāritaḥ.
a|vaśyaṃ bhavitavye ca Kurūṇāṃ vaiśase, nṛpa,
kasmāc chocasi tāñ śūrān gatān paramikāṃ gatim?
jānatā ca, mahā|bāho, Vidureṇa mah"|ātmanā

"Damn mankind and all that humanity entails. From it springs the agonies that arise at every turn. Losing one's sons, one's wealth, one's relatives and family bring such extreme pain, like poison or fire, O lord, that it burns one's limbs and destroys one's sanity. Swamped by such things a man looks favorably on death. I will find no release from the disaster that has befallen me in this reversal of my for-
tunes, except in release from life itself. I shall achieve that 8.10
very thing this very day, most virtuous of twice-borns."

After addressing this last to his noble-souled father,* most experienced in sacred wisdom, Dhrita·rashtra was stupefied, so extreme was his grief, and, lord of the earth, he remained silent, lost in his thoughts.

On hearing what his son, inflamed by grief for his sons, had said, Vyasa, the Dark Lord of the Island spoke to him.

VYASA said:

Mighty Dhrita·rashtra, listen to what I am about to tell you. You are learned, wise and astute in religion and politics. You know everything there is to know, tormenter of your enemy. Surely you must understand the impermanence of mortals.

When the world of the living is inconstant, status is 8.15
not forever and all life ends in death, on what account do you grieve, king of Bhárata's line? The hostility came about before your eyes, lord of kings, brought about by a conjunction of predestination, through the medium of your son. The slaughter of the Kurus was inevitable, protector of men. Why grieve for those champions when they have reached the highest destiny? Mighty lord of the people, the

yatitaṃ sarva|yatnena śamaṃ prati, jan'|ēśvara.
na ca daiva|kṛto mārgaḥ śakyo bhūtena kena cit
ghaṭat" âpi ciraṃ kālaṃ niyantum, iti me matiḥ.
8.20 devatānāṃ hi yat kāryaṃ
    mayā pratyakṣataḥ śrutam,
tat te 'haṃ saṃpravakṣyāmi,
    kathaṃ* sthairyaṃ bhavet tava.
pur" âhaṃ tvarito yātaḥ sabhām Aindrīṃ jita|klamaḥ.
apaśyaṃ tatra ca tadā samavetān div'|âukasaḥ
Nārada|pramukhāṃś c' âpi sarvān deva|ṛṣīṃs tathā.†
tatra c' âpi mayā dṛṣṭā Pṛthivī, pṛthivī|pate,
kāry'|ârtham upasaṃprāptā devatānāṃ samīpataḥ.
upagamya tadā Dhātrī devān āha samāgatān:
«yat kāryaṃ mama yuṣmābhir Brahmaṇaḥ sadane tadā
pratijñātaṃ, mahā|bhāgās, tac chīghraṃ saṃvidhīyatām.»
8.25 tasyās tad vacanaṃ śrutvā Viṣṇur loka|namas|kṛtaḥ
uvāca vākyaṃ prahasan Pṛthivīṃ deva|saṃsadi:
«Dhṛtarāṣṭrasya putrāṇāṃ yas tu jyeṣṭhaḥ śatasya vai,
Duryodhana iti khyātaḥ, sa te kāryaṃ kariṣyati.
taṃ ca prāpya mahī|pālaṃ kṛta|kṛtyā bhaviṣyasi.
tasy' ârthe pṛthivī|pālāḥ Kuru|kṣetre samāgatāḥ
anyonyaṃ ghātayiṣyanti dṛḍhaiḥ śastraiḥ prahāriṇaḥ.
tatas te bhavitā, devi, bhārasya yudhi nāśanam.
gaccha śīghraṃ svakaṃ sthānaṃ, lokān dhāraya, śobhane.»
ya eṣa te suto, rājaṃ, loka|saṃhāra|kāraṇāt
8.30 Kaler aṃśaḥ samutpanno Gāndhāryā jaṭhare, nṛpa,
a|marṣī, capalaś c' âpi, krodhano, duṣ|prasādhanaḥ.

noble-souled Vídura, realizing what would happen, strove
for peace with all his might. But the path had been set by
divine Fate and no living being whatsoever could prevent
it, no matter how long they tried. That is my assessment.

For I heard from the gods in person what was to be done. 8.20
I shall describe that to you, so that you might find some
peace. On an earlier occasion, I had—suppressing my fa-
tigue—gone in haste to the court of Indra. And there I saw
at that time the inhabitants of heaven assembled, as well
as all the divine seers, headed by Nárada. There too, lord
of the earth, I saw the goddess Earth. Then the Earth who
bears us aloft, who had come to meet the gods in order to
get something, approached the assembled gods and said:
"That time in the abode of Brahma you made me a promise,
most bountiful lords. It should be fulfilled. Please let it be
arranged promptly."

On hearing her speak, Vishnu, revered by the whole 8.25
world, replied smiling to the goddess Earth amid the assembly of the gods, saying: "The oldest of the hundred sons
of Dhrita·rashtra, called Duryódhana, will carry out your
mission. Your purpose will be served using that protector
of the earth. On account of him all the protectors of the
earth are now gathering in the territory of the Kurus. Fighting with powerful weapons they will kill each other. Then,
goddess, the war will have relieved you of your burden. Return quickly to your own station and support the realms
of the world, lovely woman." The man who was your son,
Your Majesty, in order to bring about the destruction of
the world, was also a chip from the god Discord planted 8.30
in Gandhári's womb, protector of men. He was intolerant,

daiva|yogāt samutpannā bhrātaraś c' âsya tādṛśāḥ,
Śakunir mātulaś c' âiva, Karṇaś ca paramaḥ sakhā.
samutpannā vināś'|ârthaṃ pṛthivyāṃ sahitā nṛpāḥ.
yādṛśo jāyate rājā, tādṛśo 'sya jano bhavet.
a|dharmo dharmatāṃ yāti svāmī ced dhārmiko bhavet.
svāmino guṇa|doṣābhyāṃ bhṛtyāḥ syur. n' âtra saṃśayaḥ.
duṣṭaṃ rājānam āsādya gatās te tanayā, nṛpa.
etam arthaṃ, mahā|bāho, Nārado veda tattvataḥ.
8.35 ātm" âparādhāt putrās te vinaṣṭāḥ, pṛthivī|pate.
mā tāñ śocasva, rāj'|êndra. na hi śoke 'sti kāraṇam.
na hi te Pāṇḍavāḥ sv|alpam aparādhyanti, Bhārata.
putrās tava dur|ātmāno, yair iyaṃ ghātitā mahī.
Nāradena ca, bhadraṃ te, pūrvam eva, na saṃśayaḥ,
Yudhiṣṭhirasya samitau rāja|sūye niveditam:
«Pāṇḍavāḥ Kauravāḥ sarve samāsādya paras|param
na bhaviṣyanti, Kaunteya. yat te kṛtyaṃ, tad ācara.»
Nāradasya vacaḥ śrutvā tad" âśocanta Pāṇḍavāḥ.
evaṃ te sarvam ākhyātaṃ deva|guhyaṃ sanātanam,
8.40 kathaṃ* te śoka|nāśaḥ syāt, prāṇeṣu ca dayā, prabho,
snehaś ca Pāṇḍu|putreṣu jñātvā daiva|kṛtaṃ vidhim.
eṣa c' ârtho, mahā|bāho, pūrvam eva mayā śrutaḥ,
kathito dharma|rājasya rājasūye krat'|ûttame.
yatitaṃ dharma|putreṇa, mayā guhye nivedite,
a|vigrahe Kauravāṇāṃ. daivaṃ tu balavattaram.

treacherous, hot-tempered and insubordinate. By divine intervention his brothers turned out just like him, as did his uncle Shákuni and Karna, his best friend. The kings were all born at the same time on this earth for the sake of this holocaust. As the king is by nature, so his people become. A lawless people will become law-abiding if only their master respects the law. Subjects can be affected by the virtues or vices of their master. There is no doubt about this. Your family has gone because of their corrupt ruler, protector of people. Nárada knew the truth of this matter.

Lord of the earth, it is their own fault that your sons have 8.35
perished. Do not grieve for them, lord of kings, for there is no reason to grieve. For Pandu's sons did not commit the slightest wrong, king of Bhárata's line. It is your evil-hearted sons who have devastated this great earth. With respect, there is no doubt that this was the news that Nárada conveyed to Yudhi·shthira earlier at the latter's court on the occasion of his coronation. "The Pándavas and Káuravas will all attack each other and none will survive, son of Kunti. You must do your duty." At hearing Nárada's words on that occasion, the Pándavas were despondent.

I have told this entire undying secret of the gods so that
you might put an end to your grief and feel kindly towards 8.40
the living, lord, as well as affection for the sons of Pandu, now that you understand that it was ordained by divine Fate. Now this matter that I had heard before, powerful lord, I discussed with the righteous king Yudhi·shthira at his coronation, that highest of rites. Once I had revealed to him the secret, the righteous king made every effort to avoid war with the Káuravas, but divine fate was stronger.

an|atikramaṇīyo hi vidhī, rājan, kathaṃ cana,
Kṛtāntasya hi bhūtena sthāvareṇa carena ca.
bhavān dharma|paro yatra, buddhi|śreṣṭhaś ca, Bhārata,
muhyate prāṇināṃ jñātvā gatiṃ c' āgatim eva ca.
8.45 tvāṃ tu śokena saṃtaptaṃ muhyamānaṃ muhur muhu
jñātvā Yudhiṣṭhiro rājā prāṇān api parityajet.
kṛpālur nityaśo, vīras tiryag|yoni|gateṣv api,
sa kathaṃ tvayi, rāj'|êndra, kṛpāṃ vai na kariṣyati?
mama c' âiva niyogena, vidheś c' âpy a|nivartanāt,
Pāṇḍavānāṃ ca kāruṇyāt prāṇān dhāraya, Bhārata.
evaṃ te vartamānasya loke kīrtir bhaviṣyati,
dharm'|ârthaḥ su|mahāṃs, tāta, taptaṃ syāc ca tapaś cirāt.
putra|śoka|samutpannaṃ hut'|āśaṃ jvalitaṃ yathā
prajñ"|âmbhasā, mahā|rāja, nirvāpaya sadā sadā.

VAIŚAMPĀYANA uvāca:

8.50 tac chrutvā tasya vacanaṃ Vyāsasy' â|mita|tejasaḥ,
muhūrtaṃ samanudhyāya Dhṛtarāṣṭro 'bhyabhāṣata.
«mahatā śoka|jālena praṇunno 'smi, dvij'|ôttama.
n' ātmānam avabudhyāmi muhyamāno muhur muhuḥ.
idaṃ tu vacanaṃ śrutvā tava daiva|niyoga|jam,
dhārayiṣyāmy ahaṃ prāṇān, ghaṭiṣye ca na śocitum.»
etac chrutvā tu vacanaṃ Vyāsaḥ Satyavatī|sutaḥ
Dhṛtarāṣṭrasya, rāj'|êndra, tatr' âiv' ântar|adhīyata.

For the injunctions of the Bringer of Death are absolutely inviolable, Your Majesty, for every living being, static or mobile. King of Bhárata's line, while you, sir, set great store by your religious duty and the highest understanding, and while you have understood that all that breathe must come and go, you are nonetheless bewildered.

Now King Yudhi·shthira, realizing that you are consumed 8.45
with grief and distraught at every moment, also plans to take his own life. Constantly compassionate and heroic even towards animals, how could he not show sympathy to you, lord of kings? Out of obligation to me and in order not to repudiate divine injunction, as well as out of compassion for the Pándavas, you must continue living, king of Bhárata's line. If you do as I suggest you will be famed throughout the world as one dedicated to duty and truly great, my son, and long will your glory shine. Whenever the grief for your sons comes upon you, Your Majesty, consuming you like fire, put it out with the water of wisdom, every time.

VAISHAMPÁYANA continued:

When he had heard those words of Vyasa whose splendor 8.50
is beyond measure, Dhrita·rashtra thought for a moment then replied: "I am shaken by such an immense web of grief, best of the twice-born, I do not recognize myself, so bewildered am I at every moment. But on hearing what you said about this being the result of divine ordinance, I shall go on living, and I shall try not to succumb to grief." When Vyasa, son of Sátyavati, heard these words from Dhrita·rashtra, lord of kings, he vanished on the spot.

JANAMEJAYA uvāca:*

9.1 GATE BHAGAVATI Vyāse Dhṛtarāṣṭro mahī|patiḥ
kim aceṣṭata, vipra'|rṣe? tan me vyākhyātum arhasi.
tath" âiva Kauravo rājā Dharma|putro mahā|manāḥ,
Kṛpa|prabhṛtayaś c' âiva kim akurvata te trayaḥ?
Aśvatthāmnaḥ śrutaṃ karma, śāpaś c' ânyonya|kāritaḥ.
vṛttāntam uttaraṃ brūhi, yad abhāṣata Sañjayaḥ.

VAIŚAṂPĀYANA uvāca:

hate Duryodhane c' âiva, hate sainye ca sarvaśaḥ,
Sañjayo vigata|prajño Dhṛtarāṣṭram upasthitaḥ.

SAÑJAYA uvāca:

9.5 āgamya nānā|deśebhyo nānā|janapad'|ēśvarāḥ
pitṛ|lokaṃ gatā, rājan, sarve tava sutaiḥ saha.
yācyamānena satataṃ tava putreṇa, Bhārata,
ghātitā pṛthivī sarvā vairasy' ântaṃ vidhitsatā.
putrāṇām, atha pautrāṇāṃ, pitṝṇāṃ ca, mahī|pate,
ānupūrvyeṇa sarveṣāṃ preta|kāryāṇi kāraya.

VAIŚAMPĀYANA uvāca:

tac chrutvā vacanaṃ ghoraṃ Sañjayasya mahī|patiḥ
gat'|âsur iva niś|ceṣṭo nyapatat pṛthivī|tale.
taṃ śayānam upāgamya pṛthivyāṃ pṛthivī|patim.
Viduraḥ sarva|dharma|jña idaṃ vacanam abravīt:

JANAM·ÉJAYA asked:

WHEN LORD VYASA had departed, what did the lord of 9.1
the earth, Dhrita·rashtra do, poet of the sages? You should relate that to me. The king of the Káuravas too, the high-souled son of Dharma and the group of three headed by Kripa, what did they all do? I have heard what Ashva·tthaman did, and of the curses mutually cast. Tell me now the further happenings which Sánjaya reported.

VAISHAMPÁYANA continued:

With Duryódhana killed, and the army completely slain, Sánjaya, whose ability to know distant events had now disappeared, reached Dhrita·rashtra.

SÁNJAYA spoke:

The rulers of many different countries who had come 9.5
here from many different regions, have all departed to the realm of the ancestors, lord, in the company of your sons. King of Bhárata's line, your son, in spite of continual entreaty, has forced the annihilation of the entire earth in his quest to wipe out his enemy. Lord of the earth, you should arrange for the performance of the funerary rites for all of them, in appropriate order: sons, grandsons and fathers.

VAISHAMPÁYANA continued:

When the lord of the earth heard those woeful words of Sánjaya, the breath went out of him, and he fell motionless on the ground. Vídura, who knows the duty of all, came up to the lord of the earth as he lay upon the ground, and said these words:

9.10 «uttiṣṭha, rājan. kiṃ śeṣe? mā śuco, Bharata'|rṣabha.
eṣā vai sarva|sattvānāṃ, lok'|ēśvara, parā gatiḥ.
a|bhāv'|ādīni bhūtāni, bhāva|madhyāni, Bhārata,
a|bhāva|nidhanāny eva. tatra kā paridevanā?
na śocan mṛtam anveti. na śocan mriyate naraḥ.
evaṃ sāṃsiddhike loke kim|artham anuśocasi?
a|yudhamāno mriyate, yudhyamānas tu jīvati.
kālaṃ prāpya, mahā|rāja, na kaścid ativartate.
kālaḥ karṣati bhūtāni sarvāṇi vividhāny uta.
na kālasya priyaḥ kaś cin, na dveṣyaḥ, Kuru|sattama.
9.15 yathā vāyus tṛṇ'|âgrāṇi saṃvartayati sarvaśaḥ,
tathā kāla|vaśaṃ yānti bhūtāni, Bharata'|rṣabha.
eka|sārtha|prayātānāṃ sarveṣāṃ tatra gāminām
yasya kālaḥ prayāty agre, tatra kā paridevanā?
yāṃś c' âpi nihatān yuddhe, rājaṃs, tvam anuśocasi,
na śocyā hi mah"|ātmānaḥ, sarve te tri|divaṃ gatāḥ.
na yajñair dakṣiṇāvadbhir, na tapobhir, na vidyayā
tathā svargaṃ upāyānti, yathā śūrās tanu|tyajaḥ.
sarve veda|vidaḥ śūrāḥ, sarve su|carita|vratāḥ,
sarve c' âbhimukhāḥ kṣīṇās. tatra kā paridevanā?
9.20 śarīr'|âgniṣu śūrāṇāṃ juhuvus te śar'|āhutī,
hūyamānāñ śarāṃś c' âiva sehur uttama|pūruṣāḥ.
evaṃ, rājaṃs, tav' ācakṣe svargyaṃ panthānam uttamam.
na yuddhād adhikaṃ kiñ cit kṣatriyasy' êha vidyate.
kṣatriyās te mah"|ātmānaḥ, śūrāḥ, samiti|śobhanāḥ,

"Get up, Your Majesty. Why are you lying there? Don't succumb to grief, bull of Bhárata's line. For, lord of the world, this is the ultimate destiny of all beings. 9.10

Beings begin in non-being. For the duration they have being. They culminate in non-being again. What is sad in that? Not by grieving does a man escort the dead. Not by grieving does he die. When the world is made this way, what purpose does sadness serve? One who does not fight may still die, while one who fights might live. Your Majesty, no-one, once the time has come, can put it off. Time drags away all beings of whatever kind. Time neither favors nor picks on anyone, most exalted of the Kurus.

Just as the wind buffets the blades of grass twisting them 9.15 this way and that, so living beings fall under the sway of Time, bull of Bhárata's line. When all beings progress as a single caravan, traveling their way, why lament the one among them whom death meets first? Sire, you grieve for those slain in battle, who do not warrant grief, since, they, noble-souled, have all gone to the third heaven. Neither gift-laden sacrifice, nor austerities, nor learning bring people to heaven, as surely as the sacrifice made by heroes when they give up their bodies. All those heroes knew the Vedas. They all lived true to their vows and they have all perished in action. What is sad about that?

They have performed their sacrifices by pouring arrows 9.20 as oblations into the heroes whose bodies were the fire. In return those most excellent men bore the arrows oblated into them. This, I tell you, Your Majesty, is the highest path to heaven. There is nothing better for a warrior in this world than a war. Those noble-souled men of the warrior caste are

āśiṣaṃ paramāṃ prāptā; na śocyāḥ sarva eva hi.
ātman" ātmānam āśvāsya mā śucaḥ, puruṣa'|rṣabha.
n' âdya śok'|âbhibhūtas tvaṃ kāryam* utsraṣṭum arhasi.

heroes, the medallions of their society. They have attained the highest blessing. Not one of them warrants grieving. Recover yourself and do not grieve, bull of mankind.

You should not abandon your duty now by falling prey to grief.

10–15
FAREWELLS AND RECONCILIATION

VAIŚAMPĀYANA uvāca:

10.1 VIDURASYA TU TAD vākyaṃ śrutvā tu puruṣa'|rṣabhaḥ
«yujyatāṃ yānam,» ity uktvā punar vacanam abravīt:
«śīghram ānaya Gāndhārīṃ, sarvāś ca Bharata|striyaḥ,
vadhūṃ Kuntīm upādāya, yāś c' ânyās tatra yoṣitaḥ.»
evam uktvā sa dharm'|ātmā Viduraṃ dharmavittamam
śoka|viprahata|jñāno yānam ev' ânvapadyata.
Gāndhārī putra|śok'|ârtā, bhartur vacana|coditā,
saha Kuntyā yato rājā, saha strībhir upādravat.
10.5 tāḥ samāsādya rājānaṃ bhṛśaṃ śoka|samanvitāḥ
āmantry' ânyonyam īyuḥ sma, bhṛśam uccukruśus tataḥ.
tāḥ samāśvāsayat kṣattā, tābhyaś c' ârtataraḥ svayam;
aśru|kaṇṭhīḥ samāropya tato 'sau niryayau purāt.
tataḥ praṇādaḥ saṃjajñe sarveṣu Kuru|veśmasu.
ā|kumāraṃ puraṃ sarvam abhavac choka|karśitam.
a|dṛṣṭa|pūrvā yā nāryaḥ purā deva|gaṇair api,
pṛthag|janena dṛśyanta* tās tadā nihat'|ēśvarāḥ.
prakīrya keśān su|śubhān, bhūṣaṇāny avamucya ca,
eka|vastra|dharā nāryaḥ paripetur a|nāthavat.

VAISHAMPÁYANA continued:

NOW, WHEN THE bull among men had heard Vídura's words, he first issued the command for his chariot to be made ready then spoke again: "Quickly, bring Gandhári here, and all the women of the Bhárata clan, including my sister-in-law Kunti, and the other women on that side." When that dutiful king had issued this request to Vídura, the foremost expert on duty, though his senses were stunned by grief, he mounted his chariot. Gandhári, afflicted by grief for her sons, was stirred to action by the words of her husband and hurried, with Kunti and with the other women, to the king. 10.1

When they reached the king, so extremely overwhelmed 10.5
by grief as they were, they called out to each other as they met together, and broke into a high wailing. As he assisted them in mounting, Vídura, the slave girl's son, tried to comfort them as their throats choked with tears, though he was himself more in sorrow than they; and then he drove with them out of the city. At that a wail became audible in every Kuru household. The entire city, even the children, was distraught with grief. Those ladies who had never been seen before even by the hosts of gods were now on public display, now that their lords were slain. They had let down their exquisite hair and removed their jewelry. Dressed in just a single shift, the ladies wandered around with no one to protect them.

10.10 śveta|parvata|rūpebhyo gṛhebhyas tās tv apākraman,
guhābhya iva śailānāṃ pṛṣatyo hata|yūtha|pāḥ.
tāny udīrṇāni nārīṇāṃ tadā vṛndāny an|ekaśaḥ
śok'|ārtāny adravan, rājan, kiśorīṇām iv' âṅgane.
pragṛhya bāhūn, krośantyaḥ putrān, bhrātṝn, pitṝn api,
darśayant' îva tā ha sma yug'|ânte loka|saṃkṣayam.
vilapantyo, rudantyaś ca, dhāvamānās tatas tataḥ;
śoken' âbhyāhata|jñānāḥ kartavyaṃ na prajajñire.
vrīḍāñ jagmuḥ purā yāḥ sma sakhīnām api yoṣitaḥ,
tā eka|vastrā, nir|lajjāḥ śvaśrūṇāṃ purato 'bhavan.
10.15 paras|paraṃ su|sūkṣmeṣu śokeṣv āśvāsayaṃs tadā
tāḥ śoka|vihvalā, rājan, na vaikṣanta paras|param.*
tābhiḥ parivṛto rājā rudatībhiḥ sahasraśaḥ
niryayau nagarād dīnas tūrṇam āyodhanaṃ prati.
śilpino, vaṇijo, vaiśyāḥ sarva|karm'|ôpajīvinaḥ
te pārthivaṃ puras|kṛtya niryayur nagarād bahiḥ.
tāsāṃ vikrośamānānām ārtānāṃ Kuru|saṃkṣaye
prādur āsīn mahāñ śabdo vyathayan bhuvanāny uta,
yug'|ânta|kāle saṃprāpte bhūtānāṃ dahyatām iva.
«a|bhāvaḥ syād ayaṃ prāpta,» iti bhūtāni menire.
10.20 bhṛśam udvigna|manasas te paurāḥ Kuru|saṃkṣaye
prākrośanta, mahā|rāja, sv|anuraktās tadā bhṛśam.

From out of the houses that towered like white mountains they poured, like dappled does emerging from the caves amid the craggy peaks, when the head of the herd has died. As left and right those herds of ladies emerged from their homes, in the shock of their grief, they ran about like fillies in an arena, Your Majesty. Clinging to each other's arms, crying out for their sons, brothers and fathers, they seemed to presage the destruction of the universe at the end of the world. Rambling and weeping they rushed about here and there; their senses stunned by grief, they had no clue what they should do. Those women who even before as close girl-friends had been shy, now though dressed only in a shift felt no shame before their mothers-in-law. 10.10

Those who had comforted each other in even the slightest sorrows, now ignored one another, Your Majesty, so distraught with grief were they. Surrounded by those women wailing in their thousands, the king, looking drawn, set out at some speed from the city to the site of the battle. Artisans, merchants, members of the vaishya clan and all those who labor for a living fell in behind the king and also went out from the city. From those women, as they wailed in their distress at the destruction of the Kurus, a great clamor arose, making the very heavens shake. They sounded like living beings being burned alive at the dawn of the apocalypse. Creatures round about reacted to the sound, convinced the end had come. 10.15

Their composure so terribly shaken at the destruction of the Kurus, great king, the citizens, who had been so devoted to them, wailed aloud. 10.20

VAIŚAMPĀYANA uvāca:

11.1 KROŚA|MĀTRAM tato gatvā dadṛśus tān mahā|rathān,
Śāradvataṃ Kṛpaṃ, Drauṇiṃ, Kṛtavarmāṇam eva ca.
te tu dṛṣṭv" âiva rājānaṃ prajñā|cakṣuṣam īśvaram,
aśru|kaṇṭhā viniḥśvasya rudantam idam abruvan:
«putras tava, mahā|rāja, kṛtvā karma su|duṣ|karam,
gataḥ s'|ânucaro, rājañ, Śakra|lokaṃ mahī|patiḥ.
Duryodhana|balān muktā vayam eva trayo rathāḥ.
sarvam anyat parikṣīṇaṃ sainyaṃ te, Bharata'|ṛṣabha.»
11.5 ity evam uktvā rājānaṃ Kṛpaḥ Śāradvatas tadā
Gāndhārīṃ putra|śok'|ārtām idaṃ vacanam abravīt:
«a|bhītā yudhyamānās te, ghnantaḥ śatru|gaṇān bahūn,
vīra|karmāṇi kurvāṇāḥ putrās te nidhanaṃ gatāḥ.
dhruvaṃ saṃprāpya lokāṃs te nir|malāñ śastra|nirjitān,
bhāsvaraṃ deham āsthāya viharanty amarā iva.
na hi kaś cidd hi śūrāṇāṃ yudhyamānaḥ parāṅ|mukhaḥ
śastreṇa nidhanaṃ prāpto, na ca kaś cit kṛt'|âñjaliḥ.
evaṃ tāṃ kṣatriyasy' āhuḥ purāṇāḥ paramāṃ gatim:
śastreṇa nidhanaṃ saṃkhye. tān na śocitum arhasi.
11.10 na c' âpi śatravas teṣām ṛdhyante, rājñi, Pāṇḍavāḥ.
śṛṇu yat kṛtam asmābhir Aśvatthāma|purogamaiḥ.
a|dharmeṇa hataṃ śrutvā Bhīmasenena te sutam,
suptaṃ śibiram āsādya Pāṇḍūnāṃ kadanaṃ kṛtam.
Pāñcālā nihatāḥ sarve Dhṛṣṭadyumna|purogamāḥ,
Drupadasy' ātmajāś c' âiva, Draupadeyāś ca pātitāḥ.

VAISHAMPÁYANA continued:

WHEN THEY HAD gone but a league they saw those great chariot warriors, Kripa of the Sharádvata tribe, Drona's son and Krita·varman. Now they in turn, on seeing the king, their lord for whom insight served as sight, said to him as he wept, their throats choked with tears, their chests heaving: "Your son, great king, after accomplishing nigh impossible feats, though a lord of this world, Your Majesty, has departed with his attendants to the world of Indra. We are the only three chariot warriors from Duryódhana's army to have escaped. The rest of the your army is wiped out, bull of Bháratas." 11.1

When they had said this to the king, Kripa of the Sharád- 11.5
vatas then turned to Gandhári, who was grief-stricken on account of her son, and said these words: "Fighting fearlessly your sons slew many hordes of enemies; they met their end performing the actions of heroes. It is certain that those killed by the sword enter the immaculate worlds where, in splendid embodiments, they live like the immortals. Not one of those heroes fled while fighting and none met their death by the sword in surrender. Death in combat by the sword—this was declared by men of old as the highest destiny of the warrior. You should not regret their death.

Moreover their enemies, the Pándavas, do not flourish, 11.10
Your Majesty. Hear what we managed under Ashva·tthaman's leadership. When we heard how your son was unlawfully murdered by Bhima·sena, we breached their camp while they slept and we slaughtered them. All the Panchálas met their death and Dhrishta·dyumna showed them the way. Drúpada's issue have all been brought down, as have

tathā viśasanaṃ kṛtvā putra|śatru|gaṇasya te
prādravāma, raṇe sthātuṃ na hi śakyāmahe trayaḥ.
te hi śūrā mah"|êṣv|āsāḥ kṣipram eṣyanti Pāṇḍavāḥ,
a|marṣa|vaśam āpannā, vairaṃ pratijihīrṣavaḥ.

11.15 te hatān ātmajāñ śrutvā, pramattāḥ puruṣa'|rṣabhāḥ
ninīṣantaḥ† padaṃ śūrāḥ kṣipram eva, yaśasvini.
teṣāṃ tu kadanaṃ kṛtvā saṃsthātuṃ n' ôtsahāmahe.
anujānīhi no, rājñi, mā ca śoke manaḥ kṛthāḥ.
rājaṃs, tvam anujānīhi,
    dhairyam ātiṣṭha c' ôttamam.
diṣṭ'|ântaṃ paśya c' âpi tvaṃ,
    kṣatraṃ dharmaṃ ca kevalam.»
ity evam uktvā, rājānaṃ kṛtvā c' âbhipradakṣiṇam,
Kṛpaś ca, Kṛta|varmā ca, Droṇa|putraś ca, Bhārata,
avekṣamāṇā rājānaṃ Dhṛtarāṣṭraṃ manīṣiṇam,
Gaṅgām anu, mahā|rāja, tūrṇam aśvān acodayan.

11.20 apakramya tu te, rājan, sarva eva mahā|rathāḥ
āmantry' ânyonyam udvignās tridhā te prayayus tataḥ.
jagāma Hāstinapuraṃ Kṛpaḥ Śāradvatas tadā.
svam eva rāṣṭraṃ Hārdikyo. Drauṇir Vyās'|āśramaṃ yayau.
evaṃ te prayayur vīrā vīkṣamāṇāḥ paras|param,
bhay'|ārtāḥ Pāṇḍu|putrāṇām, āgas kṛtvā mah"|ātmanām.

the sons of Dráupadi. Now that we have wrought such carnage on your son's clans of enemies, we have to flee, for the three of us cannot hold our own in battle. It is certain that the valiant Pándavas, great archers all, will be hot on our trail, driven by outrage, determined to take revenge for our savage act.

Maddened on hearing that we slew their sons, those 11.15
valiant bulls of men are quickly tracking us down, illustrious lady. After slaughtering their people, we dare not stand about. Give us leave, majestic queen, and do not allow yourself to be occupied with grief. Majestic king, please give us leave too, and maintain your excellent composure. And remember, death is the warrior's only duty." When they had finished speaking, Kripa, Krita·varman and Drona's son processed respectfully* around the king, king of Bhárata's line. Still gazing at the wise king Dhrita·rashtra, Your Majesty, they spurred their horses swiftly onwards, towards the Ganges.

Now once those great chariot warriors were out of eye- 11.20
shot, they also took their leave of one another and, fearing the worst, split up, each of the three heading in a different direction. So Kripa, son of Sharádvat, set out for the city of Hástina·pura. Krita·varman, son of Hrídika, went to his own kingdom. Drona's son made for Vyasa's hermitage. That is how those daring men continued their separate ways, constantly looking back towards each other, terrified of Pandu's noble-souled sons after the outrage they had committed against them.

sametya vīrā rājānaṃ tadā tv an|udite ravau,
viprajagmur mah"|ātmāno yath" êcchakam ariṃ|damāḥ.
samāsādy' âtha vai Drauṇiṃ Pāṇḍu|putrā mahā|rāthāḥ,
vyajayaṃs te raṇe, rājan, vikramya tad|anantaram.

VAIŚAMPĀYANA uvāca:

12.1 HATEṢU SARVA|sainyeṣu dharma|rājo Yudhiṣṭhiraḥ
śuśruve pitaraṃ vṛddhaṃ niryātaṃ gaja|sāhvayāt.
so 'bhyayāt putra|śok'|ārtaḥ putra|śoka|pariplutam,
śocamānaṃ, mahā|rāja, bhrātṛbhiḥ sahitas tadā,
anvīyamāno vīreṇa Dāśārheṇa mah"|ātmanā,
Yuyudhānena ca tathā, tath" âiva ca Yuyutsunā.
tam anvagāt su|duḥkh'|ārtā Draupadī śoka|karśitā
saha Pāñcāla|yoṣidbhir, yās tatr' āsan samāgatāḥ.

12.5 sa Gaṅgām anu vṛndāni strīṇāṃ, Bharata|sattama,
kurarīṇām iv' ārtānāṃ krośantīnāṃ dadarśa ha.
tābhiḥ parivṛto rājā krośantībhiḥ sahasraśaḥ,
ūrdhva|bāhubhir, ārtābhī, rudatībhiḥ priy'|â|priyaiḥ:
«kva nu dharmajñatā rājñaḥ? kva nu s" âdy' â|nṛśaṃsatā?
yac c' âvadhīt pitṝn, bhrātṝn, guru|putrān, sakhīn api.
ghātayitvā kathaṃ Droṇaṃ Bhīṣmaṃ c' âpi pitā|maham
manas te 'bhūn, mahā|bāho, hatvā c' âpi Jayad|ratham?
kiṃ nu rājyena te kāryaṃ, pitṝn bhrātṝn a|paśyataḥ,

It was at that point that those noble-souled champions, subduers of their foe, having met the king, set out on their different paths to the place of their choosing before the sun had risen. It was immediately after that, Your Majesty, that the great chariot-warrior sons of Pandu caught up with Drona's son, and, engaging him in combat, vanquished him.

VAISHAMPÁYANA continued:

THE RIGHTEOUS KING Yudhi·shthira heard that, now that 12.1
all the soldiers were slain, the aged head of his family* had set out from that city homonymous with an elephant.* He set out to meet him, one grief-stricken father toward the other, he grieving in the company of his brothers at that time, great king. He was attended by the heroic, noble-souled Krishna of Dashárha's line, along with Sátyaki the Constant Warrior and keen-fighting Yuyútsu. Behind them came Dráupadi, suffering terribly, distraught with grief, along with the Panchála women who had all gathered together there.

Towards the Ganges he could see the groups of women, 12.5
best of the Bháratas, keening like female eagles in distress. The king was surrounded by those women wailing in their thousands, their arms raised up to the sky, crying out in anguish, on account of those loved and those not:* "Now where is the king's understanding of Dharma, where his superior morality, now that he has killed his fathers, his brothers, the sons of his teachers and his friends! Now that you've brought about the death of Drona and our patriarch Bhishma, and now that you've killed Jayad·ratha, how have

Abhimanyuṃ ca durdharṣaṃ, Draupadeyāṃś ca, Bhārata?»
12.10 atītya tā mahā|bāhuḥ krośantīḥ kurarīr iva,
vavande pitaraṃ jyeṣṭhaṃ dharma|rājo Yudhiṣṭhiraḥ.
tato 'bhivādya pitaraṃ dharmeṇ' âmitra|karśanāḥ
nyavedayanta nāmāni Pāṇḍavās te 'pi sarvaśaḥ.
tam ātmaj'|ânta|karaṇaṃ pitā putra|vadh'|ârditaḥ,
a|prīyamāṇaḥ, śok'|ārtaḥ Pāṇḍavaṃ pariṣasvaje.
dharma|rājaṃ pariṣvajya sāntvayitvā ca, Bhārata,
duṣṭ'|ātmā Bhīmam anvaicchad, didhakṣur iva pāvakaḥ.
sa kopa|pāvakas tasya śoka|vāyu|samīritaḥ
Bhīmasena|mayaṃ dāvaṃ didhakṣur iva dṛśyate.
12.15 tasya saṃkalpam ājñāya Bhīmaṃ praty a|śubhaṃ Hariḥ,
Bhīmam ākṣipya pāṇibhyāṃ pradadau Bhīmam āyasam.
prāg eva tu mahā|buddhir buddhvā tasy' êṅgitaṃ Hariḥ,
saṃvidhānaṃ mahā|prājñas tatra cakre jan'|ârdanaḥ.
taṃ gṛhītv" âiva pāṇibhyāṃ Bhīmasenam ayasmayam,
babhañja balavān rājā manyamāno Vṛkodaram.
nāg'|âyuta|bala|prāṇaḥ sa rājā Bhīmam āyasam
bhaṅktvā vimathit'|ôraskaḥ susrāva rudhiraṃ mukhāt.
tataḥ papāta medinyāṃ tath" âiva rudhir'|ôkṣitaḥ,
prapuṣpit'|âgra|śikharaḥ pārijāta iva drumaḥ

you not lost your mind, great-armed warrior? What is the point of ruling, king of Bhárata's line, when you can see neither your father nor uncles nor your half-brothers, nor the irrepressible Abhimányu, nor Dráupadi's sons?"

Passing beyond the women as they continued to call out 12.10
like ospreys, the righteous king Yudhi·shthira saluted his seniormost uncle. Then the Pándavas, those harassers of their enemies, greeting their uncle with the respect due his station, each announced themselves by name. Their uncle, tormented by the killing of his own sons and oppressed by grief, reluctantly embraced that son of Pandu who had fetched his own sons to their death. When he had embraced the righteous king and spoken to him kindly, king of Bhárata's line, his heart soured as he sought for Bhima, like a fire set to burn. The fire of his anger, inflamed by the wind of his grief, looked set to burn the forest that was Bhima·sena.

Detecting Dhrita·rashtra's evil intentions towards Bhima, 12.15
Krishna removed Bhima and presented with both hands a metal Bhima in his place. From the outset Krishna, possessed of great insight, had intuited Dhrita·rashtra's secret plan, and, with great foresight, the rouser of the people had prepared the contrivance for this eventuality. With both hands the king embraced the Bhima·sena made of metal and with an extraordinary display of strength, he broke it, thinking it was Wolf-Belly. Harnessing his vital force, equivalent to that of ten thousand elephants, the king shattered the Bhima of iron, crushing his own chest in the process. Blood spewed from his mouth. Then he fell upon the

12.20 paryagṛhṇāc ca taṃ vidvān sūto Gāvalgaṇis tadā,
«m' âivam,» ity abravīc c' âinaṃ śamayan, sāntvayann iva.
sa tu kopaṃ samutsrjya gata|manyur mahā|manāḥ
«hā, hā, Bhīm'!» êti cukrośa nṛpaḥ śoka|samanvitaḥ.

taṃ viditvā gata|krodhaṃ Bhīmasena|vadh'|ârditam,
Vāsudevo varaḥ puṃsām idaṃ vacanam abravīt:

«mā śuco, Dhṛtarāṣṭra, tvaṃ. n' âiṣa Bhīmas tvayā hataḥ.
āyasī pratimā hy eṣā tvayā niṣpātitā, vibho.
tvāṃ krodha|vaśam āpannaṃ viditvā, Bharata'|rṣabha,
may' âpakṛṣṭaḥ Kaunteyo mṛtyor daṃṣṭr'|ântaraṃ gataḥ.
12.25 na hi te, rāja|śārdūla, bale tulyo 'sti kaś cana.
kaḥ saheta, mahā|bāho, bāhvor nigrahaṇaṃ naraḥ?
yath" ântakam anuprāpya jīvan kaś cin na mucyate,
evaṃ bāhv|antaraṃ prāpya tava jīven na kaś cana.
tasmāt putreṇa yā te 'sau pratimā kārit" āyasī,
bhīmasya s" êyaṃ, Kauravya, tav' âiv' ôpahṛtā mayā.
putra|śok'|âbhisaṃtaptaṃ dharmād apahṛtaṃ manaḥ
tava, rāj'|êndra, tena tvaṃ Bhīmasenaṃ jighāṃsasi.
na tv etat te kṣamaṃ, rājan, hanyās tvaṃ yad Vṛkodaram.
na hi putrā, mahā|rāja, jīveyus te kathaṃ cana.
12.30 tasmād yat kṛtam asmābhir manyamānaiḥ śamaṃ prati,
anumanyasva tat sarvaṃ, mā ca śoke manaḥ kṛthāḥ.»

ground, now splattered with blood, like the coral tree* blossoming at the tip of its crown.

Sánjaya, son of Gaválgana, his experienced charioteer 12.20
then gathered him in his arms and said to him, "Don't do this," trying to calm and sooth him. But now the noble-souled king gave up his anger and put aside his pride, overcome by grief crying out, "Oh no, oh no Bhima!"

Seeing that his anger had passed and that he that he was pained at his apparent killing of Bhima, Krishna, son of Vasu·deva, the best of men, said these words:

"There's no need to grieve, Dhrita·rashtra. This is not Bhima that you have slain since this is a metallic statue that you destroyed, powerful lord. Seeing you in the grip of wrath, bull of Bhárata, I had snatched Kunti's son out from the maw of death.

Since no one is your equal in strength, tiger of a king, 12.25
what man could survive being clenched in your embrace, strong-armed lord? Just as no living being who meets with the bringer of death can be freed, so no one who comes within the embrace of your arms could survive. For that reason I placed this metal statue that your son had caste of Bhima in front of you, king of the Kurus. Your mind had been distracted from Dharma, so distraught was it by grief for your son. So, lord of Kings, you hoped to kill Bhima·sena. But it is not right that you should kill Wolf-Belly, since
your sons would not be alive now in any case. Therefore 12.30
you should accept what we have done in the name of peace, rather than turning your thoughts to grief."

VAIŚAMPĀYANA uvāca:

13.1 TATA ENAM UPĀTIṢṬHAÑ śauc'|ârthaṃ paricārakāḥ.
kṛta|śaucaṃ punaś c' âinaṃ provāca Madhu|sūdanaḥ:
«rājann, adhītā vedās te, śāstrāṇi vividhāni ca,
śrutāni ca purāṇāni, rāja|dharmāś ca kevalāḥ.
evaṃ vidvān, mahā|prājñaḥ, samarthaḥ san bal'|â|bale
ātm'|âparādhāt kasmāt tvaṃ kuruṣe kopam īdṛśam?
uktavāṃs tvāṃ tad" âiv' âhaṃ, Bhīṣma|Droṇau ca, Bhārata,
Viduraḥ, Sañjayaś c'âiva vākyaṃ, rājan; na tat kṛthāḥ.
13.5 sa vāryamāṇo n' âsmākam akārṣīr vacanaṃ tadā,
Pāṇḍavān adhikāñ jānan bale śaurye ca, Kaurava.
rājā hi yaḥ sthira|prajñaḥ svayaṃ doṣān avekṣate
deśa|kāla|vibhāgaṃ ca, paraṃ śreyaḥ sa vindati.
ucyamānas tu yaḥ śreyo gṛhṇīte no hit'|âhite,
āpadaḥ samanuprāpya sa śocaty a|naye sthitaḥ.
tato 'nya|vṛttam ātmānaṃ samavekṣasva, Bhārata.
rājaṃs, tvaṃ hy a|vidhey'|ātmā Duryodhana|vaśe sthitaḥ.
ātm'|âparādhād āpannas tat kiṃ Bhīmaṃ jighāṃsasi?
tasmāt saṃyaccha kopaṃ tvaṃ. svam anusmara duṣ|kṛtam.

VAISHAMPÁYANA continued:

THEN HIS ATTENDANTS approached to clean him up. 13.1
When the blood had been cleaned from him, the slayer of Madhu again spoke to him: "Your Majesty, you have understood the Vedas, and many different branches of learning. You have heard the texts of ancient lore, and all the duties of kings. When you are so learned and steeped in wisdom, so capable of assessing relative strength and weakness, why do you respond angrily like this at what happened as a result of your own failings? Furthermore, I was not alone in advising you at that time—Bhishma and Drona, king of Bhárata's line, as well as Vídura and Sánjaya did so too, but you ignored that advice, Your Majesty.

Though we tried to stop you, you then went against our 13.5
advice, even though you knew that the Pándavas were superior in strength and courage. Now a king of reliable insight reflects on his own weaknesses and the particularities of the location and occasion to work out the better course. But the one who, though counseled as to the best path, as to what is beneficial or harmful, refuses to accept that advice, he later rues his conduct, once calamities befall him and he is stuck in adversity. So consider how you allowed your behavior to be directed by the behavior of another, king of Bhárata's line. For, Your Majesty, by not governing yourself you allowed Duryódhana to direct you. So why do you want to kill Bhima, when what has befallen you is the result of your own failings? For that reason you should curb your anger. You should be mindful of your own misconduct.

13.10 yas tu tāṃ spardhayā kṣudraḥ Pāñcālīm ānayat sabhām,
sa hato Bhīmasenena vairaṃ pratijihīrṣatā.
ātmano 'tikramaṃ paśya, putrasya ca dur|ātmanaḥ,
yad an|āgasi Pāṇḍūnāṃ parityāgaḥ, paraṃ|tapa.»

VAIŚAMPĀYANA uvāca:

evam uktaḥ sa Kṛṣṇena sarvaṃ satyaṃ, jan'|âdhipa,
uvāca Devakī|putraṃ Dhṛtarāṣṭro mahī|patiḥ:
«evam etan, mahā|bāho, yathā vadasi, Mādhava.
putra|snehas tu balavān dhairyān māṃ samacālayat.
diṣṭyā tu puruṣa|vyāghro balavān satya|vikramaḥ
tvad|gupto n' āgamat, Kṛṣṇa, Bhīmo bāhv|antaraṃ mama.
13.15 idānīṃ tv aham ek'|âgro, gata|manyur, gata|jvaraḥ,
madhyamaṃ Pāṇḍavaṃ vīraṃ draṣṭum icchāmi, Mādhava.
hateṣu pārthiv'|êndreṣu, putreṣu nihateṣu ca,
Pāṇḍu|putreṣu vai śarma prītiś c' âpy avatiṣṭhate.»
tataḥ sa Bhīmaṃ ca, Dhanaṃjayaṃ ca,
Mādryāś ca putrau puruṣa|pravīrau
pasparśa gātraiḥ prarudan su|gātrān;
āśvāsya kalyāṇam uvāca c' âitān.

The low villain who out of jealousy dragged the princess 13.10
of the Panchálas into the assembly was killed by Bhima out of revenge.* Look to your own transgression and that of your evil-hearted son, which led you to abandon your brother Pandu's sons, when no offense had been committed on their side, scourge of your foes."

VAISHAMPÁYANA continued:

Sovereign of the people, when Krishna, son of Dévaki, had pointed out the entire truth to Dhrita·rashtra, lord of the earth, in this manner, the latter then replied to him: "It is true what you say, strong-armed warrior of the line of Madhu. The powerful affection I feel for my son shook my composure. Thank goodness that—thanks to your protecting him, Krishna—Bhima the powerful tiger of a man, courageous in fulfilling his oath, did not come within my grasp.

But now I am composed again, my pride is extinguished 13.15
and with it my fever. I long to see that heroic middle son of Pandu, Krishna. Now that the lords of the earth have been killed and my sons all slain, my safety, and even my joy, is entirely dependent on the sons of Pandu." Then he embraced Bhima, Árjuna, the winner of the spoils, and those two eminent heroes among men, the twins of Madri, weeping as he did so, and, comforting their dear bodies with his touch, he spoke kindly to them.

VAIŚAMPĀYANA uvāca:

14.1 DHṚTARĀṢṬR'|âbhyanujñātās tatas te Kuru|Pāṇḍavāḥ
abhyayur bhrātaraḥ sarve Gāndhārīṃ saha|Keśavāḥ.
tato jñātvā hat'|âmitraṃ Yudhiṣṭhiram upāgatam,
Gāndhārī putra|śok'|ārtā śaptum aicchad a|ninditā.
tasyāḥ pāpam abhiprāyaṃ viditvā Pāṇḍavān prati,
ṛṣiḥ Satyavatī|putraḥ prāg eva samabudhyata.
sa Gaṅgāyām upaspṛśya puṇya|gandhi payaḥ śuci,
taṃ deśam upasaṃpede parama'|rṣir mano|javaḥ.
14.5 divyena cakṣuṣā paśyan manasā tad|gatena ca,
sarva|prāṇa|bhṛtāṃ bhāvaṃ sa tatra samabudhyata.
sa snuṣām abravīt kāle kalya|vādī mahā|tapāḥ,
śāpa|kālam avākṣipya śama|kālam udīrayan:
«na kopaḥ Pāṇḍave kāryo, Gāndhāri. śamam āpnuhi.
vaco nigṛhyatām, etac chṛṇu c' êdaṃ vaco mama.
ukt" âsy aṣṭādaś' âhāni putreṇa jayam icchatā,
‹śivam āśāsva me, mātar, yudhyamānasya śatrubhiḥ.›
sā tathā yācyamānā tvaṃ kāle kāle jay'|âiṣiṇā
uktavaty asi, Gāndhāri, ‹yato dharmas tato jayaḥ!›

VAISHAMPÁYANA continued:

THEN, WITH Dhrita·rashtra's permission, all the brothers, those sons of Pandu of the Kuru clan, set off to meet Gandhári, in the company of Krishna, the long-haired lord. At that, realizing that Yudhi·shthira, who had killed his enemies, had arrived, Gandhári, tormented by grief for her sons and herself uncensured, hoped to issue a curse. Recognizing her evil intentions towards the Pándavas, the seer Vyasa, son of Sátyavati, realized ahead of time what she was about to do. First sprinkling himself with purely scented fresh water in the river Ganges, the supreme seer set out for that spot, moving at the speed of thought. 14.1

With his divine eye, he could see, when he directed his mind to it, and perfectly understand the nature of all that drew breath in that realm. Great in ascetic power, speaker of the auspicious, he spoke to his daughter-in-law, discounting this as a time for cursing, extolling it as a moment for reconciliation: "You should not be angry towards the Pándava side, Gandhári, you should accept a reconciliation. Hold back the words on the tip of your tongue, and hear these words of mine. During the eighteen days while he was hopeful of victory, your son spoke to you, saying, 'Pray for an auspicious outcome for me, mother, while I am fighting with my enemies.' When, in his desire for victory, he made such a request of you time and time again, you, Gandhári, always replied, 'Victory to the righteous!' 14.5

14.10 na c' âpy atītāṃ, Gāndhāri, vācaṃ te vitathām aham
smarāmi toṣamāṇāyās, tathā praṇihitā hy asi.
vigrahe tumule rājñāṃ gatvā pāram a|saṃśayam,
jitaṃ Pāṇḍu|sutair yuddhe nūnaṃ dharmas tato 'dhikam.
kṣamā|śīlā purā bhūtvā, s" âdya na kṣamase katham?
a|dharmaṃ jahi, dharma|jñe, yato dharmas tato jayaḥ!
svaṃ ca dharmaṃ parismṛtya,
    vācaṃ c' ôktāṃ, manasvini,
kopaṃ saṃyaccha, Gāndhāri.
    m" âivaṃ bhūḥ, satya|vādini.»

GĀNDHĀRY uvāca:

bhagavan, n' âbhyasūyāmi. n' âitān icchāmi naśyataḥ.
putra|śokena tu balān mano vihvalat' îva me.
14.15 yath" âiva Kuntyā Kaunteyā rakṣitavyās, tathā mayā.
tath" âiva Dhṛtarāṣṭreṇa rakṣitavyā, yathā tvayā.
Duryodhan'|âparādhena, Śakuneḥ Saubalasya ca,
Karṇa|Duḥśāsanābhyāṃ ca kṛto 'yaṃ Kuru|saṃkṣayaḥ.
n' âparādhyati Bībhatsur, na ca Pārtho Vṛkodaraḥ,
Nakulaḥ, Sahadevo vā, n' âiva jātu Yudhiṣṭhiraḥ.
yudhyamānā hi Kauravyāḥ kṛta|mānāḥ paras|param
nihatāḥ sahitāś c' ânyais. tatra n' âsty a|priyaṃ mama.
kiṃ tu karm' âkarod Bhīmo Vāsudevasya paśyataḥ,
Duryodhanaṃ samāhūya gadā|yuddhe mahā|manāḥ.

I cannot recall you ever previously saying something that 14.10
came to nothing, Gandhári, even in appeasement, so prudent are you. Having made it through the tumultuous battle of the kings, Pandu's sons have, without a shadow of a
doubt, claimed the victory in the war, and surely the righteousness too. You have had a forgiving nature up to now,
so why be unforgiving today? Give up this unrighteous conduct, you who know what is righteous, for 'victory to the
righteous!' Bear in mind your own righteous duty as well
as the words you uttered, wise woman. Curb your anger,
Gandhári. Don't behave this way, speaker of the truth."

GANDHÁRI spoke:

Lord, I am not indignant, nor do I wish them to perish. Rather it's as if my mind is forcefully shaken by my
grief for my sons. Just as Kunti should protect her sons, so 14.15
should I mine. Just as you should protect hers, so should
Dhrita·rashtra mine. This destruction of the Kuru clan is
the result of what Karna and Duhshásana did and of the
sin committed by Duryódhana urged on by Shákuni, son
of Súbala. Árjuna the abhorrent and Wolf-Belly, son of
Pritha, did no wrong; neither did Nákula nor Saha·deva nor
Yudhi·shthira, at any time. For the warriors of the Kuru
clan fought with their hearts set against one another. The
fact that they have died along with the rest is not the source
of my hostility. But rather it is the deed Bhima did with
Krishna, the son of Vasu·deva, looking on, after haughtily
challenging Duryódhana to a duel with maces.

14.20 śikṣay" âbhyadhikaṃ jñātvā, carantaṃ bahudhā raṇe,
adho nābhyāṃ prahṛtavāṃs. tan me kopam avardhayat.
kathaṃ nu dharmaṃ dharma|jñaiḥ
samuddiṣṭaṃ mah"|ātmabhiḥ
tyajeyur āhave śūrāḥ
prāṇa|hetoḥ kathaṃ cana?

VAIŚAMPĀYANA uvāca:

15.1 TAC CHRUTVĀ vacanaṃ tasyā Bhīmaseno 'tha bhītavat
Gāndhārīṃ pratyuvāc' êdaṃ vacaḥ s'|ânunayaṃ tadā:
«a|dharmo yadi vā dharmas trāsāt tatra mayā kṛtaḥ
ātmānaṃ trātu|kāmena. tan me tvaṃ kṣantum arhasi.
na hi yuddhena putras te dharmyeṇa sa mahā|balaḥ
na śakyaḥ kena cidd hantum, ato viṣamam ācaram.
a|dharmeṇa jitaḥ pūrvaṃ tena c' âpi Yudhiṣṭhiraḥ,
nikṛtāś ca sad" âiva sma. tato viṣamam ācaram.
15.5 sainyasy' âiko 'vaśiṣṭo 'yaṃ. gadā|yuddhena vīryavān
māṃ hatvā na hared rājyam, iti c' âitat kṛtaṃ mayā.
rāja|putrīṃ ca Pāñcālīm eka|vastrāṃ rajasvalām,
bhavatyā viditaṃ sarvam uktavān yat sutas tava.
Suyodhanam a|saṃgṛhya na śakyā bhūḥ sa|sāgarā
kevalā bhoktum asmābhir. ataś c' âitat kṛtaṃ mayā.
tac c' âpy† a|priyam asmākaṃ putras te samupācarat,
Draupadyā yat sabhā|madhye savyam ūrum adarśayat.
tad" âiva vadhyaḥ so 'smākaṃ, dur|ācāraś ca te sutaḥ;
dharma|rāj'|ājñayā c' âiva sthitāḥ sma samaye tadā.

Recognizing that Duryódhana was better trained and had extensive experience of battle, Bhima struck him a blow below the navel. It is that that incites my rage. For how could champions throw out proper conduct as taught by our exalted moral experts, even to save their own life in battle? 14.20

VAISHAMPÁYANA continued:

On hearing Gandhári say this, full of trepidation, 15.1
Bhima·sena offered her these conciliatory words in reply: "My fear in that situation led me to do whatever I could to save myself, regardless of whether it was lawful or not. You should understand me doing that. For your son was so strong that no one could have killed him in a lawful fight and that is why I acted dishonorably. On top of that, he had himself previously defeated Yudhi·shthira through unlawful means and always us treated unfairly. That is why I acted dishonorably.

Your heroic son was the only survivor of your army. I did 15.5
what I did to prevent him from taking the kingdom which he could have done if he had killed me in the mace fight. You know all that your son said to the Panchálan princess when she was menstruating, and clad in but a single shift. With Duryódhana out of control it would have been impossible for us to rest easy in any part of this entire world including its oceans. For that reason too I did it. Your son committed a further despicable act against us, when he revealed his left thigh to Dráupadi in the midst of the assembly. Right then we should have killed your son when he behaved so disgracefully, but at the time we kept the

15.10 vairam uddīpitaṃ, rājñi, putreṇa tava tan mahat,
kleśitāś ca vane nityaṃ. tata etat kṛtaṃ mayā.
vairasy' âsya gataḥ pāraṃ hatvā Duryodhanaṃ raṇe.
rājyaṃ Yudhiṣṭhiraḥ prāpto, vayaṃ ca gata|manyavaḥ.»

GĀNDHĀRY uvāca:

na tasy' âiṣa vadhas, tāta, yat praśaṃsasi me sutam,
kṛtavāṃś c' âpi tat sarvaṃ yad idaṃ bhāṣase mayi,
hat'|aśve Nakule yat tu Vṛṣasenena, Bhārata,
apibaḥ śoṇitaṃ saṃkhye Duḥśāsana|śarīra|jam.
sadbhir vigarhitaṃ, ghoram, an|ārya|jana|sevitam
krūraṃ karm' âkṛthās. tasmāt tad a|yuktaṃ, Vṛkodara.

BHĪMASENA uvāca:

15.15 anyasy' âpi na pātavyaṃ rudhiraṃ, kiṃ punaḥ svakam.
yath" âiv'|âtmā tathā bhrātā. viśeṣo n' âsti kaś cana.
rudhiraṃ na vyatikrāmad dant'|oṣṭhād, amba, mā śucaḥ.
Vaivasvatas tu tad veda. hastau me rudhir'|ôkṣitau.
hat'|âśvaṃ Nakulaṃ dṛṣṭvā Vṛṣasenena saṃyuge
bhrātṝṇāṃ saṃprahṛṣṭānāṃ trāsaḥ saṃjanito mayā.
keśa|pakṣa|parāmarśe Draupadyā dyūta|kārite
krodhād yad abruvaṃ c' âhaṃ, tac ca me hṛdi vartate.
kṣatra|dharmāc cyuto, rājñi, bhaveyaṃ śāsvatīḥ samāḥ,
pratijñāṃ tām a|nistīrya. tatas tat kṛtavān aham.
15.20 na māṃ arhasi, Gāndhāri, doṣeṇa pariśaṅkitum.

truce because the righteous king Yudhi·shthira commanded
it. Your Majesty, your son always provoked great animosity 15.10
and he caused us to suffer in the forest. For that reason I
did it. Now that I have killed Duryódhana in battle, I have
moved beyond this animosity. Yudhi·shthira has won the
kingdom, and our resentment is set aside."

GANDHÁRI replied:

It is not just this murder of my son, which you have justified to me, son, since he did do all the things you have mentioned, but the fact that in the battle, when Vrisha·sena had slain Nákula's horses, scion of Bhárata, you drank the blood that flowed from Duhshásana's body. Such a disgusting act is despised by decent people. It is a practice only of barbarians. That is why your cruel behavior is unacceptable, Wolf-Belly.

BHIMA·SENA replied:

One should not drink the blood of another, let alone 15.15
one's own. A brother is just the same as one's self. There is no
distinction. His blood did not pass between my teeth and
lips, mother, don't feel anguish on that score. The God of
death is witness to that. Just my two hands were drenched
in blood. I was simply giving his brothers a fright, when
they were celebrating the sight of Vrisha·sena slaughtering
Nákula's horses in the battle. What I said in anger when
he laid his hands on Dráupadi's hair after the dice game
has never left my heart. As a warrior I would have failed
in my duty for all eternity, Your Majesty, had I failed to
discharge that vow. That is why I did what I did. Gandhári, 15.20
you should not hold this misdeed against me. Since earlier

a|nigṛhya purā putrān asmāsv an|apakāriṣu
adhunā kiṃ nu doṣeṇa pariśaṅkitum arhasi?

GĀNDHĀRY uvāca:

vṛddhasy' āsya śataṃ putrān nighnaṃs tvam a|parājitaḥ,
kasmān na śeṣayaḥ kaṃ cid, yen' âlpam aparādhitam,
saṃtānam āvayos, tāta, vṛddhayor hṛta|rājyayoḥ?
katham andha|dvayasy' âsya yaṣṭir ekā na varjitā?
śeṣe hy avasthite, tāta, putrāṇām antake tvayi
na me duḥkhaṃ bhaved etad, yadi tvaṃ dharmam ācaraḥ.

VAIŚAMPĀYANA uvāca:

evam uktvā tu Gāndhārī Yudhiṣṭhiram apṛcchata,
«kva sa rāj"?» êti sa|krodhā, putra|pautra|vadh'|ârditā.
15.25 tām† abhyagacchad rāj'|êndro vepamānaḥ, kṛt'|âñjaliḥ.
Yudhiṣṭhiras tv idaṃ tatra madhuraṃ vākyam abravīt:
«putra|hantā nṛśaṃso 'haṃ tava, devi, Yudhiṣṭhiraḥ,
śāp'|ârhaḥ, pṛthivī|nāśe hetu|bhūtaḥ. śapasva mām.
na hi me jīviten' ârtho, na rājyena, dhanena vā,
tādṛśān suhṛdo hatvā mūḍhasy' âsya suhṛd|druhaḥ.»
tam evaṃ|vādinaṃ, bhītaṃ, saṃnikarṣa|gataṃ tadā
n' ôvāca kiṃ cid Gāndhārī niḥśvāsa|paramā bhṛśam.
tasy' āvanata|dehasya, pādayor nipatiṣyataḥ
Yudhiṣṭhirasya nṛ|pater dharma|jñā dīrgha|darśinī

you did not chastise your sons, how can you now hold this misdeed against us, when in fact we have done no wrong?

GANDHÁRI replied:

When you, never suffering defeat, were killing the hundred sons of this old man, why could you not have spared just one, one who had committed only a minor wrong—just one offspring for this old couple that we are, deprived of our kingdom? How could you not leave a single staff for this blind old couple to lean on? Son, had you spared just one of the sons of mine you killed, I would not suffer so, given that you were performing your lawful duty.

VAISHAMPÁYANA continued:

When she had said this to him, Gandhári, tormented by the killing of her sons and their sons in turn, angrily called for Yudhi·shthira saying, "Where is that king?"

The sovereign approached her trembling, his hands 15.25
clasped in supplication. Then Yudhi·shthira spoke these soft words to her:

"I, Yudhi·shthira, am the despicable killer of your sons, Your Majesty. I deserve your curses. I caused the devastation of the world. Curse me. Now life holds no meaning for me, nor does kingship or wealth, since I stand here, an idiot who harms those he loves, having killed such loved ones as they."

As he fearfully spoke these words, coming close to her, Gandhári said nothing, her chest heaving heavily. As King Yudhi·shthira was bowed before her, about to prostrate himself, the long-sighted queen, who understood righteous
duty, looked at the tips of his fingers from under her blind- 15.30

15.30 aṅguly|agrāṇi dadṛśe devī paṭṭ'|ântareṇa sā.
tataḥ sa ku|nakhī|bhūto darśanīya|nakho nṛpaḥ.
taṃ dṛṣṭvā c' Ârjuno 'gacchad† Vāsudevasya pṛṣṭhataḥ.
evaṃ saṃceṣṭamānāṃs tān itaś c' êtaś ca, Bhārata,
Gāndhārī vigata|krodhā sāntvayām āsa mātṛvat.
tayā te samanujñātā mātaraṃ vīra|mātaram
abhyagacchanta sahitāḥ Pṛthāṃ pṛthula|vakṣasaḥ.
cirasya dṛṣṭvā putrān sā, putr'|ādhibhir abhiplutā,
bāṣpam āhārayad devī vastreṇ' āvṛtya vai mukham.
tato bāṣpaṃ samutsṛjya saha putrais tathā Pṛthā
15.35 apaśyad etāñ śastr' âughair bahudhā kṣata|vikṣatān.
sā tān ek'|âikaśaḥ putrān saṃspṛśantī punaḥ punaḥ,
anvaśocata duḥkh'|ārtā Draupadīṃ ca hat'|ātma|jām.
rudatīm atha Pāñcālīṃ dadarśa patitāṃ bhuvi.

DRAUPADY uvāca:

ārye pautrāḥ† kva te sarve Saubhadra|sahitā gatāḥ?
na tvāṃ te 'dy' âbhigacchanti ciraṃ dṛṣṭvā tapasvinīm.
kiṃ nu rājyena vai kāryaṃ vihīnāyāḥ sutair mama?
tāṃ samāśvāsayām āsa Pṛthā pṛthula|locanā.
utthāpya Yājñasenīṃ tu rudatīṃ śoka|karṣitām,
tay" âiva sahitā c' âpi putrair anugatā, nṛpa,
15.40 abhyagacchata Gāndhārīm ārtām ārtatarā svayam.

fold.* At that the beautiful nails of the king turned rotten. On seeing that happen, Árjuna moved to stand behind Krishna descendent of Vasu·deva. But as they fidgeted nervously, son of Bhárata's line, Gandhári's anger left her and she comforted them, like a mother. With her permission, the broad-chested brothers went together to their own mother, that mother of heroes, Kunti. On finally seeing her sons after such a long time, the royal lady, who had been filled with anxiety on their account, covered her face with the edge of her garment and allowed her tears to flow. Once
she had shed her tears in the company of her sons, she no- 15.35
ticed that they had been cut and injured many times by a veritable armory of weapons. As she repeatedly caressed her sons each in turn, tormented by her own suffering, she grieved for Dráupadi whose own sons had been killed. Then she saw that the Panchálan princess had fallen weeping on the ground.

DRÁUPADI cried out:

Madam, where have all the grandsons I gave you gone, off with Subhádra's son? They do not come to you today, though they saw you suffering so long. What use is a kingdom to me when my sons are lost to me?

Pritha, her eyes wide, tried to comfort her. She made Drúpada's weeping, grief-stricken daughter get up. Then, with her sons following on behind, she went with her, Your
Majesty, to Gandhári in her affliction, herself more afflicted 15.40
still.

VAIŚAMPĀYANA uvāca:

tām uvāc' âtha Gāndhārī saha vadhvā yaśasvinīm:
«m' âivaṃ, putr', êti śok'|ārtā paśya mām api duḥkhitām.
manye loka|vināśo 'yaṃ kāla|paryāya|noditaḥ
avaśya|bhāvī saṃprāptaḥ svabhāvāl loma|harṣaṇaḥ.
idaṃ tat samanuprāptaṃ Vidurasya vaco mahat,
a|siddh'|ânunaye Kṛṣṇe yad uvāca mahā|matiḥ.
tasminn a|parihārye 'rthe, vyatīte ca viśeṣataḥ,
mā śuco. na hi śocyās te saṃgrāme nidhanaṃ gatāḥ.
yath" âiv' âhaṃ, tath" âiva tvaṃ. ko vā m" āśvāsayiṣyati?
mam' âiva hy aparādhena kulam agryaṃ vināśitam.»

VAISHAMPÁYANA continued:

Gandhári then addressed that glorious lady and her daughter-in-law: "Don't be so racked with grief. Look at how I too am suffering. I think this devastation of the world must have been brought about by the workings of Time. This horrifying event has come about of its own course, unavoidably. This is the realization of the great speech that Vídura, great in wisdom, made, when Krishna's attempts to broker a reconciliation failed. When a matter cannot be prevented, especially when it has already occurred, you should not regret it. For those who have met their end in battle do not warrant mourning. You are in the same position as I. For who can comfort me, when I am to blame for this ruling family being reduced to nothing?"

16–25

MOTHERS AND WIDOWS IN THE CARNAGE

VAIŚAMPĀYANA uvāca:

16.1 EVAM UKTVĀ TU Gāndhārī Kurūṇām avakartanam
apaśyat tatra tiṣṭhantī sarvaṃ divyena cakṣuṣā,
pati|vratā, mahā|bhāgā, samāna|vrata|cāriṇī,
ugreṇa tapasā yuktā, satataṃ satya|vādinī,
vara|dānena Kṛṣṇasya maha"|rṣeḥ puṇya|karmaṇaḥ
divya|jñāna|bal'|ôpetā; vividhaṃ paryadevayat.
dadarśa sā buddhimatī dūrād api yath" ântike
raṇ'|âjiraṃ nṛ|vīrāṇām adbhutaṃ, loma|harṣaṇam.
16.5 asthi|keśa|vas"|ākīrṇaṃ, śoṇit'|âugha|pariplutam,
śarīrair bahu|sāhasrair vinikīrṇaṃ samantataḥ,
gaj'|âśva|ratha|yodhānām āvṛtaṃ rudhir'|āvilaiḥ,
śarīrair a|śiraskaiś ca, videhaiś ca śiro|gaṇaiḥ,
gaj'|âśva|nara|nārīṇāṃ niḥ|svanair abhisaṃvṛtam,
sṛgāla|baka|kākola|kaṅka|kāka|niṣevitam,
rakṣasāṃ puruṣ'|âdānāṃ modanaṃ kurar'|ākulam,
a|śivābhiḥ śivābhiś ca nāditaṃ, gṛdhra|sevitam.
tato Vyās'|âbhyanujñāto Dhṛtarāṣṭro mahī|patiḥ,
Pāṇḍu|putrāś ca te sarve Yudhiṣṭhira|puro|gamāḥ,
16.10 Vāsudevaṃ puras|kṛtya, hata|bandhuṃ ca pārthivam,
Kuru|striyaḥ samāsādya jagmur āyodhanaṃ prati.
samāsādya Kuru|kṣetraṃ tāḥ striyo nihat'|ēśvarāḥ

VAISHAMPÁYANA continued:

When she had finished speaking Gandhári, staying right where she was, surveyed the entire battle field of the Kurus with her divine eye, for, in her dedication to her husband, she had accrued great merit by performing the vow of making herself like him and, endowed with such strong religious power and always true to her word, she possessed—as a result of the boon granted her by the great seer Krishna, performer of purifying rites—the power of divine knowledge; the sight excited many cries of anguish from her. For even from that distance that insightful woman could see as if close by the awesome and horrifying arena of the battle between the champions of mankind. 16.1

Bones, hair and sinews lay scattered. Pools of blood had turned the ground to marsh. Thousands of dismembered bodies lay strewn all over. The ground was piled up with decapitated torsos and piles of heads detached from their bodies, from elephants, horses and chariot-fighters, all churned up with blood. Darkened under the weight of the soundless corpses of elephants, horses, men and women, the place was haunted by jackals, cranes, ravens, herons and crows, a playground for man-eating goblins, it teemed with osprey and echoed to the ominous cries of jackals; all the while vultures gathered. 16.5

Then at Vyasa's command, Dhrita·rashtra, the lord of the earth, and all of Pandu's sons with Yudhi·shthira at their head, led by Krishna, descendent of Vasu·deva, and prince 16.10
Sátyaki whose relatives had all been slain, set out for the battle ground, taking the Kuru women with them. When the women, whose men folk had been killed, arrived at

apaśyanta hatāṃs tatra putrān, bhrātṝn, pitṝn, patīn
kravy'|âdair bhakṣyamāṇān vai gomāyu|bala|vāyasaiḥ,
bhūtaiḥ, piśācai, rakṣobhir, vividhaiś ca niśā|caraiḥ.
Rudr'|ākrīḍa|nibhaṃ dṛṣṭvā tadā viśasanaṃ striyaḥ
mah''|ârhebhyo 'tha yānebhyo vikrośantyo nipetire.
a|dṛṣṭa|pūrvaṃ paśyantyo duḥkh'|ārtā Bharata|striyaḥ
śarīreṣv askhalann anyāḥ, patantyaś c' âparā bhuvi.
16.15 śrāntānāṃ c' âpy a|nāthānāṃ n' āsīt kā cana cetanā.
Pāñcāla|Kuru|yoṣāṇāṃ kṛpaṇaṃ tad abhūn mahat.
duḥkh'|ôpahata|cittābhiḥ samantād anunāditam
dṛṣṭvā yodhanam atyugraṃ dharma|jñā Subal'|ātmajā
tataḥ sā puṇḍarīk'|âkṣam āmantrya puruṣ'|ôttamam
Kurūṇāṃ vaiśasaṃ dṛṣṭvā idaṃ vacanam abravīt:
«paśy' âitāḥ, puṇḍarīk'|âkṣa, snuṣā me nihat'|ēśvarāḥ
prakīrṇa|keśāḥ, krośantīḥ kurarīr iva, Mādhava.
amūs tv abhisamāgamya smarantyo bhartṛ|jān guṇān,
pṛthag ev' âbhyadhāvantaḥ putrān, bhrātṝn, pitṝn, patīn.
16.20 vīra|sūbhir, mahā|bāho, hata|putrābhir āvṛtam,
kva cic ca vīra|patnībhir hata|vīrābhir āvṛtam,
śobhitaṃ puruṣa|vyāghrair Karṇa|Bhīṣm'|Âbhimanyubhiḥ,
Droṇa|Drupada|Śalyaiś ca, jvaladbhir iva pāvakaiḥ;
kāñcanaiḥ kavacair, niṣkair, maṇibhiś ca mah''|ātmanām,

Kuru·kshetra, the battle field of the Kurus, they saw before them their slain sons, brothers, fathers, and husbands, being eaten by flesh-eating creatures: packs of wolves, crows, ghosts, goblins and trolls, and a host of other scavengers of the night. At the sight of that carnage, the vision of wrathful Shiva's sport, the women threw themselves down from their costly carriages, screeching. Agonized by the torment of seeing such unprecedented horror, some of the women of Bhárata's line lost all the strength in their bodies, others fell to the ground.

Exhausted and bereft of the men who kept them safe, 16.15
their minds became numb. The plight of the Panchála and Kuru women was deeply pitiable. When she saw the frightful battle site, filled on every side with the clamor of these women, their hearts rent in anguish, Gandhári, daughter of Súbala, who understood Dharma, addressed the most exalted of men, the lotus-eyed lord, and, in response to seeing the slaughter the Kurus had met, made this speech to him:

"Lotus-eyed lord of the Mádhava clan, look at my daughters-in-law here. The men of their families are slain. Their hair hangs loose and they screech like osprey. Though they arrived here all as a group, recollecting all the good things about their husbands, it is alone that each now runs to son, brother, father or husband.

Everywhere you look is draped with women who brought 16.20
heroes into the world, but lost sons; who had champions for husbands, but lost their champions, strong-armed lord. The entire arena is draped in those tigers of men, Karna, Bhishma and Abhimányu; and with Drona, Drúpada and

aṅgadair, hasta|keyūraiḥ, sragbhiś ca samalaṃkṛtam,
vīra|bāhu|visṛṣṭābhiḥ śaktibhiḥ, parighair api,
khaḍgaiś ca vimalais tīkṣṇaiḥ, sa|śaraiś ca śar'|âsanaiḥ,
kravy'|âda|saṃghair muditais tiṣṭhadbhiḥ sahitaiḥ kva cit,
kva cid ākrīḍamānaiś ca, śayānair aparaiḥ kva cit.
16.25 etad evaṃ|vidhaṃ, vīra, saṃpaśy' āyodhanaṃ, vibho.
paśyamānā ca dahyāmi śoken' âhaṃ, jan'|ârdana.
Pāñcālānāṃ Kurūṇāṃ ca vināśe, Madhu|sūdana,
pañcānām api bhūtānāṃ n' âhaṃ vadham acintayam.
tān suparṇāś ca gṛdhrāś ca karṣayanty asṛg|ukṣitāḥ.
nigṛhya caraṇair gṛdhrā bhakṣayanti sahasraśaḥ.
Jayadrathasya, Karṇasya, tath" âiva Droṇa|Bhīṣmayoḥ,
Abhimanyor vināśaṃ ca kaś cintayitum arhati?
a|vadhya|kalpān nihatān, gata|sattvān, a|cetasaḥ,
gṛdhra|kaṅka|baṭa|śyena|śva|sṛgāl'|âdanī|kṛtān,
16.30 a|marṣa|vaśam āpannān, Duryodhana|vaśe sthitān
paśy' êmān puruṣa|vyāghrān, saṃśāntān pāvakān iva.
śayānā ye purā sarve mṛdūni śayanāni ca,
vipannās te 'dya vasudhāṃ vivṛtām adhiśerate.
bandibhiḥ satataṃ kāle stuvadbhir abhinanditāḥ,
śivānām a|śivā ghorāḥ śṛṇvanti vividhā giraḥ.

Shalya, who gleam like fire; festooned with gleaming armor, chest-plates and gems from the noble warriors; and embellished with their garlands and the jewelry that had adorned their arms and hands, as well as with the lances and iron-tipped clubs hurled by the arms of champions, with lustrous razor-sharp swords and bows, their arrows still in place. Here and there flesh-eating animals linger in groups enjoying themselves; in some places they even frolic, while elsewhere others lie relaxing.

Look here at the battle field in this state, powerful cham- 16.25
pion. As I look upon it, I am consumed by grief, O rouser of the people. Slayer of the demon Madhu, for me the destruction of the Panchálas and Kurus was as unthinkable as killing the five elements that make up the world. Eagles and vultures, wet with blood, yank them apart. Grasping them with their talons, the vultures gobble them in a thousand pieces. Who could have thought that Jayad·ratha and Karna, or Drona and Bhishma, or Abhimányu for that matter, could have been destroyed? Those who were slain, now lifeless and unconscious, did not deserve to die, to be made food for the vultures; for the herons and cranes; for the hyenas, the dogs and the jackals; they fell foul of the power of 16.30
antagonism, under Duryódhana's sway. See those tigers of men snuffed out like flames. Those who used to sleep on soft beds now lie exposed, distorted, on the bare ground. Once bards constantly delighted them with timely eulogies; now they hear the blood-curdling, ill-omened sounds of jackals giving tongue.

ye purā śerate vīrāḥ śayaneṣu yaśasvinaḥ,
candan'|âguru|digdh'|âṅgās, te 'dya pāṃsuṣu śerate.
teṣām ābharaṇāny ete gṛdhra|gomāyu|vāyasāḥ.
ākṣipanti śivā ghorā vinadantyaḥ† punaḥ punaḥ.

16.35 bāṇān viniśitān, pītān nistriṃśān, vimalā gadāḥ
yuddh'|âbhimāninaḥ sarve jīvanta iva bibhrati.
su|rūpa|varṇā bahavaḥ kravy'|âdair avaghaṭṭitāḥ
ṛṣabha|pratirūpāś śerate harita|srajaḥ.
apare punar āliṅgya gadāḥ parigha|bāhavaḥ
śerate 'bhimukhāḥ śūrā, dayitā iva yoṣitaḥ.
bibhrataḥ kavacāny anye, vimalāny āyudhāni ca,
na dharṣayanti kravy'|âdā, «jīvant'» îti, Jan|ârdana.
kravy'|âdaiḥ kṛṣyamāṇānām apareṣāṃ mah"|ātmanām
śātakaumbhyaḥ srajaś citrā viprakīrṇāḥ samantataḥ.

16.40 ete gomāyavo bhīmā nihatānāṃ yaśasvinām
kaṇṭh'|ântara|gatān hārān ākṣipanti sahasraśaḥ.
sarveṣv apara|rātreṣu yān anandanta bandinaḥ
stutibhiś ca par'|ârdhyābhir upacāraiś ca śikṣitāḥ,
tān imāḥ paridevanti duḥkh'|ārtāḥ param'|âṅganāḥ
kṛpaṇaṃ, Vṛṣṇi|śārdūla, duḥkha|śok'|ârditā bhṛśam.
rakt'|ôtpala|vanān' îva vibhānti rucirāṇi ca
mukhāni parama|strīṇāṃ pariśuṣkāṇi, Keśava.
ruditād viratā hy etā, dhyāyantyaḥ sa|paricchadāḥ
Kuru|striyo 'bhigacchanti tena ten' âiva duḥkhitāḥ.

Before these glorious champions lay on beds, their bodies daubed with sandal paste and aloe. Now they lie in the dust. For adornment they have these vultures and wolves and ravens. She-jackals pull at them, crying out again and again.

Each man who took such pride in fighting still holds his 16.35
pointed arrows, dressed sword or gleaming mace, as if he were still alive. Many are the handsome, fair-complexioned men now dragged apart by carrion, as they lie like bulls, draped in verdant garlands. Some warriors, their arms like iron rods, still cling to their maces, and lie turned towards them, as if toward their beloved women. Others wear spotless armor and weapons, rouser of the people. The scavengers do not touch them, thinking they are still alive. Other of the noble warriors lose their resplendent golden necklaces, as they are dragged about by scavengers, which end up scattered all around.

See how as the fearsome wolves snatch the strings of 16.40
pearls that lay around the throats of the glorious soldiers now slain, the strings explode in a thousand directions. Well-versed bards once delighted them during the last watch each night with eulogies and top-notch entertainments. Now it is these beautiful ladies, distraught with grief, who sing to them in lament, tiger of the Vrishni clan, most pitiably oppressed by their anguish and grief. Though drawn with grief, the noble ladies' faces are radiant, long-haired lord, and look like clusters of red lotuses. Now they have stopped weeping and, lost in thought, the Kuru women go here and there in anguish, their attendants trailing after them.

16.45 etāny āditya|varṇāni, tapanīya|nibhāni ca,
roṣa|rodana|tāmrāṇi vaktrāṇi Kuru|yoṣitām.
śyāmānāṃ, vara|varṇānāṃ, gaurīṇām, eka|vāsasām
Duryodhana|vara|strīṇāṃ paśya vṛndāni, keśava.
āsām a|paripūrṇ'|ârthaṃ niśamya paridevitam
itar'|êtara|saṃkrandān na vijānanti yoṣitaḥ.
etā dīrgham iv' ôcchvasya, vikruśya ca, vilapya ca,
vispandamānā duḥkhena vīrā jahati jīvitam.
bahvyo dṛṣṭvā śarīrāṇi krośanti vilapanti ca,
pāṇibhiś c' âparā ghnanti śirāṃsi mṛdu|pāṇayaḥ.
16.50 śirobhiḥ patitair, hastaiḥ, sarv'|âṅgair yūthaśaḥ kṛtaiḥ,
itar|êtara|saṃpṛktair ākīrṇā bhāti medinī.
viśiraskān atho kāyān dṛṣṭvā hy etān a|ninditān
muhyanty anugatā nāryo videhāni śirāṃsi ca.
śiraḥ kāyena saṃdhāya prekṣamāṇā vicetasaḥ
a|paśyantyo paraṃ tatra, «n' êdam asy'» êti duḥkhitāḥ.
bāh'|ūru|caraṇān anyān viśikh'|ônmathitān pṛthak
saṃdadhatyo '|sukh|āviṣṭā mūrchanty etāḥ punaḥ punaḥ.
utkṛtta|śirasaś† c' ânyān vijagdhān mṛga|pakṣibhiḥ
dṛṣṭvā kāś cin na jānanti bhartṝn Bharata|yoṣitaḥ.
16.55 pāṇibhiś c' âparā ghnanti śirāṃsi, Madhu|sūdana,
prekṣya bhrātṝn pitṝn putrān patīṃś ca nihatān paraiḥ.
bāhubhiś ca sa|khaḍgaiś ca, śirobhiś ca sa|kuṇḍalaiḥ
a|gamya|kalpā pṛthivī māṃsa|śoṇita|kardamā
babhūva, Bharata|śreṣṭha, prāṇibhir gata|jīvitaiḥ.
na duḥkheṣ' ûcitāḥ pūrvaṃ duḥkhaṃ gāhanty a|ninditāḥ.
bhrātṛbhiḥ,† patibhiḥ, putrair upākīrṇā vasuṃ|dharā.

Red as the hue of the sun or like soft copper are the 16.45
faces of the Kuru wives, from anger and from weeping. See the clusters of Duryódhana's wives and girls, dark and fair, long-haired lord. Hearing each other's lamentations, which make little sense, his women can make no sense of the resulting cacophony. Some of these valiant women, heaving deep sighs, crying out, wailing and shuddering, respond to their torment by taking their own lives. Many, when they see the corpses, scream and wail. Others beat their soft-skinned hands against their heads.

The fat earth glistens, strewn with severed heads, hands 16.50
and every other limb, forming heaps all jumbled together. Finding here familiar torsos, beyond reproof, now decapitated, and heads severed from their bodies, women lose consciousness. Placing a head with a torso, they look at them, confused, realizing to their distress, "This is not his" but are not able to find another one in its place. Piecing together one by one the various arms, thighs and feet torn apart by shafts, they faint time and time again, overwhelmed by misery. Some of the Bhárata women, seeing still other decapitated bodies mauled by beasts and birds, do not recognize them as their husbands.

Others, at seeing their brothers, fathers, sons and hus- 16.55
bands all slain by their enemies, slayer of demon Madhu, strike their heads with their hands. With arms still clutching their swords, and heads still wearing their earrings, the ground has become impassable, a mire of flesh and blood, awash with lifeless bodies, most exalted of Bhárata's line. Those innocent women, unaccustomed to any hardship before, are now steeped in misery. The earth is strewn with

yūthān' îva kiśorīṇāṃ su|keśīnāṃ, jan'|ârdana,
snuṣāṇāṃ Dhṛtarāṣṭrasya paśya vṛndāny an|ekaśaḥ.
ito duḥkhataraṃ kiṃ nu, keśava, pratibhāti me,
16.60 yad imāḥ kurvate sarvā ravam ucc'|âvacaṃ striyaḥ?
nūnam ācaritaṃ pāpaṃ mayā pūrveṣu janmasu,
yā paśyāmi hatān putrān, pautrān, bhrātṝṃś ca, Mādhava.»
evam ārtā vilapatī samābhāṣya jan'|ârdanam
Gāndhārī putra|śok'|ārtā dadarśa nihataṃ sutam.

VAIŚAMPĀYANA uvāca:

17.1 DURYODHANAṂ HATAṂ dṛṣṭvā Gāndhārī śoka|karśitā
sahasā nyapatad bhūmau, chinn" êva kadalī vane.
sā tu labdhvā punaḥ saṃjñāṃ, vikruśya ca vilapya ca,
Duryodhanam abhiprekṣya śayānaṃ, rudhir'|ôkṣitam
pariṣvajya ca Gāndhārī kṛpaṇaṃ paryadevayat.
«hā hā putr'!» êti śok'|ārtā vilalāp'|ākul'|êndriyā,
su|gūḍha|jatru|vipulaṃ, hāra|niṣka|vibhūṣitam
vāriṇā netra|jen' ôraḥ siñcantī śoka|tāpitā.
17.5 samīpa|sthaṃ Hṛṣīkeśam idaṃ vacanam abravīt:
«upasthite 'smin saṃgrāme jñātīnāṃ saṃkṣaye, vibho,
mām ayaṃ prāha, Vārṣṇeya, prāñjalir nṛpa|sattamaḥ:
‹asmiñ jñāti|samuddharṣe jayam ambā bravītu me.›
ity ukte jānatī sarvam ahaṃ sva|vyasan'|āgamam,
abruvaṃ,† ‹puruṣa|vyāghra, yato dharmas tato jayaḥ!

the corpses of their brothers, husbands and sons. See everywhere the huddles of the widows of Dhrita·rashtra's sons, rouser of the people, like herds of fine-maned fillies. What more distressing sight could there be for me, long-haired lord, than all these screaming women? Surely I must have 16.60
committed evil in all my former lives, that I now see my sons, grandsons and brothers slain, descendant of Madhu."

It was while she was, in her affliction, expressing her grief to the rouser of the people in this way, that Gandhári, already tormented by the loss of her sons, caught sight of her slain first born.

VAISHAMPÁYANA continued:

WHEN GANDHÁRI saw Duryódhana's lifeless body, grief 17.1
stole her strength. She toppled at once to the ground, like a banana tree lopped down in the wood. Then when she came to again, she screamed and wailed, as she saw Duryódhana lying there, caked in blood. Then Gandhári took him in her arms and cried a pitiful lament, "Oh oh my son," she gibbered, her senses confused in the torment of her grief. Burning with grief she soaked with the tears that streamed from her eyes his broad, muscle-bound chest,* still dressed with pearls and chest-plate.

And as she did so she said these words to the Lord of the 17.5
Senses, who was standing close by: "O descendent of Vrishni, Powerful lord, when this battle that has ended in the destruction of my relatives was imminent, this, the truest of kings, said to me, his hands raised together in supplication: 'Mother, wish me victory in this great engagement between relatives.' When he said this, I, realizing that it would all

yathā ca yudhyamānas tvaṃ na vai muhyasi, putraka,
dhruvaṃ śastra|jitāl̐ lokān prāpsyasy amaravat, prabho.›
ity evam abruvaṃ pūrvaṃ. n' âinaṃ śocāmi vai, prabho.
Dhṛtarāṣṭraṃ tu śocāmi kṛpaṇaṃ hata|bāndhavam.

17.10 a|marṣaṇaṃ, yudhāṃ śreṣṭhaṃ,
kṛt'|âstraṃ, yuddha|dur|madam,
śayānaṃ vīra|śayane
paśya, Mādhava, me sutam.
yo 'yaṃ mūrdh'|âvasiktānām agre yāti paraṃ|tapaḥ,
so 'yaṃ pāṃsuṣu śete 'dya. paśya kālasya paryayam.
dhruvaṃ Duryodhano vīro gatiṃ su|labhatāṃ gataḥ
tathā hy abhimukhaḥ śete śayane vīra|sevite.
yaṃ purā paryupāsīnā ramayanti vara|striyaḥ,
taṃ vīra|śayane suptaṃ ramayanty a|śivāḥ śivāḥ.
yaṃ purā paryupāsīnā ramayanti mahī|kṣitaḥ,
mahī|tala|sthaṃ nihataṃ gṛdhrās taṃ paryupāsate.

17.15 yaṃ purā vyajanai ramyair upavījanti yoṣitaḥ,
tam adya pakṣa|vyajanair upavījanti pakṣiṇaḥ.
eṣa śete mahā|bāhur, balavān, satya|vikramaḥ,
siṃhen' êva dvipaḥ saṃkhye Bhīmasenena pātitaḥ.
paśya Duryodhanaṃ, Kṛṣṇa, śayānaṃ rudhir'|ôkṣitam,
nihataṃ Bhīmasenena gadām saṃmṛjya, Bhārata.
akṣauhiṇīr mahā|bāhur daśa c' âikāṃ ca, keśava,
ānayad yaḥ purā saṃkhye, so 'nayān nidhanaṃ gataḥ.

lead to his own downfall, said, 'Victory to the righteous, tiger of men. As long as you are not led astray as you fight, dear son, you will win the realms won with the sword, my lord, just as an immortal.'

That is what I said to them back then, and I do not grieve on his account now, lord. Rather, it is on account of poor Dhrita·rashtra, who has lost his entire family.

Determined, the best of warriors, his weapon ready, fero- 17.10
cious in battle, look at my boy, now, descendant of Madhu, lying on the bed of champions. He walked at the head of anointed kings, a torment to the enemy. Now he lies in the mud. Observe the fickle nature of Time. Certainly Duryódhana, a hero, has gone to the world of the well-rewarded, for in action he has taken to the bed lain on by heroes. Once it was the loveliest women who gathered round to him to give him pleasure. Now as he sleeps on the hero's bed, it is ill-omened she-jackals that satisfy themselves on him. Before the sovereigns of the earth gathered round to cheer him. Now as he lies slain upon the earth, it is the vultures that gather round.

Before he was fanned by the lovely limbs of his wives. 17.15
Now it is the wings of birds that fan him. Here he lies, mighty-armed, powerful, valiant, like the elephant brought down in battle by the lion, Bhima·sena. Krishna, look at Duryódhana, lying drenched in blood, slain by Bhima·sena, brandishing his mace, scion of Bhárata. The powerful warrior who had earlier led the eleven battalions into battle, long-haired lord, thanks to his misguided strategy is now heading for his final resting place. Here lies Duryódhana,

eṣa Duryodhanaḥ śete mah"|êṣv|āso mahā|rathaḥ,
śārdūla iva siṃhena Bhīmasenena pātitaḥ.
17.20 Viduraṃ hy avamany' âiṣa, pitaraṃ c' âiva manda|bhāk,
bālo vṛddh'|âvamānena mando mṛtyu|vaśaṃ gataḥ.
niḥ|sapatnā mahī yasya trayodaśa samāḥ sthitā,
sa śete nihato bhūmau putro me pṛthivī|patiḥ.
apaśyaṃ, Kṛṣṇa, pṛthivīṃ Dhārtarāṣṭr'|ânuśāsitām
pūrṇāṃ hasti|gav'|âśvaiś ca, Vārṣṇeya, na tu tac ciram.
tām ev' âdya, mahā|bāho, paśyāmy any'|ânuśāsitam,
hīnāṃ hasti|gav'|âśvena. kiṃ nu jīvāmi, Mādhava?
idaṃ kaṣṭataraṃ paśya putrasy' âpi vadhān mama—
yad imāḥ paryupāsante hatāñ śūrān raṇe striyaḥ.
17.25 prakīrṇa|keśāṃ, su|śroṇīṃ,
Duryodhana|śubh'|âṅka|gām,
rukma|vedī|nibhāṃ paśya,
Kṛṣṇa, Lakṣmaṇa|mātaram.
nūnam eṣā purā bālā jīvamāne mahā|bhuje
bhujāv āśritya ramate su|bhujasya manasvinī.
kathaṃ tu śatadhā n' êdaṃ hṛdayaṃ mama dīryate,
paśyantyā nihataṃ putraṃ putreṇa sahitaṃ raṇe?
putraṃ rudhira|saṃsiktam upajighraty a|ninditā,
Duryodhanaṃ tu vām'|ōrūḥ pāṇinā parimārjati.
kiṃ nu śocati bhartāraṃ putraṃ c' âiṣā manasvinī,
tathā hy avasthitā bhāti; putraṃ c' âpy abhivīkṣya sā

great archer, great chariot-fighter, like the tiger struck down by the lion, Bhima·sena.

For, foolishly and wickedly disregarding Vídura and his 17.20
father, this ill-fated man has succumbed to death, all because of disregarding his elders. The earth owed its allegiance to him and no other lord these thirteen years. Now that lord of the earth, my darling son, lies on the earth, murdered. Krishna, I have seen the world under the command of Dhrita·rashtra's sons, bursting with elephants, cattle and horses. But it has not lasted long, son of Vrishni. Today I see the same world under the command of others, mighty-armed lord, stripped of its elephants, cattle and horses. How, lord of the Yadus, can I carry on living? Look at this sight, more devastating even than the death of my son—these women attending to their champions killed in the war.

Look, Krishna, at Lákshmana's full-hipped mother, her 17.25
hair hanging loose, cradling Duryódhana in her lovely lap, like the hearth of a golden altar. Surely that bright woman, when her mighty armed husband still lived, embraced within his arms, use to make carefree love to her lovely armed lord. How does this heart of mine not shatter into a hundred pieces, as I gaze upon my son slain alongside his own son in the war? The innocent woman sniffs the sweet scent of her blood-soaked son,* while on her lovely lap she strokes Duryódhana. For this bright lady grieves both her husband and her son, and she seems stuck like that; now on gazing
upon her son she beats her head with both fists, her eyes 17.30
rolling, then falls on the chest of her heroic husband, the king of the Kurus, Mádhava. She looks like a white lotus,

17.30 sva|śiraḥ pañca|śākhābhyām abhihaty' āyat'|ēkṣaṇā
patoty urasi vīrasya Kuru|rājasya, Mādhava.
puṇḍarīka|nibhā bhāti puṇḍarīk'|ântara|prabhā,
mukhaṃ vimṛjya putrasya bhartuś c' āiva tapasvinī.
yadi saty'|āgamāḥ santi yadi vā śrutayas tathā,
dhruvaṃ lokān avāpto 'yaṃ nṛpo bāhu|bal'|ârjitān.

GĀNDHĀRY uvāca:

18.1 PAŚYA, MĀDHAVA, putrān me śata|saṃkhyāñ jita|klamān
gadayā Bhīmasenena bhūyiṣṭhaṃ nihatān raṇe.
idaṃ duḥkhataraṃ me 'dya, yad imā mukta|mūrdhajāḥ
hata|putrā raṇe bālāḥ paridhāvanti me snuṣāḥ,
prāsāda|tala|cāriṇyaś caraṇair bhūṣaṇ'|ânvitaiḥ
āpannā yat spṛśant' îmāṃ rudhir'|ārdrāṃ vasuṃ|dharām.
kṛcchhrād utsārayanti sma gṛdhra|gomāyu|vāyasān,
duḥkhen' ārtā vighūrṇantyo mattā iva caranty uta.
18.5 eṣ" ānyā tv an|a|vady'|âṅgī kara|saṃmita|madhyamā
ghoram āyodhanaṃ dṛṣṭvā nipataty atiduḥkhitā.
dṛṣṭvā me pārthiva|sutām etāṃ Lakṣmaṇa|mātaram
rāja|putrīṃ, mahā|bāho, mano na vyupaśāmyati.
bhrātṝṃś c' ânyāḥ, pitṝṃś c' ânyāḥ,
putrāṃś ca nihatān bhuvi
dṛṣṭvā paripatanty etāḥ
pragṛhya su|mahā|bhujān.
madhyamānāṃ tu nārīṇāṃ vṛddhānāṃ c,' â|parājita,
ākrandaṃ hata|bandhūnāṃ dāruṇe vaiśase śṛṇu.
ratha|nīḍāni dehāṃś ca hatānāṃ gaja|vājinām
āśritya śrama|moh'|ārtāḥ sthitāḥ paśya, mahā|bhuja.

shining among white lotuses, after wiping the faces of her son and her husband, the poor woman. But if traditional lore and the scriptures be true, then certainly this king has arrived at the realms earned by the might of the arm.

GANDHÁRI continued:

LOOK AT MY sons, prince of the Yadus, one hundred in 18.1
number, who conquered exhaustion, but lost their lives in the war, mostly to Bhima with his mace. Now this further misery overtakes me: that these poor women, the widows of my sons, have lost their sons too in the war and run about the place, hair everywhere.* Accustomed only to walking on smooth terraces with their jewelry-laden feet, they have come to this: feeling their way across this blood drenched soil. They struggle to drive off the vultures, the wolves and crows, or rocked by their torment, they stagger about as if drunk.

Meanwhile this woman of faultless appearance, her waist 18.5
slender enough to be measured within a pair of hands, on seeing this gruesome battle field falls down, the suffering too much. Since seeing this daughter of rulers, the mother of the royal prince Lákshmana, my heart cannot settle, mighty armed warrior. On seeing slain on the ground either their brothers, or their fathers, or their sons, these women fall upon them, embracing their once so powerful embraces. Undefeated lord, listen to these women, those in their prime and the older alike, weeping at this pitiful slaughter, all their men folk slain. Look, powerful warrior, at these women standing here, in an agony of exhaustion

18.10 anyā† c' âpahṛtaṃ kāyāc cāru|kuṇḍalam, unnasam
svasya bandhoḥ śiraḥ, Kṛṣṇa, gṛhītvā, paśya, tiṣṭhati.*
pūrva|jāti|kṛtaṃ pāpaṃ manye n' âlpam iv', ânagha,
etābhir nir|a|vadyābhir, mayā c' âiv' âlpa|medhayā,
yad idaṃ Dharma|rājena pātitaṃ no, Janārdana.
na hi nāśo 'sti, Vārṣṇeya, karmaṇoḥ śubha|pāpayoḥ.
pratyagra|vayasaḥ paśya darśanīya|kuc|ôdarāḥ,
kuleṣu jātā, hrīmatyaḥ, kṛṣṇa|pakṣ'|âkṣi|mūrdhajāḥ,
haṃsa|gadgada|bhāṣiṇyo, duḥkha|śoka|pramohitāḥ.
sārasya iva vāśantyaḥ patitāḥ paśya, Mādhava.
phulla|padma|prakāśāni, puṇḍarīk'|âkṣa, yoṣitām
18.15 an|a|vadyāni vaktrāṇi tāpayaty eṣa raśmivān.
īrṣūṇāṃ mama putrāṇāṃ, Vāsudev', âvarodhanam
matta|mātaṅga|darpāṇāṃ paśyanty adya pṛthag|janāḥ.
śata|candrāṇi carmāṇi, dhvajāṃś c' āditya|saṃnibhān,
raukmāṇi c' âiva varmāṇi, niṣkān api ca kāñcanān,
śīrṣa|trāṇāni c' âitāni putrāṇāṃ me mahī|tale,
paśya, dīptāni, Govinda, pāvakān su|hutān iva.
eṣa Duḥśāsanaḥ śete śūreṇ' â|mitra|ghātinā
pīta|śoṇita|sarv'|âṅgo yudhi Bhīmena pātitaḥ,
18.20 gadayā Bhīmasenena paśya, Mādhava, me sutam.
dyūta|kleśān anusmṛtya Draupadī|noditena ca.

and bewilderment, supporting themselves on the cars of
chariots, or on the carcasses of slain elephants and horses.

And there stands another, clutching the head of a male 18.10
relative, with such pretty earrings and elegant nose, severed
from its body, Krishna, see! I think these innocent ladies
and I, so powerless, must have committed no small measure
of evil in our previous lives, faultless one, that the King of
Dharma visits this misfortune upon us, rouser of the people. For neither good nor evil deeds simply disappear without trace, son of Vrishni. Behold these women in the best
years of their lives, their breasts and bellies a vision to behold, born into noble families, dignified, their locks and
lashes raven, their voices cooing and soft as the call of the
swan, now bewildered with anguish and grief. See how they
have fallen, Mádhava, keening like cranes. Lotus-eyed lord,
these women's full-blown lotus-like unimpeachable faces 18.15
are getting burned in this sun.

Son of Vasu·deva, the harem of my sons, which they protected as jealously as rutting bull-elephants, is now a public spectacle. Shields like a hundred moons, and banners
radiant as the sun, the glinting armor, the golden breast
plates and helmets of my sons here on the ground, look
at them glowing, Govínda, like sacrificial fires well-stoked
with oblations. Here lies Duhshásana, whom Bhima, that
valiant slayer of adversaries, killed in battle and drained the
blood from his every limb, Bhima·sena killing him with his 18.20
mace, remembering his grievances at the dice match and
urged on by Dráupadi—look at my son, Mádhava.

uktā hy anena Pāñcālī sabhāyāṃ dyūta|nirjitā
priyaṃ cikīrṣatā bhrātuḥ Karṇasya ca, Jan'|ârdana:
«sah' âiva Sahadevena Nakulen'|Ârjunena ca
dāsī|bhūt" âsi, Pāñcāli. kṣipraṃ praviśa no gṛhān.»
tato 'ham abruvaṃ, Kṛṣṇa, tadā Duryodhanaṃ nṛpam,
«mṛtyu|pāśa|parikṣiptaṃ Śakuniṃ, putra, varjaya.
nibodh' âinaṃ su|dur|buddhiṃ mātulaṃ kalaha|priyam.
kṣipram enaṃ parityajya, putra, śāmyasva Pāṇḍavaiḥ.
18.25 na budhyase tvaṃ, dur|buddhe, Bhīmasenam a|marṣaṇam
vāṅ|nārācais tudaṃs tīkṣṇair, ulkābhir iva kuñjaram.»
tān evaṃ rahasi kruddho vāk|śalyān avadhārayan
utsasarja viṣaṃ teṣu, sarpo go|vṛṣabheṣv iva.
eṣa Duḥśāsanaḥ śete vikṣipya vipulau bhujau,
nihato Bhīmasenena, siṃhen' êva maha"|rṣabhaḥ.
aty|artham akarod raudraṃ Bhīmaseno 'ty|a|marṣaṇaḥ,
Duḥśāsanasya yat kruddho 'pibac choṇitam āhave.

GĀNDHĀRY uvāca:

19.1 EṢA, MĀDHAVA, putro me Vikarṇaḥ prājña|saṃmataḥ
bhūmau vinihataḥ śete, Bhīmena śatadhā kṛtaḥ.
gaja|madhyaṃ hataḥ śete Vikarṇo, Madhu|sūdana,
nīla|megha|parikṣiptaḥ śarad' îva divā|karaḥ.
asya cāpa|grahen' âiṣa pāṇiḥ kṛta|kiṇo mahān
kathaṃ cic chidyate gṛdhrair attu|kāmais talatravān.
asya bhāry" āmiṣa|prepsūn gṛdhra|kākāṃs tapasvinī

For in the assembly hall this son of mine, rouser of the people, seeking to please his brother and Karna, said to that Panchálan princess when she had been lost at dice, "Panchálan woman, alongside Saha·deva, Nákula and Árjuna you are now a slave. Quickly get into our house!"

At that I spoke to King Duryódhana back then, Krishna, saying, "Distance yourself from Shákuni, son. He is trammeled in the snares of death. Recognize that the intentions of this uncle of yours are entirely malevolent. He loves discord. Quickly put him aside, son, and make peace with the Pándavas. In your folly, you do not notice how you are 18.25
wounding the unforgiving Bhima·sena with the sharp arrows of your words, like an elephant with burning shafts."

Secretly irritated by this, he continued uttering such barbed words and thus spat poison at them, like a snake at bulls. Here lies Duhshásana the ill-advised, his broad arms thrown up, slain by Bhima·sena, like a great bull slain by a lion. Horrific was the act that the vengeful Bhima·sena wrought in his anger when he drank Duhshásana 's blood on the battlefield.

GANDHÁRI continued:

HERE, MÁDHAVA, is my son Vikárna, held in high esteem 19.1
by wise men, cut down upon the ground, lying dismembered into a hundred pieces by Bhima. Vikárna lies slain in the midst of elephants, slayer of Madhu, like the day-bringing sun in an autumn sky, nestled among blue clouds. Here his broad hand, calloused where he clenched his bow, sheathed in its leather fence, somehow resists the vultures

vārayaty a|niśaṃ bālā, na ca śaknoti, Mādhava.
19.5 yuvā vṛndārakaḥ śūro Vikarṇaḥ, puruṣa'|rṣabha,
sukh'|ôcitaḥ sukh'|ârhaś ca śete pāṃsuṣu, Mādhava.
karṇi|nālīka|nārācair bhinna|marmāṇam āhave
ady' âpi na jahāty enaṃ lakṣmīr Bharata|sattamam.
eṣa saṃgrāma|śūreṇa pratijñāṃ pālayiṣyatā
Durmukho 'bhimukhaḥ śete hato 'ri|gaṇa|hā raṇe.
tasy' âitad vadanaṃ, Kṛṣṇa, śvāpadair ardha|bhakṣitam
vibhāty abhyadhikaṃ,† tāta, saptamyām iva candramāḥ.
śūrasya hi raṇe, Kṛṣṇa, paśy' ānanam ath' êdṛśam.
sa kathaṃ nihato 'mitraiḥ pāṃsūn grasati me sutaḥ?
19.10 yasy' āhava|mukhe, saumya, sthātā n' âiv' ôpapadyate,
sa kathaṃ Durmukho 'mitrair hato vibudha|loka|jit?
Citrasenaṃ hataṃ bhūmau śayānaṃ, Madhu|sūdana,
Dhārtarāṣṭram imaṃ paśya pratimānaṃ dhanuṣmatām.
taṃ citra|māly'|ābharaṇaṃ yuvatyaḥ śoka|karśitāḥ
kravy'|âda|saṃghaiḥ sahitā rudatyaḥ paryupāsate.
strīṇāṃ rudita|nirghoṣaḥ, śvāpadānāṃ ca garjitam,
citra|rūpam idaṃ, Kṛṣṇa, vicitraṃ pratibhāti me.
yuvā vṛndārako, nityaṃ pravara|strī|niṣevitaḥ,
Viviṃśatir asau śete dhvastaḥ pāṃsuṣu, Mādhava.

who stab at it, longing to eat it. His wretched wife tries constantly to ward off the vultures and crows that clamor for his flesh, Mádhava, but the young thing's attempts are in vain.

The handsome young champion Vikárna, bull among 19.5
men, used to luxury and deserving luxury, lies in the dust, Mádhava. In the battle his flesh has been pierced by barbs, arrows and darts. Nonetheless glory has not forsaken this finest of the Bhárata line. Here, slain by the champion of the battle in fulfillment of his promise, Dúrmukha, who himself slew in war large numbers of foe, lies slain facing the enemy. Even half-eaten by wild beasts, Krishna, this face of his is still brilliantly resplendent, my son, like the moon at first quarter. Look how the face of a champion in battle has ended up, Krishna. How could this son of mine be slain by his enemies and end up eating dust?

No one could countenance him in the front line, gentle 19.10
one, so how could he, that same Dúrmukha,* have been faced down by his enemies and win only Indra's realm? Chitra·sena lies slain upon the ground, slayer of Madhu. Look at this son of Dhrita·rashtra, the model of archers. Around his brightly adorned and garlanded form, his young widows, haggard with grief, sit weeping, amid the huddles of flesh-eating animals. The sound of women weeping, the snarling of wild beasts, and this astonishing scene seem to dazzle me, Krishna. The handsome youth Vivínshati, always attended by the loveliest women, now lies here sunk into the dust, Mádhava.

19.15 śara|saṃkṛtta|varmāṇaṃ vīraṃ viśasane hatam
parivāry' āsate gṛdhrāḥ, paśya, Kṛṣṇa, Viviṃśatim.
praviśya samare śūraḥ Pāṇḍavānām anīkinīm
sa vīra|śayane śete paraḥ sat|puruṣ'|ôcite.
smit' ôpapannaṃ, su|nasaṃ, su|bhru, tār"|âdhip'|ôpamam,
atīva śubhraṃ vadanaṃ paśya, Kṛṣṇa, Viviṃśateḥ.
enaṃ hi paryupāsante bahudhā vara|yoṣitāḥ,
krīḍantam iva gandharvaṃ deva|kanyāḥ sahasraśaḥ.
hantāraṃ para|sainyānāṃ, śūraṃ, samiti|śobhanam,
nibarhaṇam amitrāṇāṃ Duḥsahaṃ viṣaheta kaḥ?
19.20 Duḥsahasy' âitad ābhāti śarīraṃ saṃvṛtaṃ śaraiḥ,
girir ātma|gataiḥ phullaiḥ karṇikārair iv' āvṛtaḥ.
śātakaumbhyā srajā bhāti, kavacena ca bhāsvatā,
agnin" êva giriḥ śveto, gat'|āsur api Duḥsahaḥ.

GĀNDHĀRY uvāca:

20.1 ADHYARDHA|GUṆAM āhur yaṃ bale śaurye ca, Mādhava,
pitrā tvayā ca, Dāśārha, dṛptaṃ siṃham iv' ôtkaṭam,
yo bibheda camūm eko mama putrasya dur|bhidām,
sa bhūtvā mṛtyur anyeṣāṃ svayaṃ mṛtyu|vaśaṃ gataḥ.
tasy' ôpalakṣaye, Kṛṣṇa, Kārṣṇer amita|tejasaḥ
Abhimanyor hatasy' âpi prabhā n' âiv' ôpaśāmyati.
eṣā Virāṭa|duhitā, snuṣā Gāṇḍīva|dhanvanaḥ,
ārtā bālā patiṃ vīraṃ dṛṣṭvā śocaty a|ninditā.

His armor pierced by arrows, a hero slain in the slaughter, 19.15
look Krishna, how Vivínshati is attended by the vultures gathering around him. After crossing the Pándavan lines, a champion in battle, he lies exalted on the bed of heroes, the honor of true men. Vivínshati's face, its distinguished nose and fine eyebrows, seems to smile. See how very radiant it is, Krishna, like the sovereign of the stars.* Indeed he is attended by a myriad of lovely ladies, like a charming divine musician by the heavenly maidens in their thousands.

The champion Dúhsaha, splendid in battle, who killed members of the enemy army and wrought destruction on
his opponents, who could vanquish him? Yet here Dúh- 19.20
saha's body can be seen covered in arrows, like a mountain carpeted in its native barb-flowers in bloom. With his golden garland and lustrous armor, he gleams like a white mountain by firelight, though the breath has gone from Dúhsaha.

GANDHÁRI continued:

THE MAN THEY say had more than half again the strength 20.1
and valor of his father and you, Mádhava, who was proud and powerful as a lion, descendant of Dashárha, who alone broke through the impenetrable ranks of my son's army, though once the death of others, has now succumbed to death himself. I see that even in death, the brilliance, Krishna, of your sister's son, Abhimányu, whose splendor knew no bounds, does not fade. Here the daughter of Viráta, daughter-in-law to Árjuna of the Gandíva bow, young and innocent, grieves in misery on finding her heroic husband.

20.5 tam eṣā hi samāgamya bhāryā bhartāram antike
Virāṭa|duhitā, Kṛṣṇa, pāṇinā parimārjati,
tasya vaktram upāghrāya Saubhadrasya manasvinī
vibuddha|kamal'|ākāraṃ, kambu|vṛtta|śiro|dharam.
kāmya|rūpavatī c' âiṣā pariṣvajati bhāminī
lajjamānā purā c' âinaṃ mādhvīka|mada|mūrchitā.
tasya kṣataja|saṃdigdhaṃ, jātarūpa|pariṣkṛtam
vimucya kavacaṃ, Kṛṣṇa, śarīram abhivīkṣate.
avekṣamāṇā taṃ bālā, Kṛṣṇa, tvām abhibhāṣate:
«ayaṃ te, puṇḍarīk'|âkṣa, sadṛś'|âkṣo nipātitaḥ.
20.10 bale vīrye ca sadṛśas, tejasā c' âiva te, 'n|agha,
rūpeṇa ca tath" âtyarthaṃ, śete bhuvi nipātitaḥ.
atyantaṃ sukumārasya rāṅkav'|âjina|śāyinaḥ
kaccid adya śarīraṃ te bhūmau na paritapyate?
mātaṅga|bhuja|varṣmāṇau, jy"|ākṣepa|kaṭhina|tvacau,
kāñcan'|âṅgadinau śeṣe† nikṣipya vipulau bhujau.
vyāyamya bahudhā nūnaṃ sukha|suptaḥ śramād iva,
evaṃ vilapatīm ārtāṃ na hi mām abhibhāṣase?
na smarāmy aparādhaṃ te. kiṃ māṃ na pratibhāṣase?
nanu māṃ tvaṃ purā dūrād abhivīkṣy' âbhibhāṣase.
20.15 na smarāmy aparādhaṃ te. kiṃ māṃ na pratibhāṣase?
āryām, ārya, Subhadrāṃ tvam, imāṃś ca tridaś'|ôpamān
pitṝn, māṃ c' âiva duḥkh'|ārtāṃ vihāya kva gamiṣyasi?»

Coming close to him, the wife to her supportive husband, it is she, Viráta's daughter, who strokes him with her hand. The strong-willed woman breathes in the sweet smell of the face of Subhádra's son, which looks like a full-blown lotus, atop his neck with its conch shell* lines. Seductively beautiful she who once was shy now passionately embraces him, as if emboldened by the headiness of mead. She loosens his armor, brazened with golden ore, marbled with the gore oozing from his wounds, and gazes on his body, Krishna. As she looks at him it is to you the young girl speaks, Krishna: 20.5

"He had your eyes, lotus-eyed lord, but here he is, lifeless. Your match in strength, valor and prowess, faultless 20.10
one, and exquisitely handsome like you too, but he lies here on the ground, lifeless. You were so refined, used to resting on soft deer wool and antelope hide. Doesn't it chafe your body now to lie direct upon the ground? You lie with your arms thrown up, broad and rough-skinned where the bowstring rubbed, long as the trunks of bull-elephants, clasped in golden armlets. Surely you are just sleeping peacefully as if tired after so much exertion. But why when I speak to you in distress do you not return my words? I don't remember doing anything to upset you. Why won't you reply to me? Before you would always call out to me when you saw me, even from afar. I don't remember doing anything to upset 20.15
you. Why won't you answer me? Honorable lord, where are you going, leaving honorable Subhádra, the elder men of your family here, who resemble the heavenly hosts, and me all behind?"

tasya śoṇita|digdhān keśān udyamya pāṇinā,
utsaṅge vaktram ādhāya jīvantam iva pṛcchati.
«svasrīyaṃ Vāsudevasya, putraṃ Gāṇḍīva|dhanvanaḥ
kathaṃ tvāṃ raṇa|madhya|sthaṃ jaghnur ete mahārathāḥ?
dhig astu krūra|kartṝṃs tān Kṛpa|Karṇa|Jayadrathān,
Droṇa|Drauṇāyanī c' ôbhau, yair ahaṃ vidhavā kṛtā.
ratha'|rṣabhāṇāṃ sarveṣāṃ katham āsīt tadā manaḥ
20.20 bālaṃ tvāṃ parivāry' âikaṃ mama duḥkhāya jaghnuṣām?
kathaṃ nu Pāṇḍavānāṃ ca Pāñcālānāṃ tu paśyatām
tvaṃ, vīra, nidhanaṃ prāpto nāthavān sann a|nāthavat?
dṛṣṭvā bahubhir ākrande nihataṃ tvām a|nāthavat
vīraḥ puruṣa|śārdūlaḥ kathaṃ jīvati Pāṇḍavaḥ?
na rājya|lābho vipulaḥ, śatrūṇāṃ vā parābhavaḥ
prītiṃ dāsyati Pārthānāṃ tvām ṛte, puṣkar'|êkṣaṇa.
tava śastra|jitāl̃ lokān dharmeṇa ca damena ca
kṣipram anvāgamiṣyāmi. tatra māṃ pratipālaya.
dur|maraṃ punar a|prāpte kāle bhavati kena cit,
20.25 yad ahaṃ tvāṃ raṇe dṛṣṭvā hataṃ jīvāmi dur|bhagā.
kām idānīṃ, nara|vyāghra, ślakṣṇayā smitayā girā
pitṛ|loke samety' ânyāṃ mām iv' āmantrayiṣyasi?
nūnam apsarasāṃ svarge manāṃsi pramathiṣyasi
parameṇa ca rūpeṇa, girā ca smita|pūrvayā.
prāpya puṇya|kṛtāl̃ lokān apsarobhiḥ sameyivān,
Saubhadra, viharan kāle smarethāḥ su|kṛtāni me.

Brushing back his blood-caked locks with her hand and placing his head in her lap, she asks him these things as if he were still alive. "You are the nephew of Krishna son of Vasu·deva and the son of Árjuna, who bears the Gandíva bow. So how could these great chariot-warriors kill you in the midst of the battle field? I curse those men whose actions knew no mercy, Kripa, Karna and Jayad·ratha, as well as Drona and his son, who have made me a widow. What can have been in the minds then of all those bull-like chariot warriors, when 20.20
they isolated you, so young, bent on your murder and my grief? How can it be that with the Pándavas and Panchálas all in view, you had protectors, but still ended up dead, my hero, with no one protecting you. Seeing you slain by so many in the fray, as if no one was there to help you, how can Pandu's heroic son, like a tiger among men, continue living? Neither the acquisition of this extensive kingdom nor defeat of their enemies will bring joy to Kunti's sons without you and your lotus eyes.

To the worlds you have won by the sword, through dutiful and disciplined conduct, I shall quickly follow you. Look after me there. But it must be nigh impossible to die before one's allotted time has come, or else why would I be 20.25
so unfortunate as to still be breathing, even though I have seen you slain on the battle field? With your gentle smile and voice, man-tiger, what woman will you meet now in the ancestral realm, and speak to her as you did to me? Surely you will set the hearts of the divine nymphs in heaven a-flutter with your superior looks and your winning voice. You have reached the world achieved through good deeds and met with the divine nymphs, Subhádra's son; while you

etāvān iha saṃvāso vihitas te mayā saha:
ṣaṇmāsān. saptame māsi tvaṃ, vīra, nidhanaṃ gataḥ.»
ity ukta|vacanām etām apakarṣanti duḥkhitām
20.30 Uttarāṃ mogha|saṃkalpāṃ Matsya|rāja|kula|striyaḥ.
Uttarām apakṛṣy' âinām ārtām ārtatarāḥ svayam.
Virāṭaṃ nihataṃ dṛṣṭvā krośanti vilapanti ca,
Droṇ'|âstra|śara|saṃkṛttaṃ śayānaṃ rudhir'|ôkṣitam.
Virāṭaṃ vitudanty ete gṛdhra|gomāyu|vāyasāḥ.
vitudyamānaṃ vihagair Virāṭam asit'|êkṣaṇāḥ
na śaknuvanti vihagān nivartayitum āturāḥ.
āsām ātapa|taptānām āyāsena ca yoṣitām
śrameṇa ca vivarṇānāṃ vaktrāṇāṃ viplutaṃ vapuḥ.
Uttaraṃ c', Âbhimanyuṃ ca, Kāmbojaṃ ca Sudakṣiṇam—
20.35 śiśūn etān hatān paśya! Lakṣmaṇaṃ ca su|darśanam
āyodhana|śiro|madhye śayānaṃ paśya, Mādhava.

GĀNDHĀRY uvāca:

21.1 EṢA VAIKARTANAḤ śete mah"|êṣv|āso mahā|rathaḥ
jvalit'|ânalavat saṃkhye saṃśāntaḥ Pārtha|tejasā.
paśya Vaikartanaṃ Karṇaṃ nihaty' âtirathān bahūn,
śoṇit'|âugha|parīt'|âṅgaṃ śayānaṃ patitaṃ bhuvi.
a|marṣī, dīrgha|roṣaś ca, mah"|êṣv|āso, mahā|rathaḥ
raṇe vinihataḥ śete śūro Gāṇḍīva|dhanvanā.

pass your time with them, please remember the good things I did. Your appointed life here with me has only been six months. In the seventh month you met your end, my hero."

As she said these words to him, they pulled the wretched woman away. The women of the royal house of Matsya 20.30
pulled Uttará with all her vain wishes away, Uttará in agony, themselves more agonized when they had done so. When they saw Viráta lying slain, steeped in blood, shredded by Drona's missiles and arrows, they screamed and wailed. See these vultures, wolves and crows tearing at Viráta. As Viráta is ripped apart by birds of prey, those dark-eyed ladies anxiously try to ward the birds off, but to no avail. The women, though burning up in their torment, with all their distress and effort, lose the color from their faces, and are physically overwhelmed. Úttara, Abhimányu and Sudákshina of the Kambójans, all these dear children slain here, see! And fair 20.35
Lákshmana, see him lying in the front line of the fighting, Mádhava.

GANDHÁRI continued:

HERE LIES THE son of the Sun, the great archer and great 21.1
chariot-fighter, like a blazing fire in battle, extinguished by the brilliance of Kunti's acknowledged son.* Look at Karna, son of the solar race, who had killed so many superior chariot-fighters, now lying fallen on the ground, every limb awash with streams of blood. Unforgiving and nursing a long resentment, the great archer, great chariot fighter and champion lies slain in battle by the wielder of the Gandíva bow.

yaṃ sma Pāṇḍava|santrāsān mama putrā mahā|rathāḥ
prāyudhyanta puras|kṛtya, mātaṅgā iva yūthapam,
21.5 śārdūlam iva siṃhena samare savya|sācinā,
mātaṅgam iva mattena mātaṅgena nipātitam,
sametāḥ, puruṣa|vyāghra, nihataṃ śūram āhave
prakīrṇa|mūrdha|jāḥ patnyo rudatyaḥ paryupāsate.
udvignaḥ satataṃ yasmād dharma|rājo Yudhiṣṭhiraḥ
trayodaśa samā nidrāṃ cintayann n' âdhyagacchata,
an|ādhṛṣyaḥ parair yuddhe śatrubhir Maghavān iva,
yug'|ânt'|âgnir iv' ârciṣmān, Himavān iva niścalaḥ,
sa bhūtvā śaraṇaṃ vīro Dhārtarāṣṭrasya, Mādhava,
bhūmau vinihataḥ śete, vāta|bhagna iva drumaḥ.
21.10 paśya Karṇasya patnīṃ tvaṃ Vṛṣasenasya† mātaram
lālapyamānāṃ karuṇaṃ, rudatīṃ patitāṃ bhuvi.
«ācārya|śāpo 'nugato dhruvaṃ tvāṃ,
yad agrasac cakram idaṃ dharitrī.
tataḥ śareṇ' âpahṛtaṃ śiras te
Dhanaṃjayen' āhava|śobhinā yudhi.»
hā hā dhig. eṣā patitā visaṃjñā
samīkṣya jāmbūnada|baddha|niṣkam†
Karṇaṃ mahā|bāhum a|dīna|sattvaṃ
Suṣeṇa|mātā rudatī bhṛś'|ārtā.
alp'|âvaśeṣo hi kṛto mah"|ātmā
śarīra|bhakṣaiḥ paribhakṣayadbhiḥ.

My sons, in their fear of the Pándavas, though great chariot fighters themselves, put him to the fore as they fought, as bull elephants the lord of their herd. As a tiger by a lion, 21.5
he has been brought down by the left-handed archer in the fray, as a bull elephant by a bull elephant, maddened in rut. Gathered round attending to the champion slain in battle, tiger of men, their hair hanging down disheveled, are his weeping wives. In his anxiety the just king Yudhi·shthira could not sleep for thirteen years, constantly on edge on account of this man. In battle he was as unassailable to his opponents as the bounty winning Indra to his enemies, like the flame-throwing fire of the apocalypse or the immovable mountain range, the Himalaya; that same hero, Mádhava, who had become the refuge for Dhrita·rashtra's son,* now lies slain on the ground, like a tree split by the wind.

Look at Karna's devoted wife, mother of his son Vrisha· 21.10
sena—she has fallen to the ground weeping pitifully and gibbering: "The curse of your teacher* had tracked you in tenacious pursuit, when the earth sucked down this wheel. Only then could Árjuna, winner of spoils, radiant in battle, shoot off your head with his arrow." This is too awful, too awful. Fallen, bewildered, Sushéna's mother gazes on broad-armed Karna, still dressed in his golden chest plate, his vital brilliance undinted, then weeps in violent anguish. For little now remains of her noble-souled lord, with body-snatching predators eating at him. He offers nothing pleasing to our eyes, like the moon with its hare on the fourteenth day of the waning fortnight. His wife has fallen writhing on the ground, but struggles wretchedly to her feet once more and

draṣṭuṃ na naḥ prīti|karaḥ, śaś" îva
kṛṣṇasya pakṣasya caturdaś'|âhe.
sā vartamānā patitā pṛthivyām,
utthāya dīnā punar eva c' âiṣā,
Karṇasya vaktraṃ parijighramāṇā
rorūyate putra|vadh'|âbhitaptā.

GĀNDHĀRY uvāca:

22.1 ĀVANTYAṂ BHĪMASENENA bhakṣayanti nipātitam
gṛdhra|gomāyavaḥ śūraṃ, bahu|bandhum a|bandhuvat.
taṃ paśya kadanaṃ kṛtvā śūrāṇāṃ, Madhu|sūdana,
śayānaṃ vīra|śayane rudhireṇa samukṣitam.
taṃ sṛgālāś ca, kaṅkāś ca, kravy'|âdāś ca pṛthag|vidhāḥ
tena tena vikarṣanti. paśya kālasya paryayam!
śayānaṃ vīra|śayane śūram ākranda|kāriṇam
Āvantyam abhito nāryo rudatyaḥ paryupāsate.
22.5 Prātipīyaṃ mah"|êṣv|āsaṃ hataṃ bhallena Bāhlikam
prasuptam iva śārdūlaṃ paśya, Kṛṣṇa, manasvinam.
atīva mukha|varṇo 'sya nihatasy' âpi śobhate,
somasy' êv' âbhipūrṇasya paurṇamāsyāṃ samudyataḥ.
putra|śok'|âbhitaptena pratijñāṃ c' âbhirakṣatā
Pāka|śāsaninā saṃkhye Vārddhakṣatrir nipātitaḥ.
ekādaśa camūr bhittvā rakṣyamāṇaṃ mah"|ātmanā
satyaṃ cikīrṣatā paśya hatam enaṃ Jayadratham.
Sindhu|Sauvīra|bhartāraṃ darpa|pūrṇaṃ, manasvinam
bhakṣayanti śivā gṛdhrā, jan'|ârdana, Jayadratham.
22.10 saṃrakṣyamāṇaṃ bhāryābhir anuraktābhir, a|cyuta,
bhīṣayantyo vikarṣanti gahanaṃ nimnam antikāt.
tam etāḥ paryupāsante rakṣyamāṇaṃ mahā|bhujam
Sindhu|Sauvīra|bhārtāraṃ Kāmboja|Yavana|striyaḥ.
yadā Kṛṣṇām upādāya prādravat Kekayaiḥ saha,

breathing in the familiar scent of Karna's face, she wails and wails, already devastated by the slaughter of her sons.

GANDHÁRI continued:

VULTURES AND WOLVES feast on the champion of Avánti slain by Bhima·sena. Many were those close to him. Now there is none. Look at him, slayer of Madhu. Though be brought carnage on champions, he now sleeps on the bed of heroes, sprayed in blood. Jackals, herons and every kind of carrion-eater are at him, dragging him this way and that. Observe the fickle nature of time! As he lies on the bed of heroes, the champion of Avánti, who issued war-cries, is attended on all sides by his crying wives. 22.1

Look Krishna at Báhlika, the intelligent son of Pratípa, like a sleeping tiger, the great archer killed by an arched arrow. The complexion of his face is radiant though he is slain, like the ambrosia-filled moon as it rises at full-moon. Fulfilling the oath he swore, incensed by grief for his son, the son of the slayer of the demon Paka,* has slain Vriddha·kshatra's son. Look at Jayad·ratha here; in spite of the protection afforded him by the noble Drona, the father fulfilling his vow still killed him, after breaking through the eleven battalions. The master of the Sauvíras of Sindh, Jayad·ratha, full of pride and intelligence, now she-jackals and vultures take their fill of him, rouser of the people. 22.5

Though his tender wives try to protect him, unyielding lord, the fearsome beasts drag him to a thicket in a depression nearby. Though the beasts guard him, these Kambójan and Yávana women still attend to the broad-armed master of the Sauvíras of Sindh. Jayad·ratha already deserved to 22.10

tad" âiva vadhyaḥ Pāṇḍūnāṃ, jan'|ârdana, Jayadrathaḥ.
Duḥśalāṃ mānayadbhis tu yadā mukto Jayadrathaḥ,
katham adya na tāṃ, Kṛṣṇa, mānayanti sma te punaḥ?
s" âiṣā mama sutā bālā vilapantī ca duḥkhitā
ātmanā hanti c' ātmānam ākrośantī ca Pāṇḍavān.

22.15 kiṃ nu duḥkhataraṃ, Kṛṣṇa, paraṃ mama bhaviṣyati,
yat sutā vidhavā bālā, snuṣāś ca nihat'|ēśvarāḥ?
hā hā dhig, Duḥśalāṃ paśya vīta|śoka|bhayām iva,
śiro bhartur an|āsādya dhāvamānām itas tataḥ.
vārayām āsa yaḥ sarvān Pāṇḍavān putra|gṛddhinaḥ,
sa hatvā vipulāḥ senāḥ svayaṃ mṛtyu|vaśaṃ gataḥ.
taṃ mattam iva mātaṅgaṃ, vīraṃ parama|durjayam
parivārya rudanty etāḥ striyaś candr'|ôpam'|ānanāḥ.

GĀNDHĀRY uvāca:

23.1 EṢA ŚALYO HATAḤ śete sākṣān Nakula|mātulaḥ,
dharma|jñena hatas, tāta, dharma|rājena saṃyuge.
yas tvayā spardhate nityaṃ sarvatra, puruṣa'|rṣabha,
sa eṣa nihataḥ śete Madra|rājo mahā|balaḥ.
yena saṃgṛhṇatā, tāta, ratham Ādhirather yudhi
jay'|ârthaṃ Pāṇḍu|putrāṇāṃ yadā tejo|vadhaḥ kṛtaḥ.
aho dhik, paśya! Śalyasya pūrṇa|candra|sudarśanam
mukhaṃ padma|palāś'|âkṣaṃ kākair ādaṣṭam a|vraṇam.

die at the hands of Pandu's sons back when he kidnapped the dark princess with the help of the people of Kékaya, rouser of the people. Given that they released Jayad·ratha then out of consideration for his wife Dúhshala, how come they have not shown her that consideration this time, Krishna? There she is, my poor young child, wailing in anguish, as she strikes herself and hurls reproaches at the Pándavas.

What could pain me more than this, Krishna—my 22.15
daughter, though young, is widowed and my daughter-in-laws' husbands are all slain? Oh no, look at Dúhshala. She is running about all over the place as if untouched by grief and fear, but the problem is that she has not found her husband's head.* The man who held back all the Pándavas when they were desperate to reach their son, after visiting death upon vast armies, has now succumbed to death himself. Here his wives, with faces as beautiful as moons, have gathered around their nigh-invincible hero, as round a highly charged bull elephant, and weep.

GANDHÁRI continued:

HERE LIES NÁKULA'S uncle Shalya, dead before our eyes, 23.1
my child, slain in battle by the expert in righteousness, the king of righteousness. The powerful king of Madras, who always and in everything used to vie with you, bull among men, here lies slain. By accepting the helm of the chariot of the Charioteer-king's son in the battle, since he sought to ensure the victory of Pandu's sons, he destroyed Karna's brilliance. How dreadful, see! Shalya's unsullied face, fair as a full moon, with its lotus-petal eyes, now being pecked by crows.

23.5 asya cāmīkar'|ābhasya tapta|kāñcana|sa|prabhā
āsyād viniḥsṛtā jihvā bhakṣyate, Kṛṣṇa, pakṣibhiḥ.
Yudhiṣṭhireṇa nihataṃ Śalyaṃ samiti|śobhanam
rudatyaḥ paryupāsante Madra|rājaṃ kul'|âṅganāḥ.
etāḥ su|sūkṣma|vasanā Madra|rājaṃ nara'|rṣabham
krośantyo 'tha samāsādya kṣatriyāḥ kṣatriya'|rṣabham
Śalyaṃ nipatitaṃ nāryaḥ parivāry' âbhitaḥ sthitāḥ,
vāsitā gṛṣṭayaḥ paṅke parimagnam iva dvipam.
Śalyaṃ śaraṇa|daṃ śūraṃ paśy' êmaṃ, Vṛṣṇi|nandana
śayānaṃ vīra|śayane śarair viśakalī|kṛtam.

23.10 eṣa śail'|ālayo rājā Bhagadattaḥ pratāpavān,
gaj'|âṅkuśa|dharaḥ, śrīmāñ śete bhuvi nipātitaḥ,
yasya rukmamayī mālā śirasy eṣā virājate
śvāpadair bhakṣyamāṇasya, śobhayant" îva mūrdha|jān.
etena kila Pārthasya yuddham āsīt su|dāruṇam,
roma|harṣaṇam, atyugraṃ, Śakrasya tv ahinā yathā.
yodhayitvā mahā|bāhur eṣa Pārthaṃ Dhanañjayam,
saṃśayaṃ gamayitvā ca Kuntī|putreṇa pātitaḥ.

yasya n' âsti samo loke śaurye vīrye ca kaś cana,
sa eṣa nihataḥ śete Bhīṣmo bhīṣma|kṛd āhave.
23.15 paśya Śāntanavaṃ, Kṛṣṇa, śayānaṃ sūrya|varcasam,
yug'|ânta iva kālena† pātitaṃ sūryam ambarāt.
eṣa taptvā raṇe śatrūñ śastra|tāpena vīryavān
nara|sūryo 'stam abhyeti, sūryo 'stam iva, Keśava.
śara|talpa|gataṃ Bhīṣmam ūrdhva|retasam, a|cyutam

From the mouth of this golden-hued man, glistening like molten gold, has slipped his tongue, which is being eaten by birds, Krishna. The fair women of the family shed tears as they attend Shalya, king of Madras, the medallion of the battle, but slain by Yudhi·shthira. These women of the warrior class, dressed in their flimsy clothes, have been screaming since coming upon the bull of warriors and now stand in a circle around the felled Shalya, like elephant heifers around a tusker sunk in the mud. Joy of the Vrishni clan, look at Shalya, this champion who was a source of safety, lying now on the catafalque of heroes, shredded by arrow shafts. 23.5

Here on a bed of stone lies the potent king Bhaga·datta, 23.10
the illustrious brandisher of the elephant goad, felled to the ground; the gilded garland gleams still upon his temples and seems to radiate his hair with light, even while wild beasts feast upon him. They say the fight between him and Kunti's son was savage, so fierce it set your hair on end, like the contest between Indra and the serpent. When this broad-armed warrior fought with Kunti's son, Winner of Spoils, the latter forced him into a perilous position and brought him down that way.

The awesome Bhishma, awe-inspiring in the battle, who
had no equal in heroism or valor, lies here dying. See Shán- 23.15
tanu's son lying there, Krishna, splendid as the sun, like the sun cast down, fallen at last from the sky at the end of the eon. This valiant man, who scorched his enemies in battle with the heat of his sword, this effulgence of mankind has set like the sinking orb of the sun, lord of senses. Look at Bhishma, the unyielding celibate, lain on an ascetic bed of

śayānaṃ vīra|śayane paśya śūra|niṣevite.
karṇi|nālīka|nārācair āstīrya śayan'|ôttamam
āviśya śete, bhagavān Skandaḥ śara|vaṇaṃ yathā,
a|tūla|pūrṇaṃ Gāṅgeyas tribhir bāṇaiḥ samanvitam
upadhāy' ôpadhān'|âgryaṃ dattaṃ Gāṇḍīva|dhanvanā.
23.20 pālayānaḥ pituḥ śāstram ūrdhva|retā, mahā|yaśāḥ
eṣa Śāṃtanavaḥ śete, Mādhav', â|pratimo yudhi.
dharm'|ātmā, tāta, sarva|jñaḥ pārāvaryeṇa nirṇaye,
a|martya iva martyaḥ sann eṣa prāṇān adhārayat.
n' âsti yuddhe kṛtī kaś cin, na vidvān, na parākramī,
yatra Śāntanavo Bhīṣmaḥ śete 'dya nihataḥ paraiḥ.
svayam etena śūreṇa pṛcchyamānena Pāṇḍavaiḥ
dharma|jñen' āhave mṛtyur ādiṣṭaḥ satya|vādinā.
pranaṣṭaḥ Kuru|vaṃśaś ca punar yena samuddhṛtaḥ,
sa gataḥ Kurubhiḥ sārdhaṃ mahā|buddhiḥ parābhavam.
23.25 dharmeṣu Kuravaḥ kaṃ nu paripraksyanti, Mādhava,
gate deva|vrate svargaṃ deva|kalpe nara'|rṣabhe?
Arjunasya vinetāram, ācāryaṃ Sātyakes tathā—
taṃ paśya patitaṃ Droṇaṃ Kurūṇāṃ guru|sattamam.
astraṃ catur|vidhaṃ veda, yath" âiva tridaś'|ēśvaraḥ,
Bhārgavo vā mahā|vīryas, tathā Droṇo 'pi, Mādhava.
yasya prasādād Bībhatsuḥ Pāṇḍavaḥ karma duṣkaram
cakāra, sa hataḥ śete. n' âinam astrāṇy apālayan,

arrows, lying on the bed of heroes, the final resting place of champions. He has settled himself on his ultimate bed, which he had made up of barbs, arrows and darts; he nestles there like Lord Skanda on the reed bed.* Ganga's son rests his head on a fine pillow, not stuffed with cotton, but made up of three arrows provided by the Gandíva-wielding bowman.

Here, Mádhava, lies the greatly glorious son of Shántanu, 23.20
never matched in battle, who out of filial obedience never once spilled his semen. Righteous to the core, my son, and fully aware of the outcome, he uses the choice of when to go to the life beyond granted him by his father by holding onto life, like an immortal, though die he must. It is not because there is someone more skilled, experienced or bold in battle that Shántanu's son Bhishma lies here today slain by foe. No, this champion condemned himself to death in the war, by answering truthfully when the Pándavas asked him how his own death might be achieved. The man who resurrected the extinct lineage of the Kurus will accompany them in defeat, taking his rich wisdom with him.

To whom, Mádhava, will the remaining Kurus then turn 23.25
with their questions on Dharma when this man of divine vow, a bull among men though close to divine, departs to paradise? Look now at Drona, the most excellent martial teacher to the Kurus, now fallen—he was Árjuna's guide and Sátyaki's teacher too. The greatly heroic Drona was expert in the four kinds of weapon, no different from the lord of the heaven of thirty-some gods or from Axe-wielding Rama. In his honor his pupil Árjuna the Abhorrent, the son of Pandu, performed the difficult feat,* now he lies

yaṃ purodhāya Kurava āhūyanti sma Pāṇḍavān,
so 'yaṃ śastra|bhṛtāṃ śreṣṭho Droṇaḥ śastraiḥ parikṣataḥ.

23.30 yasya nirdahataḥ senāṃ gatir agner iv' âbhavat,
sa bhūmau nihataḥ śete, śānt'|ârcir iva pāvakaḥ.
dhanur muṣṭir a|śīrṇaś ca, hast'|āvāpaś ca, Mādhava,
Droṇasya nihatasy' ājau dṛśyate jīvato yathā.
vedā yasmāc ca catvāraḥ, sarvāṇy astrāṇi, keśava,
an|apetāni vai śūrād, yath" âiv' ādau Prajāpateḥ.
vandan'|ârhāv imau tasya bandibhir vanditau śubhau
gomāyavo vikarṣanti pādau śiṣya|śat'|ârcitau.

Droṇaṃ Drupada|putreṇa nihataṃ, Madhu|sūdana,
Kṛpī kṛpaṇam anvāste duḥkh'|ôpahata|cetanā.
23.35 tāṃ paśya rudatīm, ārtāṃ, mukta|keśīm, adho|mukhīm,
hataṃ patim upāsantīṃ Droṇaṃ śastra|bhṛtāṃ varam.
bāṇair bhinna|tanu|trāṇaṃ Dhṛṣṭadyumnena, keśava,
upāste vai mṛdhe Droṇaṃ jaṭilā brahmacāriṇī.
preta|kṛtye ca yatate Kṛpī kṛpaṇam āturā
hatasya samare bhartuḥ su|kumārī, yaśasvinī.

agnīn ādhāya vidhivac, citāṃ prajvālya sarvaśaḥ,
Droṇam ādhāya gāyanti trīṇi sāmāni sāma|gāḥ.
kurvanti ca citām ete jaṭilā brahma|cāriṇaḥ
dhanurbhiḥ śaktibhiś c' âiva, ratha|nīḍaiś ca, Mādhava.
23.40 śaraiś ca vividhair anyair dhakṣyante bhūri|tejasam.

there dead. His weapons offered no protection to him, even though it is him the Pándavas hid behind when the Kurus first challenged them. Now that same Drona, the best of all those bearing arms, has been toppled by arms.

He blazed through the army consuming it, like fire. Now 23.30
he lies slain upon the ground, a torch of flames extinguished. His bow and finger guard can still be seen, unparted from his fist, so that, Mádhava, though slain Drona seems set to continue on the battle field. Neither the four Scriptures of Knowledge nor any weaponry, lord of senses, were ever lost to that champion, as was so for the lord of creation at its dawn.* His two auspicious feet that warrant worship, worshipped by bards, adored by hundreds of disciples, are now dragged apart by hyenas.

His widow Kripi the Piteous, keeps a pitiful watch over Drona, slain at the hands of Drúpada's son, slayer of Madhu,
her thoughts usurped by misery. See her weeping in distress, 23.35
her hair disheveled, her face cast down, as she attends to her slain lord Drona, the best of all who bore arms. The celibate anchorite, with her matted locks, watches over Drona in vain. His armor was already pierced in battle by Dhrishta·dyumna's arrows, lord of senses. Pitifully weak Kripi, the glorious, tender young woman, prepares for the funerary rites of her husband slain in the fray.

The priests of the "Sama Veda" have set the fire and kindled the pyre on all sides as ordained in scripture. After placing Drona upon it, they sing three Sama verses. These matted-haired celibates have made the pyre with bows,
spears and chariot cars, Mádhava. They keep it blazing 23.40
fiercely with arrows and other debris as fuel. Once they

iti Droṇam samādhāya śaṃsanti ca rudanti ca.
sāmabhis tribhir antaḥ|sthair anuśaṃsanti c' âpare.
agnāv agnim iv' ādhāya Droṇaṃ hutvā hut'|āśane,
gacchanty abhimukhā Gaṅgāṃ Droṇa|śiṣyā dvi|jātayaḥ,
apasavyāṃ citiṃ kṛtvā, puras|kṛtya Kṛpīṃ tadā.

GĀNDHĀRY uvāca:

24.1 SOMADATTA|SUTAṂ paśya Yuyudhānena pātitam,
vitudyamānaṃ vihagair bahubhir, Mādhav', ântike.
putra|śok'|âbhisaṃtaptaḥ Somadatto, jan'|ârdana,
Yuyudhānaṃ mah"|êṣv|āsaṃ garhayann iva dṛśyate.
asau tu Bhūriśravaso mātā śoka|pariplutā
āśvāsayati bhartāraṃ Somadattam a|ninditā:
«diṣṭyā n' âinaṃ, mahā|rāja, dāruṇaṃ Bharata|kṣayam
Kuru|saṃkrandanaṃ ghoraṃ yug'|ântam anupaśyasi.
24.5 diṣṭyā yūpa|dhvajaṃ putraṃ vīraṃ bhūri|sahasra|dam
an|eka|kratu|yajvānaṃ nihataṃ n' âdya paśyasi.
diṣṭyā snuṣāṇām ākrande ghoraṃ vilapitaṃ bahu
na śṛṇoṣi, mahā|rāja, sārasīnām iv' ârṇave.
eka|vastr'|ârdha|saṃvītāḥ, prakīrṇ'|â|sita†|mūrdha|jāḥ
snuṣās te paridhāvanti hat'|âpatyā, hat'|ēśvarāḥ.
śvāpadair bhakṣyamāṇaṃ tvam, aho, diṣṭyā na paśyasi
chinna|bāhuṃ nara|vyāghram Arjunena nipātitam.
Śalaṃ vinihataṃ saṃkhye, Bhūri|śravasam eva ca,
snuṣāś ca vidhavāḥ sarvā diṣṭyā n' âdy' êha paśyasi.

have consigned Drona in this way, they both sing his praises and weep. Others also echo this praise with the three Sama verses said in their hearts. As if consigning fire to fire they offer Drona in the offer-consuming blaze. The twice-born brahmins who trained under Drona circumambulate, their left side to the pyre. Then, with Kripi ahead of them, they set off towards the river Ganges.

GANDHÁRI continued:

MÁDHAVA, SEE Soma·datta's son close by, brought down 24.1
by the Constant Warrior Sátyaki, being pecked by carrion-fowl. Soma·datta, consumed with grief for his son, seems to be accusing the great archer Sátyaki, O rouser of the people. At the same time Soma·datta's widow, the innocent mother of their son Bhuri·shravas, drowning in grief herself, is on hand attempting to reassure her husband:

"It is some comfort, great king, that you do not see this cruel destruction of the Bháratas, this horrific war among
the Kurus that has ushered in the end of the world. Your 24.5
son was heroic. His emblem was the sacrificial post, and he sponsored a myriad sacrifices, distributing largesse to thousands. It is some comfort that you do not see he was slain today. It is some comfort, great king, that you do not hear the blood-curdling wailing of your daughters-in-law amid the carnage, like cranes over the churning sea. Half-undressed, just wearing a single garment, their untied hair disheveled, your daughters-in-law rush around; their sons slain, their lords slain. Oh it is some comfort that you do not see the wild beasts eating our tiger of a man, slain, his arm amputated by Árjuna; but today both Bhuri·shravas and Shala

24.10 diṣṭyā tat kāñcanaṃ chatraṃ yūpa|ketor mah"|ātmanaḥ
vinikīrṇaṃ rath'|ôpasthe Saumadatter na paśyasi.»

amūs tu Bhūriśravaso bhāryāḥ Sātyakinā hatam
parivāry' ânuśocanti bhartāram a|sit'|ēkṣaṇāḥ.
etā vilapya bahulaṃ bhartṛ|śokena karśitāḥ
patanty abhimukhā bhūmau. kṛpaṇaṃ bata, keśava:

«Bībhatsur atibībhatsaṃ karm' êdam akarot katham,
pramattasya yad acchaitsīd bāhuṃ śūrasya yajvanaḥ?
tataḥ pāpataraṃ karma kṛtavān api Sātyakiḥ,
yasmāt prāy'|ôpaviṣṭasya prāhārṣīt saṃśit'|ātmanaḥ.
24.15 eko dvābhyāṃ hataḥ śeṣe tvam a|dharmeṇa dhārmikaḥ.
kiṃ nu vakṣyati vai satsu goṣṭhīṣu ca sabhāsu ca
a|puṇyam a|yaśasyaṃ ca karm' êdaṃ Sātyakiḥ svayam?»

iti yūpa|dhvajasy' âitāḥ striyaḥ krośanti, Mādhava.
bhāryā yūpa|dhvajasy' âiṣā kara|saṃmita|madhyamā
kṛtv" ôtsaṅge bhujaṃ bhartuḥ kṛpaṇaṃ paryadevayat:

«ayaṃ sa hantā śūrāṇāṃ, mitrāṇām a|bhaya|pradaḥ,
pradātā go|sahasrāṇāṃ† kṣatriy'|ânta|karaḥ karaḥ,
ayaṃ sa rasan"|ôtkarṣī, pīna|stana|vimardakaḥ,
nābhy|ūru|jaghana|sparśī, nīvī|visraṃsanaḥ karaḥ.

have been cut down in battle and your daughters-in-law
all widowed. It is some comfort that you do not see. The 24.10
golden umbrella of your noble-souled son, whose emblem
was the sacred stake, is scattered in pieces across the platform of his chariot, Soma·datta. It is some comfort that you do not see."

Now there Bhuri·shravas' dark-eyed widows circle round the husband that Sátyaki took from them, and mourn him. Uttering long laments, hysterical with grief for their husband, they fall face down on the ground. This is so pitiful, lord of senses:

"How could Árjuna the Abhorrent do this extremely abhorrent act, cutting off the arm of the champion who performed sacrifices when his attention was taken up by Sátyaki? Then Sátyaki committed an even greater atrocity by continuing to attack him even though he had undertaken the holy fast to death.* You lie here, an honorable 24.15
man dishonorably slain, outnumbered two to one. Surely in tribunals, meetings and courts, Sátyaki will himself acknowledge that his act was wrong and ignoble?"

This is what the women of the man of the sacred stake emblem cry out, Mádhava. One of the wives of the man whose emblem was the sacred stake, whose waist he used to enclose in his hands, expresses this heart-wrenching grief for her husband's arm that she has placed in her lap:

"This is the hand that killed adversaries while ensuring the safety of friends, which bestowed thousands of cattle and brought death to warriors. This is the hand that lifted up my bodice and fondled my full breasts, that stroked my

24.20 Vāsudevasya sānnidhye Pārthen' â|kliṣṭa|karmaṇā
yudhyataḥ samare 'nyena pramattasya nipātitaḥ.
kiṃ nu vakṣyasi saṃsatsu kathāsu ca, Janārdana,
Arjunasya mahat karma, svayaṃ vā sa kirīṭa|bhṛt?»

ity evaṃ garhayitv" âiṣā tūṣṇīm āste var'|âṅganā.
tām etām anuśocanti sa|patnyaḥ, svām iva snuṣām.
Gāndhāra|rājaḥ Śakunir balavān, satya|vikramaḥ
nihataḥ Sahadevena, bhāgineyena mātulaḥ.
yaḥ purā hema|daṇḍābhyāṃ vyajanābhyāṃ sma vījyate,
sa eṣa pakṣibhiḥ pakṣaiḥ śayāna upavījyate.

24.25 yaḥ sva|rūpāṇi kurute śataśo 'tha sahasraśaḥ,
tasya māyāvino māyā dagdhāḥ Pāṇḍava|tejasā.
māyayā nikṛti|prajño jitavān yo Yudhiṣṭhiram
sabhāyāṃ vipulaṃ rājyaṃ, sa punar jīvitaṃ jitaḥ.
śakuntāḥ Śakuniṃ, Kṛṣṇa, samantāt paryupāsate
kaitavaṃ mama putrāṇāṃ vināśāy' ôpaśikṣitam.
eten' âitan mahad vairaṃ prasaktaṃ Pāṇḍavaiḥ saha
vadhāya mama putrāṇām, ātmanaḥ sa|gaṇasya ca.
yath" âiva mama putrāṇāṃ lokāḥ śastra|jitāḥ, prabho,
evam asy' âpi dur|buddher lokāḥ śastreṇa vai jitāḥ.
24.30 kathaṃ ca n' âyaṃ tatr' âpi putrān me bhrātṛbhiḥ saha
virodhayed ṛju|prajñān an|ṛjur, Madhu|sūdana?

navel, my thighs, my bottom, and loosened the fastening of my skirt.

Even while Krishna, son of Vasu·deva, looked on, Kunti's 24.20
iniquitous son severed it, while my husband's attention was elsewhere, locked in battle with another. What will you say in tribunals and inquiries, Krishna, about this great deed of Árjuna's? What will the diadem wearer himself have to say?"

Pointing the finger at them with these words the lovely, beautiful woman falls silent. Her co-wives empathize in her grief, as if she were their daughter-in-law. Shákuni, king of Gandhára, powerful and valiant to pursue his word, has been killed by Saha·deva, the uncle slain by his nephew. Once air was wafted across him by two golden-handled fans. Now his prone body is fanned by the wings of the birds.

Once able to multiply his own form a hundred or even a 24.25
thousand times, now the magical displays of their conjuring owner have all been torched by the heat of the Pándavas. An expert in deceit, he used his magic to defeat Yudhi·shthira in the assembly and win the wide kingdom, but in return he has forfeited his life. Birds now surround cocky Shákuni on all sides, the gambling cheat who trained to my sons' destruction. He pursued this great hostility towards the Pándavas that led to the slaughter of my sons, as well as of himself and those around him. Just as my sons now roam the realms won by the sword, powerful lord, so too does this
evil man roam those realms won with a sword. But what if 24.30
that crooked man sows dissent even there between my too trusting sons and their cousins, slayer of Madhu?

GĀNDHĀRY uvāca:

25.1 KĀMBOJAṂ PAŚYA dur|dharṣaṃ,
Kāmboj'|āstaraṇ'|ôcitam,
śayānam ṛṣabha|skandhaṃ
hataṃ pāṃsuṣu, Mādhava,
yasya kṣataja|saṃdigdhau bāhū candana|bhūṣitau
avekṣya karuṇaṃ bhāryā vilapaty atiduḥkhitā:
«imau tau parigha|prakhyau bāhū śubha|tal'|āṅgulī,
yayor vivaram āpannāṃ na ratir māṃ pur" âjahat.
kāṃ gatiṃ nu gamiṣyāmi tvayā hīnā, jan'|ēśvara?»
hata|bandhur a|nāthā ca vepantī madhura|svarā.
25.5 ātape klāmyamānānāṃ vividhānām iva srajām,
klāntānām api nārīṇāṃ na śrīr jahati vai tanūḥ.
śayānam abhitaḥ śūraṃ Kāliṅgaṃ, Madhu|sūdana,
paśya dīpt'|āṅgada|yuga|pratinaddha|mahā|bhujam.
Māgadhānām adhipatiṃ Jayat|senaṃ, Jan'|ârdana,
āvārya sarvataḥ patnyaḥ prarudantyaḥ su|vihvalāḥ.
āsām āyata|netrāṇāṃ su|svarāṇām, Jan'|ârdana.
manaḥ|śruti|haro nādo mano mohayat' îva me.
prakīrṇa|sarv'|ābharaṇā rudantyaḥ, śoka|karśitāḥ,
sv|āstīrṇa|śayan'|ôpetā Māgadhyaḥ śerate bhuvi.

GANDHÁRI continued:

LOOK AT THE king of Kambója, with shoulders like a bull, who seemed invulnerable. Once used to the comfort of Kambójan blankets, now he lies slain amid the dust, Mádhava. His arms once graced by sandal paste are now smeared in the gore from his wounds. Seeing them in that pitiful state the suffering is too much for his widow and she wails: 25.1

"These two arms, broad as beams, with such fine palms and fingers—being enclosed in their embrace was once my perpetual bliss. What destiny awaits me now, bereft of you, lord of the people?" The sweet-voiced woman trembles; her family all slain, there is no one to take care of her. Although 25.5
the women are exhausted, their delicate bodies retain their splendor like an array of garlands wilting in the heat.

See the valiant king of Kalínga lying close by, slayer of Madhu, wearing a pair of gleaming armlets clasped round his broad arms. The extremely distraught widows of Jayat·sena, Conquering Army, the sovereign of the Mágadhan peoples, surround him on all sides, weeping, rouser of the people. The sound of these long-eyed women with their sweet voices, rouser of the people, so captivating of the heart and ear, seems to bewilder my heart. They have broken all their jewelry* and weeping, hysterical with grief, the women of Mágadha, familiar with beds of great luxury, lie upon the bare ground.

25.10 Kosalānām adhipatiṃ rāja|putraṃ Bṛhadbalam
bhartāraṃ parivāry' âitāḥ pṛthak praruditāḥ striyaḥ.
asya gātra|gatān bāṇān Kārṣṇi|bāhu|bal'|ârpitān
uddharanty a|sukh'|āviṣṭā, mūrchamānāḥ punaḥ punaḥ.
āsāṃ sarv'|ân|avadyānām ātapena pariśramāt
pramlāna|nalin'|ābhāni bhānti vaktrāṇi, Mādhava.
Droṇena nihatāḥ śūrāḥ śerate rucir'|āṅgadāḥ
Dhṛṣṭa|dyumna|sutāḥ sarve śiśavo hema|mālinaḥ,
rath'|âgny|agāraṃ, cāp'|ârcīṃ, śara|śakti|gad"|êndhanam
Droṇam āsādya nirdagdhāḥ, śalabhā iva pāvakam.
25.15 tath" âiva nihatāḥ śūrāḥ śerate rucir'|âṅgadāḥ
Droṇen' âbhimukhāḥ sarve bhrātaraḥ pañca Kekayāḥ
tapta|kāñcana|varmāṇas, tāla|dhvaja|ratha|vrajāḥ
bhāsayanti mahīṃ bhāsā jvalitā iva pāvakāḥ.

Droṇena Drupadaṃ saṃkhye paśya, Mādhava, pātitam,
mahā|dvipam iv' āraṇye siṃhena mahatā hatam.
Pāñcāla|rājño vipulaṃ, puṇḍarīk'|âkṣa, pāṇḍuram
ātapa|traṃ samābhāti śarad' îva niśā|karaḥ.
etās tu Drupadaṃ vṛddhaṃ snuṣā bhāryāś ca duḥkhitāḥ
dagdhvā gacchanti Pāñcālyaṃ rājānam apasavyataḥ.
25.20 Dhṛṣṭaketuṃ mah"|ātmānaṃ Cedi|puṃgavam aṅganāḥ
Droṇena nihataṃ śūraṃ haranti hṛta|cetasaḥ.
Droṇ'|âstram abhihaty' âiṣa vimarde, Madhu|sūdana,
mah"|êṣv|āso hataḥ śete, nadyā hṛta iva drumaḥ.

Here the wives of the royal prince Brihad·bala, Great in Strength, sovereign of the Kósalans, come one-by-one to stand around their master, each in tears. Filled with misery and fainting time and time again, they extract from his limbs the arrows planted there by the mighty arm of Krishna's nephew. From the exhaustion of their ordeal, the faces of these irreproachable ladies look like languid lotuses. The champions slain by Drona, including all Dhrishta·dyumna's sons, young boys wearing golden garlands and lustrous armlets lie where they fell, following their encounter with Drona—they came like moths to fire, his chariot was the hearth, his bow the flame, and all was fueled by arrows, lances and maces. 25.10

So too all five Kékaya brothers lie there, armlets gleaming, slain by Drona when they confronted him in battle. Their armor of burnished gold, their banners, standards and the cars of their chariots, all cast a bright glow upon the earth with their luster, like a flaming fire. 25.15

See Drúpada, Mádhava. He was brought down in the battle by Drona, like a mighty elephant slain by a mighty lion in the forest. The broad, pale umbrella of the Panchála king shines like the fall moon at night, lotus-eyed lord. Now here old Drúpada's wretched daughters-in-law and wives have lit the Panchála king's pyre and circle round him clockwise.

There the lovely wives of the noble-souled bull of the Chedi people, Dhrishta·ketu, out of their minds with grief, take up their champion. This great archer, who warded off Drona's missile in the encounter lies here slain, Madhu-slayer, like a tree swept away by the river. 25.20

eṣa Cedi|patiḥ śūro Dhṛṣṭa|ketur mahā|rathaḥ
śete vinihataḥ saṃkhye, hatvā śatrūn sahasraśaḥ.
vitudyamānaṃ vihagais taṃ bhāryāḥ pratyupasthitāḥ
Cedi|rājaṃ, Hṛṣīkeśa, hataṃ sa|bala|bāndhavam.
Dāśārha|putra|jaṃ vīraṃ, śayānaṃ, satya|vikramam
āropy' âṅke rudanty etāś Cedi|rāja|var'|âṅganāḥ.

25.25 asya putraṃ, Hṛṣīkeśa, su|vaktraṃ, cāru|kuṇḍalam
Droṇena samare paśya nikṛtaṃ bahudhā śaraiḥ.
pitaraṃ nūnam āji|sthaṃ yudhyamānaṃ paraiḥ saha
n' âjahāt pitaraṃ vīram ady' âpi, Madhu|sūdana.
evaṃ mam' âpi putrasya putraḥ pitaram anvagāt
Duryodhanaṃ, mahā|bāho, Lakṣmaṇaḥ para|vīra|hā.
Vind'|Ânuvindāv Āvantyau patitau paśya, Mādhava,
him'|ânte puṣpitau śālau marutā galitāv iva,
kāñcan'|âṅgada|varmāṇau, bāṇa|khaḍga|dhanur|dharau,
ṛṣabha|pratirūp'|âkṣau śayānau vimala|srajau.

25.30 a|vadhyāḥ Pāṇḍavāḥ, Kṛṣṇa, sarva eva tvayā saha,
ye muktā Droṇa|Bhīṣmābhyāṃ, Karṇād Vaikartanāt, Kṛpāt
Duryodhanād, Droṇa|sutāt, Saindhavāc ca mahā|rathāt,
Somadattād, Vikarṇāc ca, śūrāc ca Kṛtavarmaṇaḥ.
ye hanyuḥ śastra|vegena devān api nara'|rṣabhāḥ,
ta ime nihatāḥ saṃkhye. paśya kālasya paryayam.
n' âtibhāro 'sti daivasya dhruvaṃ, Mādhava, kaś cana,

This valiant lord of the Chedis, the great chariot-fighter Dhrishta·ketu, who slew enemies in their thousands, lies here, himself slain in battle. While the birds peck at the king of Chedi, slain along with his army and the other men of his family, his widows stand around him, Lord of the Senses. Those fair and lovely wives of the king of Chedi take that hero born into the line of Dashárha and valiant to his word, onto their laps and weep.

See his fair-faced son, Lord of the Senses, with his sweet 25.25
earrings, who was mortally wounded by Drona's many arrows in the fray. Not once, when his father stood in combat fighting with the enemy, did he ever leave his father's side, that is certain, and he doesn't even now, Madhu-slayer. So it was, strong-armed warrior, with my grandson Lákshmana too, slayer of hostile heroes, who constantly stayed by the side of his father Duryódhana. Look, Mádhava, the two princes of Avánti, Vinda and Anuvínda have fallen like a pair of *sal* trees blossoming at the end of a frost, shriveled by the wind. Dressed in golden armlets and armor, they still clasp their sword and bow-and-arrows as they lie there decked in vivid garlands, their eyes soft as the eyes of a bull.

It must have been impossible to kill any of the Pándava 25.30
brothers, or you, since you all managed to escape Drona and Bhishma, Karna, son of Vikártana, and Kripa, Duryódhana, Drona's son and the great chariot-fighter of Sindh, Soma·datta, Vikárna and that champion Krita·varman.* Such a veritable line-up of prize-bulls among men as could have killed even the gods with the speed of their weapons, but they are the ones that lie here slain in battle. Observe the reversal wrought by time! Clearly no feat at all is too

yad ime nihatāḥ śūrāḥ kṣatriyaiḥ kṣatriya'|rṣabhāḥ.
tad" âiva nihatāḥ, Kṛṣṇa, mama putrās tarasvinaḥ,
yad" âiv' â|kṛta|kāmas tvam Upaplavyam gataḥ punaḥ.
25.35 Śaṃtanoś c' âiva putreṇa, prājñena Vidureṇa ca
tad" âiv' ôkt" âsmi, «mā sneham kuruṣv' ātma|suteṣv» iti.
tayor hi darśanaṃ n' âitan mithyā bhavitum arhati.
a|cireṇ' âiva me putrā bhasmī|bhūtā, jan'|ârdana.

VAIŚAMPĀYANA uvāca:

ity uktvā nyapatad bhūmau Gāndhārī śoka|mūrcchitā.
duḥkh'|ôpahata|vijñānā dhairyam utsṛjya, Bhārata,
tataḥ kopa|parīt'|âṅgī, putra|śoka|pariplutā,
jagāma Śauriṃ doṣeṇa Gāndhārī vyathit'|êndriyā.

GĀNDHĀRY uvāca:

Pāṇḍavā Dhārtarāṣṭrāś ca,
drugdhāḥ, Kṛṣṇa, paras|param,
upekṣitā vinaśyantas
tvayā kasmāj, Janārdana?
25.40 śaktena, bahu|bhṛtyena, vipule tiṣṭhatā bale,
ubhayatra samarthena, śruta|vākyena c' âiva ha,
icchat" ôpekṣito nāśaḥ Kurūṇāṃ, Madhu|sūdana,
yasmāt tvayā, mahā|bāho, phalaṃ tasmād avāpnuhi!
pati|śuśrūṣayā yan me tapaḥ kiñ cid upārjitam,

much for divine Fate, Mádhava, since these, the champion prize-bulls of the warrior class, lie here slain by others from that same class.

The death warrant of my courageous sons was sealed back then, Krishna, when you returned to Upaplávya empty handed.* Shántanu's son Bhishma and Vídura the wise told 25.35
me then, "Do not continue with your affection for your sons." Their vision during my audience with them could not prove futile.* Before long my sons will have been reduced to ash, rouser of the people.

VAISHAMPÁYANA continued:

On finishing these words, Gandhári, fainting in grief, fell to the ground. Though she lost consciousness in her misery, Gandhári marshaled her strength about her, son of Bhárata's line, then, her entire body suffused with anger and overwhelmed with grief for her sons, her senses agitated, she turned to Krishna in accusation.

GANDHÁRI spoke:

The sons of Pandu and the sons of Dhrita·rashtra plotted against each other, Krishna. Why did you remain impassive when they were bent on destroying themselves? You 25.40
could have been effective, positioned with a vast army and many subjects, with influence, and familiar with the arguments on both sides. Since you let the destruction of the Kurus happen you must have wanted it, broad-armed slayer of Madhu, so may you reap the result of that! By the ascetic prowess that I have built up through my obedience to my husband, earned with such great effort, I shall lay a curse on you, who wield the mace and discus. Since you looked

tena tvāṃ dur|avāpena śapsye cakra|gadā|dharam.
yasmāt paras|paraṃ ghnanto jñātayaḥ Kuru|Pāṇḍavāḥ
upekṣitās te, Govinda, tasmāj jñātīn vadhiṣyasi.
tvam apy upasthite varṣe ṣaṭ|triṃśe, Madhu|sūdana,
hata|jñātir, hat'|āmātyo, hata|putro, vane|caraḥ,
25.45 a|nāthavad, a|vijñāto, lokeṣv an|abhilakṣitaḥ
kutsiten' âbhyupāyena nidhanaṃ samavāpsyasi.
tav' âpy evaṃ hata|sutā, nihata|jñāti|bāndhavāḥ
striyaḥ paripatiṣyanti, yath" âitā Bharata|striyaḥ.

VAIŚAMPĀYANA uvāca:

tac chrutvā vacanaṃ ghoraṃ Vāsudevo mahā|manāḥ
uvāca devīṃ Gāndhārīm īṣad abhyutsmayann iva:
«jāne 'ham etad apy evaṃ. cīrṇaṃ carasi, kṣatriye.
daivād eva vinaśyanti Vṛṣṇayo. n' âtra saṃśayaḥ.
saṃhartā Vṛṣṇi|cakrasya n' ânyo mad vidyate, śubhe.
a|vadhyās te narair anyair, api vā deva|dānavaiḥ.
25.50 paras|para|kṛtaṃ nāśam ataḥ prāpsyanti Yādavāḥ.»
ity uktavati Dāśārhe Pāṇḍavās trasta|cetasaḥ
babhūvur, bhṛśa|saṃvignā, nir|āśāś c' âpi jīvite.

on while the Kurus and Pándavas, members of a single family, set about killing each other, Govínda, you will end up killing your own family. In the thirty sixth year from now, Madhu-slayer, your relatives, ministers and sons will all be murdered, and you will wander in the wilderness, where, 25.45
never knowing the words of someone to care for you, unrecognized by any peoples, you will meet a sticky end. Your wives too, their sons, friends and relatives all slain, will run around in disarray as these women of Bhárata's line do now.

VAISHAMPÁYANA continued:

On hearing her awful words, the lofty minded son of Vasu·deva spoke to Queen Gandhári, seeming to smile slightly:

"Woman of the warriors, I already know this will come true. You are doing what is already done. It is divinely ordained that the Vrishnis will perish. There is no doubt about it.* There is no one but me who can remove the Vrishnis' power, good woman. They cannot be killed by other humans, nor even by gods or demons. Rather, they, the Yá- 25.50
davas, will meet an obliteration of their own making."

When the scion of Dashárha made this declaration, fear struck into the hearts of the Pándavas. They became very alarmed, and despaired of survival.

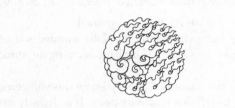

26–27
THE FUNERARY RITES

VĀSUDEVA uvāca:

26.1 UTTIṢṬH', ÔTTIṢṬHA, Gāndhāri.
mā ca śoke manaḥ kṛthāḥ.
tav' âiva hy aparādhena
Kuravo nidhanaṃ gatāḥ,
yat tvaṃ putraṃ dur|ātmānam, īrṣum, atyanta|māninam
Duryodhanaṃ puras|kṛtya duṣ|kṛtaṃ sādhu manyase,
niṣṭhuraṃ, vaira|paruṣaṃ, vṛddhānāṃ śāsan'|âtigam.
katham ātma|kṛtaṃ doṣaṃ mayy ādhātum ih' êcchasi?
mṛtaṃ vā yadi vā naṣṭaṃ yo 'tītam anuśocati,
duḥkhena labhate duḥkhaṃ. dvāv an|arthau prapadyate.

26.5 tapo|'rthīyaṃ brāhmaṇī dhatta garbhaṃ,
gaur voḍhāraṃ, dhāvitāraṃ turaṃgī,
śūdrā dāsaṃ, paśu|pālaṃ ca vaiśyā,
vadh'|ârthīyaṃ kṣatriyā rājaputrī.

VAIŚAṂPĀYANA uvāca:

tac chrutvā Vāsudevasya punar uktaṃ vaco '|priyam
tūṣṇīṃ babhūva Gāndhārī śoka|vyākula|locanā.
Dhṛtarāṣṭras tu rāja'|ṛṣir, nigṛhy' â|buddhi|jaṃ tamaḥ,
paryapṛcchata dharma|jño dharma|rājaṃ Yudhiṣṭhiram:
«jīvatāṃ parimāṇa|jñaḥ sainyānām asi, Pāṇḍava.
hatānāṃ yadi jānīṣe parimāṇaṃ, vadasva me.»

KRISHNA SON OF VASU·DEVA spoke again:

GET UP, GANDHÁRI, get up, and do not allow your heart to dwell on self-pity. For it is in fact your fault that the Kurus have met their doom, since you thought so well of your son Duryódhana, and always put him first, even though he was prone to jealousy, overbearingly arrogant and did atrocious things. He was coarse, abusively hostile and contemptuous of the instructions of elders—how can you want to lay that malignancy of your own making at my feet? Ruing the past, someone dead or something lost, one only gains further suffering though that suffering. One achieves double the undesirable outcome. 26.1

A brahmin woman conceives a child destined for asceticism, a cow bears an ox for burden, a mare a steed to run, a shudra woman provides a slave, the vaishya woman's child will tend the herd, while the child born to the princess of the warrior class is made to kill. 26.5

VAISHAMPÁYANA continued:

But on hearing those unwelcome words spoken by the son of Vasu·deva, Gandhári fell silent, her eyes welling up with grief. The royal sage Dhrita·rashtra, however, curbing the blackness that springs from lack of understanding, recognizing his duty, asked the king of righteous duty, Yudhi·shthira:

"Son of Pandu, you know how many soldiers have survived. Tell me, if you know, how many have been killed."

YUDHIṢṬHIRA uvāca:

daś' âyutānām ayutaṃ, sahasrāṇi ca viṃśatiḥ,
koṭyaḥ ṣaṣṭiś ca ṣaṭ c' âiva hy asmin, rājan, mṛdhe hatāḥ.
26.10 a|lakṣitānāṃ vīrāṇāṃ sahasrāṇi catur|daśa,
daśa c' ânyāni, rāj'|êndra, śataṃ ṣaṣṭiś ca pañca ca.

DHṚTARĀṢṬRA uvāca:

Yudhiṣṭhira, gatiṃ kāṃ te gatāḥ, puruṣa|sattama?
ācakṣva me, mahā|bāho, sarva|jño hy asi me mataḥ.

YUDHIṢṬHIRA uvāca:

yair hutāni śarīrāṇi hṛṣṭaiḥ parama|saṃyuge,
deva|rāja|samāl̐ lokān gatās te satya|vikramāḥ.
ye tv a|hṛṣṭena manasā, «martavyam» iti, Bhārata,
yudhyamānā hatāḥ saṃkhye, te gandharvaiḥ samāgatāḥ.
ye ca saṃgrāma|bhūmi|ṣṭhā yācamānāḥ, parāṅ|mukhāḥ
śastreṇa nidhanaṃ prāptā, gatās te guhyakān prati.
26.15 pātyamānāḥ parair ye tu hīyamānā, nir|āyudhāḥ,
hrī|niṣevā mahātmānaḥ parān abhimukhā raṇe,
chidyamānāḥ śitaiḥ śastraiḥ kṣatra|dharma|parāyaṇāḥ,
gatās te Brahma|sadanaṃ hatā vīrāḥ su|varcasaḥ.
ye tv atra nihatā, rājann, antar āyodhanaṃ prati

YUDHI·SHTHIRA replied:

Ten thousand times one hundred thousand, plus twenty thousand more then a further sixty six *crore*, makes one billion, six hundred and sixty million and twenty thousand slain in this campaign, Your Majesty. Unaccounted 26.10
for, chief of kings, are fourteen thousand heroes, plus a further ten thousand and one hundred and sixty, and five, i.e. twenty four thousand one hundred and sixty five.

DHRITA·RASHTRA asked:

To what destiny have they all departed, broad-armed Yudhi·shthira, most exalted of men? Tell me, for I regard you as knowing everything.

YUDHI·SHTHIRA replied:

Those who happily offer up their bodies in the supreme war, intrepid in their undertaking, go to the realms resident to the king of gods himself. Those whose hearts were, in contrast, unhappy when they realized they were sure to die, king of Bhárata's line, once killed in action, they join the ranks of the heavenly musicians. But those who met their death by the sword while seeking mercy on the battle field or fleeing, go to the realm of the deformed treasurers of the god of the north.

On the other hand, those high-minded soldiers who, 26.15
though brought down or maimed by their enemies or though deprived of their weapon, still faced their enemies in battle out of a sense of dignity and focused on fulfilling their duty as a warrior, while cut apart with whetted weapons, when slain they went to the palace of God Brahma as

yathā kathañ cit puruṣās te, gatās t' Ûttarān Kurūn.

DHṚTARĀṢṬRA uvāca:

kena jñāna|balen' âivaṃ, putra, paśyasi siddhavat?
tan me vada, mahā|bāho, śrotavyaṃ yadi vai mayā.

YUDHIṢṬHIRA uvāca:

nideśād bhavataḥ pūrvaṃ vane vicaratā mayā
tīrtha|yātrā|prasaṅgena samprāpto 'yam anugrahaḥ.
26.20 deva'|rṣir Lomaśo dṛṣṭas. tataḥ prāpto 'smy anusmṛtim.
divyaṃ cakṣur api prāptaṃ jñāna|yogena vai purā.

DHṚTARĀṢṬRA uvāca:

a|nāthānāṃ janānāṃ ca, sa|nāthānāṃ ca, Bhārata,
kaccit teṣāṃ śarīrāṇi dhakṣyase vidhi|pūrvakam.
na yeṣām asti saṃskartā, na ca ye 'tr' āhit' āgnayaḥ,
vayaṃ ca kasya kuryāmo bahutvāt, tāta, karmaṇām?
yān suparṇāś ca gṛdhrāś ca vikarṣanti yatas tataḥ
teṣāṃ tu karmaṇā lokā bhaviṣyanti, Yudhiṣṭhira.

heroes in resplendent armor. While those men slain here, somehow caught up in the fighting, have departed for the idyllic region of the Northern Kurus.*

DHRITA·RASHTRA asked further:

What miraculous power of knowledge allows you to see such things, as if you were a saint?* Tell me that, my broad-armed son, if indeed I could withstand the hearing of it.

YUDHI·SHTHIRA replied:

Earlier when, as a result of your decree, I was roving in
the forest I gained this blessing while engaged on a pilgrim-
age of the holy sites. I was blessed with seeing the divine 26.20
seer Lómasha, which led to me gaining the power of perfect focus on any chosen question. I had also gained the power of divine sight earlier through my practice of gnostic meditation.

DHRITA·RASHTRA spoke again:

Son of Bhárata's line, I am assuming you will perform the cremation and preparatory rites both of those people who have family to take care of them and of those who do not. For which of those who have no-one to perform their rites and have no sacred fire set for them here shall we conduct the rites, given how many there are? For it is through ritual that the next worlds are created for those whom the birds and vultures now drag all over the place, Yudhi·shthira.

VAIŚAMPĀYANA uvāca:

evam ukto, mahā|rāja, Kuntī|putro Yudhiṣṭhiraḥ
ādideśa Sudharmāṇaṃ, Dhaumyaṃ, sūtaṃ ca Sañjayam,
26.25 Viduraṃ ca mahā|buddhiṃ, Yuyutsuṃ c' âiva Kauravam,
Indrasena|mukhāṃś c' âiva bhṛtyān sūtāṃś ca sarvaśaḥ,
«bhavantaḥ kārayantv eṣāṃ preta|kāryāṇy a|śeṣataḥ,
yathā c' â|nāthavat kiñ cic charīraṃ na vinaśyati.»

śāsanād dharma|rājasya Kṣattā, sūtaś ca Saṃjayaḥ,
Sudharmā Dhaumya|sahita, Indrasen'|ādayas tathā
candan'|âguru|kāṣṭhāni, tathā kālīyakāny uta,
ghṛtaṃ, tailaṃ ca, gandhāṃś ca, kṣaumāṇi vasanāni ca
samāhṛtya mah"|ârhāṇi, dārūṇāṃ c' âiva sañcayān,
rathāṃś ca mṛditāṃs tatra, nānā|praharaṇāni ca,
26.30 citāḥ kṛtvā prayatnena, yathā|mukhyān nar'|âdhipān
dāhayām āsur a|vyagrāḥ śāstra|dṛṣṭena karmaṇā.

Duryodhanaṃ ca rājānaṃ, bhrātṝṃś c' âsya śat'|âdhikān,
Śalyaṃ Śalaṃ ca rājānaṃ, Bhūriśravasam eva ca,
Jayadrathaṃ ca rājānam, Abhimanyuṃ ca, Bhārata,
Dauḥśāsaniṃ, Lakṣmaṇaṃ ca, Dhṛṣṭaketuṃ ca pārthivam,
Bṛhantaṃ, Somadattaṃ ca, Sṛñjayāṃś ca śat'|âdhikān,
rājānaṃ Kṣemadhanvānaṃ, Virāṭa|Drupadau tathā,
Śikhaṇḍinaṃ ca Pāñcālyaṃ, Dhṛṣṭadyumnaṃ ca Pārṣatam,
Yudhāmanyuṃ ca vikrāntam, Uttamaujasam eva ca,

VAISHAMPÁYANA continued:

When prompted in this way, Your Supreme Majesty, Yudhi·shthira, son of Kunti, directed Sudhárman, Dhaumya
and Sánjaya of the bardic charioteer class, along with Ví- 26.25
dura, steeped in wisdom, and Yuyútsu of the line of Kuru, as well as the attendants, led by Indra·sena, and the charioteers from all sides, saying, "I command you to ensure the performance of the funerals of all these men with no exceptions, so that no corpse whatsoever might be lost because of having no one to take care of him."

At the just king's command, Vídura the slave woman's son and Sánjaya the bard, as well as Sudhárman with Dhaumya, Indra·sena and the rest, set about collecting sandal, aloe and other kindling, and dark sandalwood, ghee, oils and perfumes, as well as linen. Then they heaped up the most valuable kinds of wood, along with the broken down
chariots and all kinds of weapons to be found there. Once 26.30
they had created the pyres, they cremated the kings in order of rank, with painstaking care, unwavering from the ritual as found in the sacred treatises.

His Majesty Duryódhana and his hundred brothers, O king of Bhárata's line, as well as Shalya, Shala and His Majesty Bhuri·shravas, His Majesty Jayad·ratha and Abhimányu, Duhshásana's son and Lákshmana, and His Royal Highness Dhrishta·ketu, Brihánta and Soma·datta, in addition to the hundred Sríñjayas, as well as His Majesty Kshema·dhanvan, Viráta and Drúpada too, Shikhándin of the Panchálas and Dhrishta·dyumna of Prishata's line, and
Yudha·manyu the brave, along with Uttamáujas too, the 26.35
king of Kósala, the sons of Dráupadi as well as Shákuni,

26.35 Kausalyaṃ, Draupadeyāṃś ca, Śakuniṃ c' âpi Saubalam,
Acalaṃ Vṛṣakaṃ c'âiva, Bhagadattaṃ ca pārthivam,
Karṇaṃ Vaikartanaṃ c' âiva saha|putram a|marṣaṇam,
Kekayāṃś ca mah"|êṣv|āsāṃs, Trigartāṃś ca mahā|rathān,
Ghaṭotkacaṃ rākṣas'|êndraṃ, Baka|bhrātaram eva ca,
Alambusaṃ rākṣas'|êndraṃ, Jalasandhaṃ ca pārthivam—
etāṃś c' ânyāṃś ca su|bahūn pārthivāṃś ca sahasraśaḥ
ghṛta|dhār"|āhutair dīptaiḥ pāvakaiḥ samadāhayan.

pitṛ|medhāś ca keṣāṃ cit prāvartanta mah"|ātmanām,
sāmabhiś c' âpy agāyanta te, 'nvaśocyanta c' âparaiḥ.
26.40 sāmnām ṛcāṃ ca nādena, strīṇāṃ ca rudita|svanaiḥ
kaśmalaṃ sarva|bhūtānāṃ niśāyāṃ samapadyata.
te vidhūmāḥ, pradīptāś ca, dīpyamānāś ca pāvakāḥ
nabhas' îv' ânvadṛśyanta grahās tanv|abhra|saṃvṛtāḥ.
ye c' âpy a|nāthās tatr' āsan nānā|deśa|samāgatāḥ,
tāṃś ca sarvān samānāyya, rāśīn kṛtvā sahasraśaḥ,
citvā dārubhir a|vyagraiḥ prabhūtaiḥ, sneha|tāpitaiḥ
dāhayām āsa tān sarvān Viduro rāja|śāsanāt.
kārayitvā kriyās teṣāṃ Kuru|rājo Yudhiṣṭhiraḥ,
Dhṛtarāṣṭraṃ puras|kṛtya Gaṅgām abhimukho 'gamat.

son of Súbala, both Áchala and Vríshaka, and His Highness Bhaga·datta, Karna the unforgiving, son of Vikártana, with his sons, and the great archers the Kékayas and the great chariot-fighting Tri·gartas, Ghatótkacha, the goblin chief, as well as Baka's brother, the goblin chief Alámbusha, and His Highness Jala·sandha—these and other fair-armed rulers of the earth in their thousands were cremated there on fires blazing with offerings of streams of ghee.

As the ancestral rites for some of the noble-souled deceased were performed, Sama priests sang hymns while the others gave expression to their mourning for the deceased. With the intonation of the hymns of sacrifice and 26.40
the hymns to the gods, and the sound of women weeping, despond descended on all living beings that night. The fires, blazing smokeless and kept ablaze, looked like the planets in the firmament, amid fine strands of cloud. Now those who had none to care for them in that place, having come from diverse places, they were all brought together and piled up in heaps by the thousands. When many people, moved by sympathy, had carefully heaped up firewood, Vídura, at the king's command, set them all alight. When Yudhi·shthira, now king of the Kurus, had finished having the rites performed for the deceased, he set off in the direction of the river Ganges, placing Dhrita·rashtra at the head of the procession.

VAIŚAMPĀYANA uvāca:

27.1 TE SAMĀSĀDYA Gaṅgāṃ tu śivāṃ puṇya|jal'|ôcitām,
hradinīṃ ca prasaṃpannāṃ, mahā|rūpāṃ, mahā|balām,
bhūṣaṇāny, uttarīyāṇi, veṣṭanāny avamucya ca,
tataḥ pitṝṇāṃ, bhrātṝṇāṃ, pautrāṇāṃ, sva|janasya ca,
putrāṇām, āryakāṇāṃ ca, patīnāṃ ca Kuru|striyaḥ
udakaṃ cakrire sarvā rudantyo bhṛśa|duḥkhitāḥ.
suhṛdāṃ c' âpi dharma|jñāḥ pracakruḥ salila|kriyāḥ.
udake kriyamāṇe tu vīrāṇāṃ vīra|patnibhiḥ
27.5 s'|ûpatīrth" âbhavad Gaṅgā, bhūyo viprasasāra ca.
tan mah"|ôdadhi|saṃkāśaṃ, nir|ānandam, an|utsavam,
vīra|patnībhir ākīrṇaṃ Gaṅgā|tīram aśobhata.

tataḥ Kuntī, mahā|rāja, sahasā śoka|karśitā
rudatī mandayā vācā putrān vacanam abravīt:

«yaḥ sa vīro, mah"|êṣv|āso ratha|yūthapa|yūthapaḥ
Arjunena jitaḥ saṃkhye vīra|lakṣaṇa|lakṣitaḥ,
yaṃ sūta|putraṃ manyadhvaṃ Rādheyam iti Pāṇḍavāḥ,
yo vyarājac camū|madhye divākara iva prabhuḥ,
pratyayudhyata yaḥ sarvān purā vaḥ† sa|pad'|ânugān,
27.10 Duryodhana|balaṃ sarvaṃ yaḥ prakarṣan vyarocata,
yasya n' âsti samo vīrye pṛthivyām api pārthivaḥ,
yo 'vṛṇīta yaśaḥ śūraḥ prāṇair api sadā bhūvi,
Karṇasya satya|sandhasya, saṃgrāmeṣv a|palāyinaḥ,

VAISHAMPÁYANA continued:

NOW WHEN THEY had reached the auspicious and de- 27.1
lightful river Ganges, with its purifying waters, deep-
pocketed, clear, vast and powerful, the Kuru women discarded their ornaments, upper garments and bodices. Then,
weeping bitterly, they all performed the water offering both
for their fathers, brothers and junior male relatives in the
families of their birth and for the men in the families they
married into, including their sons and husbands. Familiar
with the religious rules, they also performed the water rites
for deceased allies. Now with all the water offerings being
performed for the heroes of the war by their devoted widows, the Ganges came right up to the lip of her banks and 27.5
flowed more broadly still, such that it looked like the great
ocean and its banks, crowded with all the devoted widows
of those heroes, though joyless and solemn, looked glorious.

At that point, Your Majesty, Kunti, distraught with grief, suddenly started speaking to her sons in a trembling voice, weeping:

"That great archer hero who led the pack for the leader
of the chariot fighters, the hero that Árjuna defeated in the
battle, who was marked with all the signs of a hero, yet
whom you sons of Pandu assumed was the son of the charioteer and Radha, the powerful lord who shone like the sun
himself at the heart of the battalion, who had previously
repelled all of you and your attendant infantry, resplendent 27.10
as he led the entire might of Duryódhana's army, to whom
there was no earthly ruler his equal in valor in the entire
world, the champion who always chose glory even over life
on this earth, yes Karna, who always kept his promise and

kurudhvam udakaṃ tasya bhrātur a|kliṣṭa|karmaṇaḥ.
sa hi vaḥ pūrva|jo bhrātā Bhāskarān mayy ajāyata
kuṇḍalī, kavacī, śūro, divākara|sama|prabhaḥ.»

śrutvā tu Pāṇḍavāḥ sarve mātur vacanam a|priyam,
Karṇam ev' ânuśocanto bhūyaḥ klāntatar" âbhavan.*

tataḥ sa puruṣa|vyāghraḥ Kuntī|putro Yudhiṣṭhiraḥ
27.15 uvāca mātaraṃ vīro, niḥśvasann iva pannagaḥ.
«yaḥ śar'|ōrmir, dhvaj'|āvarto, mahā|bhuja|mahā|grahaḥ,
tala|śabd'|ânunadito, mahā|ratha|mahā|hradaḥ,
yasy' êṣu|pātam āsādya n' ânyas tiṣṭhed Dhanaṃjayāt,
kathaṃ putro bhavatyāḥ sa deva|garbhaḥ pur" âbhavat?
yasya bāhu|pratāpena tāpitāḥ sarvato vayam,
tam agnim iva vastreṇa kathaṃ chāditavaty asi?
yasya bāhu|balaṃ nityaṃ Dhārtarāṣṭrair upāsitam,
upāsitaṃ yath" âsmābhir balaṃ Gāṇḍīva|dhanvanaḥ,
bhūmi|pānāṃ ca sarveṣāṃ balaṃ, balavatāṃ varaḥ,
27.20 n' ânyaḥ Kuntī|sutāt Karṇād agṛhṇād rathināṃ rathī,
sa naḥ prathama|jo bhrātā sarva|śastra|bhṛtāṃ varaḥ!

never turned his back in any battle, for him you must perform the water offering due a brother of unblemished conduct, for he is your first-born older brother sired by the radiant Sun and born of me, born already wearing the earrings and armor, a champion whose appearance mirrored that of his day-bringing father."

Now when Pandu's sons all heard this shocking revelation from their mother they began to mourn for Karna of all people and became even more despondent than before.

At this, that tiger among men, Kunti's son Yudhi·shthira
said to his mother, the hero letting out his breath like a 27.15
hissing snake:

"His arrows came in waves, his banner eddied, his huge arms were great snatching crocodiles resounding with the clap of his palms, his great chariot the depths of his ocean-floor, the onslaught of his arrows none could withstand save spoil-winning Árjuna, how can it be that he was your son, divinely conceived ahead of us? We were seared from every angle by the hot prowess of his arms. How could you have hidden him like fire under your skirt? The might of his arms deployed always in the service of Dhrita·rashtra's men, just as on our side we deployed the might of the deployer of the bow Gandíva, and of all the protectors of this earth,
only the mightiest among the powerful, the charioteer of 27.20
charioteers, none but a fellow son of Kunti, could take that power from Karna, for as it turns out that champion among all who bear arms was our eldest brother!

asūta taṃ† bhavaty agre katham adbhuta|vikramam?
aho bhavatyā mantrasya gūhanena vayaṃ hatāḥ,
nidhanena hi Karṇasya pīḍitāḥ sma† sa|bāndhavāḥ.
Abhimanyor vināśena, Draupadeya|vadhena ca,
Pāñcālānāṃ vināśena, Kurūṇāṃ patanena ca,
tataḥ śata|guṇaṃ duḥkham idaṃ mām aspṛśad bhṛśam.
Karṇam ev' ânuśocāmi, dahyāmy agnāv iv' āhitaḥ.
n' êha sma kiñ cid a|prāpyaṃ bhaved api divi sthitam,
27.25 na ca sma† vaiśasaṃ ghoraṃ Kaurav'|ântakaraṃ bhavet.»

evaṃ vilapya bahulaṃ dharma|rājo Yudhiṣṭhiraḥ
vyarudac. chanakai, rājaṃś, cakār' âsy' ôdakaṃ prabhuḥ.
tato vineduḥ sahasā striyas tāḥ khalu sarvaśaḥ,
abhito yā sthitās tatra. tasminn udaka|karmaṇi
tata ānāyayām āsa Karṇasya sa|paricchadāḥ
striyaḥ Kuru|patir dhīmān bhrātuḥ premṇā Yudhiṣṭhiraḥ.
sa tābhiḥ saha dharm'|ātmā preta|kṛtyam an|antaram
cakāra vidhivad dhīmān dharma|rājo Yudhiṣṭhiraḥ.
«pāpen' āsau mayā śreṣṭho bhrātā jñātir nipātitaḥ.
ato manasi yad guhyaṃ strīṇāṃ, tan na bhaviṣyati.»

How can it be that you gave birth to that man of extraordinary valor before any of us? Alas, you have destroyed us by keeping this information, since, as his brothers, we are devastated by Karna's demise. More than by the loss of Abhimányu and the killing of Dráupadi's sons, more than by the loss of the Panchálas and the fall of the Kurus, a hundred times more devastating than all of that is the impact of this new grief on me. For Karna I am consumed by grief like one cast into the fire. Nothing here, nor even what is
found in heaven, need have been unattainable, nor need 27.25
there have been this horrific carnage that exterminated the Káuravas."

So it was that the righteous king Yudhi·shthira gave full voice to his sense of loss, then wept. With great care, Your Majesty, the powerful lord performed the water offering for Karna, at which all at once a roar went up from the women, from those on both sides. When the water offering had been performed, Yudhi·shthira, the wise lord of the Kurus, the embodiment of honor, then, displaying the kind affection of a brother, had the wives and dependents of Karna, who were close by, brought to him. That wise and righteous king immediately performed the ancestral rites for Karna with the women of his brother's household in accordance with ritual prescriptions. Then he declared, "This was my older brother, my own flesh and blood whose death I sinfully brought about. Whatever curse any of the women of his household have conceived in their hearts on account of this, may none of that come to pass!"

27.30 ity uktvā sa tu Gaṅgāyā uttatār' ākul'|êndriyaḥ,
bhrātṛbhiḥ sahitaḥ sarvair Gaṅgā|tīram upeyivān.

After this, though his senses were overwhelmed, he emerged from the waters of Ganges and returned to the river bank, accompanied by all his remaining brothers. 27.30

NOTES

Bold *references are to the English text;* ***bold italic*** *references are to the Sanskrit text. An asterisk (*) in the body of the text marks the word or passage being annotated.*

'Dead of Night'

Benediction **Naráyana** is the son of **Nara**, the original man, and is often coupled with him. These two names are also frequently applied to Krishna and Árjuna, respectively. **Sarásvati** is the goddess of speech and learning.

1.1 **Sánjaya** is continuing his narration to Dhrita·rashtra of the events following the Pándavas' apparent victory and Bhima's slaying of Dhrita·rashtra's son, the leader of the Káuravan side, Duryódhana. The warriors he refers to in the opening line are the three surviving combatants of the Káurava side: Ashva·tthaman, Kripa and Krita·varman, who here return to the Káurava camp, only to find that it has been captured by the Pándavas and Panchálas, who are rejoicing at their victory and claiming the spoils of war.

1.6 The compound ***krodh'|âmarṣa|vaśaṃ***, consisting of the terms for "rage," "non-tolerance" (*amarṣa*) and "power" could equally well be analyzed as *krodh'|āmarṣa|vaśaṃ* where *āmarṣa* means "state of mind." The phrase should then be translated as "They succumbed to rage."

1.6 The **king** who has been slaughtered is Duryódhana, whose illegal killing at the hands of Bhima is recounted in the preceding book of the "Maha·bhárata." In fact, Duryódhana still clings to life, and the three will return to him the following morning to inform him of the events of the night to come.

1.25 The phrase **vision good** has a double meaning—the night is beautiful and the visibility good.

1.38 **Gáruda** is a divine bird of prey, the most powerful of all birds.

1.53–55 These verses about moments when an army is vulnerable are cited as a quotation, yet attacking an enemy sleeping at night is against the rules of combat (see JOHNSON 1998: 105). It is possible that they are a warning about times of weakness, when an army should be particularly wary, rather than advocating attack at such points. They therefore offer Ashva·tthaman a useful ambiguity.

1.60 **Eleven battalions**: when the different kshatriya groups of the region form into battalions in anticipation of war, the Káurava side is in the majority with eleven while the Panchála-Pándava side has seven.

1.67 The phrase **alteration of time** (*kālasya paryaya*) seems to be a double or even triple entendre, referring to the reversal of fortune or fate for the strong and skilled Káurava side, but also to the actual alteration of time that allowed the Pándava side to massacre the Káuravas: the Pándava side had carried out the trick of covering the sun to make the Káuravas think the truce of night had begun, thus altering time. A further meaning of *kālasya paryaya* is "loss of time," i.e. that this is a setback in their own eventual victory.

2.7 In Indian religions rain is attributed to the cloud god, Parjánya, or one of the more powerful gods, who incorporates his attributes, such as Indra. Translations omitting the divine reference in this idiom lose the analogy of shared divine and human roles in human success.

3.4 Nila·kantha's commentary understands ***sarvātmānam*** as resulting from double sandhi: *sarvaḥ ātmānam* > *sarva ātmānam* > *sarvātmānam*.

3.18 **The Lord of Beings**, Praja·pati, is the god who presides over creation, sometimes identified with the creator god Brahma.

3.19 The allocation of qualities to the different classes is a reference to the fourfold division of man into brahmin (priest), kshatriya (ruler/warrior), vaishya (trade and husbandry) and shudra (servant) respectively. The **Text of Wisdom** is the Veda, the hymns for brahmanical rituals that are the preserve of the brahmin class.

3.21 Ashva·tthaman's father Drona was a brahmin, and a teacher as is appropriate for a brahmin, but of martial arts, the preserve of the warrior. He was the martial arts instructor of the Pándavas and Káuravas. Hence Ashva·tthaman's profession is that of a warrior, in spite of his priestly birth.

3.28 **Indra** is one of the chief gods of Vedic Hinduism who remains important, particularly in warrior imagery and in some of the background myths of major characters, in the "Maha·bhárata." His slaying of the antigods, the **Dánavas**, is one of the feats of his that is praised in Vedic hymns dedicated to him.

3.30 **Rudra** "Fierce" or "Cruel" is the wrathful form of the god Shiva, whose bow is called **Pináka**. Ashva·tthaman's invoking of Rudra for this onslaught develops to new heights in the forthcoming scenes.

4.23 The nominative present participle ***anusmaran*** does not accord with classical Sanskrit grammar here, since the agent of remembrance, Ashva·tthaman, is represented by the genitive *me* and the participle should agree. Nila·kantha's commentary therefore glosses this with the genitive present participle *anusmarataḥ*.

4.26 Sandhi has been performed twice, so that the anticipated *hata iti* has become ***hateti***.

4.26 **Dhrishta·dyumna** illegally killed Ashva·tthaman's father Drona, when the latter had already put down his weapons. Drona had entered a meditative state in preparation for death, despairing of life at Yudhi·shthira, the embodiment of truth, lying to him that his son Ashva·tthaman, is dead. In fact Drona's soul has already departed to heaven by the time Dhrishta·dyumna decapitates him.

4.27 The sovereign whose **thigh was shattered** is the Káurava leader Duryódhana tricked by Bhima's foul play in the previous book.

5.12 **Loose hair** is sign of formal mourning.

5.21 **Shikhándin** had turned himself from woman to man in order to take revenge on Bhishma who, vowed to celibacy, had rejected her advances after first also causing her betrothed to reject her—in a previous lifetime—by abducting her. Since Bhishma knew this, he laid down his arms, unwilling to fight a woman. The other deaths described are all examples of the Pándavas gaining advantage in the war by breaking the rules of engagement. See under their names in the glossary.

5.22 In the battle between Bhuri·shravas and Sátyaki (book VII), Bhuri·shravas initially beats and humiliates Sátyaki in single combat. To save Sátyaki, Árjuna breaks the dharmic rules of combat against outside help intervening in a one-on-one fight, by shooting Bhuri·shravas' arm off as he is about to slay Sátyaki. Bhuri·shravas then undertakes a fast to the death, but dharmic conduct is again broken by Sátyaki who takes this opportunity to kill the doubly unarmed Bhuri·shravas.

6.4 The **sacred thread**, usually made of cotton, marks out a higher caste Hindu who performs the traditional Vedic sacrifices. It is worn across the chest, over one shoulder.

6.17 The apparently threatening snake, representing the sword, is swallowed up into the lair of its traditional enemy, the mongoose.

6.30–34 **Great Deity** (*Mahādeva*) is the god Shiva, and many of the epithets listed above for the terrible apparition at the entrance of the camp which Ashva·tthaman did not recognize, as well as those that follow, are standard attributes of his. His consort is called **Uma. The Destroyer**, Hara, is the name of Shiva. The role of creating, sustaining and destroying the universe are attributed to each of the triad of Hindu gods, Vishnu, Brahma and Shiva respectively. **Bhaga** ("Share") the god responsible for apportioning a share of the sacrifice is blinded by Shiva when he destroys the sacrifice of the gods, described at the end of 'Dead of Night' by Krishna.

7.3 Shiva has an **uneven** number of eyes, because he has three—the third eye being in the middle of his forehead. In some versions of the primordial sacrifice of the gods destroyed by Shiva, described by Krishna at the end of 'Dead of Night,' the officiant is Daksha, one of the Praja·patis, "lords of creation," sons of the god Brahma created in order to create the universe of living beings. He is killed by Shiva for not inviting him to the sacrifice.

7.5 The **three citadels** of the demon architect Maya, built on each of the three levels of the world, earth, atmosphere and heaven, were destroyed by Shiva because of the havoc wreaked on the universe by their demonic inhabitants.

7.8 **Gauri** is another name of Shiva's consort Párvati, an incarnation of Uma.

7.9 *Kumāra* "young man/prince" is one of the names of **Karttikéya**, the youthful god of war. The **excellent bull** is Shiva's *vahana* or vehicle, Nandin.

7.19 **Mákara** is a fresh-water crocodile or dolphin with mythical attributes. It frequently appears carved as part of the supporting structures in Indian-influenced architecture.

7.41 The three parts of the **universe** are heaven, atmosphere and earth.

7.42 The **eight kinds of supremacy** are the ability to shrink, become light, increase one's size, obtain what one wishes, have irresistible will, mastery over others, sovereignty, and ability to control desires.

7.47 The **one whose insignia is the trident** and the **Being** are both references to Shiva.

7.56 **Ángiras** is the name of a sage who realized many of the Rigvedic hymns used for Vedic sacrifice. *Āṅgirasa* means a descendent of Ángiras and is also a synonym for "sacrificial fire." Drona is citing his innate authority to offer oblations.

8.4 ***svapatāṃ***: epic Sanskrit sometimes does not add the *a*-augment in the formation of the imperfect.

8.3 The **highest path in battle** is the one to heaven.

8.21 The anticipated sandhi between the vowels at the end and start of *pādas* *c* and *d*, which would give the reading *Pañcāla/rājasy' ākrānto,* has rather been left as a hiatus here, retaining correct metrical scansion and a clear break between *pādas*.

8.58 The term **twice-born** for a brahmin refers to the second "birth" of initiation into the study of the Vedas.

8.70 The syntax here is unclassical, the agent of the absolutive ***bad-dhvā*** not being the grammatical agent of the sentence.

8.84 The **Night of Time** (*kālarātri*) is the night of destruction at the end of the universe, personified either as the goddess Durga, or as Yama's (Death's) sister.

8.87 The term *dvipa*, "twice drinking," for elephant seems to be chosen here to hint at the elephant's use of his trunk in water, hence the non-literal translation **water-tossing.**

8.110–113 In these verses the imagery of the battle field as a sacrificial ground is heightened, with Ashva·tthaman's ambiguous role as both warrior and member of the priestly class emphasized. The description of him as a joy to his fore-fathers, refers both to his acts to avenge his father's death as well as his offering the enemy soldiers as oblations to his ancestors.

8.129 **Lord of Animals**, Pashu·pati, is an epithet of Shiva.

8.155 The **lord of the wind gods** (Maruts) is the god Indra.

9.14 Duryódhana is the **first-born** of his one hundred brothers.

9.19 The **God of Treasure**, *dhan'/âdhyakṣa*, is the god of wealth as well as the god of war, also called Kubéra.

9.19 **The Powerful Plowman,** Krishna's older brother Bala·rama whose weapon is a plowshare, is the teacher of both Duryódhana and Bhima. Bala·rama is officially neutral in battle, but leans towards the Káuravas and Duryódhana in particular, to whom he gave his sister in marriage. His epithet here come from the great feats of strength he performed using his plowshare—using it to drag the entire Yámuna river to him for the latter's failure to come to him and bathe, and to drag the entire city of Hástina·pura after him.

9.22 **Wolf-belly** is an epithet of Bhima. In the preceding book, Duryódhana has been defeated in single combat by Bhima using a blow to the thigh, at Krishna's instigation, thus breaking a rule of combat.

9.31 ***Upekṣatām***: imperfect without augment.

9.43 The **teacher** is a reference to Ashva·tthaman's own father, Drona, the teacher of all the others, avenging whose death Ashva·tthaman killed Dhrishta·dyumna.

11.24 Bhima rescued the rest of the family from the flammable house, built for the Pándavas by the Káuravas at **Varanávata**, before it was consumed by fire in the arson attack ("Maha·bhárata" Book 1, 'The Beginning').

11.26 Book Four of the "Maha·bhárata" describes the exploits of the Pándavas while working in disguise in the king's service in exile after the dice game, during which Bhima killed the ogre **Hidímba** and married the ogre's sister, and killed the general **Kíchaka** for pressing his affections on Dráupadi.

12.5 Drona **bestowed the gift** of the missile on Árjuna during his studentship, marking his favoritism of Árjuna over even his own son (Book One of the "Maha·bhárata"). This means that both Árjuna and Ashva·tthaman have the knowledge of how to invoke the Brahma-head missile.

12.31 **Rúkmini** was one of Krishna's lovers, and mother to **Pradyúmna**, an incarnation of the god of love, identified with the god Sanat·kumára, "eternal youth," usually understood to be Shiva's son. This is a conflation of the myth of the birth Kumára to Shiva and Parvati after the asceticism of both culminated in Shiva ejaculating at the sight of Parvati and Kumára immediately developing from his semen. The reference therefore claims attributes of Shiva for Krishna.

12.33 **Rama** and **Gada** are Krishna's brothers; **Samba** is the son by Krishna out of Jámbavati.

12.34 **Ándhaka** is a name given to the descendants of Ándhaka, a descendant in turn of Yadu, as is Krishna.

13.2 **Finest Kambójan horses**: Kambója was an area of India famous for horse-breeding.

13.3 **Stallion of Shibi** (*Śaibya*), **Fine-neck** (*Sugrīva*), **Cloud Blossom** (*Meghapuṣpa*) and **Thunder** (*Balāhaka*) are the names of the four divine stallions that draw Vishnu's chariot, harnessed four abreast.

13.4 The god **Crafter of All**, Vishva·karman, is the divine smith, the god attributed with the creation of the physical universe in early Hindu literature.

13.5 **Vínata** is the mother of the Gáruda bird, Vishnu's emblem, and the traditional enemy of his half-siblings, snakes.

15.9 **Brahma's path**: *Brahmacarya* comes to mean the celibate studentship in classical Hinduism, but here is meant in the earlier meaning of a religious life dedicated to the ascetic-god Brahma. For Árjuna this is probably a reference to his period of lone asceticism on Indra·kila Mountain ("Maha·bhárata" Book III, 'The Forest').

16.2 **Viráta's daughter** is Uttará. She had married Árjuna's son Abhimányu ("Maha·bhárata" Book IV, 'Viráta'). Their son Paríkshit, saved from this missile by the event retold here, lives to become the king of Hástina·pura after Yudhi·shthira.

16.4 **Paríkshit, the Extensive**: *parikṣittvaṃ* is hard to translate, meaning literally "spreadingness, extending (as the earth)." There is a play contrasting the meaning of *pari√kṣi* to decay, be lost, and *pari√kṣi* to extend, and linking the latter to the name of Paríkshit. It is to Paríkshit's son Janam·éjaya, that the "Maha·bhárata" is being related by Vaishampáyana.

16.35 The **sacred remains**, *ucchiṣṭam*, left over after a sacrificial offering to a god.

17.14 **Grandfather** (*pitāmaha*) is one of the epithets of the creator god Brahma. The **first being** here refers to Shiva.

17.12 The **other born** here is the creator god Praja·pati. The term for living beings here, *prajā* means creatures, literally "born forth" and is being contrasted with *agrajo* "born first."

17.12 **Immovable** (*sthāṇu*) is one of the epithets of Shiva because of his motionless stance when practicing austerities.

17.21 It seems that here the outcome of Shiva's long stint of asceticism, undertaken to create beings without the inevitable flaws, is his ***linga***, or penis, the phallic icon emblematic of Shiva, which now has no purpose, so he uproots it and casts it in the ground.

18.5 This description and the relationship of Shiva's bow to the sacrifice is rather terse. A fuller explanation which makes more sense of these connections is provided Nila·kantha's commentary, which states:

"The act of devotion to the world takes the form of the aspiration, 'May all people know me as a good person.' The performance of rites takes the form of the rites of passage beginning with the rite of purifying the womb [performed after menstruation to ensure conception, so the first rite in the life of the prospective human]. The household sacrifices are the rites performed into the sacred fire obligatory for the married householder. Man's sacrifice of the five elements takes the form of whatever is pleasing to men through the qualities, such as sound, derived from the five elements. Pleasure that arises from the senses is the meaning. It is with these four ritual acts that all this universe is created."

One of the difficulties of translating this passage into English is the broad interpretation of *yajña* "sacrifice/offering" in Hindu traditions to incorporate all aspects of life, and the terse terminology used in referring to it—because of its familiarity in contrast to its abstruse nature for those outside of such a context. See also the following note.

18.6 **Five spans**: The measurement given is *kiṣku*. A *kiṣku* is the breadth of twenty four thumbs. The seventeenth-century commentator on the "Maha·bhárata," Nila·kantha, says that a *kiṣku* is the same as a *hasta*, a spread hand, corresponding to the old "span" measurement, the distance from the end of a man's thumb to his little finger when spread (23cm). Nila·kantha also explains the relationship between this verse and the previous. Shiva is using two of the types of sacrifice mentioned in the preceding verse but in a different sense. His sacrifice of the world is because he intends to destroy the world, and the bow measuring five spans is equated with it measuring the five elements.

18.16 These three gods, **Savítri**, **Bhaga** and **Pushan** are all associated with the light of the sun.

18.21 This is a reference to the fire believed to burn at the base of the ocean.

'The Women'

1.21 This statement is Dhrita·rashtra's resolution to die, as noted by Nila·kantha commenting on this verse, perhaps by traveling until one dies by exhaustion, one of the means of suicide permitted by Hindu dharma codes. For a detailed discussion with references, see FITZGERALD (2004: 661).

2.30 The **three advantages** in life are material, religious/social and sensual well-being mentioned in the previous verses.

4.11 This verse, particularly the middle line, is accepted as difficult to interpret by all who have worked on it. I think the middle line acts as a simile—one ignores what one is doing to oneself because one does not in fact perceive or understand it, just as one might pay no attention to something a mute is trying to say simply because one is not accustomed to perceiving it, regardless of whether he is trying to say something important. I understand *kṛtaṃ* rather than *uktaṃ* is being used here because the mute may attempt to speak but does not actually speak. This is different from the interpretation of the commentary, followed by GANGULI who translates it rather than the main text. The commentary, clearly seeing this verse as needing interpretation, reads:

tasyaivaṃ yamadūtair nīyamānasya vāgghīnasya sarvendriya-vikalasya yanmātraṃ yat kiñ cid iṣṭāniṣṭaṃ puṇyaṃ pāpaṃ tan mukhe prathamaṃ kṛtaṃ bhavati. tatrāpi puṇyaphalaṃ viṣayeṣu yogāt ātmānaṃ badhyamānaṃ garbhavāsādinā pātyamānaṃ upekṣate na tu svahitaṃ kāmayate. "Of one thus being taken away by Yama's minions, whose voice is gone = all his faculties are impaired, even what = whatever desirable and undesirable thing = meritorious or evil [act] that in the mouth/at the outset = first is made = becomes. Although there is the reward of meritorious action, he is, as a result of the contact with the sense objects, indifferent to the fact that his self is being bound=being destroyed by living in the womb, etc. and at the same time he does not desire what is good for him." There are two main problems with the commentary's reading. The first is that it requires a shift from the person being reborn being the agent—and in the nominative case in both the first third and final third of the sentence—to being in the genitive in the middle third. The second is that it interprets, *mukhe*, "in the mouth," to mean "at the outset," which seems odd in a line where absence of speech has already been mentioned.

FITZGERALD (2004: 665) also notes that there is difficulty here, while reaching a different conclusion.

8.10 The **noble-souled father** is Krishna of the Island, birth-father of Dhrita·rashtra, Pandu and Vídura.

8.20 ***kathaṃ*** is used here in the less familiar sense of "such that," "so that" rather than as a question mark.

8.40 See note to 8.20.

9.1 Chapter Nine is not included in the main text of the critical edition. While the first verse of this chapter nine is the same as the first verse in chapter nine of the critical edition, they only coincide again in chapter ten of our text, equivalent to chapter nine of the critical edition. Much of this chapter from verse ten onwards is repeated, albeit slightly altered, from chapter five of our text. The commentary recognizes it as a repetition—not as a mistake—and writes: *śokasyātigāḍhatvāt punar vidureṇoktam abhāvādīnītyādi*: Because he [Dhrita·rashtra] had sunk so deep in grief, Vídura repeated the passage beginning with the phrase, "Beings begin in non-being."

9.23 In the first occurrence of this the reading is *kāyam*, "body," not ***kāryam***, "duty."

10.8 ***Dṛśyanta*** is the imperfect form without its augment.

10.15 ***rājan, na vaikṣanta***: The reading here is unusual, since *vekṣ*, probably shortened from *avekṣ*, is usually a class ten *parasmaipada* verb. An alternative is to emend to *n' âvaikṣanta* or to accept the reading as *rājann avaikṣanta*, which however, would mean they looked at each other, whereas the meaning seems to be that they did not even look at each other.

11.18 **Processed respectfully**: the Sanskrit reads, "Made the king on the right," meaning that they walked around the king, keeping him to the right, a sign of respect when taking leave of a senior.

12.1 **The aged head of the family** is Dhrita·rashtra.

12.1 **That city homonymous with an elephant** (*gajasāhvayāt*): Although the city Hástina·pura, "city by Hastin," is so called because it was founded by a man called Hastin, the term *hastin* "having hands or having a trunk" also means "elephant."

12.6 The commentary explains that **those loved and those not** refers to men of the two sides—they weep because of those who have died and because of those who killed them.

12.19 The **coral tree**, *Erythrina indica*, has crimson flowers.

13.10 This refers to Duryódhana's humiliation of Dráupadi in the assembly at the game of dice, Bhima's oath to avenge her and Bhima's subsequent killing of Duryódhana with a foul and fatal blow with his mace to Duryódhana's thighs.

15.30 Gandhári wears a **blindfold** to make her as blind as her husband Dhrita·rashtra.

17.4 **His broad, muscle-bound chest**: literally [chest which was] broad with collarbone, *jatru*, well hidden.

17.28 Although not familiar in modern Western imagery—in spite of the experience of parents—sniffing a child is a sign of affection, and also occurs in classical Greek drama.

18.2 The women's hair is everywhere because loose hair is a visible indication of mourning.

18.10 Here *paśya* and the vocative are inserted within an active, nominative sentence.

19.10 A play is being made on **Dúrmukha**'s name, literally "Hardface" or "Hard to countenance."

19.17 The **sovereign of the stars** is the moon.

20.6 A neck marked with three lines lines like a **conch shell** is an auspicious characteristic and a mark of beauty.

21.1 Karna, the **son of the Sun** (*Vaikartana*) is the abandoned first born son of Kunti by the sun-god, and was killed by Árjuna, one of Kunti's acknowledged sons.

21.9 Karna, not knowing his true birth status, became Duryódhana's closest friend and a sworn enemy of his own brothers.

21.11 **The curse of your teacher**: Karna was cursed by his teacher Rama Jamad·agnya when the latter realized he must be of the warrior and not the priestly class, as he had claimed, because of his fortitude against pain.

22.7 The **slayer of the demon Paka** (*pāka/śāsani*) is Indra; by extension the name is also given to Árjuna, with reference to Indra being his divine father. Árjuna killed Vriddha·kshatra's son Jayad·ratha, in revenge for Jayad·ratha's murder of Abhimányu.

22.16 Dúhshala cannot find **her husband's head** because, when Árjuna killed Jayad·ratha, he decapitated him, sending his head flying into the lap of Jayad·ratha's father.

23.18 The image of Bhishma lying as snugly on the nails as **Lord Skanda on the reed bed** is a reference to the birth of Shiva's son Skanda. He was aborted when his six mothers (collectively) were turned into stars, but the river Ganga ensured he safely reached term by harboring him amid her reeds.

23.28 **The difficult feat** referred to here is Árjuna's defeat of Drona's arch-enemy Drúpada—Drona now lies beheaded at the hands of Drúpada's son.

23.32 The creative utterances of Praja·pati, **the lord of creation**, at the dawn of creation, contain or represent the entirety of the Vedas and all sciences, before the allotment of certain sciences to certain classes of man, especially the sacrificial Vedas to the brahmin and the martial sciences to the warrior class. Thus Drona, as a brahmin in a warrior role, contains all sciences within him as did the originator of all knowledge.

24.14 Árjuna intervened as Bhuri·shravas was about to kill Sátyaki by severing his right arm from behind, thus contravening the rule of single-handed combat (no pun intended!), and Sátyaki then proceeded to kill Bhuri·shravas even though the latter had given up his weapon, thus contravening the rules of engagement.

25.8 Women break their **jewelry** on becoming widows.

25.31 **Drona's son** is Ashva·tthaman. The chariot fighter of Sindh is Jayad·ratha. Not all the warriors Gandhári lists here are in fact dead. While Bhishma lies dying, Kripa and Krita·varman are still unharmed.

25.34 **Krishna** made a diplomatic mission to Hástina·pura as both sides were preparing for war in an attempt to persuade Duryódhana to restore part of the kingdom to the Pándavas. This would have been in accordance with the terms of the agreement following the Pándavas' defeat in the dice game and subsequent exile, but Duryódhana refuses and Krishna returns to Upaplávya empty handed ("Maha·bhárata" Book v, 'Preparations for War').

25.36 The phrase **their vision during my audience** is an attempt to convey both senses of *darṣanam*.

25.48 The prophecy comes true in the 'Book of the Clubs,' when a drunken fight escalates, urged on by Krishna. Most of the Vrishnis die, battering each other with clubs, while Krishna himself later allows himself to be killed by a hunter who mistakes him for a deer.

26.17 **The idyllic region of the Northern Kurus** (*Uttara Kuru*): a part of the human world where all aspects of life are better: longevity, supply of food, etc.

26.18 **As if you were a saint...**: *siddha* is a "perfected one," an adept who has achieved magical powers, *siddhi*, through his ascetic practice or spiritual achievement. The divine eye here allows the *siddha* to see the karmic consequences of a person's actions and their destiny after death (and thus we find the Buddha being asked a similar question in Buddhist texts).

27.14 The hiatus that would be left by the normal sandhi of *-āḥ* + *a-* has been resolved by performing sandhi twice to give *klāntatar" âbhavan* rather than the anticipated ***klāntatarā abhavan***, perhaps for the sake of the meter.

EMENDATIONS TO THE SANSKRIT TEXT

'Dead of Night'

1.14 *mahātmanaḥ* CE : *mahātmanā* K. The K reading is not recorded in CE.

1.33 *krodhāmarṣavaśaṃ* CE : *krodhāmarṣaśataṃ* K. CE does not record the K reading.

1.42 *kṣaṇenāhan sa* CE : *kṣaṇenāhanad* K

1.45 *'nvacintayat* em : *'nvattintayat* K : *vyacintayat* CE

1.50 *vācyaṃ* CE : *vākyaṃ* K

1.69 *bhavatos tu* CE : *bhavato 'stu* K

5.13 *pāñcālā* CE : *pañcālā* K

6.5 *svāyataiḥ* CE : *svāyateḥ* K

6.14 *yugānte* CE : *yugmānte* K

7.59 *pratigṛhāṇa* CE : *pratigrahāṇa* K

7.64 *tasya* CE : *tāta* K

8.8 *yathā* CE : *yayā* K

8.9 *bhavadbhyāṃ* em : *bhayadbhyāṃ* K

8.42 *°aṅgaḥ* CE : *°aṅga°* K

8.44 *°raktasya* CE : *°siktasya* K

8.45 *ajāgrata* em : *ajāgranta* K : *ajāgrata* CE

8.50 *bhāradvājas tu* CE : *bhāradvājaḥ sa* K

8.58 *muktacakraṃ* CE : *muktacakra* K

8.62 *kāyād* CE : *kāyātu* K

8.63 *bhīṣmanihantā taṃ* CE : *bhīṣmanihantāram* K. CE's reading means that Shikhándin, responsible for Bhishma's lingering death (he is not yet dead), attacked Ashva·tthaman with the help of the Prabhádrakas, and appears to follow the line of action better. K's reading means that Ashva·tthaman attacked Shikhándin at this point, meaning that this verse has to function as an introduction to the next events in the story, which include that attack. Because this then also requires an unspecified change of subject in 8.64, I have emended to follow CE here.

8.75 *paurvakālikam* CE : *pūrvakālikam* K

8.89 *tathāvadan* CE : *tathā vadan* K

8.117 *madhyakāyān* CE : *madhyadeśe* K

8.131 *yodhā anayan* CE : *yodhān anayad* K

8.136 *paścādaṅgulayo* CE : *paścādaṅguleyā* K

8.138 *param* CE : *varam* K

8.153 *kṣatre* CE : *kṣudraṃ* K

9.27 *suśiṣyo* em : *sa śiṣyo* K : *suśiṣyo* CE

9.28 *kṣatriyasyāhuḥ* CE : *kṣatrisyāhuḥ* K

9.36 *nānugacchāmas* CE : *nānugacchāma* K

9.60 *tava* CE : *droṇa* K

9.60 *prādhāvaṃ* CE : *prādravan* K

10.19 *paramo 'sti* CE : *paramasti* K

11.13 *āśayam* CE : *āśrayam* K

12.15 *°haraṃ* CE : *°hanaṃ* K

13.6 *anvārohadd Hṛṣīkeśaṃ* em : *anvārohaddhṛṣīkeśaḥ* CE : *athārohaddhṛṣīkeśaḥ* K

17.23 *caitad utpāṭya* CE : *cedaṃ utpādya* K

18.13 *sa|pāvakaḥ* CE : *sa pāvakaḥ* K

18.23 *babhūva* CE : *bebhūva* K

'The Women'

2.7 *anveti* em : *anvetti* K

2.19 *mahātmānaḥ* em : *mahātmanaḥ* K

6.6 *adhitiṣṭhati* CE : *adhitiṣṭhata* K

7.10 *majjamānaṃ mahāpaṅke* CE : *majjamāṃsamahāpaṅke* K

8.22 *nāradapramukhāṃś cāpi sarvān devarṣīṃs tathā* CE : *nāradapramukhāś cāpi sarve devarṣayo 'nagha* K

11.15 *ninīṣantaḥ* CE : *nirīkṣantaḥ* K

15.8 *taccāpy* CE : *tathāpy* K

15.25 *tām* CE : *tam* K

15.31 *'gacchad* CE : *'gacchād* K

15.37 *pautrāḥ* em : *putrāḥ* K : *pautrāḥ* CE

16.34 *vinadantyaḥ* em : *vinidantyaḥ* K : *vinadantaḥ* CE

16.54 *utkṛttaśirasaś* CE : *utkṛtya śirasaś* K

16.58 *bhrātṛbhiḥ* CE : *bhātṛbhiḥ* K

17.7 *abruvaṃ* CE : *abruva* K

18.10 *anyā* em : *anyāṃ* K : *anyā* CE

19.8 *abhyadhikaṃ* CE : *abhyadhika* K

20.12 *śeṣe* CE : *śete* K

21.10 *vṛṣasenasya* CE : *vṛṣasegasya* K

21.12 *°niṣkam* CE : *°kakṣam* K

23.15 *kālena* CE : *kālana* K

24.7 *prakīrṇāsita°* CE : *prakīrṇāḥ sita°* K

24.18 *go/sahasrāṇāṃ* em : *go/sahasraṇāṃ* K

27.9 *yaḥ sarvān purā vaḥ* CE : *vaḥ sarvān purā yaḥ* K

27.21 *taṃ* em : *ta* K : *taṃ* CE

27.22 *pīḍitāḥ sma* em : *pīḍitās tu* K : *pīḍitāḥ sma* CE

27.25 *ca sma* em : *cedam* K : *ca sma* CE

GLOSSARY OF PROPER NAMES AND EPITHETS

Abhimányu "Proud/heroic." Alternative name: Karshni, "son of Krishna's sister." Son by Árjuna of Krishna's sister Subhádra. Husband of Uttará. Father of Paríkshit, the only Káurava-Pándava male to survive the war, revived by Krishna after being still-born. It is through this lineage that the Bhárata line continues, and it is to Abhimányu's grandson Janam·éjaya that the "Maha·bhárata" is related at the outer level of the narrative.

Ádhiratha "Charioteer." Karna's foster father, the king of Anga.

Árjuna Alternative names: Dhanan·jaya, "winner of bounty;" Kauntéya, "son of Kunti;" Paka·shásani, "son of Indra who slew the demon Paka;" Kirítabhrit, "wearer of the diadem;" Bibhátsu "abhorrent." A son of Pandu, his divine father is Indra. The middle Pándava.

Ashva·tthaman "Horse-strength." Alternative names: several names all meaning Drona's son: Drona·putra, Drona·suta, Draunáyani and Drauni; Bharadvája "descendent of Bharad·vaja" (also an epithet of Drona). He is brahmin by birth, but warrior by nature, being the son of Drona, the instructor in martial arts to both Pándavas and Káuravas. Because he is functioning as an avenging son to his father's death in 'Dead of Night,' he is referred to almost entirely as Drona's son throughout that book. Leader of the surviving combatants on the Káurava side once Duryódhana is out of action, he is also the fifth and final general of the Káurava army. Side: Káurava.

Bala·rama Krishna's brother. Side: neutral.

Bhaga·datta King of Prag·jyótisha.

Bhárata Ancestral king ruling northern India; ancestor of most of the characters of the "Maha·bhárata." For both reasons, the address "scion/son of Bhárata" is a frequent term of address for kings in the "Maha·bhárata."

BHIMA "Terrible." Alternative names: Bhima·sena, "terrible army;" Vrikódara, "wolf-belly." Father: Pandu; divine father: Vayu, god of wind, hence his tempestuous nature; mother: Kunti. The second eldest of the five Pándava brothers, and the favorite of their shared wife Dráupadi. Bhima used an illegal move to kill Duryódhana in a duel by hitting him across the thigh with his mace, the event immediately preceding the events of 'Dead of Night.' Side: Pándava.

BHISHMA "Awesome," because of the awesome vow he undertakes so that his father can marry (see below). Alternative names: Gangéya, "son of Ganga," who had become human temporarily to give birth to seven gods cursed to become human, each of which she immediately kills, except for Bhishma, because she is interrupted by her husband; Shántanava, "son of Shántanu;" Grandfather, because he is the seniormost male ancestor of the Káuravas and Pándavas. When Shántanu fell in love with Sátyavati, mother of Krishna Dvaipáyana, the composer of the "Maha·bhárata," her father's consent to their union is dependent on Bhishma giving up his right to the Káurava throne. Bhishma agrees and, further, takes a vow of celibacy to avoid a future challenge to Shántanu and Sátyavati's line, earning the blessing from his father that he should choose his own time of death. He avails himself of this blessing, once "killed" by Árjuna and Shikhándin, by lingering on his deathbed until after the outcome of the battle. Although he remains on the Káurava side in the war, and acts as their first general, he informs the Pándavas of the means of killing him: "no man can kill me"—the once female Shikhándin is crucial to his eventual downfall. Side: Káurava.

BHURI·SHRAVAS "Great fame." Son of Soma·datta. Illegally killed by Sátyaki with Árjuna's assistance. Side: Káurava.

BRAHMIN A member of the priestly class, the highest of the four castes of the varna system.

BRIHAD·BALA King of the Kósalans. Side: Káurava.

CHITRA·SENA A son of Dhrita·rashtra and Gandhári. Side: Káurava.

DHRISHTA·DYUMNA Drúpada's son, Dráupadi and Shikhándin's brother. He kills his father's enemy, Drona, and, in revenge, is killed by Drona's son, Ashva·tthaman. General of the Panchála-Pándava army. Side: Pándava.

DHRISHTA·KETU "Emblem of the courageous." King of the Chedi people. Grandson of Dashárha. Side: Pándava.

DHRITA·RASHTRA "Regent/one by whom the kingdom is maintained." Alternative names: Prajña·chakshus, "wisdom-eye;" Vaichítra·virya, "son of Vichítra·virya," the blind king of the Kurus. Father of the one hundred Káurava brothers and uncle of the Pándavas. Wife: Gandhári. Father: the divine seer Krishna Dvaipáyana. Mother: Ámbika. The person to whom Sánjaya is narrating the "Maha·bhárata" at the innermost layer of the narrative framework. Eventually dies in a forest fire, after the end of the war. Side: Káurava.

DRAUPADÉYA "Sons of Dráupadi." The five sons of Dráupadi by each of the different Pándavas a year apart: Prativíndhya, son of Yudhi·shthira; Suta·soma, son of Bhima; Shruta·kirti, son of Árjuna; Shataníka, son of Nákula, and Shruta·karman, son of Saha·deva. All five are slaughtered by Ashva·tthaman. See HILTEBEITEL (1976: 325) for the suitability of the specific manner of their deaths.

DRÁUPADI "Daughter of Drúpada." Alternative names: Krishná, "dark;" Panchâli, "princess of Panchála." Yajña·seni, "daughter of Yajña·sena." The wife of all five Pándava brothers. The daughter of King Drúpada. The mother of five sons, all of whom are killed in the war. Her humiliation at the hands of the Káuravas in the Great Hall is the source of much of the bad blood between the cousins and, in particular, the inspiration for Bhima's illegal slaying of Duryódhana. Side: Pándava.

DRONA "Vessel," so called after the sperm that fathered him was preserved in a wooden vessel. Alternative name: Bharadvája "son of Bharad·vaja," Vedic seer. His wife is Kripi. His son is Ashva·tthaman. The brahmin teacher of weaponry and military skills to both the Káurava and Pándava cousins. While favoring Árjuna, his loyalty to the Káurava side is established by his earlier falling out with, and aggression towards, the Pándavas' ally Drúpada, king of the Panchálas and father of the Pándavas' shared wife, Dráupadi. He acts as the second general of the Káurava army. By the time of the 'Dead of Night' he is already dead, killed by Dhrishta·dyumna on the fifteenth day of the war. The invincible Drona laid down his arms, allowing himself to be killed on hearing that his son Ashva·tthaman had been killed. This is a trick played on him, for the Ashva·tthaman who has been killed is not his son but an elephant of the same name. Initially Bhima announces Ashva·tthaman's death, but Drona knows not to trust Bhima. It is when Yudhi·shthira, until then incapable of lying, repeats the untruth, that Drona despairs—perhaps more at a world where even Yudhi·shthira lies, than because he actually believes the lie. It is because of this trick that his son Ashva·tthaman seeks to avenge his father's murder in 'Dead of Night.' Side: Káurava.

DRÚPADA Alternative name: Yajña·sena, "whose army is sacrifice." Name of the king of the Panchálas, allies of the Pándavas. He is also the father of Dráupadi, Dhrishta·dyumna and Shikhándin. Side: Pándava.

DÚHSAHA One of Dhrita·rashtra and Gandhári's sons. Side: Káurava.

DUHSHÁSANA "Ill-advising." One of Dhrita·rashtra and Gandhári's sons. He dragged Dráupadi by her hair at the dice game. In revenge, Bhima kills him in battle and drinks his blood. Side: Káurava.

DURYÓDHANA "Dirty fighter/difficult to fight." Alternative name: Suyódhana "good fighter." Eldest of the Káurava brothers, and chief antagonist of the war.

GANGA The river Ganga. A goddess, the mother of Bhishma.

GANDHÁRI "Princess of Gandhára (a region in the north of the Indian subcontinent)." Alternative name: Saubalá, "daughter of Súbala." Father: Súbala; brother: Shákuni, king of Gandhára. Mother of Duryódhana and the other ninety-nine Káurava brothers, queen to blind king Dhrita·rashtra, in devotion to whom she always keeps her eyes blindfolded. The main interlocutor for the second half of 'The Women.' Eventually dies in a forest fire, after the end of the war. Side: Káurava.

GHATÓTKACHA *Rákshasa* son of Bhima, killed by Karna. Side: Pándava.

INDRA Chief of the gods in the Vedic and early epic period, during which he is already beginning to be eclipsed by Shiva, as well as by Brahma and Vishnu. Myths of his exploits in slaying certain enemies, including the *ásuras*, the titans or antigods, and his slaying of the Dánava demons, play an important part in similes to praise the prowess of certain warriors in this text. Alternative names: Vásava, "head of the group of gods called the Vasus;" Shakra, "powerful;" Mághavat, "possessor of bounty."

JAMAD·AGNI One of the Seven Seers and father of Parashu·rama.

JANAM·ÉJAYA Son of Paríkshit, and so great grandson of Árjuna. He becomes king of Hástina·pura and it is to him that Vaishampáyana relates the entire "Maha·bhárata" for the first time.

JAYAD·RATHA Alternative name: Sáindhava, a reference to his position as "king of Sindh." Son of Vriddha·kshatra. Brother-in-law of Duryódhana. He assists in the unlawful killing of Árjuna's son Abhimányu by cutting him off from the rest of the Pándava army. Árjuna kills him in revenge. Side: Káurava.

KARNA "Ear" (due to his golden earrings). Alternative names: Vaikártana, "son of the Sun;" Radhéya, "son of Radha" (his foster mother); Partha, "son of Pritha (Kunti)"; Ádhirathi, "son of Ádhiratha" (his foster father). The first born son of Kunti using her mantra to summon the sun-god. He is the eldest brother to the Pándavas, but unbeknownst to them since she had kept his birth a secret. Karna is Duryódhana's closest ally and friend. Even after finding out from Krishna that he is the oldest brother of the Pándavas, and could thus bring the two sides together, he keeps his true parentage secret, preferring to remain loyal to Duryódhana. He is the third

Káurava general in the war, killed illegally by Árjuna when disadvantaged by his chariot wheel being stuck in the mud. Side: Káurava.

KÉKAYAS Five brothers. Side: Pándava.

KÍCHAKA A Matsyan general killed by Bhima for attempting to seduce Dráupadi.

KRIPA "Pity/tender" (after the pity that inspired his adoptive father to look after him). Alternative name: Gáutama, "grandson of Gótama." Father: birth father, Sharádvat. Adoptive father, Shántanu. Sister: Kripi, Drona's wife. Born, with Kripi as his twin, from the semen emitted by the warrior-ascetic Sharádvat at the sight of a nymph sent to seduce him by the warrior god Indra, hoping to reduce his military and ascetic power. He inherited his birth father's military ability and became martial arts teacher, alongside Drona, to the Káurava and Pándava cousins, and will, after the war, become the teacher of the heir to the Káurava-Pándava throne, Paríkshit. Like Drona and Ashva·tthaman he is a brahmin by birth, but a warrior by profession. In the 'Dead of Night' he first proposes caution and abiding by the rules of engagement, but then assists Ashva·tthaman in carrying out the massacre of the Panchála camp at night. Survives the war to become the teacher of Paríkshit, the surviving descendent of the Pándava alliance. Side: Káurava.

KRIPI "Pity/tender" (after the pity that inspired her adoptive father to look after her). Wife of Drona.

KRISHNA "Black." Some alternative names: Késhava, "hirsute;" Janárdana, "rouser/tormenter of the people;" Hari; Hrishikésha, perhaps "lord of the senses;" Mádhava, "descendant of Madhu;" Madhu·súdana, "slayer of the demon Madhu;" Pundarikáksha, "lotus-eyed;" Vasudéva "son of Vasu·deva;" Dévaki·putra, "son of Dévaki;" Dashárha, "descendant of Dashárha;" Varshnéya, "of the Vrishni clan;" Vrishni·nándana, "joy of the Vrishnis." Father: Vasu·deva, mother: Dévaki. Sister: Subhádra. Árjuna's charioteer and the main adviser to the Pándava side, acting both as go-between between the two sides and instigator of some of the foul play that gives the Pándavas their victory. Identified as an incarnation of the god Vishnu to varying degrees throughout the "Maha·bhárata." Side: Pándava.

KRISHNA DVAIPÁYANA "Krishna of the Island." See Vyasa.

KRITA·VARMAN Alternative names: Hardíkya, "son of Hrídika/good-hearted;" Sátvata, "of the Satvats," the name of the tribe to which he belongs; Bhoja, "king of the Bhojas." He is a prince of the Vrishni (Satvat) clan, i.e. the same clan as Krishna, of whom he is a friend, although he allies himself against Krishna and the Pándavas in the war. He assists Ashva·tthaman in carrying out the massacre of the Panchála camp at night. He survives the war, but is killed later in the fighting that breaks out among the Vrishni clan following a dispute between him and Sátyaki. Side: Káurava.

KUNTI Alternative name: Pritha. Mother of Karna and three of the five Pándava brothers and matriarch of the Pándava side. Her children, and their two brothers out of Madri, all have different divine fathers invoked through the use of a mantra granted to her by the sage Durvásas. Eventually dies in a forest fire, after the end of the war. Side: Pándava.

LÁKSHMANA A son of Duryódhana.

MADRI Junior wife of Pandu, mother of Nákula and Saha·deva.

MATSYA Name of a country and a people in alliance with the Panchálas. The king is Viráta, the capital Upaplávya. The Pándavas spend their thirteenth year of exile, which resulted from losing the dicing match again the Káuravas, in the service of Viráta. His allegiance is gained when they protect him from a cattle raid by the Káuravas. Side: Pándava.

NÁKULA AND SAHA·DEVA The twin sons of Madri, junior wife of Pandu, their human father; their divine father(s) are the Ashvins.

NÁRADA An ancient divine sage.

PANCHÁLA Group of people, main allies of the Pándavas, from whom, under Drona's leadership, the Káuravas confiscate land, leading to the underlying animosity that forms the basis of the war. Dráupadi's clan. The Pándavas break away from the Káuravas, through their marriage with Dráupadi, to form an alliance with this group.

PÁNDAVA "Son of Pandu." The five sons of Pandu, three from his wife Kunti, namely Yudhi·shthira, Bhima, Árjuna, and two from his wife Madri, namely the twins Nákula and Saha·deva.

PRABHÁDRAKA Name of a people forming one of the divisions of the Panchála army. Side: Pándava.

PRATIVÍNDHYA Son of Yudhi·shthira and Dráupadi. Side: Pándava.

RADHA Foster mother of Karna.

RÁKSHASA A type of ogre.

SÁNJAYA "Victory." Alternative name: Gaválgani, "son of Gaválgana," who was his father. Charioteer and adviser to King Dhrita·rashtra, he keeps Dhrita·rashtra abreast with the events of the war, to some extent acting as his eyes. In this capacity, he functions as one of the main narrators of the "Maha·bhárata" within the innermost framework of narration. He escapes the massacre at night, the only one to leave the camp alive. Side: Káurava, but personally neutral—he is a failed peacemaker.

SHÁNTANU Bhishma's father. See Bhishma.

SÁTYAKI "Son of Sátyaka." Alternative name: Yuyudhána, "constant warrior." A Vrishni king. Krishna's charioteer. Eventually killed after the end of the war in the fighting that destroys the Vrishni clan, as cursed by Gandhári. Side: Pándava.

SHATANÍKA "Commander of one hundred columns." Alternative name: Nákuli, "son of Nákula," his father. One of the sons of Dráupadi. Side: Pándava.

SHÁKUNI Alternative name: Sáubala. King of Gandhára. Brother of Gandhári and uncle of Duryódhana. Side: Káurava.

SHALYA "Spear." King of Madra, brother of Madri, and so uncle of Nákula and Saha·deva. Acted as Karna's charioteer. Fourth general of the Káurava army, killed by Yudhi·shthira. Side: Switched from Pándava to Káurava.

SHIKHÁNDIN Son (originally daughter) of Drúpada. Sister/brother to Dhrishta·dyumna and Dráupadi. Pivotal in Árjuna's victory over Bhishma, who can be killed by "no man," he is the only person who can bring about Bhishma's death, because of the ambiguity of his gender. In a previous lifetime he was a woman, Amba. She was abducted by Bhishma and although released to her betrothed untouched by Bhishma, her betrothed rejected her because of the abduction. Bhishma in turn also refuses to wed her, because of his vow of celibacy. She seeks the god Shiva's assitance to become a man to avenge herself on Bhishma. She is reborn female, but raised as a boy, now called Shikhándin, and eventually swaps her female genitalia for male genitalia. In this apparently male form, though "no man," he/she can approach Bhishma, who knows his/her true identity, shielding Árjuna and thus allowing Árjuna to kill Bhishma. Side: Pándava.

SHIVA One of the dominant gods of the Hindu pantheon, he is associated particularly with ascetic practice, granting of weapons to those who win his favor, his destruction of the universe and, especially in 'Dead of Night,' with the primordial sacrifice. Alternative names are many, including: Rudra, "wrathful," Pashu·pati, "lord of the beasts;" Kritti·vasa "skin-clad;" Sthanu, "Immovable." There is a tension between his power versus that of Vishnu-Krishna in the "Maha·bhárata" as a whole, which we see addressed in 'Dead of Night' through stories of their essential collaboration with Vishnu-Krishna ultimately calling the shots. It is this fearsome god who possesses Ashva·tthaman, giving him the power to perform the massacre in the night.

SHRUTA·KARMAN "Of famous deed." One of the sons of Dráupadi, fathered by Saha·deva. Side: Pándava.

SHRUTA·KIRTI "Of regaled renown." One of the sons of Dráupadi, fathered by Árjuna. Side: Pándava.

SÓMAKA Name of a people, sometimes allies of the Panchálas, sometimes an alternative name for Panchála. Side: Pándava.

SRÍNJAYA Name of a people, allied with the Panchálas, sometimes synonymous with them. Side: Pándavas.

SUBHÁDRA Wife of Árjuna. Sister of Krishna. Mother of Abhimányu.

SUDÁKSHINA A king of the Kambójas. Side: Káurava.

SUTA·SOMA One of the sons of Dráupadi, fathered by Bhima. Side: Pándava.

UTTAMÁUJAS "Supreme energy." A Panchála prince. Side: Pándava.

UTTARÁ Daughter of Viráta. Wife of Abhimányu. Mother of Paríkshit.

VAISHAMPÁYANA Pupil of Vyasa. Narrator of the epic to Janam·éjaya.

VICHÍTRA·VIRYA "Of dazzling heroism." Nominal father of Dhrita·rashtra and Pandu, who were born from his widows using Vyasa as the posthumous surrogate father. See Vyasa.

VIRÁTA King of the Matsyas, under whom the Pándavas served in disguise during their thirteen years of enforced exile after losing the dice game. Father of Uttará, wife of Árjuna's son, Abhimányu, and so grandfather of Paríkshit, the only male offspring of the Pándavas to survive the war. Side: Pándava.

VIVÍNSHATI A son of Dhrita·rashtra and Gandhári. Side: Káurava.

VRISHA·SENA Son of Karna. Alternative name: Sushéna. Side: Káurava.

VRISHNI The Yádava tribe, from which Krishna hails. Allies with the Pándavas.

VYASA Alternative names: Krishna, "dark;" Dvaipáyana, "of the island," because of where he was born. Son by the seer Paráshara of Sátyavati, future wife of Shántanu. He is the divine seer who dictates the "Maha·bhárata" to the elephant god Ganésha, as well as teacher of Vaishampáyana, who narrates the epic to Janam·éjaya. Yet Vyasa also appears within the action of the "Maha·bhárata." When Shántanu and Sátyavati's two sons Chitrángada and Vichítra·virya fail to produce heirs, Bhishma arranges for Vyasa to father children with their respective widows, Ámbika and Ambálika. Disgusted by Vyasa, Ámbika closes her eyes, with the result that her son, Dhrita·rashtra ("the regent") is born blind, barring him from legitimate kingship. Ambálika forces herself to keep her eyes open, but turns pale, so that her son is born pale, "Pandu," the sole heir who can legitimately reign. Vyasa has a further son when Ámbika substitutes her servant in her place. The result is the wise Vídura, who also cannot reign, as a child of mixed caste with a low caste mother. Thus Vyasa is the biological father of the half-brothers Dhrita·rashtra and Pandu, the sons of whom—following the premature death of Pandu, remain locked in bitter rivalry, the outcome of which is the "Maha·bhárata" war.

YÁDAVA See Vrishni.

YUDHA·MANYU "Zealous in battle." Warrior of the Panchála clan. The first main player to find Dhrishta·dyumna murdered. Side: Pándava.

YUDHI·SHTHIRA "Steadfast in battle." Alternative names: Ajamídha, "descendent of Aja·midha the Goat-Sacrificer;" Dharma·raja, "righteous king;" Kauntéya, "son of Kunti." Eldest of the five Pándava brothers. Known for his honesty and allegiance to the dharma, he is nonetheless repeatedly compromised: his addiction to dicing, coupled with his vow to refuse nothing to anyone, leads to the fateful dice game in which he loses everything, and the Pándavas end up in exile; he tricks Bhishma into explaining how he can be killed and by confirming that Ashva·tthaman (the elephant) has been slaughtered, reduces Drona to despair, allowing the latter's death. Side: Pándava.

THE CLAY SANSKRIT LIBRARY

For further details please consult the CSL website.

1. The Emperor of the Sorcerers (*Bṛhatkathāślokasaṃgraha*) (vol. 1 of 2) by *Budhasvāmin*. SIR JAMES MALLINSON
2. Heavenly Exploits (*Divyāvadāna*). JOEL TATELMAN
3. Maha·bhárata III: The Forest (*Vanaparvan*) (vol. 4 of 4) WILLIAM J. JOHNSON
4. Much Ado about Religion (*Āgamaḍambara*) by *Bhaṭṭa Jayanta*. CSABA DEZSŐ
5. The Birth of Kumára (*Kumārasaṃbhava*) by *Kālidāsa*. DAVID SMITH
6. Ramáyana I: Boyhood (*Bālakāṇḍa*) by *Vālmīki*. ROBERT P. GOLDMAN. Foreword by AMARTYA SEN
7. The Epitome of Queen Lilávati (*Līlāvatīsāra*) (vol. 1 of 2) by *Jinaratna*. R.C.C. FYNES
8. Ramáyana II: Ayódhya (*Ayodhyākāṇḍa*) by *Vālmīki*. SHELDON I. POLLOCK
9. Love Lyrics (*Amaruśataka, Śatakatraya & Caurapañcāśikā*) by *Amaru, Bhartṛhari & Bilhaṇa*. GREG BAILEY & RICHARD GOMBRICH
10. What Ten Young Men Did (*Daśakumāracarita*) by *Daṇḍin*. ISABELLE ONIANS
11. Three Satires (*Kaliviḍambana, Kalāvilāsa & Bhallaṭaśataka*) by *Nīlakaṇṭha, Kṣemendra & Bhallaṭa*. SOMADEVA VASUDEVA
12. Ramáyana IV: Kishkíndha (*Kiṣkindhākāṇḍa*) by *Vālmīki*. ROSALIND LEFEBER
13. The Emperor of the Sorcerers (*Bṛhatkathāślokasaṃgraha*) (vol. 2 of 2) by *Budhasvāmin*. SIR JAMES MALLINSON
14. Maha·bhárata IX: Shalya (*Śalyaparvan*) (vol. 1 of 2) JUSTIN MEILAND
15. Rákshasa's Ring (*Mudrārākṣasa*) by *Viśākhadatta*. MICHAEL COULSON

16. Messenger Poems (*Meghadūta, Pavanadūta & Haṃsadūta*)
by *Kālidāsa, Dhoyī & Rūpa Gosvāmin*. Sir James Mallinson
17. Ramáyana III: The Forest (*Araṇyakāṇḍa*)
by *Vālmīki*. Sheldon I. Pollock
18. The Epitome of Queen Lilávati (*Līlāvatīsāra*) (vol. 2 of 2)
by *Jinaratna*. R.C.C. Fynes
19. Five Discourses on Worldly Wisdom (*Pañcatantra*)
by *Viṣṇuśarman*. Patrick Olivelle
20. Ramáyana V: Súndara (*Sundarakāṇḍa*) by *Vālmīki*.
Robert P. Goldman & Sally J. Sutherland Goldman
21. Maha·bhárata II: The Great Hall (*Sabhāparvan*)
Paul Wilmot
22. The Recognition of Shakúntala (*Abhijñānaśākuntala*) (Kashmir Recension) by *Kālidāsa*. Somadeva Vasudeva
23. Maha·bhárata VII: Drona (*Droṇaparvan*) (vol. 1 of 4)
Vaughan Pilikian
24. Rama Beyond Price (*Anargharāghava*)
by *Murāri*. Judit Törzsök
25. Maha·bhárata IV: Viráta (*Virāṭaparvan*)
Kathleen Garbutt
26. Maha·bhárata VIII: Karna (*Karṇaparvan*) (vol. 1 of 2)
Adam Bowles
27. "The Lady of the Jewel Necklace" & "The Lady who Shows her Love" (*Ratnāvalī & Priyadarśikā*) by *Harṣa*.
Wendy Doniger
28. The Ocean of the Rivers of Story (*Kathāsaritsāgara*) (vol. 1 of 7)
by *Somadeva*. Sir James Mallinson
29. Handsome Nanda (*Saundarananda*)
by *Aśvaghoṣa*. Linda Covill
30. Maha·bhárata IX: Shalya (*Śalyaparvan*) (vol. 2 of 2)
Justin Meiland
31. Rama's Last Act (*Uttararāmacarita*) by *Bhavabhūti*.
Sheldon Pollock. Foreword by Girish Karnad

32. "Friendly Advice" (*Hitopadeśa*) by *Nārāyaṇa* &
"King Víkrama's Adventures" (*Vikramacarita*). Judit Törzsök

33. Life of the Buddha (*Buddhacarita*)
by *Aśvaghoṣa*. Patrick Olivelle

34. Maha·bhárata V: Preparations for War (*Udyogaparvan*) (vol. 1 of 2)
Kathleen Garbutt. Foreword by Gurcharan Das

35. Maha·bhárata VIII: Karna (*Karṇaparvan*) (vol. 2 of 2)
Adam Bowles

36. Maha·bhárata V: Preparations for War (*Udyogaparvan*) (vol. 2 of 2)
Kathleen Garbutt

37. Maha·bhárata VI: Bhishma (*Bhīṣmaparvan*) (vol. 1 of 2)
Including the "Bhagavad Gita" in Context
Alex Cherniak. Foreword by Ranajit Guha

38. The Ocean of the Rivers of Story (*Kathāsaritsāgara*) (vol. 2 of 7)
by *Somadeva*. Sir James Mallinson

39. "How the Nagas were Pleased" (*Nāgānanda*) by *Harṣa* &
"The Shattered Thighs" (*Ūrubhaṅga*) by *Bhāsa*.
Andrew Skilton

40. Gita·govínda: Love Songs of Radha and Krishna (*Gītagovinda*)
by *Jayadeva*. Lee Siegel. Foreword by Sudipta Kaviraj

41. "Bouquet of Rasa" & "River of Rasa" (*Rasamañjarī & Rasataraṅgiṇī*) by *Bhānudatta*. Sheldon Pollock

42. Garland of the Buddha's Past Lives (*Jātakamālā*) (vol. 1 of 2)
by *Āryaśūra*. Justin Meiland

43. Maha·bhárata XII: Peace (*Śāntiparvan*) (vol. 3 of 5)
"The Book of Liberation" (*Mokṣadharma*). Alexander Wynne

44. Little Clay Cart (*Mṛcchakaṭikā*) by *Śūdraka*.
Diwakar Acharya. Foreword by Partha Chatterjee

45. Bhatti's Poem: The Death of Rávana (*Bhaṭṭikāvya*)
by *Bhaṭṭi*. Oliver Fallon

46. "Self-Surrender," "Peace," "Compassion," and "The Mission of the Goose": Poems and Prayers from South India
(*Ātmārpaṇastuti, Śāntivilāsa, Dayāśataka & Haṃsasaṃdeśa*)
by *Appayya Dīkṣita, Nīlakaṇṭha Dīkṣita & Vedānta Deśika*.

Yigal Bronner & David Shulman
Foreword by Gieve Patel

47. Maha·bhárata VI: Bhishma (*Bhīṣmaparvan*) (vol. 2 of 2)
Alex Cherniak

48. How Úrvashi Was Won (*Vikramorvaśīya*) by *Kālidāsa*
Velcheru Narayana Rao & David Shulman

49. The Quartet of Causeries (*Caturbhāṇī*)
by *Śūdraka, Śyāmilaka, Vararuci & Īśvaradatta.*
Csaba Dezső & Somadeva Vasudeva

50. Garland of the Buddha's Past Lives (*Jātakamālā*) (vol. 2 of 2)
by *Āryaśūra*. Justin Meiland

51. Princess Kadámbari (*Kādambarī*) (vol. 1 of 3)
by *Bāṇa*. David Smith

52. The Rise of Wisdom Moon (*Prabodhacandrodaya*)
by *Kṛṣṇamiśra*. Matthew T. Kapstein
Foreword by J.N. Mohanty

53. Maha·bhárata VII: Drona (*Droṇaparvan*) (vol. 2 of 4)
Vaughan Pilikian

54. Maha·bhárata X & XI: Dead of Night & The Women
(*Sauptikaparvan & Strīparvan*). Kate Crosby

55. Seven Hundred Elegant Verses (*Āryāsaptaśatī*)
by *Govardhana*. Friedhelm Hardy

56. Málavika and Agni·mitra (*Mālavikāgnimitram*) by *Kālidāsa*.
Dániel Balogh & Eszter Somogyi